［Revised Edition］

An Introduction to Japanese Grammar and Communication Strategies

Senko K. Maynard

日本語の文法とコミュニケーション・ストラテジー

［改訂版］

泉子・K・メイナード

The Japan Times

First edition: November 1990
Revised edition: March 2009

English copyreading: Cindy Mullins of 4M Associates
Layout design and typesetting: Asahi Media International
Illustrations: Senko K. Maynard
Jacket design: Hiroki Yamaoka

Published by The Japan Times, Ltd.
5-4, Shibaura 4-chome, Minato-ku, Tokyo 108-0023, Japan
Tel: 03-3453-2013
http://bookclub.japantimes.co.jp/

ISBN978-4-7890-1338-3

Printed in Japan

To Michael

Preface

Many years ago, when I began teaching Japanese as a foreign language at Rutgers University, a student came to me and said, "I'm still not exactly sure when to use *ga* and when to use *wa*." Also, a student who returned from a year's study abroad in Japan confided in me that he wasn't sure which style to use when he interacted with Japanese people of different social status.

Many students of Japanese have voiced questions about the basic grammatical rules. They wonder about how to combine bits of various phrases in order to make sense. Equally so, they are sometimes lost when it comes to choosing the appropriate expression in face-to-face interaction. They wonder what to say, what not to say, when to say, when not to say, and, most of all, how to say it—to whom.

I addressed these and other issues in my original 1988 manuscript of this book, which was first published in 1990. The book reached many English-speaking students worldwide, and in 1998 it was translated into Thai.

Since the book's first publication, the field of Japanese language pedagogy has grown exponentially, and long lists of textbooks and reference books have been published. The Japanese language itself has undergone remarkable changes. I have continued my path as a teacher and researcher of Japanese language and linguistics, and over the past twenty years I have written over a dozen books, some theoretical and some pedagogical.

Two years ago, my original publisher, The Japan Times, agreed to produce a revised and updated version, and what you have in your hands is the result. The purpose of this book has not changed. It is to explain, in great detail, not only how Japanese grammar operates, but how you should use it strategically in conversation so that you are both grammatically correct and socially competent. The readers I address in this book have not changed. The book is written with English speakers in mind. Whether English is your native language or not, English is a world language through which I can reach many readers. As a result, explanations and characterizations of the Japanese language are presented in contrast with the English language.

Incorporating shifts in styles that have evolved over the years, I have updated some entries with new information, and with new up-to-date examples. The Japanese language seems to change very quickly, particularly the version rampantly and quickly spreading among youth. You will find some such examples frequently used at the time of this writing. Despite the reality that language will always undergo changes, the basics remain stable.

You need no prior knowledge of Japanese to learn from this book. I have deliberately structured the content to flow from easy-to-grasp material to more difficult topics and more refined grammatical points. Each successive entry builds upon information that comes before it, so were you to study the book page by page from beginning to end, your knowledge would be progressive.

You may be taking Japanese language courses at high school or college. You may be learning on your own. Whatever your situation, this book will be a useful guide. It will help you grasp the Japanese grammar and communication strategies covered in elementary and intermediate levels.

Because this book is virtually an anthology of grammar and communication strategies, Japanese teachers may also find it a useful reference to add to their personal library.

For many years I have enjoyed teaching Japanese language and linguistics at American institutions (in chronological order, the University of Hawai'i, Connecticut College, Harvard University, and Princeton University), and especially at Rutgers University. I thank students and colleagues I have met at various locales for their friendship, inspiration, and encouragement. This book is dedicated to past, present, and future students of the Japanese language at Rutgers University. It is also dedicated to students learning Japanese on their own or at many institutions worldwide.

I thank Rutgers University for awarding me a sabbatical leave for the fall semester of 2008, during which I have worked on this revision.

My special thanks go to Chiaki Sekido of The Japan Times for her scrupulous attention to detail in editing the book. She edited the book's first edition, and it has been a pleasure to work with her again. Last but not least, thank you, Michael, for being my ever enthusiastic cheerleader.

SKM
November, 2008
"On the Banks of the Old Raritan"

Table of Contents

List of Entries

Part II: FUNDAMENTALS

Part III: **CORE**

To the Reader

This book presents, in 130 entries, basic Japanese grammar and communication strategies. These entries contain essential, if not introductory, information necessary to become proficient in the Japanese language. Some bear grammatical headings, such as "Negation of Verbs," while others are labeled with functional notions, such as "Requesting."

The rationale for this mixture of categories is simple. I believe a student of Japanese must possess a combination of at least these two related but different types of knowledge. I have made an effort in this book to make connections between grammatical structures and communication strategies, both of which are necessary to realize various communicative functions.

Ultimately, as a student of Japanese, you must be able not only to comprehend Japanese but to express your thoughts in Japanese. Language learning is not imitation, but creation. We should not end up simply memorizing a few "conversational expressions" without understanding how those expressions mean what they mean. We should also remind ourselves that just being able to order a cup of coffee in Japanese is not enough to thrive in today's complex world.

To communicate in Japanese meaningfully, study of the basic grammar is indispensable, particularly for adult non-native speakers. Knowing the grammar will help you acquire Japanese. It makes comprehension easier, and provides a basis on which you can judge the appropriateness of your own speech. But you need more than grammatical correctness to participate in real conversations. Understanding communication strategies introduced in this book will assist your successful participation in Japanese communication.

Still, understanding grammar and knowing "about" the language is not enough to be proficient in a foreign language. Far from it. Varied experiences, which ideally include living in Japan and using the language in context, are necessary to become totally competent in Japanese. Participating in structured language classes, if possible, is quite useful. This will offer the opportunity to learn the basics of the Japanese language, and to interact with teachers and other students in Japanese. When learning a foreign language, it is essential to actually use the language. Language cannot be mastered simply by reading about it.

Beyond learning the language itself, because language is a part of the society and culture of which it is a part, one must always remain curious and sensitive to the language community as a whole. Knowing about various social and cultural aspects of Japan is an important part of language education, which should be incorporated into your learning experience.

A book such as this one cannot possibly explain everything about Japanese. Learning Japanese involves a variety of activities, and learning through this book is only one part of a large project. But after having studied 130 entries discussed in this book, you will have taken an important step toward achieving your goal.

1. Organization of the Book

This book is divided into four parts. Part I, Preliminaries, offers introductory remarks, and discusses the general background of the Japanese language. Here I introduce ten basic grammatical and strategic characteristics of Japanese, which will be referred to throughout the book, whenever relevant.

Part II, Fundamentals, covers entries 1 through 40, and introduces the very basics of the grammar and communication strategies. Here, basic words, case markers, and different types of adjectives and verbs are introduced. Verbs such as the *be*-verb, existential verbs, and both *i*-type and *na*-type adjectives are discussed. Also presented are the information structure of topic and comment and the basic word order. Part II covers basic communication strategies, such as greetings, introducing, and inquiring.

The heart of this book is Part III, Core, which includes entries 41 through 100. Here the meat of the Japanese grammar and strategies is presented in detail. Grammatically more complex issues are dealt with, such as negative questions, different types of sentences based on verb categories, and complex sentences of various kinds. Part III contains clausal modifiers, conditionals, the relationship between proposition and modality, and so on. This part also provides important communication strategies, such as requesting, inviting, apologizing, and leave-taking. Also discussed are expressions that communicate emotions, such as sentential adverbs and interjections. In Part III, we also study conversation management, i.e., those skills necessary to participate in real verbal interactions.

Part IV, Expansion, discusses advanced materials of introductory or elementary Japanese. Various modal expressions as well as passive and causative structures are presented. In this part we also study how direct and indirect quotations work, and how multiple sentences are organized in Japanese discourse. Communication strategies covered in Part IV touch upon advising someone, visiting someone's place, and designing your own utterances.

This book also contains Appendixes, List of Author's Works, Subject Index, and the Japanese-English Word List.

On the cover page of Part I through IV and Appendixes, you will find my watercolor paintings. I hope you will enjoy a few samples of the American scenes that I have been painting over the years.

2. Arrangement of Each Entry

Each entry consists of some of the following.

■ Target Expression(s)

Target expressions are the main focus. We concentrate on these expressions and learn how they are structured, and what they mean when used in communication. Some target expressions are formulaic, and should be memorized word for word.

Some target expressions are structural representations of grammatical patterns. For these entries, it is important to understand the grammatical process.

■ Grammatical or Strategic Explanation

Depending on the entry, either a grammatical or strategic explanation is provided. For grammatical explanation, it is particularly important to understand how various components are structurally ordered in forming the phrase or sentence. For strategic explanation, it is more important to understand how the target expression should or should not be used in actual social settings. Cultural background information and relevant social knowledge are provided to substantiate the appropriate strategies.

■ Examples

Phrases and sentences similar to the target expression(s) are given to illustrate the point. These additional examples should help you to further understand the structure and the strategy of the target expression.

■ Additional Information

You are not expected to learn everything in one reading. Information provided here is not critical at each level. So you may ignore this section first, and then come back to it later.

■ Warning

For some entries, there are warnings especially useful for beginning and intermediate students. These warnings often originate from frequent errors that have been made by students of Japanese who are at the beginning and intermediate levels.

When possible, Japanese items are listed in the *a-i-u-e-o* order. The *a-i-u-e-o* order is based on the list of Japanese sounds given in Sound System on page 2. Vowels starting from top to bottom, i.e., *a, i, u, e, o* are first, followed by *ka, ki, ku, ke, ko,* and so forth. For lines 3, 5, 7, and 10, voiced sounds follow voiceless counterparts: *ga* after *ka, gi* after *ki,* and so on. Sounds in line 11 follow voiced counterparts; i.e., *pa* follows *ba,* and *pi* follows *bi,* and so forth. *N* is the last sound in the *a-i-u-e-o* order.

Items in the Japanese-English Word List are transcribed in Romanization, and are arranged in alphabetical order.

When thought useful, example sentences are accompanied by glossing—a word-by-word translation—written directly under the Japanese.

3. Abbreviations

The following list provides abbreviations in alphabetical order.

Adj basic	basic form of the adjective
Adj-*i*	*i*-type adjective
Adj-*na*	*na*-type adjective
Adj stem	stem of the adjective
Adj *te*	gerundive *te*-form of the adjective
AuxAdj	auxiliary adjective
AuxV	auxiliary verb
IO	indirect object
IP	interactional particle
L	linker
lit.	literal translation
N	noun (including noun phrases)
O	direct object
Q	question marker
QT	quotation marker
S	subject marker
T	topic marker
V	verb (including existential verbs and the *be*-verb)
Vbasic	basic form of the verb
Vformal	formal style of the verb
Vinformal	informal style of the verb
Vnon-past	non-past form of the verb
Vpast	past form of the verb
Vstem	stem of the verb
V*te*	gerundive *te*-form of the verb
[ ]	grammatical pattern
*	non-existent, ungrammatical and unacceptable form
‘ ’	English translation
( )	optional or additional

See Appendix 1 for the definition of some grammatical terms listed above.

Part I:
PRELIMINARIES

Where Hawai'i's Ocean Meets the Rocks

1. Sound System

Although it is best to actually hear the sound of spoken Japanese first-hand, the information to follow may be useful before reading the Romanized Japanese. The chart provides the single vowel, consonant-plus-vowel cluster, and consonant-plus-semivowel *y*-plus-vowel cluster, which form Japanese sounds. Additionally, the sound of *n*, if it appears by itself (as in the third sound of *ni-ho-n-go*) constitutes an independent sound unit. Each sound listed below constitutes one mora (or the so-called syllable), and receives one beat (or mora) when pronouncing Japanese.

Note that a long vowel is considered a combination of single vowels, and is spelled out *aa* or *oo* and so forth throughout this book. These vowels receive as many beats as represented by the number of single vowels. Consonants *k, s, p,* and *t* receive one beat in a double consonant environment. For example, *hakkiri* is a four-mora word (*ha-k-ki-ri*). It should be pointed out that the consonant g is optionally nasalized in all environments, except at the word-initial position.

Japanese Sound System

1	2	3	4	5	6	7	8	9	10	11	12	13	14	15
a	*ka*	*ga*	*sa*	*za*	*ta*	*da*	*na*	*ha*	*ba*	*pa*	*ma*	*ya*	*ra*	*wa*
i	*ki*	*gi*	*shi*	*ji*	*chi*		*ni*	*hi*	*bi*	*pi*	*mi*		*ri*	
u	*ku*	*gu*	*su*	*zu*	*tsu*		*nu*	*hu*	*bu*	*pu*	*mu*	*yu*	*ru*	
e	*ke*	*ge*	*se*	*ze*	*te*	*de*	*ne*	*he*	*be*	*pe*	*me*		*re*	
o	*ko*	*go*	*so*	*zo*	*to*	*do*	*no*	*ho*	*bo*	*po*	*mo*	*yo*	*ro*	
														n
	kya	*gya*	*sha*	*ja*	*cha*		*nya*	*hya*	*bya*	*pya*	*mya*		*rya*	
	kyu	*gyu*	*shu*	*ju*	*chu*		*nyu*	*hyu*	*byu*	*pyu*	*myu*		*ryu*	
	kyo	*gyo*	*sho*	*jo*	*cho*		*nyo*	*hyo*	*byo*	*pyo*	*myo*		*ryo*	

2. Writing System and Romanization

Japanese employs a combination of three different types of writing systems: *hiragana, katakana,* and *kanji. Hiragana* is used for native Japanese words. Conjugating endings of verbs and adjectives, grammatical particles, and auxiliary verbs are written in *hiragana. Katakana* is used for transcribing foreign loan words (other than Chinese) and some onomatopoeic words. *Katakana* is also used for stylistic reasons, for example, to attract special attention from the reader.

The *hiragana* and *katakana* lists follow.

Hiragana（ひらがな）

a	*ka*	*ga*	*sa*	*za*	*ta*	*da*	*na*	*ha*	*ba*	*pa*	*ma*	*ya*	*ra*	*wa*
あ	か	が	さ	ざ	た	だ	な	は	ば	ぱ	ま	や	ら	わ
i	*ki*	*gi*	*shi*	*ji*	*chi*	*ji*	*ni*	*hi*	*bi*	*pi*	*mi*		*ri*	
い	き	ぎ	し	じ	ち	ぢ	に	ひ	び	ぴ	み		り	
u	*ku*	*gu*	*su*	*zu*	*tsu*	*zu*	*nu*	*hu*	*bu*	*pu*	*mu*	*yu*	*ru*	
う	く	ぐ	す	ず	つ	づ	ぬ	ふ	ぶ	ぷ	む	ゆ	る	
e	*ke*	*ge*	*se*	*ze*	*te*	*de*	*ne*	*he*	*be*	*pe*	*me*		*re*	
え	け	げ	せ	ぜ	て	で	ね	へ	べ	ぺ	め		れ	
o	*ko*	*go*	*so*	*zo*	*to*	*do*	*no*	*ho*	*bo*	*po*	*mo*	*yo*	*ro*	*(w)o*
お	こ	ご	そ	ぞ	と	ど	の	ほ	ぼ	ぽ	も	よ	ろ	を
														n
														ん

When reading *hiragana*, note the following transcription rules:

1. The particle *wa* is spelled は, particle *e* as へ, and particle *o* as を.

2. The verb *yuu* 'to say' is spelled いう.

3. *Oo* is normally represented as おう with a few exceptions, such as:

おおきい	*ookii*	big
とおい	*tooi*	far
とおる	*tooru*	to go through
こおる	*kooru*	to freeze

4. The *zu* sound is transcribed in two ways. The general rule is to spell as ず. The alternative writing, づ, is used where the sound *zu* corresponds with つ in a related word. For example, *kizuku* 'to notice' is transcribed きづく, because it is related to *tsuku* of きがつく 'to notice.' Also, when the preceding *hiragana* is つ, づ is used as in つづく 'to continue.'

5. Similar phenomenon exists for the sound *ji*. Although generally じ is used, in rare cases, ぢ is used where the sound *ji* corresponds with ち in a related word. For example, はなぢ *hanaji* 'nosebleed' is transcribed with ぢ, because it is associated with the word ち 'blood.' The continuation of ちぢ occurs in ちぢむ *chijimu* 'to shrink.'

6. Combinations of *kk*, *ss*, *tt*, and *pp* are spelled with small *tsu*. For example, さっき *sakki* 'a while ago' and さっさと *sassato* 'quickly.'

Katakana（カタカナ）

a ア	*ka* カ	*ga* ガ	*sa* サ	*za* ザ	*ta* タ	*da* ダ	*na* ナ	*ha* ハ	*ba* バ	*pa* パ	*ma* マ	*ya* ヤ	*ra* ラ	*wa* ワ
i イ	*ki* キ	*gi* ギ	*shi* シ	*ji* ジ	*chi* チ	*ji* ヂ	*ni* ニ	*hi* ヒ	*bi* ビ	*pi* ピ	*mi* ミ		*ri* リ	
u ウ	*ku* ク	*gu* グ	*su* ス	*zu* ズ	*tsu* ツ	*ze* ヅ	*nu* ヌ	*hu* フ	*bu* ブ	*pu* プ	*mu* ム	*yu* ユ	*ru* ル	
e エ	*ke* ケ	*ge* ゲ	*se* セ	*ze* ゼ	*te* テ	*de* デ	*ne* ネ	*he* ヘ	*be* ベ	*pe* ペ	*me* メ		*re* レ	
o オ	*ko* コ	*go* ゴ	*so* ソ	*zo* ゾ	*to* ト	*do* ド	*no* ノ	*ho* ホ	*bo* ボ	*po* ポ	*mo* モ	*yo* ヨ	*ro* ロ	*(w)o* ヲ
														n ン

Note that for long vowels in *katakana*, ー is used.

You may notice the similarity between ソ (*so*) and ン (*n*), as well as ツ (*tsu*) and シ (*shi*). When distinguishing ソ (*so*) and ン (*n*), watch out for the direction of the second stroke. *Katakana* ン (*n*) has the upward stroke similar to *hiragana* ん (*n*). A good way to remember the difference between ツ (*tsu*) and シ (*shi*) is that they follow the basic stroke direction of their *hiragana* counterparts つ (*tsu*) and し (*shi*), respectively.

Because loan words carry sounds absent in Japanese, the transcription process has resulted in the use of special *katakana* combinations. The following are established cases.

ティ	*ti*	ディ	*di*				
シェ	*she*	ジェ	*je*	チェ	*che*		
ファ	*fa*	フィ	*fi*	フェ	*fe*	フォ	*fo*

Some examples include フォ (*fo*) as in フォーク (*fo*rk), フィ (*fi*) as in フィラデルフィア (*Phi*ladel*phi*a), ティ (*ti*) as in パーティー (par*ty*), ジェ (*je*) as in ジェーン (*Ja*ne), ディ (*di*) as in ディーゼル (*di*esel), and so on.

As for *kanji*, this book contains only the most frequently used *kanji* selected from *Jooyoo Kanji* characters. Depending on your textbook or the program you enroll in, you will learn these writing symbols at different stages and at different speeds. In this book, Japanese examples are first presented in the Japanese writing method commonly used, i.e., a combination of all three systems.

Examples are then followed by Romanization. The Romanization system used in this book is of a modified Hepburn style. Long vowels are spelled out (for example, as *aa, ii,* etc.) rather than marking them with a lengthening diacritical mark. The independent sound *n* is spelled as *n'* when followed by a vowel or a semivowel, *y*.

Although the Japanese writing system does not separate each word, for convenience, in the Romanization presentation in this book, words are separated. Some hyphens are used to mark separation of morphological units (i.e., smallest meaningful units). Proper nouns are spelled with capital letters, and interrogative sentences are punctuated with a question mark when the question marker *ka* is absent.

3. Characteristics of the Japanese Language

Japanese is the national language of Japan, and is spoken by approximately 127 million people. Japanese is also spoken in Japanese emigrant communities around the world, most prominently in Hawai'i and Brazil. In addition, it is estimated that a few million people speak Japanese as a second or a foreign language. Still, unlike English, which is spoken by hundreds of millions worldwide, Japanese is very much the language of a single national entity.

Japanese is suggested to be distantly related to Korean, and therefore to the Altaic languages (among them, Mongolian and Turkish). Japanese is a topic-comment prominent language with a basic word order of the verb placed at the final position. This contrasts with English, which is a subject-predicate prominent language with a basic word order of subject-verb-object. Japanese has particles or postpositions that express not only grammatical relationships but interpersonal feelings as well. Non-specification of topics, subjects, objects, and particles is common.

In what follows I list the ten most basic characteristics of Japanese. We will refer to them whenever these and other related characteristics become relevant throughout the book.

1. *Verb-final*
   The basic Japanese word order is verb-final.

2. *The I-type Adjective*
   The *i*-type adjective behaves like a verb in that it can constitute a predicate by itself.

3. *Topic-comment Prominence*
   The notion of topic plays a vital part in organizing information in an utterance or a sentence. Topic is marked by topic-marking particles such as *wa, tte* and *mo*.

4. *Not Saying the Obvious*
   Not specifying the elements which are obvious to the communication participants is frequent. As long as the information is recoverable, there is no need to specify. Little structural constraint blocks such omission.

5. *Speech Style—formal/informal and honorifics*
   Different devices are used to mark formal or informal styles. Additionally, a speaker shows reverence to those of higher social status by using respectful and humble forms of the honorific system.

6. *Modifier Precedes the Modified*
   Beyond being verb-final, the basic word order in Japanese is that a modifier (such as adjectives and clausal modifiers) precedes the modified.

7. *Postpositional Particles*
   Two types of particles, grammatical and interactional, are used to show grammatical and interpersonal relations respectively. Particles are postposed to the element whose relation is defined.

8. *Verb/Adjective Conjugation*
   Verbs and adjectives change forms based on tense, and on how the speaker views the event and the state.

9. *Numbers and Counters*
   Japanese does not make the distinction between grammatical singular and plural. When specifying quantity, it employs a set of counters.

10. *Non-agent Orientation*
    Japanese tends to view and describe the world as a natural state, or a change brought about by some force. Specification of subject or agent is not as prominent a concern as observed in English.

4. Simple and Complex Sentences

Each utterance or sentence may obtain single or multiple propositional contents. By simple sentences, we mean sentences with a single predicate—regardless of whether or not it appears on the surface. By complex sentences, we mean those that contain more than one predicate.

Most Japanese simple sentences end with one of the following structures: (1) Verb (including existential verbs), (2) Adj-*i*, (3) [Adj-*na* + *da*], and (4) [N + *da*], all optionally followed by auxiliary verbs, auxiliary adjectives, and particles.

More than one predicate may be incorporated into a sentence by choosing one of the following methods:

1. Continue by using the stem of the verb and the verb gerundive form.
2. Add another clause and connect it with a conjunction.
3. Add clausal modification or clausal explanation to modify the noun.
4. Use nominalizers *koto* and *no*, which makes clauses into noun phrases.
5. Use quotations to include simple or complex sentences within them.

The relationship between two clauses is either "coordinate" or "subordinate." In a coordinate connection, two clauses are connected without subordinating one to the other. Coordinate relationships are expressed by the "and" and "but" connection.

In a subordinate connection, a clause is incorporated within another (main) clause. Of the three types of subordinate connection, the first shows, among other things, relationships such as cause-effect, condition-result, duration or sequencing of time, and quotation. The second is noun modification, including both clausal modification and clausal explanation. The third is nominalization using the nominalizers *koto* and *no*.

Most of the complex sentence structures are introduced in Part III. In the beginning, attention should be paid to the structure of the simple sentence only.

5. Variations of the Japanese Language

When we refer to "the Japanese language," we tend to assume there is one language. In reality, however, the Japanese an individual speaks represents one variety among many, all of which belong to the Japanese language. Moreover, a single Japanese speaker chooses different variations depending on social and personal needs, sometimes shifting between multiple styles and variations in a single conversational encounter.

There are at least four major aspects related to the variation in language, i.e., style, gender, generation, and region.

In this book, constraints on variations are so noted when warranted. Needless to say, depending on social and interpersonal situations, using the wrong variation can be quite detrimental. It is important to pay attention to specific features and restrictions. Particularly restricted are blunt expressions often associated with masculine speech style.

I should also point out that speakers use different variations as a tool for expressive and creative needs. By "borrowing" styles stereotypically associated with other speakers, a speaker may achieve certain effects.

Style:

By style, I refer to linguistic styles such as formal versus informal, and spoken versus written. The basics of these styles are covered in Entry 3.

Regarding the distinction between spoken and written styles, there has been a recognizable tendency for Japanese to become more casual, i.e., the casualization of speech is in progress. In the early 1980s, a handful of writers introduced a casual writing style bearing straightforward and unconventional characteristics. By the 1990s, this speech-like written style (called *shin-genbun-itchitai*) began to gain recognition as a stylistic trend. It is a style written as if talking to a friend. This more casual style frequently uses interjections, particles, sound change, and its discourse tends to be simple, sporadic, and emotionally laden. Currently, the speech-like written style has become so prevalent it is used in publications addressed to adult readers, including some of the magazine articles, essays, and novels.

Gender:
Variations associated with gender, i.e., somewhat politer feminine speech versus more blunt masculine speech, are discussed in Entry 39.

Regarding the issue of gender and language, we should keep in mind that Japanese women's speech has taken on more of the masculine speech features, and that gender-associated differences in language use, particularly among youth, are becoming something of a myth. Young female speakers use increasingly more blunt expressions and shy away from the traditional feminine speech style.

Traditionally, a proper woman was expected to use feminine speech. However, such gender-restricted discourse itself reflects an ideology that discriminates against women. It makes more sense to understand feminine and masculine speech styles as options available for all speakers.

Currently, it is more acceptable for a woman to be more aggressive than in the past, particularly in private and casual situations. The language targeted to young women in the media also has taken on features traditionally considered restrictively masculine.

Generation:
Among generational variations, the youth language is often noted for its newness, cleverness, and peculiarity. Youth language is the language spoken, under certain circumstances, by teens and those in their twenties. Some features of the so-called youth language, however, span generations. Some youth expressions have taken root in the speech style of people in their thirties, and even in their forties.

Here are some of the characteristics of youth language.

1. Shortening of existing phrases
2. Change of meanings
3. Frequent use of special emphatic expressions
4. Use of objectifying and self-alienating expressions

Region:
Among many regional variations in Japan, the major dialect divisions are recognized between the Ryukyuan dialects (of Okinawa) and the mainland. The mainland dialects are customarily divided into three large groups: eastern Japan, western Japan, and Kyushu. There are, however, major differences between the eastern group on the one hand and the western and Kyushu group on the other.

The language of the western (Kansai) area is called the "Kansai dialect," and, more restrictedly, the "Osaka dialect." It shows some contrast with the dialect of the Kanto area, or Tokyo speech.

The principal differences are in the word usages and in the tone. For example, the verb form *moo haratta* 'already paid' in the Tokyo speech is *moo haroota* in Kansai dialect. Adverbs also differ; *takaku natta* 'became expensive' in Tokyo speech is *takoo natta* in Kansai dialect. For the negative *nai* in Tokyo speech, the Kansai dialect uses *n* or *hen*, as in *Kyoo wa ikanai* 'I won't go today' versus *Kyoo wa ikan* or *Kyoo wa ikahen*.

The tone system difference between the two varieties is also quite noticeable. For example, *ko-ko-ro* 'heart' is pronounced in Tokyo with low-high-low tone, and with high-low-low tone in Osaka.

Among Japanese, ideal speech is that spoken by announcers on NHK (*Nippon Hoosoo Kyookai* [Japan Broadcasting Corporation], the public broadcast in Japan) when reading the daily news. It is a good idea to listen to their Japanese as a model for the most acceptable accent, speed, and tone of the Japanese language.

Part II:
FUNDAMENTALS

Iowa Wintry Country Road

1. Greetings (1)—Common Greetings

■ Target Expressions

Good morning.

おはようございます。
Ohayoo gozaimasu.
おはよう。
Ohayoo.

■ Strategic Explanation

Three basic strategies. Typical Japanese greetings consist of a set of formulaic expressions. The following expressions are used when you see a person for the first time in a day, depending on the time of your encounter.

(a) おはよう（ございます）。*Ohayoo (gozaimasu).* 'Good morning.'
Gozaimasu makes the greeting formal and polite; when greeting your social superior, *gozaimasu* should be added. Among close colleagues and friends, *ohayoo* in a positive tone of voice suffices.

(b) こんにちは。*Konnichiwa.* 'Good afternoon.'
Remember that *n* is syllabic in Japanese. This word contains five beats, pronounced as *ko-n-ni-chi-wa*. Be careful not to pronounce it as *ko-ni-chi-wa*.

(c) こんばんは。*Konbanwa.* (pronounced as *ko-n-ba-n-wa*) 'Good evening.'

As in English, when greeted with these expressions, answering by identical greetings will suffice. If you bow—even slightly—as you say these greetings, you are adding a greater degree of politeness. If you can witness actual native speakers' behavior or watch it in television programs, movies, and on the Internet, observe how the Japanese move their heads and upper torsos when greeting each other.

Not greeting strangers. Among complete strangers, greetings as introduced here are not customarily exchanged, unless you greet a person so that you can start a business interaction, or unless the environment defines some social relationship between you and the addressee. Although at least in some parts of the United States it is common to greet complete strangers in an elevator, such greeting exchanges are not customary in Japan.

■ Warning

- *Konnichiwa* and *konbanwa* are not used among family members. Likewise, among familiar company employees, when meeting each other at the company, instead of *konnichiwa*, other brief greetings such as *aa doomo* or nodding are used to acknowledge each other.

- Many Americans greet each other by saying "How are you?" Although it is possible to literally translate this phrase into Japanese *ikaga desu ka?* 'how are you?' this expression is not normally used, unless you are specifically concerned about the physical condition of the other as, for example, when asking a person how he or she feels after being sick.
- Another possible translation of 'how are you?' is *(o)genki desu ka?* which is also rarely used by Japanese speakers. *(O)genki desu ka?* is used when you meet your friend after a while and you are concerned about how he or she has been; this expression is similar to the English 'how have you been?'
- Instead of *how are you*, the Japanese strategy of greeting requires, first, the appropriate greeting formula introduced here, and second, innocuous comments on the weather. Talking about the weather, or, really, any noncontroversial or universal topic is a widely exercised strategy (also in many parts of the world) to express the speaker's interest in the person addressed; such expressions show a friendly attitude.

2. Describing State (1)—Adjectival Predicate

■ Target Expression

(It's) hot, isn't it?

あついですね。
Atsui-desu ne.

[Adj-*i*]

■ Grammatical Explanation

Five ways of modification. These are five ways of modifying nouns in Japanese: (1) the use of what is called *i*-type adjectives, [Adj-*i*], (2) using demonstratives, (3) modifying another noun connected with the particle *no*, [N + *no*], (4) using *na*-type adjectives, and (5) through clausal modifiers. Here we focus on the first type.

***I*-type adjectives.** The *i*-type adjectives all end with -*i*. (Not all words ending with -*i* are adjectives, however.) They precede the nouns they modify (refer to characteristic 6). Thus, 'hot day' in Japanese is *atsui hi*, *atsui* 'hot' preceding *hi* 'day.'

Japanese adjectives differ from English adjectives in this respect: [Adj-*i*] may also be used as a predicate (refer to characteristic 2). *Atsui* is a predicate meaning '(*it*) is hot' and is used independently in casual or informal situations. [Adj-*i*], when used as a predicate, may be followed by *-desu*, a suffix to indicate a formal style. Thus, *atsui-desu* also means '(it) is hot,' but it is a more formal expression of *atsui*. This is the safest style for beginning language learners since it is applicable to many social situations. In general, it is better to be a little more formal.

About particles. Japanese has a rich system of particles—functional words normally consisting of only a few syllables—which function grammatically and interactionally. Japanese particles are "postpositional" (placed immediately after) to the element whose relation to other elements is being defined (refer to characteristic 7).

***Ne* and *nee*.** Among interactional particles, *ne* and its lengthened version *nee* are most frequently used. *Ne* and *nee* roughly function as English tag-questions (such as *don't you* in *you like to read, don't you?*) used when soliciting assurance and/or agreement from the listener. *Ne* and *nee* are attached to declarative sentences, both affirmative and negative. In general, interactional particles are used in spoken Japanese. When used in written discourse, it gives a flavor of being in a speaking-directly-to-the-reader style, as one finds in personal letters.

What happened to *it*. You may be wondering what happened to *it* in the English target expression, *(It's) hot, isn't it?* As will be explained later, pronouns are frequently unmentioned in Japanese. There is no need to match each English word with its Japanese equivalent (refer to characteristic 4). Unlike English, the grammatical subject does not require overt expression in a Japanese sentence. A word-by-word translation is hardly a recommended strategy for learning Japanese. Note that the *it* in the target structure does not refer to something identified earlier—the "anaphoric" function of pronouns. The *it* is placed in English only because it is grammatically required.

Commenting on the weather. Commentary on the weather is frequently used as a greeting. It is a safe subject to bring up to communicate that you are not a threat to the other person and you want to maintain a friendly attitude. The best response to a comment like *atsui-desu nee* is *soo desu nee* '(lit., that is so) yes, indeed'—regardless of whether you truly think so or not.

List of Commonly Used *I*-Type Adjectives

新しい	*atarashii*	new
温かい	*atatakai*	(pleasantly) warm
暑い/熱い	*atsui**1	hot
厚い	*atsui**1	thick, heavy
忙しい	*isogashii*	busy

美しい	*utsukushii*	beautiful
おいしい	*oishii*	delicious
多い	*ooi*[*2]	many, much
大きい	*ookii*	large
遅い	*osoi*	late, slow
おもしろい	*omoshiroi*	interesting, funny
きびしい	*kibishii*	strict, demanding
暗い	*kurai*	dark
寂しい	*sabishii*	lonely
寒い	*samui*	cold (in reference to the atmosphere)
すばらしい	*subarashii*	splendid
少ない	*sukunai*[*2]	a few, little
すごい	*sugoi*	breathtaking, enormous
せまい	*semai*	narrow
涼しい	*suzushii*	cool
高い	*takai*[*3]	tall
高い	*takai*[*3]	expensive
小さい	*chiisai*	small
近い	*chikai*	near
冷たい	*tsumetai*	cold (to touch)
遠い	*tooi*	distant
長い	*nagai*	long
早い/速い	*hayai*	early, quick
低い	*hikui*	low
広い	*hiroi*	wide, spacious
古い	*hurui*[*4]	old
まずい	*mazui*	with bad taste
短い	*mijikai*	short
むずかしい	*muzukashii*	difficult
やさしい	*yasashii*	kind, easy
やばい	*yabai*	risky
安い	*yasui*	inexpensive
良い	*yoi/ii*	good
若い	*wakai*[*5]	young
悪い	*warui*	bad

*1. The word *atsui* represents two separate adjectives. When the three morae *a-tsu-i* are pronounced with low/high/low pitch, *atsui* means 'hot'; when pronounced with low/high/high pitch it means 'thick, heavy.'

*2. *Ooi* and *sukunai* must not be used as direct modifiers of nouns. They are used as predicates only. [*Ooku no* + N] and [*sukoshi no* + N] are used for noun modification. It is possible to use *ooi* and *sukunai* as clause modifiers when *ooi* and *sukunai* are used as predicates, as in *chokin no sukunai hito* 'a person with little savings.' For the adjectives *chikai* and *tooi*, both forms (*chikai* and *chikaku no, tooi* and *tooku no*) are possible when used for noun modification.

*3. The adjective *takai* has two separate meanings, one meaning 'tall' as in tall person and tall building, the other meaning 'expensive.'

*4. The adjective *hurui* is not used to express a person's old age. 'Old (in age)' is expressed by an expression *toshi o totta* 'lit., gained age,' a clausal modifier preceding the noun.

*5. Adjective *wakai* normally refers to a young adult; *wakai hito*, for example, means a young or younger adult. *Wakai*, however, is never used with *kodomo* 'child.' Instead, *osanai* is used to refer to an infant.

■ Additional Information

- *I*-type adjectives may be shortened for exclamatory purposes in very casual speech. For example, instead of *atsui*, a person may cry out "*Atsu-tt*" as he or she touches a hot cup. Shortened *i*-type adjectives create sentences such as (a).

  (a) はやっ!
  Haya-tt!
  (Boy, it's quick!)

- Another sound change in *i*-type adjectives is observed in casual conversation in peer groups, especially among young male speakers. For example, *yabai* may be pronounced as *yabee*. The adjective *yabai* 'risky' is used ironically in positive contexts as well. Retaining the meaning of 'threatening,' when something is so overwhelmingly moving, *yabai* or *yabee* may be used, for example, when one tastes an extremely delicious food. This use of *yabai* is limited to very casual situations among intimates.

3. Speech Style (1)—Spoken, Written, Formal, and Informal Styles

■ Target Expressions

(It's) early, isn't it?

早いですね。
Hayai-desu ne.
早いねえ。
Hayai nee.

[Adj-*i* + -*desu*]

■ Strategic Explanation

Just as in English, Japanese has different language styles, depending on the genre and situational contexts. We concentrate on two fundamental feature differences here: written and spoken language on one hand, and the formal and informal (casual) style on the other.

Written and spoken styles. In writing, we create a planned discourse addressed to a nonspecific audience. In spontaneous speaking, we create unplanned discourse addressed directly to the interaction partner. This means that speech is featured by increased levels of fragmentation with devices emotionally appealing to the listener. It encourages personal and emotional involvement. On the other hand, in written language, you are more likely to see complex sentence structures into which information is richly packed.

Features of spoken Japanese.

1. Language is much more fragmented with shorter utterances and phrases.
2. Interactional particles are frequently used at the end of phrases and utterances.
3. Fillers and hesitation noises (*uh-huh, um*...), and interactional conjunctions occur frequently.
4. What is understood and obvious is not expressed to the extent it is expressed in written discourse.
5. Postposing fragments after the final verb is frequently observed.
6. Verbs end with gerundive and other continuing forms at the end of utterances.
7. Remarks on communication itself (metacommunication) are made.
8. Utterances may be co-created by both speakers.

Formal and informal styles. Differences between formal and informal styles are important in Japanese. Just as in English, but more distinctly in Japanese, we find different speech styles depending on the social situation and the social status of the participants. Formal social situations such as school, business ceremonies or other public gatherings require formal and careful style. Formal style is also recommended toward social superiors even in less formal situations. Normally a higher social status is attributed to speakers who are older or higher in rank in the workplace, or who are considered to hold a higher social status—a holder of a more prestigious occupation, for example. The speech style chosen by a speaker who represents a different social level is not reciprocal. Friendly informal speech used by a social superior does not mean that one should respond in the same style.

An informal, casual style is used among social equals; an extremely casual style is reserved for close friends. Even among speakers representing a socially different status, if the situation of speech is personal and informal, as during casual chatting while drinking *sake*, the style chosen is likely to be informal. Choosing the appropriate style in different social encounters, however, requires social sensitivity and experience. It is best to play it safe by using the formal style until you know when you are expected to use an informal speech style.

Speech style and *uchi/soto*. Closely related to the choice of speech style is the well-discussed tendency of a Japanese to identify himself or herself as a member of a group. An individual is simultaneously a member of various social groups—family, university from which one has graduated, or the company where one is employed. Depending on the situational context, one of these and other groups is emphasized. Inside the group is called *uchi* 'inside,' whereas outside the group is referred to as *soto* 'outside,' and a different social orientation and behavior is observed in these two contrasting social territories. Within *uchi*, a feeling of *amae* 'dependence' prevails. When the *amae* relationship is mutually recognized, the speech style becomes informal and casual. In fact, contrary to the common belief that Japanese are inherently formal and polite, Japanese people enjoy casual and familiar relationships, and often expose an emotional vulnerability to a surprising degree.

As a foreigner learning Japanese, an overly casual style is not recommended until a strong *amae* relationship is established. Foreign nationals are generally excluded from membership in the most basic group recognized in Japan, that is, being Japanese. The style chosen by Japanese toward a foreigner, a person who belongs to *soto*, at least during initial encounters, is most likely to be formal. Viewed from the outside, this gives the impression that Japanese are always formal and polite.

Learning to choose appropriate styles. Choosing appropriate speech style is an important aspect of communication in any society. In Japanese, the distinction between these styles is somewhat clearer than it is in English, and Japanese society tends to penalize an inappropriate speech style more severely than other societies do. Naturally, speech styles vary in gradations. Some spoken styles are more careful and softer than others, while other styles may be more or less blunt and straightforward. We all acquire a sensitivity to speech styles in our own culture. The key is to learn the meaning of different styles in a foreign language and to cultivate a sensitivity in accordance with the norms of that society.

At this point we should be aware of two styles, one formal and the other informal (or plain). In using [Adj-*i*], when the *-desu* ending is added, it is formal, while the form without *-desu* is considered informal and plain.

■ Additional Information

- Informal style is used in written Japanese in fiction, non-fiction, prose and modern poetry. In writing letters, however, formal style is used if the relationship and the situation call for it. Business letters are always written in a formal style. Personal letters exchanged between social intimates may be in formal or informal style reflecting the particular relationship between the parties.

- Throughout this book, both formal and informal styles appear without specific markings. Only when necessary, stylistic features are noted in square brackets.

4. Describing State (2)—Adjectival Predicate with Topic

■ Target Expression

It's warm today, isn't it?

今日は暖かいですねえ。
Kyoo wa atatakai-desu nee.

[N + *wa*]

■ Grammatical Explanation

Topic and comment. The target expression above contains a formal style of [Adj-*i*]; that is, *atatakai-desu* preceded by a noun, *kyoo* 'today,' and *wa*, a topic marker. *Wa* is a particle which marks the "topic" of an utterance/a sentence or a topic activated across several utterances/sentences (refer to characteristic 3). Topic is defined simply as "something that is being talked about." In the sentence *kyoo wa atatakai-desu nee, kyoo* is marked as a topic; the statement is about *kyoo* 'today.' The remaining portion of the utterance, that is, *atatakai-desu nee,* is called "comment" and provides information pertinent to the topic. The concepts of topic and comment are extremely important for understanding how Japanese organize sentences. We will return to this issue later.

Characteristics of Japanese nouns. Since this entry marks the first appearance of Japanese nouns, we must note one grammatical characteristic of Japanese nouns very different from English.

There is no grammatical distinction between singular and plural nouns in Japanese (refer to characteristic 9). Thus for both one apple and two apples, *ringo* suffices. Whether *ringo* is singular or plural depends on the context and is not marked in the noun form. Since a grammatical singular and plural distinction is not required in Japanese, learning whether or not an English noun is countable, that is, whether or not the plural *-s* should be attached, is difficult for Japanese students learning English. It is sometimes difficult to remember that the English noun *chalk* is uncountable (*two *chalks* is not acceptable in English when counting two pieces of chalk) while the noun *pencil* is (one must say two *pencils*).

■ Examples

(1) 英語はむずかしいです。
Eigo wa muzukashii-desu.
(English is difficult.)

(2) 仕事はきびしい。
Shigoto wa kibishii.
(The job is demanding.)

(3) **A:** 東京は寒いですね。
Tookyoo wa samui-desu ne.
(It's cold in Tokyo, isn't it?)

B: ええ、本当に。
Ee, hontooni.
(Yes, indeed.)

(4) りんごはおいしいです。
Ringo wa oishii-desu.
(Apples are delicious.)

■ Additional Information

- Some Japanese proper nouns written in the conventional alphabet in Western literature are misrepresentations of original Japanese words. For example, Tokyo, so spelled in English literature worldwide, is pronounced with four beats *To-o-kyo-o* in Japanese. In this book when Japanese transliteration is given, it is given in such a manner as to reflect the actual mora structure and the pronunciation of each word.
- In conversation, instead of *wa, tte* is frequently used.

(a) 英語**って**むずかしいですね。
*Eigo **tte** muzukashii-desu ne.*
(English is difficult, isn't it?)

(b) 仕事**って**きびしい。
*Shigoto **tte** kibishii.*
(Working is hard.)

5. Loan Words

■ Target Expressions

coffee, hamburgers, personal computers

コーヒー、ハンバーガー、パソコン

koohii, hanbaagaa, pasokon

■ Grammatical Explanation

History of loan words. Throughout history, the Japanese language has borrowed many words from foreign countries, first from China as early as the Nara period (710-794 A.D.). Throughout the Heian and the Edo periods (eighth century to nineteenth century), Chinese words continued to enter into the Japanese language, and many were integrated into Japanese to the extent that they are no longer considered foreign "loan" words. Today, most Chinese words are written in *kanji* compounds and carry the Chinese reading (*on*-reading).

Around 1600 A.D., the Japanese language began to borrow many Western words, particularly from Portuguese and Dutch (during the Edo period). Additionally, German, French, and, most of all, English loan words have been introduced since the beginning of the Meiji era (1868 A.D.). Western loan words are written in *katakana* and are pronounced according to the Japanese phonological rules, mostly in the form of available Japanese morae. Therefore, the sounds you hear for English words in Japanese may be very different from the original English, and may in fact be incomprehensible.

Loan words take on different meanings. Sometimes a homonym in English may be introduced into Japanese as words with two distinct pronunciations. For instance, the word *strike* has been borrowed in two distinct ways: *sutoraiku* to mean 'strike' as in baseball, and *sutoraiki* to mean 'strike' as in the labor movement. *Sutoraiki* is often shortened as *suto*. A loan word may be specialized in meaning in such a way as to share the same semantic field with a related Japanese word. For example, the word *biru*, a shortened version of the English word *building,* normally refers to Western style tall buildings only, while the Japanese word *tatemono* 'building' refers to other types of buildings.

As shown here in the case of *biru* and others (*hankachi* for handkerchief, *maiku* for microphone), long foreign words are often shortened. Multiple words may be shortened also, often into four syllable words; *pasokon* for *per*sonal *com*puter.

Generating new words from loan words. A loan word can be generative. It can be combined with Japanese or other foreign words to produce a compound noun.

The word *pan* 'bread'—from Portuguese *pão*—for example, is combined with several morphemes (smallest meaningful units that constitute a word) and other words to form the following:

食**パン**	*shoku***pan**	loaf of bread
フランス**パン**	*Huransu***pan**	French bread
ライ麦**パン**	*raimugi***pan**	rye bread
ロール**パン**	*rooru***pan**	rolls
むし**パン**	*mushi***pan**	steamed bread

Loan words as nouns. Most loan words are integrated into Japanese as nouns and may make morphological changes accordingly. Drive, *doraibu* in Japanese, is combined with the verb *suru* 'do,' as in *doraibu-suru*, to mean 'to drive' (as in *to drive a car*). English adjectives are normally loaned as adjectives which end with *-na*. For example, unique, *yuniiku* in Japanese, is used as *yuniikuna hito* 'a unique person' (*na*-type adjectives are discussed later). As a peculiar type of loan word, the verb *get* is transformed as *getto-suru* to mean 'to obtain.'

For those who are interested in learning loan words in Japanese, there are loan word dictionaries published from time to time.

Pseudo-loan words. There are also pseudo-loan words made in Japan. These are foreign words but they are created by Japanese with meanings different from the original language. For example, *naitaa* made of the English word *night* followed by a morpheme *-er* refers to baseball night games. Roman letters of the alphabet are also used. The nationwide railway network is called JR (pronounced *jeiaaru*) with the Roman letters as its authentic written symbols. You may also find foreign words appearing in Japanese writing with the original writing symbols. These are "foreign words" and are not considered "loan words" which constitute a part of Japanese vocabulary.

List of Foreign Proper Nouns and Common Loan Words

Country names:

アメリカ	*Amerika*	America (United States of)
イギリス	*Igirisu*	England
イタリア	*Itaria*	Italy
オランダ	*Oranda*	Holland
カナダ	*Kanada*	Canada
スペイン	*Supein*	Spain
ドイツ	*Doitsu*	Germany
フランス	*Huransu*	France

City names:

サンフランシスコ	*Sanhuranshisuko*	San Francisco
シカゴ	*Shikago*	Chicago
トロント	*Toronto*	Toronto
ニューヨーク	*Nyuuyooku*	New York
ホノルル	*Honoruru*	Honolulu
パリ	*Pari*	Paris
ボストン	*Bosuton*	Boston
ロンドン	*Rondon*	London
ロサンゼルス	*Rosanzerusu*	Los Angeles

Personal names:

ジョン	*Jon*	John
スミス	*Sumisu*	Smith
ターナー	*Taanaa*	Turner
チョー	*Choo*	Cho
ナンシー	*Nanshii*	Nancy
ビル	*Biru*	Bill
ブラウン	*Buraun*	Brown

Drinks:

ウイスキー	*uisukii*	whiskey
コーヒー	*koohii*	coffee
ジュース	*juusu*	juice, fruit drinks
ビール	*biiru*	beer
ミルク	*miruku*	milk
ワイン	*wain*	wine

Food:

アイスクリーム	*aisukuriimu*	ice cream
カステラ	*kasutera*	sponge cake [from *pão de Castella*]
ケーキ	*keeki*	cake
サンドイッチ	*sandoitchi*	sandwich
ステーキ	*suteeki*	steak
ハンバーガー	*hanbaagaa*	hamburger (served with hamburger buns)
ハンバーグ	*hanbaagu*	hamburger (served with food items other than hamburger buns, like Salisbury steak)
パスタ	*pasuta*	pasta
パン	*pan*	bread [from Portuguese *pão*]

Sports:

ゴルフ	*goruhu*	golf
サッカー	*sakkaa*	soccer
スケート	*sukeeto*	skate
スキー	*sukii*	ski
ジョギング	*jogingu*	jogging
ダンス	*dansu*	dance
テニス	*tenisu*	tennis
バスケ(ットボール)	*basuke(ttobooru)*	basketball

Transportation:

タクシー	*takushii*	taxi
バス	*basu*	bus
モノレール	*monoreeru*	monorail

Others:

(アル)バイト	*(aru)baito*	part-time job [from German *Arbeit*]
(インター)ネット	*(intaa)netto*	Internet
カメラ	*kamera*	camera
スーパー	*suupaa*	supermarket
デジカメ	*dejikame*	digital camera
デパート	*depaato*	department store
テレビ	*terebi*	television
バー	*baa*	bar
パソコン	*pasokon*	personal computer
ホテル	*hoteru*	hotel
マンション	*manshon*	upscale apartment or condominium [from English word *mansion*]
ラジオ	*rajio*	radio
レストラン	*resutoran*	restaurant
ワイシャツ	*waishatsu*	solid colored dress shirt [from *white shirt*]

6. Personal Names and Occupations

■ Target Expressions

Ms. Yamada, Mr. Jones

山田さん、ジョーンズさん
Yamada-san, Joonzu-san

[-*san*]

■ Strategic Explanation

Address terms. In most cases Japanese prefer to address a person by his or her last name plus *-san*. *-San* applies to both genders and all marital statuses. There is no distinction between *Miss, Mrs., Ms.,* and *Mr.* (In the English translation appearing in this book, one of these titles is chosen for convenience.) In Japanese, surnames appear first and the given names follow. Most Japanese do not have middle names. Thus, Makio Yamada (*Yamada Makio* in Japanese) is most often addressed and referred to as *Yamada-san*. In reference to foreign names, there is no need to reverse the order. Bill Johnson will be *(Biru) Johnson-san*. Other similar suffixes include: *-sama* (polite and formal), *-chan* (familiar) and *-kun* (primarily used in reference to younger males).

About using first names. In familiar situations, first names with *-san* may be used. For example, *Makio-san* and *Biru-san*. Among youth, particularly in familiar and casual situations, first names without *-san* are often used, for example, *Makio* and *Biru*.

Occupational terms. Japanese may address others by referring to the occupational title, for example, *sensei* 'teacher' as in *Tanaka-sensei* 'Professor Tanaka.' This is used both as referential and addressing terms. Some occupations may be used with *-san*, as in *moderu-san*, when referring to the occupation and when addressing a fashion model, particularly when personal names are not known. These include *ten'in-san* 'store attendant,' and *untenshu-san* (or *doraibaa-san*) 'driver' or 'chauffeur.' Some occupational titles are used for self-address when communicating with social subordinates. For example, a teacher may refer to himself or herself by saying *sensei* toward students. (The term for university professor *kyooju* is not used for self-addressing purposes, however.)

■ Warning

Do not use *-san* when referring to yourself. Although in English it is possible to say "I'm Ms. Jones," in Japanese *-san* should not be attached for self-referencing. This also applies to the situation when you are referring to a member of your *uchi* group toward the member of your *soto* group. This is because in-group members are considered so close to oneself that they should be treated as one treats oneself, that is, without *-san*.

List of Common Last Names

市川	*Ichikawa*	高橋	*Takahashi*
伊藤	*Itoo*	田中	*Tanaka*
上田	*Ueda*	中川	*Nakagawa*
小川	*Ogawa*	原	*Hara*

加藤	*Katoo*	松本	*Matsumoto*
小林	*Kobayashi*	山田	*Yamada*
斉藤	*Saitoo*	山中	*Yamanaka*
佐藤	*Satoo*	山下	*Yamashita*
鈴木	*Suzuki*	渡辺	*Watanabe*

List of Common Occupations

医者	*isha*	medical doctor
エンジニア	*enjinia*	engineer
(大学) 教授	*(daigaku) kyooju*	university professor
会社員	*kaishain*	company employee
歌手	*kashu*	singer
学生	*gakusei*	student
学者	*gakusha*	scholar
銀行員	*ginkooin*	banker, bank employee
建築家	*kenchikuka*	architect
公務員	*koomuin*	public servant, government employee
政治家	*seijika*	politician
先生	*sensei*	teacher, professor
主婦	*shuhu*	housewife
店員	*ten'in*	store attendant
秘書	*hisho*	secretary
ピアニスト	*pianisuto*	pianist
モデル	*moderu*	(fashion) model

7. Self-identification by *Da*

■ Target Expression

I'm Anderson.

アンダーソンです。
Andaason desu.

[*da*]

■ Grammatical Explanation

Japanese *be*-verb. The verb *be* in Japanese is *da* (its formal counterpart is *desu*). There is no grammatical subject-verb agreement in Japanese. *Da* is used for the present tense of the *be*-verb regardless of the person and number of the subject, i.e., in place of English *am, is,* as well as *are.*

Structuring *be*-verb sentences. In expressing *I'm Anderson* in Japanese, since whom "I" refers to is obvious, there is no need to specify it (refer to characteristic 4). Japanese is a verb-final language, and therefore, *desu* is placed after the personal name *Anderson* (refer to characteristic 1). We construct an utterance *Andaason desu* 'I'm Anderson.'

When considering the structure of a Japanese sentence, think of it as verb-centered; the most important part of the sentence is the verbal element, and all other aspects are specified only when necessary, all added before the verbal element. Contrast this with English sentence structure where a grammatical subject, verb, and sometimes object are required.

***-Desu* as suffix.** So far, we have studied two predicate types: (1) [Adj-*i*], and (2) *da*. It is important to recognize here that the suffix *-desu* attached to [Adj-*i*] is different from the verb *da* discussed here. *-Desu* attached to [Adj-*i*] does not function as a verbal predicate *be*; it only assigns a stylistic feature. Remember that while the verb *be* takes either *da* or *desu*, the [Adj-*i*] predicate takes only *-desu* (**takai-da*). When *-desu* is used for stylistic purposes, we mark it with a hyphen to indicate that it is a suffix, rather than an independent verb.

■ Warning

The informal form *da* is often deleted completely. In spoken language, the informal form of *Nihon-jin desu* 'I'm Japanese' is simply *Nihon-jin*.

8. Deictic Expression (1)—The *Ko-so-a-do* System

■ Target Expressions

this book, that book

この本、あの本

kono hon, ano hon

[*kono, sono, ano, dono*]

[*kore, sore, are, dore*]

■ Grammatical Explanation

Ko-so-a-do. Japanese demonstratives and pronouns are marked by prefixes *ko-*, *so-*, *a-*, and *do-*. Depending on how the speaker views the referent in terms of physical or psychological distance from where the speaker is situated, references such as *this*, *it*, and *that* (these are called deictic expressions) are assigned. *Ko-* is assigned when referring to an item closest to the participants, especially to the one closest to the speaker. *So-* is assigned when an item is closest to the listener, while *a-* is used to identify those items that are away from both the speaker and listener. *Do-* is used when making interrogative (question) words.

Using the *ko-so-a-do* system. The *ko-so-a-do* system is useful in distinguishing items in a defined conceptual discourse. When a new item is introduced within a frame of reference and when it is anaphorically referred to (i.e., referred back to an element identified earlier), the *so-* reference is used. On the other hand, if the referent is assumed to be known by both participants and can be recalled into the current frame of reference of discourse, the *a-* reference is used.

Thus, for example, if you introduce Tracy first in conversation and then refer back to her, you would use *sono* reference as in 'There's this person called Tracy and that person (*sono hito*)...' If you know that the listener already knows about the person you are going to talk about, *ano* reference is used, as in 'Is that person (*ano hito*) well? You know, that person (*ano hito*) we met in Kyoto last month.' By using *a*-reference, you share a common experience with your companion. This strategy may be used to create empathy.

List of *Ko-so-a-do* Words

Demonstratives (used as in *kono hon* 'this book'):

この	*kono*	this (close to the speaker)
その	*sono*	that (close to the listener)
あの	*ano*	that (away from but identified by both speakers)
どの	*dono*	which

Pronouns:

これ	*kore*	this one
それ	*sore*	that one
あれ	*are*	that one over there
どれ	*dore*	which one

The *ko-so-a-do* system generates additional sets:

Locative nouns:

ここ	*koko*	this place
そこ	*soko*	that place
あそこ	*asoko*	that place over there (over there)
どこ	*doko*	which place (where)

Directional nouns:

こちら	*kochira*	this way
そちら	*sochira*	that way
あちら	*achira*	direction toward that way over there
どちら	*dochira*	which way, which one

Directional nouns are also used as polite versions of personal pronouns; *kochira* meaning 'this person,' *dochira* meaning 'which person,' etc.

Adjectives:

こういう	*kooyuu*	such as this
そういう	*sooyuu*	such as that
ああいう	*aayuu*	such as that
どういう	*dooyuu*	such as what, of what kind

Manner adverbs:

こう	*koo*	this way
そう	*soo*	that way
ああ	*aa*	that way
どう	*doo*	what way, which way

■ Examples

(1) こちらは山中さんです。
Kochira wa Yamanaka-san desu.
(This is Ms. Yamanaka.)

(2) この本、むずかしい。
Kono hon, muzukashii.
(This book is difficult.)

(3) 阿佐ヶ谷アパートはあのビルです。
Asagaya Apaato wa ano biru desu.
(Asagaya Apartment is that building over there.)

■ Warning

When using demonstratives in imaginary discourse, the following points should be noted. *Ko*-demonstratives often convey the impression that things are familiar or close to self, *so*-demonstratives are often used as cohesive ties, and *a*-demonstratives are used for the purpose of appealing to empathy and emotion.

Because these characteristics do not precisely match English demonstratives, special care is required. When you are not referring to things in physical terms, it is particularly important to avoid using *a*-demonstratives for purely referential purposes. So, for example, *asoko* in (b) is wrong, unless a special emotional reason justifies its usage. Use *soko*, instead.

(a) 昨日、渋谷に行きました。
Kinoo, Shibuya ni ikimashita.
(Yesterday, I went to Shibuya.)

(b) *あそこで友だちに会いました。

(c) **そこ**で友だちに会いました。
***Soko** de tomodachi ni aimashita.*
(There I met my friend.)

9. Introducing—Expressions for Social Introduction

■ Target Expressions

I'm Smith. How do you do?
はじめまして、スミスです。どうぞよろしく。
Hajimemashite, Sumisu desu. Doozo yoroshiku.

■ Strategic Explanation

Introducing ritual. When introducing people at social gatherings and meetings, formulaic expressions are used. *Hajimemashite* '(lit., for the first time) how do you do?,' *doozo yoroshiku* '(lit., please be favorable to me) how do you do?' are prototypical examples. For formal occasions, a politer version, *doozo yoroshiku onegai-shimasu* should be used.

Study the following interaction.

浅田： ああ、スミスさん、こちらは中川さんです。
Asada: *Aa, Sumisu-san, kochira wa Nakagawa-san desu.*
(Oh, Mr. Smith, this is Ms. Nakagawa.)

中川： はじめまして、中川です。どうぞよろしく。
Nakagawa: *Hajimemashite, Nakagawa desu. Doozo yoroshiku.*
(I am Nakagawa. How do you do?)

スミス： スミスです。こちらこそどうぞよろしく。
Smith: *Sumisu desu. Kochira koso doozo yoroshiku.*
(I am Smith. How do you do?)

Kochira koso 'lit., this side also' is used by Smith to express the greeting from her side also; this expression is used when someone already gives the greeting and you want to return the same, similar to the English expression *same here*, or *same to you*.

Bowing. Utterances *hajimemashite and doozo yoroshiku* should be accompanied by bowing. Bowing expresses sincerity and goodwill; it is important to bow, particularly when you are introduced to a social superior. The timing to raise your head when bowing can be tricky. Theoretically, a social subordinate should not raise his or her head before the superior does. Check the height of your superior's bowing before you raise your head completely. You can also perform multiple bowings if needed.

Engaging in small talk. When introduced for the first time to a person at a social occasion, people engage in non-offensive small talk. A favored strategy among Japanese for "breaking the ice," is to mention common acquaintances or common backgrounds, leading to questions that would mean 'do you know so-and-so?' or 'have you worked with so-and-so?' 'where are you from?' and so forth.

■ Additional Information

- With increasing encounters with Westerners, Japanese expect to shake hands when introduced. Hand-shaking is appropriate, particularly when introductions are conducted in English without an interpreter. However, if you are introduced to a Japanese superior in Japanese under formal circumstances, it is best to express your respect by following the custom of the superior, and bow respectfully. If the other party offers their hand, you should, of course, shake hands. You may also notice that Japanese bow and shake hands simultaneously. Japanese are only trying to adopt the Western way, while expressing greetings in a Japanese style.
- In business meetings, *meishi* 'business cards' are often exchanged. Hand the card to whomever you meet so that the writing faces him or her. As you hand your business card, bow slightly to show respect; as you receive the business card, bow slightly again to express gratitude. Silently you read the title and the name carefully. This shows respect; the information you gain by reading the business card is useful for defining the person's relative social status, and therefore for deciding on what speech style you should choose.

10. Verbal Predicate (1)—Common Verbs: Non-past

■ Target Expression

A friend will come.

友だちが来ます。
Tomodachi ga kimasu.

[Vnon-past]

■ Grammatical Explanation

Japanese verbs. We already learned the *be*-verb, that is, *da/desu*. All other verbs in Japanese end with the vowel *-u*. (Needless to say, not all words that end with *-u* are verbs, however.) The verbs change ending forms according to features associated with the verb, and they take specific forms when the auxiliary verbs are attached (refer to characteristic 8). For example, verb endings are changed to indicate past tense, negation, as well as causative and passive features.

Verb forms and non-past tense. Here we focus on the non-past tense, so called since it expresses English equivalents of both present and future tenses. In other words, the basic purpose of non-past tense is to convey that the action or the state referred to has not yet occurred. Verb forms are considered by many students of Japanese to be a rather difficult aspect to learn. Although it requires a certain amount of memorization, the system itself is rather simple. Unlike the more complex verb conjugation of Romance and some Germanic languages, in Japanese there is no correspondence between the person (such as the first-, second-, and third-person), the number (singular and plural) and the verb form. In fact, since the changing process of verb forms differs substantially from Romance and Germanic languages, "conjugation" may be a misnomer; we use this term only for convenience.

Three verb conjugation types. Verb conjugation follows rules specific to the types of verbs, and for that reason verbs are categorized into three types based on the endings of the "basic" ([Vbasic]) or "dictionary" form. (There are different ways to explain Japanese verbs—some categorize verbs into five groups instead—but here we use one of the simplest.) The three groups are: *U*-verbs, *RU*-verbs and Irregular verbs. *U*-verbs include all verbs that are neither *RU*- nor Irregular verbs. *RU*-verbs end with *-iru* and *-eru* in their basic forms. There are only two irregular verbs, the verb *suru* 'to do' and *kuru* 'to come.' There are some special honorific verbs ending with *-aru*. There are special irregular verbs that will be studied in Entry 86.

The basic form is the form listed in the dictionary, and is the informal, non-past affirmative form of the verb. For deriving the formal version from the basic form, the following rules apply.

U-verbs:	Delete final *-u* and add *-imasu*.				
	e.g. 飲む	*nom**u***	→	*nom**imasu***	to drink
RU-verbs:	Delete final *-ru* and add *-masu*.				
	e.g. 食べる	*tabe**ru***	→	*tabe**masu***	to eat
Irregular Verbs:	する	***suru***	→	***shimasu***	to do
	来る	***kuru***	→	***kimasu***	to come

There are a few exceptions to the basic rules of verb categorization. The following verbs, although ending with *-iru* and *-eru* forms, are *U*-verbs and are conjugated likewise.

入る	*hair**u***	→	*hair**imasu***	to enter
減る	*her**u***	→	*her**imasu***	to decrease
要る	*ir**u***	→	*ir**imasu***	to need
帰る	*kaer**u***	→	*kaer**imasu***	to return
切る	*kir**u***	→	*kir**imasu***	to cut
参る	*mair**u***	→	*mair**imasu***	to go [humble]
しゃべる	*shaber**u***	→	*shaber**imasu***	to chat
しめる	*shimer**u***	→	*shimer**imasu***	to dampen
すべる	*suber**u***	→	*suber**imasu***	to slide, to slip

In cases of *iru*, *kaeru*, *kiru*, and *shimeru*, there are *RU*-verbs with identical mora structure: *iru* 'to be, to exist,' *kaeru* 'to change, to exchange,' *kiru* 'to wear,' and *shimeru* 'to close.'

Stative and active verbs. Japanese verbs are further categorized based on their tendency to describe either a state or a dynamic action. The prototypical stative verbs are the existential verbs *iru* and *aru*, both meaning 'there exists.' The *i*-type adjective predicates are also stative. Prototypical active verbs are *iku* 'to go,' *oyogu* 'to swim,' and *nomu* 'to drink.'

The meaning of non-past form. When a non-past form of the verb is used, it means the following:

1. *Description of the present state* (for stative verbs):

(1a) 子供が**います**。

Kodomo	*ga*	***imasu.***
child	S	there is

(There is a child.)

2. *Description of definite future* (for active verbs):

(2a) 会議は十時に**始まる**。

Kaigi	*wa*	*juu-ji*	*ni*	***hajimaru.***
meeting	T	ten o'clock	at	begin

(The meeting will start at ten.)

3. *Personal will* (for active verbs when the subject is 'I'):

(3a) 新しい会社でいっしょうけんめい**働きます**。

Atarashii	*kaisha*	*de*	*isshookenmei*	***hatarakimasu.***
new	company	at	hard	work

(I will work hard at the new company.)

4. *Pointing out principles or the nature of things* (for both stative and active verbs):

(4a) 水は摂氏零度で**凍る**。

Mizu	*wa*	*sesshi*	*reido*	*de*	***kooru.***
water	T	centigrade	zero degree	at	freeze

(Water freezes at zero degree centigrade.)

5. *Description of rules, regulations, and habits*:

(5a) 毎朝八時に会社へ**行く**。

Maiasa	*hachi-ji*	*ni*	*kaisha*	*e*	***iku.***
every morning	eight o'clock	at	company	to	go

(Every morning I go to the office at eight.)

6. *Description of procedures*:

(6a) 玉ねぎは薄く**切ります**。

Tamanegi	*wa*	*usuku*	***kirimasu.***
onion	T	thinly	slice

(Onions are sliced thinly. [as in a cookbook])

Japanese verbs tend to have an abstract and more generalized meaning when used in non-past tense as shown in categories numbered 4, 5, and 6 above. In order to express the present tense of the action verbs, the present progressive tense (to be discussed under Entry 51) is used.

More about verbs. The formal non-past verb form is also called *masu*-form due to the obvious reason of ending with *-masu*. *Masu*-form minus *-masu* is the "stem" of the verb, [Vstem]. The verb stems become useful later when we learn to attach to them other grammatical elements.

Because the formal non-past affirmative form takes *desu* (for the *be*-verb *da*) and *masu* endings, it is also called *desu/masu* style. Formal forms of adjectives also fall under the *desu/masu* style.

Note the verb position in a sentence. In normal situations, it appears at the end of the sentence (refer to characteristic 1). You may consider this phenomenon as an extension of characteristic 6 in that verbs are modified by all preceding modifying elements, including subjects, objects, and other adverbial phrases.

Particles *ga* and *o*. At this point, we note two grammatical particles, the subject-marker *ga* and the object-marker *o*, both of which will be discussed in detail later.

■ Examples

(1) 友だちが 来ます。
Tomodachi ga kimasu.[*1]
(A friend is coming.)

(2) サンドイッチを食べます。
Sandoitchi o tabemasu.[*1]
(I will eat sandwiches.)

*1. It is important to note that case-marking grammatical particles follow the nouns whose case the particles assign. These are postpositions in contrast with English prepositions which precede nouns.

List of Common Verbs

Basic form		English	Formal form
U-verbs:			
会う	*au*	to meet	*aimasu*
開く	*aku*	to open	*akimasu*
遊ぶ	*asobu*	to play	*asobimasu*
洗う	*arau*	to wash	*araimasu*
歌う	*utau*	to sing	*utaimasu*
送る	*okuru*	to send	*okurimasu*
おこる	*okoru*	to be angry	*okorimasu*
落とす	*otosu*	to drop	*otoshimasu*[*2]
おどろく	*odoroku*	to be surprised	*odorokimasu*
踊る	*odoru*	to dance	*odorimasu*
終わる	*owaru*	to end	*owarimasu*
買う	*kau*	to buy	*kaimasu*
帰る	*kaeru*	to return	*kaerimasu*
聞く	*kiku*	to hear	*kikimasu*

閉まる	*shimaru*	to close [intransitive]	*shimarimasu*
すわる	*suwaru*	to sit down	*suwarimasu*
しゃべる	*shaberu*	to chatter	*shaberimasu*
泣く	*naku*	to cry	*nakimasu*
ぬぐ	*nugu*	to take off (clothes, etc.)	*nugimasu*
飲む	*nomu*	to drink	*nomimasu*
働く	*hataraku*	to work	*hatarakimasu*
待つ	*matsu*	to wait	*machimasu*[*2]
持つ	*motsu*	to possess	*mochimasu*[*2]
もらう	*morau*	to receive	*moraimasu*
言う	*yuu*	to say	*iimasu*[*3]
読む	*yomu*	to read	*yomimasu*
笑う	*warau*	to laugh	*waraimasu*

RU-verbs:

-*iru* ending verbs:

いる	*iru*	to exist	*imasu*
落ちる	*ochiru*	to drop [intransitive]	*ochimasu*
起きる	*okiru*	to get up	*okimasu*
着る	*kiru*	to wear	*kimasu*
信じる	*shinjiru*	to believe	*shinjimasu*
できる	*dekiru*	can do	*dekimasu*
見る	*miru*	to see	*mimasu*

-*eru* ending verbs:

開ける	*akeru*	to open [transitive]	*akemasu*
あげる	*ageru*	to give	*agemasu*
入れる	*ireru*	to pour in	*iremasu*
教える	*oshieru*	to teach	*oshiemasu*
答える	*kotaeru*	to answer	*kotaemasu*
閉める	*shimeru*	to close [transitive]	*shimemasu*
捨てる	*suteru*	to throw away	*sutemasu*
出る	*deru*	to go out	*demasu*
寝る	*neru*	to sleep, to go to bed	*nemasu*

---

*2. There is a phonological (sound) change to be noted when conjugating verbs. For verbs that end with -*su* and -*tsu* in their basic forms, the formal non-past forms are -*shimasu* and -*chimasu*, respectively. There is no "si" or "ti" sound in Japanese, except in some special case of loan words as in *paatii*.

*3. When handling conjugation of the verb *yuu* 'to say,' think of it spelled '*iu*,' (which is the way it is actually written in Japanese, but nonetheless pronounced as '*yuu*'). Thus, the formal version of *yuu* (*iu*) is *iimasu*.

■ Additional Information

- The irregular verb *suru* is very productive. It is combined with nouns (of Chinese origin) to make a noun into a verb. For example:

研究する	*kenkyuu* (research)-*suru*	to conduct research
入浴する	*nyuuyoku* (taking a bath)-*suru*	to take a bath
販売する	*hanbai* (sale)-*suru*	to sell
勉強する	*benkyoo* (study)-*suru*	to study
旅行する	*ryokoo* (trip)-*suru*	to travel
輸出する	*yushutsu* (export)-*suru*	to export

- Additionally, foreign loan words become verbs by adding -*suru*; for example, *fookasu* (focus)-*suru* 'to focus,' and *shanpuu* (shampoo)-*suru* 'to shampoo.'
- Another form resembling the *desu/masu* style is used in casual conversation, primarily in masculine speech. For example, *nomu-ssu*, instead of *nomu* (or *nomimasu*), which affords a style between *nomu* and *nomimasu*. Adding -*ssu* after [V/Adj pre-Aux] form provides a style that sustains a casual friendly atmosphere without completely abandoning a formal tone.

(a) 暑い**ッス**ねえ。
*Atsui-**ssu** nee.*
(It's hot, isn't it?)

11. Verbal Predicate (2)—Existential Verbs: Non-past

■ Target Expression

Mrs. Yamada is there.

山田さんがいます。
Yamada-san ga imasu.

[*aru, iru*]

■ Grammatical Explanation

Existential verbs. We have learned two kinds of verbs: (1) the *be*-verb, *da*, and (2) common verbs ending with the -*u* sound. Additionally, we have noted that in Japanese [Adj-*i*] may be used as an independent predicate. The existential verbs *iru* and *aru* constitute another Japanese verb predicate type. The verbs *iru* and *aru*, both of which can be translated into English 'there is/are,' are called existential verbs—their basic meaning is to state that something exists.

The verb *iru* conjugates according to the *RU*-verb conjugation rules; *aru* which is a *U*-verb does not follow the *U*-verb rules entirely. At this point, we will learn four forms only: *aru*, *arimasu* (the formal non-past of *aru*) and *iru*, *imasu* (the formal non-past of *iru*). The meaning and the usage surrounding these two verbs differ from English existential verbs, and they deserve special attention.

Meanings of *iru* and *aru*. There are basic and extended meanings in these existential verbs, and, in some cases, there is a preference for one or the other, as described below.

1. *Physical existence:*
   For expressing physical existence, as shown in the target expression, if what exists is animate, *iru* is used; if inanimate, *aru*. Thus we have:

(1a) ねこが**います**。

Neko	*ga*	***imasu.***
cat	S	there is

(There is a cat.)

(1b) テーブルが**あります**。

Teeburu	*ga*	***arimasu.***
table	S	there is

(There is a table.)

If the cat is dead, *neko no shigai ga arimasu* 'there is a dead cat' is used.

In some cases, for expressing the existence of a person, both *aru* and *iru* are used, with *iru* implying a person's concrete existence (sometimes in a certain location), and *aru* implying a more abstract existence.

(1c) あの人は敵が**いる**。

Ano	*hito*	*wa*	*teki*	*ga*	***iru.***
that	person	T	enemy	S	there

([lit., As for that person there are enemies.] He has some enemies.)

(1d) あの人は敵が**ある**。

Ano hito wa teki ga ***aru.***

(There are enemies against him.)

2. *Possession*:
   Aru is used for inanimate possession.

(2a) 田中さん(に)は(お)金が**あります**(*います)。

Tanaka-san	*(ni)*	*wa*	*(o)kane*	*ga*	***arimasu*** *(*imasu).*
Ms. Tanaka	for	T	money	S	there is

(Ms. Tanaka has money.)

In the examples above, what exists and what is possessed are marked by the subject marker *ga*. One may wonder about this characterization; as shown in the English translation, the money is not the "subject"; it is rather the object that Ms. Tanaka possesses. We will return to this point later. For now, just note that what exists and what is possessed are marked by *ga*, unless of course it is a topic, in which case it is marked by *wa*. The possessor is marked by the topic marker *wa*, optionally preceded by another particle *ni*. *Ni* indicates location in this usage. We will discuss many functions of the particle *ni* later.

Extended meanings of *aru*. *Aru* is used to express occurrence of incidents. (In this use, the locative particle *de*—instead of another locative particle *ni* which is normally used—co-occurs.)

(a) この部屋**で**パーティーがあります。

Kono heya	***de***	*paatii*	*ga*	*arimasu.*
this room	in	party	S	there is

(There is a party in this room.)

(b) 東京**で**地震があった。 (*Atta* is an informal past tense form of *aru*.)

Tookyoo	***de***	*jishin*	*ga*	*atta.*
Tokyo	in	earthquake	S	there was

(There was an earthquake in Tokyo.)

■ Additional Information

- The existential verb *aru* is idiomatically used as *ari* 'possible' and *arienai* 'impossible.' These expressions are casual, and mostly spoken in conversation.

(a) そんなのってアリ？
Sonna no tte ari?
(Is it possible for that to happen?)

(b) ありえなーい！ そんなこと。
Arienaai! Sonna koto.
(Impossible! Such a thing.)

- Another expression associated with the existential verb *aru* should be mentioned in passing. The expression *dearu* 'to be,' may be used in place of *da* in written Japanese. For example, a well known novel by Soseki Natsume is titled *Wagahai wa neko dearu* (I am a cat). The conjugation of *dearu* follows that of *aru*.

(c) 日本人は働き者**である**。

Nihon-jin	*wa*	*hatarakimono*	***dearu.***
Japanese	T	hard worker	are

(Japanese are industrious.)

12. Deictic Expression (2)—Personal Pronouns

■ Target Expressions

I, we

わたし、わたしたち
watashi, watashi-tachi

■ Strategic Explanation

Personal pronouns. The use of personal pronouns in Japanese is far more restricted than in English. Although a variety of pronoun-like forms are used in Japanese, depending on the gender of the speaker and the referent, or on the speech style chosen, in reality there is a tendency to avoid their use. First, however, let us look at the system.

Personal Pronouns

	First person 'I'	Second person 'you'	
Very formal:	わたくし *watakushi*	おたく(さま) *otaku(-sama)*	そちら(さま) *sochira(-sama)*
Formal:	わたし *watashi*	あなた *anata*	
Informal:	僕 [masculine speech] *boku*	君 *kimi*	
	あたし [feminine speech] *atashi*		
Casual/Blunt:	おれ [masculine speech] *ore*	お前 [masculine speech] *omae*	あんた *anta*

For the third person, limited use of *kare* 'he (often meaning boyfriend or male lover)' and *kanojo* 'she (often meaning girlfriend or female lover)' are used. A frequently used form for the third person is *ano hito* 'that person,' meaning either 'he' or 'she.'

Avoiding personal pronouns. Learning how to use Japanese personal pronouns is important, but more important is to understand how not to use them. Since pronouns are anaphoric expressions referring to referents uniquely identifiable, they are normally avoided (refer to characteristic 4). Recall that in Japanese there is no strict requirement in grammar as in the case of English for every sentence to have a grammatical subject. Simply put, whatever is assumed to be known is easily left unsaid. This is why earlier we introduced an expression *Andaason desu* without the grammatical subject *watashi* 'I' (see Entry 7).

Anata* and *omae. The pronoun *anata* is used by wives as a vocative when they address their husbands. Husbands address their wives by their first name without *-san*, or by a very informal version of the second-person pronoun, *omae*. The pronominal address terms chosen by husbands and wives are not reciprocal.

Plural forms. Plural forms of personal pronouns are made by adding a suffix-*tachi*; *watakushi-tachi, watashi-tachi, boku-tachi, kimi-tachi, atashi-tachi, ore-tachi, omae-tachi* and *anata-tachi*. For *anata, -gata* may also be added, that is, *anata-gata*. The suffix, *-tachi*, can be added to some other nouns referring to persons as well. For instance, *kodomo-tachi* meaning 'children.' *Yamamoto-san-tachi* is also possible. This refers not to a group of people with the same last name, Yamamoto, but to 'Yamamoto and others.' For 'they,' plural of *ano hito, ano hito-tachi* is often used. In casual speech, a suffix *-ra* is also used as in *ore-ra* and *omae-ra*.

■ Warning

If there is a need to use the second-person personal pronoun *anata*, it should be avoided when addressing your superior. Normally it is safer to address the listener by name. Instead of asking Mr. Anderson by saying *Anata wa gakusei desu ka?* 'Are you a student?,' *Andaason-san wa gakusei desu ka* is preferred. If the name of the listener is not known, use the politer version of *anata*, namely, *otaku(-sama)* or *sochira(-sama)*.

13. Particles (1)—Basic Case Markers

■ Target Expression

Mr. Araki drinks beer.

荒木さんがビールを飲みます。
Araki-san ga biiru o nomimasu.

[*ga*] [*o*] [*ni*]

■ Grammatical Explanation

Relatively free word order. One major difference between English and Japanese sentence structure is the word order. Japanese has a basic topic-comment and subject-object-verb order, in contrast with the English subject-verb-object order (refer to characteristic 1). In Japanese, word order is relatively free, although there is a preferred word order which we will study later. In English, the position in relation to the verb defines the grammatical case of the noun. In Japanese, instead of word order, particles are used to mark cases. Consider the difference in meaning between the following sentences.

(a) Mary kills John. メアリーがジョンを殺す。/ ジョンをメアリーが殺す。
Mearii ga Jon o korosu. *Jon o Mearii ga korosu.*

(b) John kills Mary. ジョンがメアリーを殺す。/ メアリーをジョンが殺す。
Jon ga Mearii o korosu. *Mearii o Jon ga korosu.*

Case-marking by particles. As shown in the Japanese translation given above, different particles mark the subject and object case; the position of the noun does not assign cases. Three particles which we concentrate on are:

ga	subject marker	(abbreviated as S)
o	object marker	(abbreviated as O)
ni	indirect object marker	(abbreviated as IO)

"Subject" and "primary predicate focus." At this point, we must go back to the question posed earlier about the notion of "subject" in Japanese. In Japanese, the subject, not in a strict grammatical sense (as in "subject-verb agreement"), refers to the element that is most prominent and focused upon, and is directly associated with and predicated by the verb in active (not passive) sentences. We will refer to this subject as an element of "primary predicate focus." *Ga* identifies the element in primary predicate focus as defined by the specific verbal predicate. For action verbs introduced earlier, subject is the agent or the performer of the action. For a group of verbs that express a direct sensory perception, the primary predicate focus is placed on the items that cause such perception. These expressions will be learned in time. For stative verbs, the noun marked by subject marker *ga* is the element whose state is described. For existential sentences the subject is what exists, for an existential possessive sentence a subject is what is possessed.

"Subject" and verb types. There are four possible ways in which different types of verbs interact with the concept of "subject," as shown below.

Verb types	N + *ga*
1. *Active transitive:*	N is the doer, the agent (N + *o* designates object). **友だちが**本を読む。 ***Tomodachi ga*** *hon o yomu.* (My friend reads a book.)
2. *Active intransitive:*	N is the doer, the agent (N + *o* is not used). **友だちが**来る。 ***Tomodachi ga*** *kuru.* (My friend comes.)

3. *Stative:*	N is what is described. **あの人が**先生です。 ***Ano hito ga*** *sensei desu.* (That person is the teacher.) **建物が**ある。 ***Tatemono ga*** *aru.* (There is a building.)
4. *Reactive:*	N is the source for response and reaction. **アイスクリームが**好きだ。 ***Aisukuriimu ga*** *suki da.* ice cream S like (I like ice cream.)

In the first case, the agent, or the doer of the action, is the subject and what is acted on is the object. In the second type, the agent of the intransitive verb is the subject. In sentences with stative verbs, what is described is the subject, i.e., the element of primary predicate focus. In the fourth type, which will be called "reactive" description, the source that causes reaction or response in the experiencer (the person who experiences this response process) is the subject. Only a limited number of verbal and adjectival predicates fall into this category (see Appendix 5 for the listing of predicates for "reactive" description. The reactive predicate may be active stative). In all types, noun phrases are marked by *ga*, unless the noun becomes the topic, in which case it is marked by *wa*.

Reactive structures. In some "reactive" structures, it is possible to add another dimension; the experiencer of the event described may appear in a sentence or an utterance by N followed by *ga*.

(c) **私が**アイスクリームが好きだ。
Watashi ga *aisukuriimu ga suki da.*
(I like ice cream.)

The term "reactive" is chosen because the [N + *ga* + reactive predicate] structure primarily postulates that something existing out there causes the experiencer's response and reaction. We will learn more about the predicates of "reactive" description in Entry 46.

***Wa* overtaking *ga*.** Remember, not all *ga*-marked noun phrases appear on the surface of the sentence. If they are topics and/or assumed to be known among participants, they are likely to be left unsaid. When the element of primary predicate focus is chosen to become the topic of utterance or across several utterances, *ga* is taken over by *wa*, the topic marker. Thus, it is possible to say, for example, *hon wa arimasu*, in which case, *hon* conveys shared information and becomes the topic.

■ Examples

(1) 友だちが来ます。

Tomodachi	*ga*	*kimasu.*
friend	S	come

(A friend will come.)

(2) 友だちに本をあげます。

Tomodachi	*ni*	*hon*	*o*	*agemasu.*
friend	IO	book	O	give

(I will give my friend a book.)

(3) 大きい建物があります。

Ookii	*tatemono*	*ga*	*arimasu.*
large	building	S	there is

(There is a large building.)

(4) (お)金があります。
(O)kane ga arimasu.
(I have money.)

Note that in all examples, case-marking particles are placed immediately after the nouns whose cases are defined. In sentence (2), it is possible to change the order of case-marked phrases. *Hon o tomodachi ni agemasu* is a grammatical sentence, with identical cases assigned as in sentence (2).

■ Additional Information

For many nouns of Chinese origin, the following choice regarding the use of object marker *o* should be noted. For the word *benkyoo* 'study,' either *benkyoo o suru* or *benkyoo-suru* is acceptable. If, however, the noun is modified by [N + *no*], adjectives, or adjectival clauses, only the [*benkyoo o suru*] pattern is acceptable. Note that sentence (a) is correct while sentence (b) is not. It is of course possible to use *benkyoo-suru* as a single verb preceded by its object [N + *o*], as shown in (c). When the [N + *o*] phrase appears as an object of the verb, the verb cannot take another noun marked by *o*, as shown in the ungrammatical example sentence (d).

(a) 日本語の勉強をする。 *Nihongo no benkyoo o suru.*
(b) *日本語の勉強する。 **Nihongo no benkyoo-suru.*
(c) 日本語を勉強する。 *Nihongo o benkyoo-suru.*
(d) *日本語を勉強をする。 **Nihongo o benkyoo o suru.*

14. Not Saying the Obvious

■ Strategic Explanation

Mentioning only necessary information. In this entry, we examine our characteristic 4. Generally speaking, in Japanese any and all elements are left unsaid as long as what is unsaid is generally "understood." Nouns, verbs, and even particles are frequently deleted, particularly in spoken style. In Japanese, expressions are more closely tied to the surrounding situation than in English. The subject-predicate axis is not as rigid or as strongly felt in Japanese. Instead of following the rule of subject-verb-object, as it is the case in English, only what needs to be mentioned in a specific context is added before the sentence-final verbal elements.

Leaving things unsaid. Mentioning unnecessary bits of information is, in fact, a sign of clumsiness in Japanese conversation; it only indicates a lack of conversational skill. The guideline provided below should be followed when leaving things unsaid.

1. *Topic of the sentence and discourse:*
   Once a topic is introduced in discourse, it normally remains unmentioned unless a specific need arises. For example, when the topic continues in a new conversation segment or a new paragraph, it may be restated to signal that the same topic is still active.

2. *Answer to a question:*
   In an answer to a question, what is already stated in the question is often not repeated.

3. *Information situationally interpretable:*
   Pronouns which are situationally interpretable are often unmentioned; *watashi* 'I' and *anata* 'you' are self-evident.

4. *Culturally and socially shared information:*
   There is no need to explain the already shared knowledge of one's culture and society.

5. *Grammatical particles:*
   Deletion of grammatical particles is normally restricted to informal spoken language only.

■ Additional Information

- In spoken Japanese, even the main clause may be left unsaid. This is possible when participants readily understand the context.

(a) 帰ったら（どうですか）？
Kaettara *(doo desu ka)?*
return (how about)
([How about] returning?)

(b) 高いから（買いません）。
Takai *kara* *(kaimasen).*
expensive because (don't buy)
(Because it is expensive [I don't buy].)

- Emphasis on not mentioning the obvious does not exclude repetition or redundancy in conversation. In fact, repetition occurs frequently in spoken Japanese. What is emphasized here is that compared to English, Japanese has less grammatical constraints that block this "tendency to mention less."
- The tendency for mentioning less is exercised in the process of word-formation as well. Long noun phrases tend to be shortened into four-mora words, often combining the initial two sounds from two words. See, for example:

東大 *Toodai*	= **東**京**大**学 ***Too**kyoo **Dai**gaku*	The University of Tokyo
卒論 *sotsuron*	= **卒**業**論**文 ***sotsu**gyoo **ron**bun*	graduation thesis, dissertation
入試 *nyuushi*	= **入**学**試**験 ***nyuu**gaku **shi**ken*	enterance examination
マスコミ *masukomi*	= **マスコミ**ュニケーション ***masu komy**unikeeshon*	mass communication

15. Structure of the Japanese Sentence (1)—Topic and Comment

■ Grammatical Explanation

We are already familiar with the terms "topic" and "comment." But what are they really? Why are they important in Japanese? How do they interact with another structural relation, subject and predicate?

Topic-comment versus subject-predicate. First, as we defined earlier, topic is what is being talked about. It can be the subject, object, or any other grammatical element. Topic and comment themselves are not strictly grammatical notions. The topic-comment relation is based on how information is structured in communication. It is an overall umbrella-like system of distinguishing what is being talked about (topic) in actual communication, and what is being introduced as information added (comment) to the topic.

The comment consists of a subject and a predicate. In Japanese as we have already seen, subject is interpreted broadly. We defined subject as an item of primary predicate focus directly associated with the verb. Predicate consists of the verb, which is located at the end of an utterance, preceded by other elements such as adverbs, adjectives, and nouns.

Overall organization of a sentence. In order to understand how topic-comment and subject-predicate relate to each other, examine the schematization presented below. The elements in square brackets become the topics in the example sentences; these phrases are no longer mentioned.

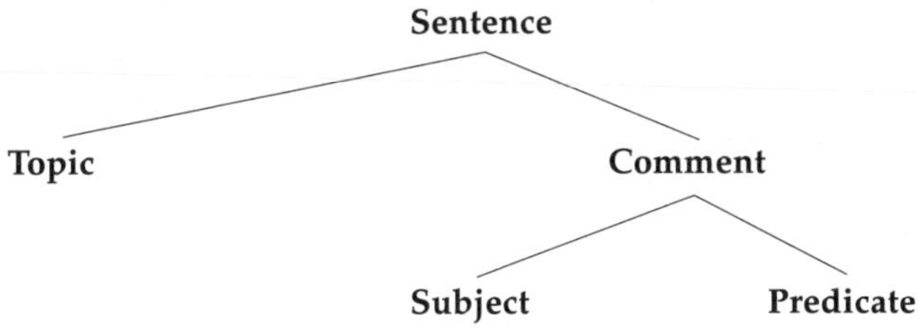

(1)	ここには *Koko ni wa*	くだものが *kudamono ga*	[ここに] あります。 [*koko ni*] *arimasu.*
(2)	田中さんは *Tanaka-san wa*	[田中さんが] [*Tanaka-san ga*]	日本人です。 *Nihon-jin desu.*
(3a)	(No topic selected)	友だちが *Tomodachi ga*	来ます。 *kimasu.*
(3b)	その友だちは *Sono tomodachi wa*	[友だちが] [*Tomodachi ga*]	アメリカ人です。 *Amerika-jin desu.*
(3c)	[友だちは] [*Tomodachi wa*]	[友だちが] [*Tomodachi ga*]	テレビを見ます。 *Terebi o mimasu.*

In sentence (1), the topic chosen is the locative phrase *koko ni* 'here.' The subject, locative phrases, and verb constitute the predicate, with the subject being *kudamono* 'fruit,' marked by *ga*. In this sentence the focus is placed on what exists there, namely, *kudamono*, which is the subject of the sentence. What is introduced as topic (that is, locative phrase *koko ni*) defines the general framework into which the information described by comment is incorporated. Once the locative phrase is promoted to be the topic, it becomes defunct within the predicate framework.

In sentence (2), *Tanaka-san* is identified as topic, which coincides with the subject of the sentence. When topic and subject coincide, topic takes over the subject phrase and is no longer mentioned. Of course, the topic itself is also deletable, as shown in sentence (3c). Only grammatical particles *ga* and *o* are overridden by *wa* (and other topic markers). For other particles, *wa* is attached to them, as in *ni wa*, *to wa*, *de wa*, and so forth.

Establishing topic. Imagine a situation where you describe your friend to a listener. In sentence (3a), the subject *tomodachi* is introduced into discourse with *ga*, and no topic is yet assigned. When a piece of information new to the listener is introduced, it does not yet constitute a topic. But in sentence (3b), *sono tomodachi* anaphorically refers to the same individual and it is marked with *wa*, now becoming the topic. Further, in sentence (3c) the topic which coincides with the subject is deleted. This process follows a three-step progression:

1. The new information is introduced as subject [N + *ga*].
2. The topic is established [N + *wa*].
3. The established topic is deleted.

Although not all cases of topic establishment follow this sequence, it represents a prototypical case. (Especially in narratives, the dramatic characters may be introduced with *wa*, although they appear for the first time in the story. By virtue of introducing a character as if consisting of already given information, the character is accepted as the topicalized main character of the story.)

Topic as a framework. Think of topic as a framework or notion shared by the interactants. Into this framework, information provided by the subject-predicate axis which constitutes comment, is incorporated. Whereas in English this process is not normally reflected in sentential structures, in Japanese we have an overt topic marker *wa* (and other topic markers) to do precisely that. Hence, Japanese is known as a topic-comment prominent language. The topic-comment structure may roughly be translated into English 'as for X/speaking of X, it is Y,' meaning that there is a special relationship between X and Y.

Topic-comment preference. Japanese prefer the topic-comment structure when describing events. Instead of creating a sentence that would mean 'John speaks Japanese well,' Japanese would prefer *Jon-san wa Nihongo ga joozu desu* 'as for John, his Japanese is good,' where *joozu desu* means 'be good at.' (Note here that *joozu da* is a "reactive" predicate with the element of primary predicate focus marked by *ga*.) What *wa* marks creates an overall informational framework, and what *ga* marks identifies the element of primary predicate focus.

Topic-comment in English. In spoken English the topic-comment structure may appear as in:

(a) Ryan's Cafe ... I won't go there. It's too expensive.

(b) John. I don't know about him.

In these utterances, topics are placed in the initial position. Phrases *Ryan's Cafe* and *John* are announced as something about which comments follow. Although this type of topicalized utterance structure has restricted usage in English, in Japanese, topic-comment is the predominant structure.

***Ga* question and *ga* for "exhaustive listing."** A related fact regarding the subject marker *ga* should be mentioned at this point. Imagine a situation where you are interested in knowing which one is Mr. Smith among a group of people in the room. In this case, the utterance you make is something like:

(c) どの人がスミスさんですか。 (*Ka* is a question marker.)
Dono hito ga Sumisu-dan desu ka.
(Which person is Mr. Smith?)

In providing an answer to such a question, your friend would point to Mr. Smith and answer by using the [X *ga* Y *da*] pattern.

(d) あの人がスミスさんです。
Ano hito ga Sumisu-san desu.
(That person is Mr. Smith.)

Since *ano hito* 'that person' provides new information and points out an item that satisfies the condition of being Mr. Smith exhaustively (that person and that person alone), this use of *ga* is called *ga* for "exhaustive listing." [X *ga*] in this pattern carries with it a connotation of "X and only X is the Y in question." A special feature of exhaustive listing *ga* is that the item marked with *ga* normally receives phonological prominence.

***Wa* question.** You might be wondering about another possible way of asking a question in the situation described above. By making *Sumisu-san* the topic, you may ask a question:

(e) スミスさんはどの人ですか。
Sumisu-san wa dono hito desu ka.
(As for Mr. Smith, which person is he?)

An answer to this question may take the form:

(f) (スミスさんは)あの人です。
(Sumisu-san wa) ano hito desu.
(Mr. Smith is that person over there.)

Sumisu-san is the topic marked by *wa*, and *ano hito desu* provides comment, a piece of new information. Different strategies of questioning and answering occur depending on how a speaker chooses the topic, that is, how a speaker organizes given and new information.

16. Identifying Topics—Topic Marker *Wa*

Target Expression

Mr. Takagi goes to Osaka every week.

高木さんは毎週大阪へ行きます。

Takagi-san wa maishuu Oosaka e ikimasu.

[*wa*] [*mo*]

Grammatical Explanation

The topic, being that which is talked about, can be a grammatical subject, object, locative, and so forth. In the example sentence above, *Takagi-san* 'Mr. Takagi' is a subject as well as a topic marked by *wa*.

***Wa-ga* and whole versus part.** Going a step further, there could be sentences containing two separate items, one a topic and the other a subject. For example, study the following sentence.

(a) このホテルはサービスがいいですよ。

Kono hoteru	*wa*	*saabisu*	*ga*	*ii desu*	*yo.*
this hotel	T	service	S	good	IP

([lit., As for this hotel, service is good.] The service of this hotel is good.)

Here we have a topic *kono hoteru* which offers the framework, and the comment, *saabisu ga ii* which in turn consists of subject *saabisu* and predicate *ii*. Topic defines the "whole" and subject focuses on its "part." This example leads us to one of the most well-known (among grammarians) Japanese sentences:

(b) ぞうは鼻が長い。

Zoo	*wa*	*hana*	*ga*	*nagai.*
elephant	T	trunk	S	long

([lit., As for elephants, trunks are long.]) Elephants' trunks are long.)

Again, this sentence makes sense when you know that topic can be practically any element of the sentence, and it exists outside the subject-predicate axis. The relationship between the topic and the subject in this sentence is also that of whole-part.

Multiple topics. Going even a step further, we can conceive of sentences with multiple topics.

(c) 渡辺さんはあしたは会社を休みます。

Watanabe-san	*wa*	*ashita*	*wa*	*kaisha*	*o*	*yasumimasu.*
Ms. Watanabe	T	tomorrow	T	company	O	will be absent

(Ms. Watanabe will be absent from the company tomorrow.)

In this case, the topic framework is a combination of *Watanabe-san* and the temporal phrase *ashita*.

Particle *mo*. An additional topic-marking particle should be introduced at this point. *Mo* which signals topic with the meaning of 'also' and 'in addition' functions similarly with *wa*. (*Mo* takes over particles *ga* and *o* as in the case of *wa*.) For example:

(d) 佐々木さん**も**休みます。
Sasaki-san ***mo*** *yasumimasu.*
(Ms. Sasaki will also be absent.)

The particle *mo* will be discussed in detail in Entry 97.

Topic marker in subordinate clauses. Before proceeding, an issue concerning the topic marker in relation to subordinate clauses needs to be discussed. Since the topic is what is being talked about, it does not normally occur in a subordinate clause. This is because a subordinate clause is less important than the main clause in terms of its contribution to the overall information structure.

When a noun phrase appears in subordinate clauses, the use of *wa* is normally avoided, and the noun phrase is marked by another appropriate grammatical particle. Even when that noun phrase conveys information shared by participants, the topic marker *wa* is avoided. This usage of particles other than *wa* is best described as non-topicalization, that is, the avoidance of topic marker based on the structure of the relevant information. Among subordinate clauses, there are some types in which this change is not obligatory, as in subordinate clauses marked *noni* 'despite,' and *keredomo* 'although.'

Contrastive *wa*. A phenomenon closely associated with the topic *wa* is a special use of it, often called "contrastive *wa*." When a *wa*-marked phrase together with *wa* is pronounced with phonological prominence, it implies contrast, regardless of whether the contrastive item is specified or not. When there are multiple topics within an utterance or a sentence, it is often the case that some in fact carry a contrastive meaning. In example (e), *Bosuton e wa* is pronounced prominently (in a higher tone and with more volume than normal), and it carries the contrastive meaning as described below.

(e) 山川さんはボストンへ**は**行きます。
Yamakawa-san wa Bosuton e ***wa*** *ikimasu.*
(Mr. Yamakawa goes to Boston.)

Here the intended message is that Mr. Yamakawa goes at least to Boston, although he may not go to the contrasted implied place, for example, New York City.

■ Additional Information

In addition to *wa* and *mo*, several expressions are used to mark the topic. These include *tte*, *nara(ba)*, and *to ieba*, as shown below. *Tte* is used in casual style; and *nara* and *to ieba* carry additional meanings, as given in the English translation. We will study the details of these markers later.

(a) ボストン**って**有名ですよね。
Bosuton ***tte*** *yuumei-desu yo ne.*
(Boston is famous, right?)

(b) ボストン**なら**行く。
Bosuton ***nara*** *iku.*
(If it's Boston, I'll go.)

(c) ボストン**といえば**有名な教会があります。
Bosuton ***to ieba*** *yuumeina kyookai ga arimasu.*
(Speaking of Boston, there is a famous church there.)

17. Particles (2)—Markers for Time, Location, Methods, etc.

■ Target Expression

I'm going back to the United States at Christmas.

クリスマスにアメリカへ帰ります。
Kurisumasu ni Amerika e kaerimasu.

[*ni*] [*e*] [*de*] [*to*] [*made*]

■ Grammatical Explanation

Grammatical particles. We spend some time here familiarizing ourselves with a number of frequently used grammatical particles. These are attached to nouns and define grammatical relationships between that noun and other elements. Recall that we have studied subject marker *ga*, object marker *o*, and indirect object marker *ni* earlier.

(a) ***ni*** Locative marker (*in*, *at*), also directional

(お)金はここ**に**あります よ。
(O)kane wa koko ***ni*** *arimasu yo.*
(There is money here.)

(b) ***ni*** Temporal marker—point of time (*at*)

八時**に**行きます。
*Hachi-ji **ni** ikimasu.*
(I'll go at eight o'clock.)

(c) ***ni*** Marker of source (*from*)

友だち**に**借りる。
*Tomodachi **ni** kariru.*
(I'll borrow from my friend.)

(d) ***e*** Directional marker (*to, toward*)

学校**へ**行く。
*Gakkoo **e** iku.*
(I'm going to school.)

(e) ***de*** Locative marker—place of dynamic action (*in, at*)

ここ**で**勉強します。
*Koko **de** benkyoo-shimasu.*
(I'll study here.)

(f) ***de*** Instrumental marker (*by, through*)

これ**で**切ります。
*Kore **de** kirimasu.*
(I'll cut (it) with this.)

(g) ***to*** Joint action (*with*)

佐々木さん**と**行きます。
*Sasaki-san **to** ikimasu.*
(I'll go with Ms. Sasaki.)

(h) ***to*** Enumerative (*and*)

トースト**と**ハムエッグを食べる。
*Toosuto **to** hamueggu o taberu.*
(I will have toast and ham-and-eggs.)

(i) ***ka*** Alternative (*or*)

コーヒー**か**紅茶を飲む。
*Koohii **ka** koocha o nomu.*
(I'll drink coffee or tea.)

(j) ***kara*** Starting point (*from*)

あした**から**夏休みです。
*Ashita **kara** natsuyasumi desu.*
(It's summer vacation from tomorrow.)

(k) ***made*** Ending point (*till, up to, to*)

あした**まで**待ちます。
*Ashita **made** machimasu.*
(I'll wait until tomorrow.)

(l) ***made ni*** Deadline (*by*)

あした**までに**手紙を書く。
*Ashita **made ni** tegami o kaku.*
(I'll write a letter by tomorrow.)

***Ni* versus other particles.** The explanation to follow is given to help you distinguish between some of the particles, particularly that ubiquitous *ni*, which can be used to mark indirect object, location, direction, time, goal, and so forth.

1. *Directional e and ni:*
The differences between the two directional markers *e* and *ni*, which are interchangeable in many cases, are the following. *E* is used to express the direction associated with an action and is used when emphasizing its process. The verbs such as *iku* 'to go,' *kuru* 'to come,' and *kaeru* 'to return' can be and often are used to focus on the process of the actions referred to. For example, *Tookyoo-eki e iku* 'to go to Tokyo Station.'
Ni, on the other hand, is used when emphasizing the result of the action. The verbs such as *hairu* 'to enter,' *ireru* 'to put in,' *tsukeru* 'to attach,' *tsuku* 'to arrive' and *atsumaru* 'to gather' can be and often are used to focus on the result of the action and are preferably marked by *ni*. For example, *heya ni hairu* 'to enter a room.'
Parenthetically, *made*, which can also be used for direction, describes the destination of the action focusing on the goal. The verbs such as *hakobu* 'to carry,' and *aruku* 'to walk' often co-occur with *made*, for example, *uchi made aruku* 'walk (to) home.'

2. *Locative de and ni:*
When describing the location where the dynamic action takes place, *de* is obligatory. On the other hand when the stative verb is used, the location in which that state exists is described by *ni*. The verbs that co-occur with the locative *ni* are limited. Frequently used examples are *iru, aru, sumu* 'to live,' and *oku* 'to place (something).' Locative particles introduced here may be followed by topic markers *wa* and *mo*.

(2a) アメリカで勉強します。日本**でも**します。
*Amerika de benkyoo-shimasu. Nihon **de mo** shimasu.*
(I'll study in America. I'll also study in Japan.)

(2b) 部屋**には**友だちがいます。
*Heya **ni wa** tomodachi ga imasu.*
(In the room there is my friend.)

3. *Ni for 'source' and kara for 'starting point':*
As we already discussed, *ni* is a particle of location. Location here is to be interpreted in a broad sense; it could indicate various points of locations involved in an action. Depending on the verb, *ni* can indicate the location from where the source of action is sought. In this case, it is interchangeable with *kara*.

(3a) 友だち**に**聞きましたよ。
*Tomodachi **ni** kikimashita yo.*[*1]
(I heard from a friend.)

(3b) 友だち**から**聞きましたよ。
*Tomodachi **kara** kikimashita yo.*[*1]
(I heard from a friend.)

*1. *Kikimashita* is the formal past-tense form of the verb *kiku*. *Yo* is an interactional particle which marks introduction of new information, often with emphasis.

■ Examples

(1) ジョンソンさんはクリスマスにニュージャージーへ帰ります。
Jonson-san wa Kurisumasu ni Nyuujaajii e kaerimasu.
(Mr. Johnson will return to New Jersey for Christmas.)

(2) 友だちと車でニューヨークへ行く。
Tomodachi to kuruma de Nyuuyooku e iku.
(He will go to New York by car with his friend.)

(3) デパートでプレゼントを買います。
Depaato de purezento o kaimasu.
(He will buy some presents at a department store.)

(4) ジョンソンさんは二週間ニュージャージーにいます。
Jonson-san wa nishuukan Nyuujaajii ni imasu.
(Mr. Johnson will be in New Jersey for two weeks.)

(5) 店でりんごとみかんを買う。
Mise de ringo to mikan o kau.
(I'll buy some apples and tangerines at the store.)

■ Additional Information

- Concerning locative particles, the following should be noted. For verbs of motion (such as *tooru* 'to pass through,' *aruku* 'to walk,' *noboru* 'to climb,' *magaru* 'to turn,' *tobu* 'to fly' and *yokogiru* 'to cross'—often with the English meaning of 'on,' 'across,' and 'through')—the relevant location is expressed by the object marker *o*. A similar phenomenon is observed in English; *crossing the street*—where *the street* does not take a locative preposition. Compare this with *working in the room*—where *the room* is preceded by the preposition *in* indicating location.

- With some active verbs, both *o* and *de* can co-occur; but they convey different meanings.

  (a) 子供たちは川**を**泳いで向こう岸に行く。
  Kodomo-tachi wa kawa ***o*** *oyoide mukoo gishi ni iku.*
  (Children swim across the river and reach the other side.)

  (b) 子供たちは川**で**泳ぐ。
  Kodomotachi wa kawa ***de*** *oyogu.*
  (Children swim in the river.)

  When one swims across the river following basically a straight line, the object marker *o* is used, while when the swimming takes place in the river at various locations between the two banks, *de* is used.

■ Warning

The enumerative *to* connects only nouns and noun phrases. Do not use it to connect verbs, adjectives, and clauses.

18. Word Order (1)—Preferred Word Order

■ Target Expression

Ms. Turner will go to Hakata by Bullet Train.

ターナーさんは新幹線で博多へ行きます。
Taanaa-san wa Shinkansen de Hakata e ikimasu.

■ Grammatical Explanation

Preferred word order. Although the grammatical word order in Japanese is relatively free, there is a preferred order of elements within the sentence. First, topics, if they appear, come in the initial position. This is because by identifying a topic, both the speaker and listener align themselves to appreciate a common starting point. Recall the two characteristics regarding basic word order in Japanese, characteristics 1 (verb-final) and 6 (modifier precedes the modified). Under normal circumstances, verbal elements always come at the very end of the utterance. The preferred order is schematized below. Numbers under the column Roman Numeral II show the preferred order of elements within that slot.

I		II		III		IV
Topic	+	1. temporal 2. locative 3. subject 4. joint action (*to*) 5. method (*de*) 6. starting point (*kara*) 7. direction (*ni, e*) 8. object (*o*)	+	Verbal/ Adjectival Predicate	+	Interactional Particles

■ Examples

(1) 原さんはあした子供たちと電車で東京へ行きますね。

Hara-san	*wa*	*ashita*	*kodomo-tachi*	*to*	*densha*	*de*	*Tookyoo*	*e*
Ms. Hara	T	tomorrow	children	with	train	by	Tokyo	to

ikimasu	*ne.*
go	IP

(Ms. Hara goes to Tokyo tomorrow by train with her children, doesn't she?)

(2) 子供たちは先生と図書館にいますね。

Kodomo-tachi	*wa*	*sensei*	*to*	*toshokan*	*ni*	*imasu*	*ne.*
children	T	teacher	with	library	at	there are	IP

(Children are at the library with the teacher, aren't they?)

The best strategy here is to memorize a few sentences which contain various correctly ordered elements, and to use these sentences as reference points. Examples (1) and (2) serve as a good start.

■ Additional Information

As we have seen, the order of elements in the Japanese sentence is quite different from that of English. The difference in order is not limited to syntactic elements alone. Recall that in Japanese the family name (a more general group identification) precedes the given name (a more specific individual identification). In specifying addresses, Japanese starts from a larger area to a specific area, while in English the reverse is true. For example, *Tookyoo no Oota-ku* 'Tokyo's Ota Ward' versus Los Angeles, California. Likewise, addresses written on the envelopes and cards follow this basic principle. In Japanese, the larger area designation precedes the smaller area designation.

19. Temporal Expressions

■ Target Expressions

morning, today, this week

朝、今日、今週

asa, kyoo, konshuu

■ Grammatical Explanation

A host of time-indicating nouns can be used as adverbs modifying the verbs. A parallel phenomenon is observed in English where a time-indicating phrase such as *today* may be used as a noun in *today is Sunday*, as well as an adverb in *today I must work all day*. These phrases are mostly deictic, that is to say, they are specified by the speaker's relation to the here-and-now world.

List of Useful Temporal Expressions

1. *General*:

朝	*asa*	morning
今	*ima*	now
いつも	*itsumo*	always
今朝	*kesa*	this morning
今夜	*kon'ya*	tonight
午後	*gogo*	afternoon
午前中	*gozenchuu*	morning, before noon
夕べ	*yuube*	last night
昨晩	*sakuban*	last night
さっき	*sakki*	shortly before
早朝	*soochoo*	early morning
昼間	*hiruma*	daytime
真夜中	*mayonaka*	midnight
夕方	*yuugata*	evening
夜	*yoru*	night

2. *A systematized list of temporal phrases*:
   The list below shows past, present, and future phrases for (a) day, (b) week, (c) month, and (d) year. For example, *ototoi* 'the day before yesterday,' *kinoo* 'yesterday,' *kyoo* 'today,' *ashita* 'tomorrow,' *asatte* 'the day after tomorrow.' The last column lists words 'every . . .' as in *mainichi* 'every day.' For the word 'tomorrow,' both *ashita* and *asu* are used, with the former being more colloquial.

	-2	-1	now	+1	+2	every
(a)	おととい *ototoi*	きのう *kinoo*	今日 *kyoo*	あした/あす *ashita/asu*	あさって *asatte*	毎日 *mainichi*
(b)	先々週 *sensenshuu*	先週 *senshuu*	今週 *konshuu*	来週 *raishuu*	さ来週 *saraishuu*	毎週 *maishuu*
(c)	先々月 *sensengetsu*	先月 *sengetsu*	今月 *kongetsu*	来月 *raigetsu*	さ来月 *saraigetsu*	毎月 *maitsuki*
(d)	おととし *ototoshi*	去年 *kyonen*	今年 *kotoshi*	来年 *rainen*	さ来年 *sarainen*	毎年 *mainen*

3. *Four seasons* (may take temporal particle *ni*):

春	*haru*	spring
夏	*natsu*	summer
秋	*aki*	fall
冬	*huyu*	winter

4. *Days of the week* (normally takes temporal particle *ni*):

月曜日	*getsuyoobi*	Monday
火曜日	*kayoobi*	Tuesday
水曜日	*suiyoobi*	Wednesday
木曜日	*mokuyoobi*	Thursday
金曜日	*kin'yoobi*	Friday
土曜日	*doyoobi*	Saturday
日曜日	*nichiyoobi*	Sunday

■ Examples

(1) 佐々木さんは朝早く起きます。
Sasaki-san wa asa hayaku okimasu.
(Mr. Sasaki gets up early in the morning.)

(2) いつもコーヒーを飲みます。
Itsumo koohii o nomimasu.
(He always drinks coffee.)

(3) 朝から勉強します。
Asa kara benkyoo-shimasu.
(He begins studying in the morning.)

(4) 午後はいろいろなことをします。
Gogo wa iroirona koto o shimasu.
(In the afternoon he does various things.)

(5) 月曜日はテニスをします。
Getsuyoobi wa tenisu o shimasu.
(On Mondays he plays tennis.)

(6) 水曜日は夕方友だちに会います。[*1]
Suiyoobi wa yuugata tomodachi ni aimasu.
(On Wednesdays he meets his friends in the evening.)

(7) 金曜日は家にいます。
Kin'yoobi wa uchi ni imasu.
(On Fridays he stays home.)

*1. The verb *au* 'to see someone, to meet someone,' takes *ni* as an object marker. This usage is idiomatic; the use of *ni* will be explained again in Entry 29.

■ Warning

- Although some of the temporal expressions introduced here do not normally take the temporal particle *ni*, there are some cases where they must, as in days of the week. As will be mentioned later, when a temporal expression contains numerals (as in the date of the month and time of the day), the temporal particle *ni* is required. Some temporal phrases have slightly different meanings depending on whether or not they are followed by temporal particles. For example, *san-nen kan* 'for three years' points to the whole duration of three years, while *san-nen kan ni* 'in three years/within three years' may point to a specific time within those three years. Among temporal nouns without numerals, some may be optionally accompanied by *ni*, as in *haru ni*, in which case the time defined by the expression is in focus or in contrast with other possibilities (for example, in contrast with winter).
- Regarding the expression *mai* 'every,' it is important not to use this morpheme to create new phrases, for example, **mai kin'yoobi* for 'every Friday.' Use only those listed in the chart.

20. Modifying (1)—Nominal Modifiers with *No*

■ Target Expressions

a Japanese car, the author of this book

日本の車、この本の著者
Nihon no kuruma, kono hon no chosha

[N + *no*]

■ Grammatical Explanation

Modifying with [N + *no*]. Regarding the modification of nouns, we have already learned [Adj-*i*] in Japanese. Here is another way to modify or explain about a noun phrase. Place a [N + *no*] before the noun to be modified (refer to characteristic 6). *No* is a particle; we will call *no* used in this way as a linker (abbreviated as L) which links nouns. In the target expression *Nihon* 'Japan' and *no* are placed before the noun *kuruma* 'car.' The phrase *Nihon no* describes what kind of car it is. *Kono hon no chosha* 'the author of this book' is a combination of a phrase *kono hon* (which consists of a demonstrative *kono* specifying *hon*) plus *no* which in turn specifies *chosha* 'author.'

Multiple linkers. To go a step further, we can generate phrases with multiple linkers.

(a) 日本の果物の品種の名前

Nihon	*no*	*kudamono*	*no*	*hinshu*	*no*	*namae*
Japan	L	fruit	L	variety	L	name

(names of the varieties of fruits of Japan)

Again, it is important to remember that the order of nouns in Japanese is the reverse of the English [noun + of + noun] structure. The literal translation may be something like 'Japan's fruits' varieties' names' in which case the order is identical. Thinking of the [N + *no*] pattern as equivalent to the English [N + possessive marker (')] may be helpful in confirming the order of nouns, as in 'Japan's fruits' varieties' names.'

Modifying with pronouns. The use of *no* discussed here applies to pronouns as well; for example, *watashi no hon* '(lit., I's book) my book,' *kare no otoosan* 'his father.' Again, pronoun forms are not as frequently used in Japanese. Unless there is a special need, these pronominal forms are avoided in Japanese. It is also possible to add *no* to a noun phrase which already has particles attached. For example, *Tookyoo kara no tegami* 'a letter from Tokyo,' where *Tookyoo kara* 'from Tokyo' is linked to *tegami* 'letter' by the linker *no*. The [N + *no*] structure can modify noun phrases which are already modified by adjectives; for example, *Yamada-san no atarashii kuruma* 'Yamada's new car,' and *Tookyoo no atarashii depaato* 'Tokyo's new department store.'

[N + *no*] as apposition. The [N + *no*] phrase is also used to express apposition, that is, in an expression such as *musume no Yuki* which means 'my daughter, Yuki.' In a broader perspective, we see a common semantic origin in this use of *no* as the one we already noted above in that the phrase *musume no* specifies and adds information to *Yuki*.

■ Examples

(1) これは渡辺さんの部屋ですね。
Kore wa Watanabe-san no heya desu ne.
(This is Mr. Watanabe's room, isn't it?)

(2) アメリカ人の友だちのサリーさんとデパートへ行きます。

Amerika-jin	*no*	*tomodachi*	*no*	*Sarii-san*	*to*	*depaato*	*e*	*ikimasu.*
American	L	friend	L	Sally	with	department store	to	go

(I'm going to a department store with my American friend, Sally.)

(3) フランスのワインはおいしいね。
Huransu no wain wa oishii ne.
(French wine is delicious, isn't it?)

■ Additional Information

- There are some conventionalized uses and non-uses of the linking particle *no*. These are exceptions to the phenomenon mentioned above. First, there are groups of words that can appear either as [N + *no* + N] or as complex nominals; for example, *seiyoo* 'Western world' and *bunka* 'culture' may appear as *seiyoo no bunka* or as a complex nominal *seiyoobunka*.
- There are some cases where the linking *no* cannot be used. For example, a complex noun *nyuugakushiken* (combination of *nyuugaku* 'entrance' and *shiken* 'examination') but not **nyuugaku no shiken*; and *shakaishugi* 'socialism' (combination of *shakai* 'society' and *shugi* 'ideology') but not **shakai no shugi*. In some cases *no*-linked nouns and complex nominals differ in meaning: *Tookyoo Daigaku* 'The University of Tokyo,' and *Tookyoo no daigaku* 'university (located) in Tokyo,' for example. These conventions must be learned one by one.

21. Inquiring (1)—Questions and Interrogative Words

■ Target Expressions

Do you go? (Are you going?)

行きますか。
Ikimasu ka.

When is the exam?

試験はいつですか。
Shiken wa itsu desu ka.

Which one is Mr. Yamada's book?

どれが山田さんの本ですか。
Dore ga Yamada-san no hon desu ka.

■ Grammatical Explanation

Question marker *ka*. In phrasing a formal question, the particles *ka* (glossed as Q) is added at the end of the sentence. *Ka* may follow both formal and informal endings of verbs, existential verbs, and [Adj-*i*]. The [V/Adj informal + *ka*] combination, however, is extremely blunt. For practical purposes, only use the [V/Adj formal + *ka*] combination. For the *be*-verb *da*, only the [*desu* + *ka*] combination is possible; **da ka* is an incorrect form. The interrogative particle *ka* receives a slight rising intonation.

Using interrogative words. When an interrogative word (question words equivalent to English *what, when, where,* and so forth) is inserted, unlike English, it is inserted in the place where its answer would normally appear. For example, in *shiken wa ashita desu* 'the exam is tomorrow,' the word *itsu* 'when' is inserted in the same place where the temporal phrase *ashita* 'tomorrow' appears. In Japanese, there is no need to start questions with interrogative words. Simply follow the principle of the preferred word order studied earlier (Entry 18).

Rising intonation. In conversation when asking a question, a rising intonation at the end of the utterance—without *ka*—may be used. Thus *iku* or *ikimasu* with rising intonation (on the last mora only) means 'do you go?' For sentences with *da*, delete *da* and just use rising intonation, *shiken wa ashita?* suffices as a plain version of *shiken wa ashita desu ka? *Shiken wa ashita da?* must be avoided. For [Adj-*i*], *takai?* and *takai-desu?* may be used, the latter being a gentle style used only occasionally.

Choosing *wa* or *ga* in questions. At this point let's look more closely at the two target sentences *shiken wa itsu desu ka?* and *dore ga Yamada-san no hon desu ka?* Notice that in these sentences we find the topic marker *wa* and subject marker *ga*. In the question *shiken wa itsu desu ka?*, new information (the time of the exam) is sought about the topic, that is, *shiken* 'exam.' Therefore *shiken* is marked as a topic. In other words, exam is the starting point of this question, a piece of information assumed to be shared between the speaker and the listener.

In the question *dore ga Yamada-san no hon desu ka?*, the information sought is the identification of Yamada's book. Therefore *dore* is not marked with a topic marker; the information corresponding to *dore* is the information sought. *Dore* is marked with a case marker appropriate to the case defined in the sentence structure, in this case the subject marker *ga*.

The answer to this question is constructed with *ga*; *kore ga Yamada-san no hon desu* 'this is Mr. Yamada's book.' Again this is because *kore* 'this' constitutes a new piece of information, a newly provided answer. Although *kore* itself is a deictic expression and therefore has potential to become the topic marked with *wa*, *kore* is given as a piece of new information in this specific context.

List of Interrogative Words

Pronouns:		
いくつ	*ikutsu*	how many
いくら	*ikura*	how much
誰	*dare*	who
どこ	*doko*	which place, where
どちら	*dochira*	which one (of the two), where [politer than *doko*]
どれ	*dore*	which one (among many)
何	*nani*	what
Adverbs:		
どう	*doo*	how
いかが	*ikaga*	how [polite]
なぜ/どうして	*naze/dooshite*	why
なんで	*nande*	why [casual style]

Asking which one. For forming a question to ask which of the two, use the pattern [N + *to* + N + *to* + *dochira ga*].

(a) これ**と**それ**とどちらが**おいしいですか。

Kore	***to***	*sore*	***to***	***dochira***	***ga***	*oishii-desu*	*ka.*
this	and	that	and	which	S	delicious	Q

(Which is delicious, this or that?)

Using alternate questions. For forming alternate questions, simply repeat single questions.

(b) **A:** 高いですか。安いですか。
Takai-desu ka. Yasui-desu ka.
(Is it expensive or inexpensive?)

B: 高いです。
Takai-desu.
(It is expensive.)

(c) **A:** 今日行く？ あした行く？
Kyoo iku? Ashita iku?
(Do you go today or tomorrow?)

B: あした行く。
Ashita iku.
(I'll go tomorrow.)

■ Examples

(1) **A:** 原さんはいつ誰とどこへ行きますか。

Hara-san	*wa*	*itsu*	*dare*	*to*	*doko*	*e*	*ikimasu*	*ka.*
Mr. Hara	T	when	who	with	where	to	go	Q

(As for Mr. Hara, when, with whom, and where is he going?)

B: 来週スミスさんとイギリスへ行きます。
Raishuu Sumisu-san to Igirisu e ikimasu.
(He will go to England with Mr. Smith next week.)

(2) **A:** あれは何ですか。
Are wa nan desu ka.
(What is that?)

B: ああ、あれは病院ですよ。
Aa, are wa byooin desu yo.
(Ah, that is a hospital.)

A: そうですか。大きい病院ですね。
Soo desu ka. Ookii byooin desu ne.
(Is that so? It's a large hospital, isn't it?)

■ Additional Information

- Other informal questions are used in casual conversation. In masculine speech, *kai* and *no kai* are used for yes/no questions, and *n dai* is used for questions with interrogative words. *Kai, no kai,* and *n dai* follow informal verb forms as in (a) and (b). The *be*-verb *da* preceding these forms is deleted as in (c).

For gentle style, the particle *no* is sometimes added to informal verb forms, transforming the statements into questions. For sentences ending with informal *da*, instead of **da no, na no* is used.

(a) 行く**のかい**?
Iku ***no kai****?*
(Are you going?)

(b) いつ行くん**だい**?
Itsu iku n ***dai****?*
(When are you going?)

(c) あの人誰**だい**?
Ano hito dare ***dai****?*
(Who's that?)

(d) 行く**の**?
Iku ***no****?*
(Are you going?)

(e) これ何**なの**?
Kore nan ***na no****?*
(What's this?)

- Question sentences using *nani* are often used rhetorically. They express different attitudes and emotions, including surprise, disbelief, disgust, and anger. See some idiomatic examples to follow. These are to be interpreted based on the contexts in which they appear.

(f) **なに**、それ!
Nani *sore!*
(What? What do you mean by that!)

(g) **なに**を! [blunt style]
Nani *o!*
(What! Don't give me that!)

(h) **なん**だと! [blunt style]
Nan *da to!*
(What [are you talking about]!)

- Another point to be noted: when the question marker *ka* appears with falling intonation, it marks a statement which acknowledges something curious not known before.

(i) ああ、田島さんです**か**。↘
Aa, Tajima-san desu ***ka****.* ↘
(Oh, you are Ms. Tajima, I see.)

- Questions in casual conversation often take the topic marker *tte*, instead of *wa*.

  (j) 友だちって誰？
  Tomodachi tte dare?
  (Your friend, who is it?)

  (k) 夏休みっていつから？
  Natsuyasumi tte itsu kara?
  (Summer vacation, from when is it?)

22. Verbal Predicate (3)—Past

■ Target Expression

Ms. Kasai went to the art museum yesterday.

河西さんはきのう美術館へ行きました。
Kasai-san wa kinoo bijutsukan e ikimashita.

[Vpast]

■ Grammatical Explanation

Past tense forms. The verb form we have studied so far primarily refers to the description of present and future events and states. Although some argue that Japanese does not have a strict "tense system," the form to be introduced here is best understood as the past tense form of the verb since it functions similarly to English past and (past) perfect tenses (refer to characteristic 8). Formal and informal past tense forms are derived as follows:

U-verbs:
formal: replace *-u* with *-imashita*
informal: verbs ending with *-ku*, replace *-ku* with *-ita*
verbs ending with *-gu*, replace *-gu* with *-ida*
verbs ending with *-u*, *-tsu* and *-ru*, replace them with *-tta*
verbs ending with *-nu*, *-bu*, and *-mu*, replace them with *-nda*
verbs ending with *-su*, replace *-su* with *-shita*

RU-verbs:
formal: take off *-ru*, and add *-mashita*
informal: take off *-ru*, and add *-ta*

Irregular verbs:
formal: *suru* takes *shimashita, kuru* takes *kimashita*
informal: *suru* takes *shita, kuru* takes *kita*

Existential verbs:
formal: *iru* takes *imashita, aru* takes *arimashita*
informal: *iru* takes *ita, aru* takes *atta*

Be-verb:
da takes *deshita* (formal) and *datta* (informal)

"*Ta*" song. It is easiest to memorize the conjugation of [Vinformal past] forms if you put it to the tune of "John Brown's Body"—what I call the "*Ta*" song. (For gerundive -*te* forms, change *ta* and *da* to *te* and *de*, respectively.)

(1) *taberu — tabeta; miru — mita;*
(2) *-tsu, -ru, -u — -tta; -su — -shita;*
(3) *-ku, -gu — -ita, -ida;*
(4) *-mu, -bu, -nu — -nda;*
(5) *suru — shita, kuru — kita.*

Line (1) shows *RU*-verb changes, and lines (2) through (4) show verb final changes for *U*-verbs. Line (5) lists irregular verb changes for *suru* and *kuru*.

Functions of past tense forms. The past tense form is generally used for the following purposes:

1. *Descriptions of past events:*

(1a) きのうは雨が**降りました**。 (*hurimashita* is past tense of *huru* 'to rain')

Kinoo	*wa*	*ame*	*ga*	***hurimashita.***
yesterday	T	rain	S	fell

(It rained yesterday.)

2. *Commentary on fulfillment of a wish or desire:*

(2a) バスが**来た**！ (*kita* is past tense of *kuru* 'to come')
*Basu ga **kita**!*
(The bus came!)

This expression implies that you were waiting for the bus, and finally you see the bus coming. It refers to the current realization of a wish.

(2b) 本当によく**晴れた**！ (*hareta* is past tense of *hareru* 'to clear up')
*Hontooni yoku **hareta**!*
([lit., It cleared up completely.] How nice, it has cleared up!)

3. *Reaffirmation of an assumption:*

(3a) 田中さん**でした**ね。 (*deshita* is past tense of *da*)
*Tanaka-san **deshita** ne.*
(You are [lit., were] Mrs. Tanaka, right?)

4. *Expressions of urging someone to act or to perform*—used only in situations which allow for manipulation (only in past informal forms):

(4a) さあ、**買った**、**買った**！ (*katta* is past tense of *kau* 'to buy')
*Saa, **katta**, **katta**!*
(Come on, buy these!)

(4b) 子供たちは**帰った**、**帰った**！ (*kaetta* is past tense of *kaeru* 'to return')
*Kodomo-tachi wa **kaetta**, **kaetta**!*
(Children, come on, go home!)

■ Examples

(1) **A:** きのうは何をしましたか。
Kinoo wa nani o shimashita ka.
(What did you do yesterday?)

B: 本を読みました。
Hon o yomimashita.
(I read a book.)

(2) ホワイトさんはおとといからきのうまで京都にいました。
Howaito-san wa ototoi kara kinoo made Kyooto ni imashita.
(Mr. White was in Kyoto from the day before yesterday until yesterday.)

(3) **A:** きのうはよく降ったねえ。
Kinoo wa yoku hutta nee.
(It rained a lot yesterday, didn't it?)

B: ええ、本当に。私は一日中うちにいました。
Ee, hontooni. Watashi wa ichinichijuu uchi ni imashita.
(Yes, indeed. I was at home all day.)

(4) ああ、そうだ、エリカのふるさと、山梨だよね。
Aa, soo da, Erika no hurusato, Yamanashi da yo ne.
(Oh, that's right, Erika, your hometown is Yamanashi, right?)

■ Additional Information

- The [Vpast] has different meanings depending on whether the verb is active or stative, especially when the verb appears in subordinate clauses. When the active [Vpast] appears in a subordinate clause, it expresses the completion of action prior to the tense defined by the main verb, while the active [Vnon-past] indicates an action not yet completed prior to the tense defined by the main verb.

(a) あの人に**会った**から父に電話した。

Ano	*hito*	*ni*	***atta***	*kara*	*chichi*	*ni*	*denwa-shita.*
that	person	O	met	because	my father	IO	called

(Because I met him, I called my father.)

(b) あの人に**会う**から父に電話した。
*Ano hito ni **au** kara chichi ni denwa-shita.*
(Because I am going to meet him, I called my father.)

Additional information regarding the tense in subordinate clauses will be given when necessary throughout this book.

- Mainly because of the phenomenon observed in examples above, some grammarians call the Japanese [Vpast] a "perfective." We will continue to call it [Vpast] because in case of stative verbs, [Vpast] does not carry a strong sense of "perfectiveness." Note also that although [Vpast] in simple sentences can carry a strong perfective sense—particularly when accompanied by an adverb *moo* 'already'—as shown in (c), it can also refer to a straightforward past-tense event as in (d).

(c) もう食べた？
Moo tabeta?
([lit., Did you eat?] Have you eaten already?)

(d) きのう行きました。
Kinoo ikimashita.
(I went yesterday.)

23. Verbal Predicate (4)—Future

■ Target Expression

I'll go to Japan next year.

来年日本へ行きます。
Rainen Nihon e ikimasu.

[Vnon-past]

■ Grammatical Explanation

Certainty about the future. As mentioned earlier, the non-past verb form is used not only to express the present tense but also to indicate definite future events and actions. This is why we prefer the term "non-past," which describes both present and future tenses. Here we examine this and other ways to express the future tense in Japanese.

First, the [Vnon-past] form describes definite future. It expresses the speaker's strong belief that those events are likely to occur. When the subject is in the first-person, it also expresses the speaker's intentions.

Uncertainty about the future. For expressing the speaker's uncertainty about future events and states, use [Vbasic] followed by auxiliary verb [AuxV] *-daroo*. For formal style, use [Vbasic] followed by *-deshoo*. When combined with [Vbasic] (including existential verbs *iru* and *aru*), this strategy expresses one's doubt about the future events and states described. For the *be*-verb, replace *da* with *daroo/deshoo*. We will study *-daroo/-deshoo* in detail in Entry 99.

Other future expressions are also used, such as *rainen Nihon e iku tsumori/yotei desu* 'I intend to go to Japan next year,' but these expressions will be learned later.

■ Additional Information

- The auxiliary verb *-daroo* is also used for making the conversation more smooth and comfortable. By expressing some doubt, *-daroo* gives a hesitant and therefore less domineering flavor to one's comments and opinions. Instead of asking, for example, *Shinjuku eki wa doko desu ka?* 'where is Shinjuku Station?,' *Shinjuku eki wa doko deshoo ka?* may be used. This is less straightforward and shows the speaker's consideration toward others.
- Another extended use of *-daroo* is to show sympathy toward or understanding of another's feelings. Instead of saying *isogashii-desu ne* 'you are busy,' *isogashii-deshoo ne* is preferred to mean something like 'oh, you must be busy . . .' showing sympathy. This contrasts with American English in which softness and sympathy are often communicated by intonation and tone of voice.

24. Expressions of Location

■ Target Expressions

in front of the bank, inside the room
銀行の前、部屋の中
ginkoo no mae, heya no naka

■ Grammatical Explanation

[N + *no*] locatives. Noun phrases linked with *no* and locative particles are used to describe locations. For example, a noun *naka* 'inside' is modified by an [N + *no*] structure. For expressing 'inside the box,' *hako no naka* is used (be warned of the word-order here).

List of Locative Expressions

間	*aida*	ビルの**間**	*biru no* ***aida***	between the buildings
上	*ue*	机の**上**	*tsukue no* ***ue***	on (top of) the desk
うしろ	*ushiro*	建物の**うしろ**	*tatemono no* ***ushiro***	behind the building
先	*saki*	この**先**	*kono* ***saki***	up ahead
下	*shita*	机の**下**	*tsukue no* ***shita***	under the desk
そば	*soba*	駅の**そば**	*eki no* ***soba***	near the station
近く	*chikaku*	駅の**近く**	*eki no* ***chikaku***	near the station
となり	*tonari*	家の**となり**	*uchi no* ***tonari***	next door to my house
中	*naka*	箱の**中**	*hako no* ***naka***	inside the box
前	*mae*	家の**前**	*uchi no* ***mae***	(in) front of the house
向こう	*mukoo*	川の**向こう**	*kawa no* ***mukoo***	beyond the river
横	*yoko*	建物の**横**	*tatemono no* ***yoko***	beside the building

Locatives and particles. Both *naka* and *hako no naka* are noun phrases. Depending on how the location functions in a predicate, *hako no naka* takes any of the grammatical particles. Thus, we have *hako no naka ni* 'inside the box,' *hako no naka e* 'into the box,' and *hako no naka kara* 'from inside the box.' *Hako no naka* can also become the grammatical topic, subject or object as in *hako no naka o miru* 'to look inside the box.'

Using locatives with *da*. The locative phrase can also appear preceding the *be*-verb *da* as in *naihu to fooku wa hikidashi no naka desu* 'knives and forks are inside the drawer.' Note that in this use, locative particle *ni* is not used. In other words, in Japanese there are two ways for describing locations, although the English translation is identical. Recall the concept of topic in interpreting this example.

Here 'knives and forks' are not the location 'inside the drawer.' The topic-comment relation requires extended interpretation as discussed in Entry 15.

(a) ナイフとフォークは引き出しの中**にあります**。

Naihu	*to*	*fooku*	*wa*	*hikidashi*	*no*	*naka* ***ni***	***arimasu.***
knife	and	fork	T	drawer	L	inside	there are

(Knives and forks are in the drawer. This is closer to 'there are knives and forks in the drawer.')

(b) ナイフとフォークは引き出しの中**です**。
Naihu to fooku wa hikidashi no naka ***desu.***
(Knives and forks are in the drawer.)

■ Examples

(1) 机の上にノートを置く。
Tsukue no ue ni nooto o oku.
(I put a notebook on the desk.)

机の下にくつの箱を置く。
Tsukue no shita ni kutsu no hako o oku.
(I will put a shoe box under the desk.)

(2) **A:** あそこに本屋さんがあるよね。
Asoko ni hon'ya-san ga aru yo ne.
(There is a bookstore over there, right?)

B: どこ？
Doko?
(Where?)

A: あの大きいビルのとなり。

Ano	*ookii*	*biru*	*no*	*tonari.*
that	large	building	L	next to

(Next to that large building.)

B: ああ、ある、ある。
Aa, aru, aru.
(Ah, there is.)

A: あの本屋できのうジムに会った。
Ano hon'ya de kinoo Jimu ni atta.
(I saw Jim at that bookstore yesterday.)

B: 本当？
Hontoo?
(Really?)

25. Indefinite Pronoun *No*

■ Target Expression

I bought the expensive one.

高いのを買いました。
Takai no o kaimashita.

[modifier + *no*]

■ Grammatical Explanation

Adjective plus *no*. The indefinite pronoun *no* (different from the linker *no*) functions like the English indefinite pronoun *one*, and *ones*. *No* cannot be used alone, nor with demonstratives alone; it must be accompanied by a modifier. As shown in the target expression, *takai no* 'expensive one' may be used when what is expensive is already shared among interactants. In such a case, it is unnecessary and is considered redundant to specify the item with a regular noun, for example, *takai kuruma*.

Personal pronoun plus *no*. *No*, when combined with personal pronouns and nouns indicating possessor, adds the meaning of possession in two ways. For example, first, *watashi no* is used independently to mean 'mine.' Second, *watashi no* means 'my' when it precedes a noun, for example, *watashi no okane* 'my money' (in this case *no* is a linker). Note other examples of the indefinite pronoun *no*; *ano hito no* 'his/her,' *Yamada-san no* 'Ms. Yamada's,' and so forth. When the indefinite pronoun *no* is preceded by demonstratives such as *kono*, instead of **kono no*, *kore* must be used.

■ Examples

(1) ここに大きいのがあるよ。
Koko ni ookii no ga aru yo.
(Here is the large one.)

(2) **A:** 赤いのと白いのとどちらがいいですか。
Akai no to shiroi no to dochira ga ii-desu ka.
(Which one is better, the red one or the white one?)

B: 赤いのがいいです。
Akai no ga ii-desu.
(The red one is good [for me].)

(3) **A:** これ、誰の？ [holding a book]
Kore, dare no?
(Whose is this?)

B: スミスさんのです。
Sumisu-san no desu.
(That is Mr. Smith's.)

26. Negating (1)—Negation of Verbs

■ Target Expression

I'm not going to the office today.

今日は会社へ行きません。
Kyoo wa kaisha e ikimasen.

■ Grammatical Explanation

Negative forms. To form negation in Japanese, verb endings are changed into negative forms (refer to characteristic 8). Japanese does not operate like English, which negates with [auxiliary verbs + not] as in *do/does/did not*. Negation in Japanese is somewhat similar to the English process of adding negative prefixes such as *discontinue* and *uncover*, except that in Japanese, the endings of the verbs are changed to form the negative. Negative verb forms in Japanese are as follows:

U-verbs:

informal non-past:	replace the final vowel with *-anai* (For *U*-verbs ending in a [vowel + *-u*], replace the final verb with *-wanai*.)
formal non-past:	replace *-masu* of *-masu* form with *-masen*
informal past:	replace *-nai* of *-anai* form with *-nakatta*
formal past:	add *-deshita* to *-masen* form

RU-verbs:

informal non-past:	replace *-ru* with *-nai*
formal non-past:	replace *-masu* of *-masu* form with *-masen*
informal past:	replace *-nai* with *-nakatta*
formal past:	add *-deshita* to *-masen* form

Existential verbs:
Iru follows *RU*-verb conjugation. For *aru*:

informal non-past:	*nai* (There is no form **aranai*.)
formal non-past:	*arimasen*
informal past:	*nakatta*
formal past:	*arimasen-deshita*

Irregular verbs:

informal non-past:	*suru* takes *shinai*, *kuru* takes *konai*
formal non-past:	*suru* takes *shimasen*, *kuru* takes *kimasen*
informal past:	*suru* takes *shinakatta*, *kuru* takes *konakatta*
formal past:	*suru* takes *shimasen-deshita*, *kuru* takes *kimasen-deshita*

Be-verb:

informal non-past:	*dewa-nai*, *ja-nai* [contracted form]
formal non-past:	*dewa-arimasen*, *ja-arimasen* [contracted form]
informal past:	*dewa-nakatta*, *ja-nakatta* [contracted form]
formal past:	*dewa-arimasen-deshita*, *ja-arimasen-deshita* [contracted form]

Note that the negative of *da* has alternative formal forms: *ja-nai desu* (non-past) and *ja-nakatta* desu (past).

Sample Verb Negative Forms

[Vbasic]	informal non-past	formal non-past	informal past	formal past
U-verbs:				
書く	書かない	書きません	書かなかった	書きませんでした
kaku	*kakanai*	*kakimasen*	*kakanakatta*	*kakimasen-deshita*
遊ぶ	遊ばない	遊びません	遊ばなかった	遊びませんでした
asobu	*asobanai*	*asobimasen*	*asobanakatta*	*asobimasen-deshita*
RU-verbs:				
食べる	食べない	食べません	食べなかった	食べませんでした
taberu	*tabenai*	*tabemasen*	*tabenakatta*	*tabemasen-deshita*
Be-verb:				
だ	ではない	ではありません	ではなかった	ではありませんでした
da	*dewa-nai*	*dewa-arimasen*	*dewa-nakatta*	*dewa-arimasen-deshita*
	じゃない	じゃありません	じゃなかった	じゃありませんでした
	ja-nai	*ja-arimasen*	*ja-nakatta*	*ja-arimasen-deshita*

Negation with *wa*. The topic marker *wa* in the target sentence *kyoo wa kaisha e ikimasen* must now be explained in the context of negation. When we negate a statement, we negate what is known. In this sense, *wa* appearing in negative sentences is a special case of topic marking. In fact *wa* defines what we are negating. It defines the negative scope. This usage of *wa* is often called "negative *wa*." Negative *wa* also implies contrastiveness, another quality associated with the topic marker *wa* as mentioned earlier (Entry 16). Negation implies a contrast with the assumed affirmative statement. Note that qualities associated with *wa*, namely, contrastiveness and negation, are simply consequences of the fundamental function of *wa*, that is, the identification of topic in communication.

Specifying negative scope. We can create another version of the target sentence by adding *wa* to another noun phrase as in *kyoo wa kaisha e* <u>*wa*</u> *ikimasen*. This sentence defines the negative scope one step further than the original target sentence. It implies 'I don't go to the office today, although I may go somewhere else.' It negates the possibility of going specifically to the office, but not necessarily the possibility of going somewhere else. *Wa* in negative sentences then is a useful tool for defining what exactly a speaker wishes to negate.

***Dewa-nai* and *ja-nai*.** We noted that for negative sentences of the *be*-verb, *dewa-nai/dewa-arimasen* are used. Consider that in these negative expressions, *wa* also appears. It literally negates what precedes *wa*, that is, *de*, the gerundive *-te* form of the verb *da*. In the sentence *Nihon-jin dewa-arimasen*, what is negated is 'being Japanese,' implying that the person is of some other nationality. *Dewa-nai* and *dewa-arimasen* have contracted versions used in casual speech, i.e., *ja-nai* and *ja-arimasen*.

Negating without *wa*. A point of caution: the reader is reminded that the discussion above does not exclude the possibility of negating without *wa*. It is possible to negate with other case markers without *wa*, in the context where the relevant phrase does not constitute topic. Consider the following. Speaker A at least knows that someone else is not coming; A asks who that might be. In response to this question, B answers as (a).

(a) 山田さんが来ません。
Yamada-san ga kimasen.
(Mr. Yamada is not coming.)

Here (a) provides an answer by marking with *ga* the piece of new information—the name of the person who is not coming. In this case what is known is the fact that someone is not coming; *Yamada-san* cannot be marked by *wa*, since it is not a piece of shared information.

Negating with *mo*. Another important point to be studied in relation to negative sentences; the interrogative words in negative statements take the [interrogative word + *mo*] structure. *Dare-mo*, *nani-mo*, and *doko e mo* are frequently used. These are equivalent to 'anyone,' 'anything,' and 'anywhere,' meaning total negation. When the [interrogative word + *mo*] combination is used for affirmative sentences, it adds the meaning of total positiveness, as in 'all' and 'every.' (See Appendix 6 for the list regarding this point.)

Wakannai **and** ***ikanee.*** In rapid colloquial speech, *ra* in *-ranai* and *-ranakatta* becomes *n*, creating *wakannai* (instead of *wakaranai*) and *wakannakatta* (instead of *wakaranakatta*). Also in blunt masculine speech, *-nai* in informal negative endings changes to *-nee*. This creates forms such as *ikanee* instead of *ikanai*, *tabenee* instead of *tabenai*. These expressions are considered extremely colloquial and often rude; they should be avoided under most circumstances. It is important to know that these expressions are limited to intimate and casual situations only.

■ Examples

(1) きのう近くの公園へ行った。
Kinoo chikaku no kooen e itta.
(Yesterday I went to a nearby park.)

きのうはあまりいい天気じゃなかった。
Kinoo wa amari ii tenki ja-nakatta.
(Yesterday the weather was not so good.)

とても寒かった。
Totemo samukatta.
(It was very cold.)

公園には誰もいなかった。
Kooen ni wa dare-mo inakatta.
(There was no one [else] in the park.)

(2) **A:** あの人はイタリア人じゃありませんよ。
Ano hito wa Itaria-jin ja-arimasen yo.
(He is not an Italian.)

B: そうですか。知りませんでした。
Soo desu ka. Shirimasen-deshita.
(Is that so? I didn't know that.)

(3) **A:** スーザンは行かなかったよ。
Suuzan wa ikanakatta yo.
(Susan didn't go.)

B: 本当？ 私も行かなかった。
Hontoo? Watashi mo ikanakatta.
(Really? I didn't go either.)

■ Additional Information

- Although less frequently used and in use primarily in written discourse, another negative ending *-mai* should be mentioned in passing. *-Mai* expresses the negative intention of the speaker, and is attached to the [Vnon-past] form, and optionally to the [Vstem] of the *RU*-verb. For existential verbs *aru* and *iru*, *arumai* and *imai* are used. For the verbs *kuru* and *suru*, *kurumai* and *surumai* (as well as *kimasumai* and *shimasumai*) are used. For the verb *da/desu*, *dewa-arumai* is used; for [Adj-*i*], *-ku(wa)-arumai* is used.

(a) そんなことは言う**まい**。
*Sonna koto wa yuu**mai**.*
(I won't say such a thing.)

(b) もう酒は飲む**まい**。
*Moo sake wa nomu**mai**.*
(I won't drink *sake* any more.)

(c) 甘い物は食べ(る)**まい**。
*Amai mono wa tabe(ru)**mai**.*
(I won't eat sweet things.)

- In spoken Japanese, *to omou* 'to think' is added to create the expression *mai to omou* 'to think not to.'
- Another negative form used primarily in the written style is *-nu*. To obtain *-nu* and its gerundive form *-zu*, replace *-nai* of negative verb forms with *-nu* or *-zu*.

  For the *i*-type adjective, replace the final *-i* with *-karazu (da)*.

(d) それはわから**ぬ**。
*Sore wa wakara**nu**.*
(I don't know that.)

(e) 今日は寒から**ず**、暑から**ず**だ。
*Kyoo wa samukara**zu**, atsukara**zu** da.*
(Today is neither hot nor cold.)

■ Warning

It is a good idea to remind ourselves that not all negative expressions mean negation of a statement. Two main exceptions are: (1) negation used for the purpose of invitation as in (a), and (2) negative endings used in exclamatory expressions as in (b).

(a) 買い物に行かない？

Kaimono	*ni*	*ikanai?*
shopping	for	don't go

(Don't you want to go shopping?)

(b) あっ、大貴君じゃない！
Att, Daiki-kun ja-nai!
(Oh, that's Daiki!)

27. Quantity (1)—Quantifiers of Adverbial Phrases

Target Expressions

many, a little, not at all

たくさん、すこし、ちっとも

takusan, sukoshi, chittomo

Grammatical Explanation

Adverbial quantifiers. Quantifiers, or degree words, are used as adverbial phrases, and are normally placed immediately after the noun whose quantity is described. For example, *ringo o takusan kaimashita* 'I bought many apples.' Note in English the quantifier *many* precedes the noun, *apples*.

When degree words are used to modify adjectives, they immediately precede them, as in *taihen muzukashii* 'very difficult.' Here is a list of frequently used adverbial quantifiers.

大勢	*oozei*	many (only in reference to people)
かなり	*kanari*	considerably
少し	*sukoshi*	a few, a little
ずいぶん	*zuibun*	very much
大変	*taihen*	much
たくさん	*takusan*	many, much
ちょっと	*chotto*	a little
ちょっぴり	*choppiri*	very little, a wee bit

Adverbial quantifiers *takusan* and *oozei* cannot be used to modify adjectives (**takusan ookii*).

Negative adverbial quantifiers. There are some adverbial quantifiers used with negative statements only, similar to the English *at all*, which is always used in negative statements. These include:

あまり	*amari*	(not) so
少しも	*sukoshimo*	(not) at all
ちっとも	*chittomo*	(not) at all

***Dake* and *shika*.** Another useful quantifying strategy is to express 'only' and 'no more than.' For example, *dake* 'only' as in *ringo wa sukoshi dake kaimashita* 'I bought only a few apples,' and *shika* in negative sentences as in *ringo wa sukoshi shika kaimasen-deshita* 'I didn't buy more than a few apples,' or 'I bought only a few apples.'

The difference between the *dake* and the *shika* sentences lies in the speaker's intention as to whether she/he emphasizes that there is something, or there isn't as much as there should be. See for example:

(a) 千円**しか**ありませんからレストランへは行けませんよ。

Sen-en	***shika***	*arimasen*	*kara*	*resutoran*	*e*	*wa*	*ikemasen*	*yo.*
one thousand yen	only	there isn't	because	restaurant	to	T	cannot go	IP

(Since I have only one thousand yen, I can't go to a restaurant.)

■ Examples

(1) A: 遅くなりますか。
Osoku narimasu ka.
(Will you be late?)

B: ええ、少し。
Ee, sukoshi
(Yes, a little.)

(2) 酒はあまり飲みません。ビールはたくさん飲みます。
Sake wa amari nomimasen. Biiru wa takusan nomimasu.
(I don't drink too much *sake*. I drink a lot of beer.)

(3) A: このデジカメ、ちょっと高いねえ。
Kono dejikame, chotto takai nee.
(This digital camera is a bit expensive, isn't it?)

B: そうですか。こちらのはいかがですか。
Soo desu ka. Kochira no wa ikaga desu ka.
(Is that so? How about this one over here?)

■ Additional Information

- The quantifier *chotto* has additional functions; (1) when using vocative phrase 'excuse me!' or 'hey' to catch the attention of someone, and (2) when making a request, to add the meaning of 'just' in, for example, *kore chotto karite mo ii-desu ka?* 'could I just borrow this?' These expressions will be discussed later.
- In casual conversation, especially among youth, adverbial phrases such as *choo*, *mecha*, and *metcha* are used to exaggerate the extreme.

(a) **超**むずかしい。
Choo *muzukashii.*
(It's extremely difficult.)

(b) ヨシキって、**めっちゃ**かわいい。
Yoshiki tte, ***metcha*** *kawaii.*
(Yoshiki is so cute.)

28. Quantity (2)—Numerals and the Number System

Target Expressions

one, ten, one hundred

一、十、百
ichi, juu, hyaku

Grammatical Explanation

Numbers up to 10. There are two number systems up to number 10, one originally Japanese and the other of Chinese origin. The number system consisting of indigenous Japanese vocabulary is limited in its use. It is used for counting objects without counters (to be explained later), and for describing ages up to 10 years old. Its variation is also used for dates up to the 10th of the month, as well as for a few other combinations. The number system of Chinese origin is more extensively used. It is used for mathematical calculation, for combinations that make higher numbers, and in combination with various counters.

		Japanese Origin		Chinese Origin	
1	one	ひとつ	*hitotsu*	いち	*ichi*
2	two	ふたつ	*hutatsu*	に	*ni*
3	three	みっつ	*mittsu*	さん	*san*
4	four	よっつ	*yottsu*	し/よん	*shi/yon*
5	five	いつつ	*itsutsu*	ご	*go*
6	six	むっつ	*muttsu*	ろく	*roku*
7	seven	ななつ	*nanatsu*	しち/なな	*shichi/nana*
8	eight	やっつ	*yattsu*	はち	*hachi*
9	nine	ここのつ	*kokonotsu*	きゅう/く	*kyuu/ku*
10	ten	とお	*too*	じゅう	*juu*

Numbers beyond 10. For combining numbers higher than 10, use the Chinese origin numbering system according to the following rules:

Numbers beyond 10 to 100:

1. For number 11, add one to the word for 10, for number 12, add two to the word for 10, and so forth:

juu ichi, juu ni, juu san, juu shi (juu yon), juu go, juu roku, juu shichi (juu nana), juu hachi, juu kyu (juu ku)

2. For numbers in ten's, numbers one to nine plus *juu* are used:

ni-juu, san-juu, yon-juu, go-juu, roku-juu, shichi-juu (nana-juu), hachi-juu, kyuu-juu; nan-juu (how many tens)

3. Continue to use the number 20 for numbers in twenties such as *ni-juu hachi* for 28, and the number 30 for numbers in thirties, and so forth until 100 (*hyaku*):

Numbers beyond 100 to 10,000:

4. For numbers beyond 100, start with the word for 100; the numbers from 1 to 10 and then to 99 should follow until you reach 200 (*ni-hyaku*); then repeat the process until you reach 1,000 (*sen*):

hyaku, ni-hyaku, san-byaku, yon-hyaku, go-hyaku, rop-pyaku, nana-hyaku, hap-pyaku, kyuu-hyaku; nan-byaku (how many hundreds) ex. 253: *ni-hyaku go-juu san* 368: *san-byaku roku-juu hachi*

Note that after *san* and *nan*, *byaku* is used (instead of *hyaku*), as in *san-byaku* (three hundred) and *nan-byaku* (how many hundred). For *roku* and *hachi*, *rop-pyaku* and *hap-pyaku* combinations are used.

5. For numbers beyond 1,000, start with the word for 1,000, and work downward in units of 100 and 10 until you reach 10,000 (*man*):

sen, ni-sen, san-zen, yon-sen, go-sen, roku-sen, nana-sen, has-sen, kyuu-sen; nan-zen (how many thousands) ex. 1,508: *sen go-hyaku hachi* 7,945: *nana-sen kyuu-hyaku yon-juu go*

Note the sound change in *san-zen, nan-zen* and *has-sen*.

Numbers beyond 10,000:

6. For numbers beyond 10,000, start with 10,000, then 1,000 and so on until 100,000 (*juu-man*):

ichi-man, ni-man, san-man, yon-man, go-man, roku-man, nana-man (shichi-man), hachi-man, kyuu-man; nan-man (how many ten thousands) ex. 84,321: *hachi-man yon-sen san-byaku ni-juu ichi*

7. *Man* is combined with numbers up until 9,999. Thus *kyuu-sen kyuu-hyaku kyuu-juu kyuu-man* is 99,990,000. 100,000,000 is *ichi-oku*:
   ex. 28,410,763: *ni-sen hap-pyaku yon-juu ichi-man nana-hyaku roku-juu san*

From zero to one hundred billion. Note that from 1 through 9,999 Japanese and English have equivalent expressions. At the 10,000 mark, however, Japanese counts in units of *man*, thus 20,000 is two-*man*, 30,000, three-*man*, etc. The same holds true for the unit *oku* which designates 100,000,000.

100,000,000,000	*is-sen-oku*	one hundred billion
10,000,000,000	*hyaku-oku*	ten billion
1,000,000,000	*juu-oku*	one billion
100,000,000	*ichi-oku*	one hundred million
10,000,000	*is-sen-man*	ten million
1,000,000	*hyaku-man*	one million
100,000	*juu-man*	one hundred thousand
10,000	*ichi-man*	ten thousand
1,000	*sen*	one thousand
100	*hyaku*	one hundred
10	*juu*	ten
1	*ichi*	one
0	*rei, zero*	zero

Example numbers:

48	*yon-juu hachi* (or *shi-juu hachi*)
105	*hyaku go*
136	*hyaku san-juu roku*
3,792	*san-zen nana-hyaku kyuu-juu ni*
756,248	*nana-juu go-man roku-sen ni-hyaku yon-juu hachi*

Useful phrases using the number system.

Days of the Month:
(From the 1st to the 10th)

一日	*tsuitachi*	二日	*hutsuka*	三日	*mikka*	四日	*yokka*
五日	*itsuka*	六日	*muika*	七日	*nanoka*	八日	*yooka*
九日	*kokonoka*	十日	*tooka*				

(For days beyond the 10th)
Add the number and *nichi*; *juu go-nichi* '15th,' *ni-juu san-nichi* '23rd.' Exceptions are *juu yokka* '14th,' *hatsuka* '20th,' and *ni-juu yokka* '24th.' For 'which date,' use *nan-nichi*.

Durations of Days:
For the duration of one day, use *ichi-nichi*. For the duration of more than one day, forms identical to dates of the month are used optionally followed by *-kan*, as in *juu go-nichi-kan* 'for fifteen days.' *Nan-nichi* can also mean 'how many days.'

Month:
Add *gatsu* to the numbers of Chinese origin up to 12.

一月	*ichi-gatsu*	二月	*ni-gatsu*	三月	*san-gatsu*	四月	*shi-gatsu*
五月	*go-gatsu*	六月	*roku-gatsu*	七月	*shichi-gatsu*	八月	*hachi-gatsu*
九月	*ku-gatsu*	十月	*juu-gatsu*	十一月	*juu ichi-gatsu*	十二月	*juu ni-gatsu*

Only these combinations are used. For 'which month,' use *nan-gatsu*.

Time:

秒	*byoo*	seconds
分	*hun* (*-pun*)	minutes
時	*ji*	hours
時間	*jikan*	duration of hours
半	*han*	thirty minutes

For *hun*, a phonological change occurs as shown below:

一分	*ip-pun*	one minute
三分	*san-pun*	three minutes
六分	*rop-pun*	six minutes
八分	*hap-pun*	eight minutes
十分	*jup-pun/jip-pun*	ten minutes

***Sugi* and *mae*.** Additional useful phrases for time indication is *sugi* 'past,' and *mae* 'before.'

10:30	十時半	*juu-ji han*
3:57	三時五十七分（すぎ）	*san-ji go-juu nana-hun (sugi)*
	四時三分前	*yo-ji san-pun mae*
2:00 p.m.	午後二時	*gogo ni-ji*
7:05 a.m.	午前七時五分（すぎ）	*gozen shichi-ji go-hun (sugi)*

Remember to attach the particle *ni* when indicating specific time, as in *san-ji ni* 'at three o'clock.'

■ Examples

(1) **A:** シカゴは今何時ですか。
Shikago wa ima nan-ji desu ka.
(What time is it in Chicago now?)

B: 二時です。
Ni-ji desu.
(Two o'clock.)

A: 午前二時ですか。
Gozen ni-ji desu ka.
(Two a.m.?)

B: いいえ、午後二時です。
Iie, gogo ni-ji desu.
(No, two p.m.)

(2) 三時半に電車が来ます。
San-ji han ni densha ga kimasu.
(The train comes at three thirty.)

■ Additional Information

For phone numbers, just as in English, each number is read as a single digit number. For example, 832-5601 will be read, *hachi san ni no go roku zero ichi*. The particle *no* is added at the hyphen. The area code (*kyokuban*) is also read as a signal digit number.

29. Particles (3)—More about Particles

■ Target Expression

Both Ms. Sasaki and I are university students.

佐々木さんも私も大学生です。
Sasaki-san mo watashi mo daigakusei desu.

[*mo*] [*to*] [*ni*] [*ka*] [*kara*] [*o*]

■ Grammatical Explanation

Beyond the particles we have studied so far, we should make note of some others (refer to characteristic 7). Here we focus on specifics of some frequently used particles and patterns.

Enumerative particles. A number of particles are used for the enumeration of nouns.

[A *mo* B *mo*]*1	both A and B
[A *to* B *to* C]	A and B and C
[A *ya* B (*ya* C) *nado*]	A and B (and C) and others
[A *ni* B *ni* C]	A, additionally B, additionally C
[A *yara* B *yara*]	A and B and perhaps others also
[A *ka* B]*2	A or B

[A *toka* B *toka*]	such things as A and B (perhaps)
[A *dano* B *dano*]	such things as A and B

*1. The negation of [A *mo* B *mo*] pattern negates both. Thus: *Biiru mo uisukii mo dame desu.* '(lit., Both beer and whiskey are not good.) I drink neither beer nor whiskey.'
*2. Further discussion on the use of *ka* is available in Entry 102.

(a) 佐々木さん**も**三上さん**も**大学生です。
Sasaki-san ***mo*** *Mikami-san* ***mo*** *daigakusei desu.*
(Both Ms. Sasaki and Ms. Mikami are university students.)

(b) きのう本屋でこの本**と**その本を買いました。
Kinoo hon'ya de kono hon ***to*** *sono hon o kaimashita.*
(I bought this and that book at the bookstore yesterday.)

(c) コーヒー**とか**紅茶**とか**いろいろな物があった。
Koohii ***toka*** *koocha* ***toka*** *iroirona mono ga atta.*
(There were various things such as tea and coffee.)

(d) この本**か**あの本を買います。
Kono hon ***ka*** *ano hon o kaimasu.*
(I'm going to buy this book or that book.)

Use of particle *ni*. Beyond the locative, directive, and source-indicating use of *ni* discussed in Entry 17, the following points should be taken into consideration.

1. *Ni* is used to show the goal, location, and grammatical object of some verbs; these are considered idiomatic:

   noru as in *basu* ***ni*** *noru* 'to get on the bus'
   kotaeru as in *shitsumon* ***ni*** *kotaeru* 'answer the question'
   au as in *tomodachi* ***ni*** *au* 'see a friend'
   niru as in *chichioya* ***ni*** *niru* 'resemble one's father'

2. *N*i marks what one emotionally responds to when using a group of intransitive verbs that express feelings and emotions.

あきる	*akiru*	to get bored, to get tired of
あきれる	*akireru*	to be surprised, to be amazed
あこがれる	*akogareru*	to long for, to pine for
甘える	*amaeru*	to be dependent upon
気づく	*kizuku*	to notice
こだわる	*kodawaru*	to be bothered, to be concerned about
困る	*komaru*	to be troubled

こりる	*koriru*	to learn by experience
なつく	*natsuku*	to become attached to
ほれる	*horeru*	to fall in love, to be infatuated
迷う	*mayou*	to be puzzled

(e) 勉強**に**あきた。
*Benkyoo **ni** akita.*
(I'm tired of studying.)

(f) いろいろなこと**に**よく気づきますねえ。
*Iroirona koto **ni** yoku kizukimasu nee.*
(You [lit., notice things well, don't you] are rather perceptive, aren't you?)

3. *Ni* co-occurs with some of the [Adj-*i*] predicates as shown below. In these examples, similarly to the case in B above, *ni* identifies the specific item that the adjective predicate applies to, i.e., 'resistant (specifically) to heat.'

暑さ**に**強い	*atsusa **ni** tsuyoi*	resistant to heat
資源**に**乏しい	*shigen **ni** toboshii*	poor in resources
駅**に**近い	*eki **ni** chikai*	close to the station

Use of particle *o*. Let's sum up the usage of the particle *o*.

1. Marks direct object:

(g) ミルク**を**飲む。
*Miruku **o** nomu.*
(I drink milk.)

2. Indicates directional movement—along, across, or through:

(h) 駅前の通り**を**歩いた。
*Ekimae no toori **o** aruita.*
(I walked along the street in front of the station.)

3. Indicates the starting point of an action:

(i) 会社**を**何時に出ますか。
*Kaisha **o** nan-ji ni demasu ka.*
(What time do you leave the company?)

Locatives *kara* and *o*. When using *kara* and *o* for indicating location (meaning 'from'), the following distinctions are made. *Kara* means 'from a certain physical location,' while *o* may also indicate an abstract source, and it is sometimes used idiomatically.

(j) 大学**から**出ないでください。
*Daigaku **kara** denaide-kudasai.*
(Please do not leave the [university] campus.)

(k) 何年に大学**を**出ましたか。
*Nannen ni daigaku **o** demashita ka.*
(In what year did you graduate from the university?)

(l) 子供がうち**を**出ました。
*Kodomo ga uchi **o** demashita.*
(My child left home. [i.e., ran away from home or married into some other family])

Use of particle *de*. Beyond the locative and instrumental use of *de* studied earlier, *de* is used for the following purposes.

1. Amount of time or money:

(m) 五千円**で**この本を買った。
*Go-sen-en **de** kono hon o katta.*
(I bought this book for 5,000 yen.)

2. Cause or reason:

(n) かぜ**で**会社を休みました。

Kaze	***de***	*kaisha*	*o*	*yasumimashita.*
cold	due to	company	O	was absent

(I was absent from the office due to a cold.)

3. Limit or extent of something:

(o) 会議はあと十五分**で**終わります。

Kaigi	*wa*	*ato*	*juu go-hun*	***de***	*owarimasu.*
meeting	T	more	fifteen minutes	in	be over

(The meeting will be over in fifteen minutes.)

(p) 東京**で**一番有名なレストランへ行きました。

Tookyoo	***de***	*ichiban*	*yuumeina*	*resutoran*	*e*	*ikimashita.*
Tokyo	in	most	famous	restaurant	to	went

(We went to the most famous restaurant in Tokyo.)

■ Additional Information

Toka is used independently to imply choice in questions and invitations in casual conversation. Because of the implied choice, the question becomes less direct, thus having a softening effect.

(a) ビール**とか**、買う？
*Biiru **toka** kau?*
(Shall we buy beer [or something]?)

(b) 大阪**とか**、行く？
*Oosaka **toka**, iku?*
(Are you going to Osaka?)

30. Requesting (1)—Asking for Items and Services

■ Target Expression

Please (take me) to the airport. [said to a taxi driver]

空港までお願いします。

Kuukoo made onegai-shimasu.

■ Strategic Explanation

Onegai-shimasu* and *kudasai. There are two formulaic expressions in asking for items and services. First, *onegai-shimasu* 'I make a request' for the addressee's services, and second, *kudasai* 'please give (or hand over),' primarily used in the transaction of objects and things. When handing in forms at a bank or at public service offices, for example, *onegai-shimasu* should be used since you are requesting their service. When purchasing some items, *kore o kudasai* is frequently used, although the politer expression *kore o onegaishimasu* may also be used. When asking for someone on the phone, as in 'Mari, please' or 'May I speak to Mari?' *Mari-san onegai-shimasu* is used. For making requests that involve verbs, another pattern is used, which we will learn later (Entry 40).

When not to request. One point to be noted regarding requests. Normally one should avoid making straightforward requests to social superiors. A more polite way of making requests is to turn it into a question, something similar to English *could you ...?* or *would it be possible for you to ...?* Imagine a situation where you want to obtain an information packet from your professor. Instead of saying *kore kudasai*, one should say *kore itadaite mo yoroshii deshoo ka?* 'would it be all right if I received this?' This form will be studied later (Entry 110).

■ Examples

(1) 東京駅へ/までお願いします。 [said to a taxi driver]
Tookyoo eki e/made onegai-shimasu.
(Please [take me] to Tokyo Station.)

(2) これお願いします。 [at a bank]
Kore onegai-shimasu.
(Please take care of this.)

(3) これください。 [at a store]
Kore kudasai.
(I'll take this.)

31. Negating (2)—Past Tense and Negation of the *I*-type Adjective

■ Target Expression

This book wasn't so interesting.
この本はあまりおもしろくなかったです。
Kono hon wa amari omoshirokunakatta-desu.

■ Grammatical Explanation

More [Adj-*i*] forms. As we have already learned, [Adj-*i*] behaves like a verb. They conjugate just like verbs (refer to characteristic 8). Here we concentrate on the past tense and the negative forms of [Adj-*i*].

Past tense forms:

informal past:	replace the final -*i* with -*katta*
formal past:	add -*desu* to informal past

Negative forms:

informal non-past:	replace -*i* with -*kunai*
formal non-past:	add -*desu* to informal non-past
informal past:	replace -*i* with -*kunakatta*
formal past:	add -*desu* to informal past

The negative affix -*nai* which was introduced for the negation of verbs is in fact an *i*-type adjective, and therefore it is essential that you master how [Adj-*i*] conjugates. There is also a variation in the formal negative forms of [Adj-*i*].

formal non-past:	replace -*i* with -*kuarimasen*
formal past:	add -*deshita* to -*kuarimasen*

The -*kuarimasen* negation is considered slightly more polite than the -*kunai-desu* negation.

Using *wa* in negatives. *Wa* is optionally inserted to form the negative expression *-ku(wa)-nai*. The conjugation with the particle *wa* focuses on what is negated slightly more than the conjugation without. For example, *takakuwa-arimasen* has an interpretation of not being expensive, similar to the English expression *at least it's not expensive*.

Sample *I*-Type Adjective Conjugation

		non-past	past
[Affirmative]	informal:	広い *hiroi*	広かった *hirokatta*
	formal:	広いです *hiroi-desu*	広かったです *hirokatta-desu*
[Negative]	informal:	広くない *hirokunai*	広くなかった *hirokunakatta*
	formal:	広くないです *hirokunai-desu*	広くなかったです *hirokunakatta-desu*
		広くありません *hirokuarimasen*	広くありませんでした *hirokuarimasen-deshita*

■ Examples

(1) **A:** このレストランは高いですか。安いですか。
Kono resutoran wa takai-desu ka. Yasui-desu ka.
(Is this restaurant expensive? Is it inexpensive?)

B: 先週ここで食べましたが、とても高かったです。
Senshuu koko de tabemashita ga, totemo takakatta-desu.
(I ate here last week, but it was quite expensive.)

A: そうですか。おいしかったですか。
Soo desu ka. Oishikatta-desu ka.
(I see. Was it good?)

B: あまりおいしくなかったですね。
Amari oishikunakatta-desu ne.
(It wasn't very delicious.)

(2) **A:** 九州の冬はあまり寒くありません。テキサスの冬はいかがですか。
Kyuushuu no huyu wa amari samukuarimasen. Tekisasu no huyu wa ikaga desu ka.
(Kyushu's winter is not too cold. How is it in Texas?)

B: テキサスもあまり寒くないですよ。
Tekisasu mo amari samukunai-desu yo.
(It isn't so cold in Texas either.)

■ Warning

The informal non-past negative form of the adjective *ii* 'good' is *yokunai*. Other forms include; *yokunai-desu, yokuarimasen-deshita, yokunakatta, yokunakatta-desu*.

32. Responding to Questions (1)—Answering Yes/No Questions

■ Target Expressions

yes, no, yeah, nope

はい、いいえ、うん、ううん
hai, iie, un, uun

■ Strategic Explanation

Saying yes and no. In answering questions, *hai, ee,* and *un* are used to indicate agreement. Although each is a way of saying "yes," one should be aware of the different situations in which each is optimally used. *Hai* is most neutral; *ee* is conversational; *un* is casual and restricted to communication among familiar *uchi* (in-group) members. Another interjection *haa* 'yes' is formal and polite, often used as a humble form toward social superiors.

For negative answers, *iie, iiya* (or *iya*) and *uun* are used. *Iie* is most neutral; *iiya* (or *iya*) is conversational and frequently preferred in masculine speech. The use of *uun* is casual and should be used among familiar *uchi* members under informal circumstances.

Using short answers. It is possible to answer question (a) with *hai, Nihongo wa totemo muzukashii-desu*. However, in real conversation, there is no need to repeat. Short answers are perfectly acceptable (refer to characteristic 4) and in fact are preferred.

(a) A: 日本語はむずかしいですか。
Nihongo wa muzukashii-desu ka.
(Is Japanese difficult?)

B: ええ、とても。/いいえ、ちっとも。
Ee, totemo. / Iie, chittomo.
(Yes, very much so. / No, not at all.)

About *soo desu*. When answering a question with the verb *be* as in question (b), *soo desu* is preferred to an answer in a complete sentence. *Hai, Yamada desu* would not be used unless there was a need for repeating. For the *be*-verb sentences, answer with *hai soo desu* 'yes, it is so,' or *iie soo dewa-arimasen* 'no, it isn't so.'

(b) **A:** 山田さんですか。
Yamada-san desu ka.
(Are you Ms. Yamada?)

B: はい、そうです。
Hai, soo desu.
(Yes, I am.)

Avoiding *soo desu*. Even when the sentence has a *da/desu* expression, if it is an adjective, *soo da* and *soo dewa-nai* forms are not normally used. When answering the question *takai-desu ka?, hai, takai-desu* is used. Likewise, in answer to the question *benri desu ka?, hai, benri desu* is appropriate but not **hai soo desu*. *Benri desu* is a formal version of *benri da*, another type of adjectival predicate, which we will learn in Entry 37.

■ Additional Information

- You may hear Japanese people saying *hai* quite frequently in conversations. If you were to interpret every *hai* as agreement and affirmation, these conversations would sound quite silly. But as we will discuss later, *hai* does not always nor simply mean 'yes.' Actually *hai* has a very important social function. It is a respectful listener response (called *aizuchi* 'back-channel' responses), which is equivalent to English *uh-huh* and *yeah*. When conversing with a Japanese person you should understand that the *hai* you hear, more often than not, means 'I hear what you're saying. And?'
- Additionally, *hai* has ritualistic functions; it is the preferred utterance (1) as when responding to your name in a roll-call, equivalent to *here* as an answer, (2) as a movement-accompanying utterance when you hand something to someone, equivalent to *here you go* or *here it is*, and (3) as an energetic signal to get something started, equivalent to the English *go*.

33. Quantity (3)—Counters

■ Target Expressions

three hours, ten dollars, two pairs (of shoes)

三時間、十ドル、二足

san-jikan, juu-doru, ni-soku

■ Grammatical Explanation

Counting different things. Each language provides different ways for counting objects. Just as Japanese people learning English must simply memorize things like *an ear of corn, a kernel of corn,* or *a litter of kittens,* one must learn a set of counters (or classifiers) when counting in Japanese. These counters are used for a set group of items and are attached immediately following the number. Here are some examples:

Objects:

階	*kai*	for the floors of a building
個	*ko*	used for a broad category of small and compact objects, including round fruit, balls, boxes, etc.
冊	*satsu*	for bound objects such as books, notebooks, magazines, etc.
足	*soku*	for pairs of shoes, socks, stockings, etc.
台	*dai*	for vehicles, machines, bicycles, etc.
通	*tsuu*	for letters and documents
杯	*hai*	for liquid in cups, glasses, bowls, buckets, etc.
本	*hon*	for long, cylindrical objects including trees, sticks, pens, bananas, fingers, etc.
枚	*mai*	flat, thin objects including paper, dishes, stamps, blankets, boards, etc.

Measuring units:

キロ	*kiro*	used for both kilometers and kilograms
グラム	*guramu*	gram
センチ	*senchi*	centimeter
メートル	*meetoru*	meter
リットル	*rittoru*	litter

Animal world:

匹	*hiki*	for insects, fish, small animals such as cats and dogs
頭	*too*	for large animals such as horses, bears, lions, etc.
羽	*wa*	for birds

Frequency:

回	*kai*	times, as in *ik-kai* 'once'
度	*do*	times, as in *ichi-do* 'once'

Order:

番	*ban*	as in *ni-ban* 'number two, second place'
等	*too*	as in *san-too* 'third place'

Duration:

時間	*jikan*	hour, as in *yo-jikan* 'four hours'
週間	*shuukan*	week, as in *ni-shuukan* 'for two weeks'
分	*hun*	minute, as in *hap-pun* 'eight minutes'
秒	*byoo*	second, as in *go-juu-byoo* 'fifty seconds'
年間	*nen kan*	year, as in *juu-nen kan* 'for ten years'

People:

一人 *hitori* and 二人 *hutari* for one and two persons. When there are more than two people, use the appropriate number and add *-nin*; 三人 *san-nin*, 四人 *yo-nin*, 五人 *go-nin*, 六人 *roku-nin*, 七人 *shichi-nin* (or *nana-nin*), 八人 *hachi-nin*, 九人 *ku-nin*, 十人 *juu-nin*, 十一人 *juu ichi-nin*, and so forth.

Phonological changes. In combining numbers with classifiers, phonological changes may occur. Some examples are given below.

	mai	***hiki***	***hon***	***satsu***
1	一枚 *ichi-mai*	一匹 *ip-piki*	一本 *ip-pon*	一冊 *is-satsu*
2	二枚 *ni-mai*	二匹 *ni-hiki*	二本 *ni-hon*	二冊 *ni-satsu*
3	三枚 *san-mai*	三匹 *san-biki*	三本 *san-bon*	三冊 *san-satsu*
4	四枚 *yon-mai (yo-mai)*	四匹 *yon-hiki*	四本 *yon-hon*	四冊 *yon-satsu*
5	五枚 *go-mai*	五匹 *go-hiki*	五本 *go-hon*	五冊 *go-satsu*
6	六枚 *roku-mai*	六匹 *rop-piki*	六本 *rop-pon*	六冊 *roku-satsu*
7	七枚 *shichi-mai* *(nana-mai)*	七匹 *shichi-hiki* *(nana-hiki)*	七本 *shichi-hon* *(nana-hon)*	七冊 *shichi-satsu* *(nana-satsu)*
8	八枚 *hachi-mai*	八匹 *hap-piki*	八本 *hap-pon*	八冊 *has-satsu*
9	九枚 *kyuu-mai*	九匹 *kyuu-hiki*	九本 *kyuu-hon*	九冊 *kyuu-satsu*
10	十枚 *juu-mai*	十匹 *jup-piki* *(jip-piki)*	十本 *jup-pon* *(jip-pon)*	十冊 *jus-satsu* *(jis-satsu)*
	何枚 *nan-mai*	何匹 *nan-biki*	何本 *nan-bon*	何冊 *nan-satsu*

Indicating frequency. For expressing frequency, [duration of time + *ni* + frequency] is used; *ichi-nichi ni ichi-do* 'once a day,' *mikka ni ichi-do* 'once in three days,' *is-shuukan ni san-jikan* 'three hours in a week,' etc.

■ Examples

(1) 切手を十枚ください。
Kitte o juu-mai kudasai.
(I'd like ten stamps.)

(2) ここから大学まで約四キロです。
Koko kara daigaku made yaku yon-kiro desu.
(It is about four kilometers from here to the university.)

(3) **A:** これいくら？
Kore ikura?
(How much is this?)

B: 三千円です。
San-zen-en desu.
(It's three thousand yen.)

A: これも三千円？
Kore mo san-zen-en?
(Is this also three thousand yen?)

B: いいえ、それは三千五百円です。
Iie, sore wa san-zen go-hyaku-en desu.
(No, that is three thousand and five hundred yen.)

■ Additional Information

- Useful phrases which specify quantity are those which express approximation. The phrases *hodo*, *kurai*, *gurai*, *bakari*, and *yaku* all express approximation of quantity equivalent to the English *about*. The phrase *yaku* precedes the quantifier while all others follow it. The phrase *goro* is used only to express approximation of a point in time meaning 'approximately the time (when).'
- Another strategy for approximation is to use two consecutive numbers which limit the quantity to somewhere between the two numbers; *ni-san-nin* 'two to three people,' *go-rop-pun* 'five to six minutes.' Approximations bring forth ambiguity which is advantageous in certain situations. Particularly when making a request, approximation is preferred. It is easier for the listener to accept the request when it is made in approximation.

(a) じゃあ、それ**一時間ぐらい**貸してください。
*Jaa, sore **ichi-jikan gurai** kashite-kudasai.*
(Well then, please loan that to me for about one hour.)

34. Inviting and Suggesting (1)—Inviting and Suggesting Items

■ Target Expression

How about some coffee?

コーヒーでもいかがですか。
Koohii demo ikaga desu ka.

[*ikaga desu ka*]

■ Strategic Explanation

Ikaga* and *doo. *Ikaga desu ka* 'how about it' or its informal version *doo desu ka* are useful for making suggestions and invitations by specifying items. *Ikaga deshoo ka,* a more polite version is also used for people one must be polite toward.

Using *demo.* When suggesting or inviting, the items you specify are often followed by the particle *demo. Demo* is used when other choices are expected to exist and the speaker lists only one of the possible alternatives. *Demo* adds the English meaning of 'or something,' making the suggestion less specific, and therefore less imposing. It doesn't confine the partner to the choice offered. Such usage of a particle expresses interpersonal sensitivity and consideration toward the listener, and it is preferred among Japanese.

■ Examples

(1) A: 食事いっしょにいかがですか。
Shokuji isshoni ikaga desu ka.
(How about eating together?)

B: ええ、いいですねえ。
Ee, ii-desu nee.
(Yes, that will be nice.)

(2) A: 今夜一杯どう？
Kon'ya ip-pai doo?
(How about going for a drink tonight?)

B: いいねえ。
Ii nee.
(That will be nice.)

(3) A: あのう、飲みものでもいかがですか。
Anoo, nomimono demo ikaga desu ka.
(How about something to drink?)

B: ええ、お願いします。
Ee, onegai-shimasu.
(Yes, please.)

35. Appealing to the Listener (1)—Interactional Particles

■ Target Expression

> *Mr. Johnson, right?*
>
> ジョンソンさんですね。
> ***Jonson-san desu ne.***

■ Strategic Explanation

Interactional particles. We have already learned interactional particles *ne* and *yo*. *Ne* is a confirmation seeker similar to English expressions *right*? and *don't you agree?*, normally tagged at the end of an utterance. *Yo* is a particle of assertion which adds moderate emphasis. It is chosen when the speaker provides information that he or she assumes the partner does not know or is not quite familiar with. Several other particles convey the speaker's attitude and feelings toward the content of the statement and toward one's partner. Frequently attached at the sentence-final position, they are also called sentence-final particles (refer to characteristic 7). In spoken language, however, some of these particles may occur at the end of phrases within an utterance.

Characteristics of common interactional particles. Commonly used particles are listed below. When using them, note the relative social status of the participants.

	Relative social status	Implications and effects
ne (nee)		confirmation and friendliness
na (naa)	S higher than L*1	confirmation, often self-addressed
yo	S higher than L	assertion providing new information, while adding moderate emphasis
sa	S higher than L	insistence of obviousness
wa (with high tone)	primarily in feminine speech	femininity, mild insistence
wa (with low tone)	primarily in masculine speech	mild insistence
ze	among friends, primarily in masculine speech	strong insistence

na	S higher than L, blunt	negative imperative
no		question and empathy

*1. S=Speaker, L=Listener

As shown above, interactional particles make interaction more expressive. Of the particles listed here, *ne* is the most frequently used, often appearing not only sentence-finally but also within an utterance boundary at locations where some type of feedback expression is requested.

Note that feminine *wa* and its combination such as *wa yo ne* are rarely used among youth. This form is gradually disappearing. Younger female speakers prefer *iku yo* to *iku wa yo*, for example.

Ka could be considered an interactional particle since it appears sentence-finally and expresses the speaker's interrogative attitude toward the statement.

Restrictions on particle use. It is important to note that some of the particles are restricted in terms of the verb-ending forms that immediately precede them. *Ne* and *yo* can be attached to all informal and formal verb and adjective endings as well as immediately after a noun. *Wa* can be used with both formal and informal endings but not with a noun immediately preceding it. *Sa* is used primarily for informal endings as well as immediately after a noun. *Ze* is used with informal forms and cannot co-occur with nouns immediately preceding them. *Na* and *naa* are used with informal endings, but not used immediately following a noun. When *no* is used, the preceding informal *be*-verb, *da*, changes to *na*; *Nihon-jin na no?*

Using multiple particles. There are also cases where multiple particles are attached for combined effects as shown below.

(a) 今の仕事はむずかしいです**よね**。

Ima *no* *shigoto* *wa* *muzukashii* *desu* ***yo*** ***ne.***
now L work T difficult be IP IP
(Your present job is difficult, isn't it?)

■ Examples

(1) あのう、ちょっとお願いがありましてね……

Anoo, *chotto* *onegai* *ga* *arimashite* *ne . . .*
well a little request S exist IP
(Well, I have some request to make . . .)

(2) あのね、ちょっとね、お願いがあってね……

Ano ne, *chotto* *ne,* *onegai* *ga* *atte* *ne . . .*
well IP a little IP request S exist IP
(Well, uhh . . . I have a request . . .)

(3) **A:** あの女の子ね、誰の子供なの？
Ano onna no ko ne, dare no kodomo na no?
(Whose child is that girl?)

B: さあ、誰の子供ですかね。
Saa, dare no kodomo desu ka ne.
(Well, whose child is she?)

■ Additional Information

- As a variation of the interactional particle, you may hear *desu ne* inserted many times.

  (a) それで**ですね**、あしたまでに**ですね**、お願いしますよ。
  *Sore de **desu ne**, ashita made ni **desu ne**, onegai-shimasu yo.*
  (So, by tomorrow, could you take care of it?)

  Desu ne carries a slightly more formal flavor than *ne;* it is used in a way similar to *ne* and *nee*.

- *Yo* may be combined with the question marker *ka*, to form *ka yo*. The *ka yo* combination is used in masculine casual speech to express surprise and disappointment. For example, when being surprised that one member of the group left the restaurant without paying for his share, the leader of the group may comment, *kuinige ka yo* 'just eating and running away, is he?' This is blunt, and rarely used in feminine speech.

■ Warning

- When used sentence-internally, interactional particles add a more colloquial flavor to speech. One should refrain from overly frequent insertion of particles in formal speech and in situations where politeness is expected.
- Since *yo* appears frequently, some caution is necessary. Because *yo* is used in statements to provide new bits of information while asserting an opinion, claim, advice, warning, etc., one should avoid using it with one's social superior. This is because the presumption of one's social superior's lack of knowledge is unadvisable.
- Note that particles under normal circumstances receive no phonological stress. For example, although *yo* is used to express slight emphasis in that by adding *yo*, *yo* itself does not receive stress.
- Interactional particles *ne(e)* and *sa(a)* may sometimes appear independently to solicit listener responses or as conversational fillers.

36. More about Interrogative Words

■ Target Expressions

Is anyone there?

誰かいますか。
Dare-ka imasu ka.

No one is there.

誰もいません。
Dare-mo imasen.

[*dare-ka*] [*nani-mo*]

■ Grammatical Explanation

Although we have already learned interrogative words, the use of these words needs re-examination because they have special meanings when combined with different particles.

Dare-ka. When an interrogative word is followed by the particle *ka*, it adds the meaning of 'some' in, for example, *doko-ka e ikimashita* 'he went somewhere.' In English, however, in question sentences 'any' is preferred. So when the [interrogative word + *ka*] is used in question sentences, it is best to say that it adds the meaning of the English 'any.' See for example, *nani-ka arimasu ka* 'is there anything?' Although the basic meaning added by the use of [interrogative word + *ka*] is that of 'some,' different interrogative words bear slightly different meanings. We will study them in example sentences. See Appendix 6 for the complete listing of these forms discussed here.

Dare-mo* and *dare de mo. When interrogative words are followed by *mo* in affirmative sentences, they add the meaning of 'every.' Therefore, *dare* 'who' plus *mo* means 'everybody,' *dore-mo* 'everything,' *dochira-mo* 'both,' and so forth. (Note that *nani-mo* does not occur in affirmative sentences, however.)

When the [interrogative word + *mo*] pattern appears in negative sentences, it adds a meaning of total negation, as in *doko-mo* 'anywhere,' *doko e mo* 'to anywhere' *itsu-mo* 'any time,' and *nani-mo* 'anything,' and so forth. In Japanese, unlike English, negation must be completed by the negative verb ending as well. Thus, *nani-mo arimasen* 'there isn't anything' or 'there is nothing.'

When interrogative words are followed by *de mo*, the meaning of 'any' is added. *Dare de mo* means 'any person,' in a sentence such as *dare de mo ii-desu* 'any person is good (fine).'

■ Examples

(1) A: 誰か来ますか。
Dare-ka kimasu ka.
(Is someone coming?)

B: いいえ、誰も来ませんよ。
Iie, dare-mo kimasen yo.
(No, no one will come.)

(2) 近くにどこかいいファミレスない？
Chikaku ni doko-ka ii famiresu nai?
(Is there any nice family restaurant [diner] nearby?)

(3) いつかアフリカへ行きます。
Itsu-ka Ahurika e ikimasu.
(Someday I will go to Africa.)

(4) きのうはどこへも行かなかった。
Kinoo wa doko e mo ikanakatta.
(Yesterday I didn't go anywhere.)

■ Additional Information

The interrogative pronoun *nan-ka* is used further for two other purposes. First, it appears as a filler in conversation; second, it is used to introduce a topic emphatically. An example below shows an emphatic topic introduction by *nan-ka*, which has a similar function of *such as* in English.

(a) 都会**なんか**危険で、きたなくて、大きらいだ。
*Tokai **nan-ka** kiken de, kitanakute, daikirai da.*
(Places such as large cities are dangerous and filthy, I hate them.)

37. Describing State (3)—*Na*-type Adjectives

■ Target Expression

It's quiet, isn't it?

静かですね。
Shizuka desu ne.

[Adj-*na*]

■ Grammatical Explanation

Using [Adj-*na*] as modifier. We have studied two ways to modify nouns so far. The first by [Adj-*i*] and the second, modifying by the [N + *no*] structure. The third method is to use a group of adjectives called nominal adjectives, or "*na*-type adjectives," [Adj-*na*], that modify nouns that follow (refer to characteristic 7). They are sometimes called nominal adjectives because although they function as adjectives, grammatically they behave similarly to nouns, although not totally. They are called *na*-type adjectives because *na* obligatorily marks this group of phrases when directly modifying nouns. (All nominal adjectives end with *na*, but not all words ending with *na* are nominal adjectives.)

Using [Adj-*na*] as predicate. Unlike [Adj-*i*], [Adj-*na*] cannot be used as they are as predicates. They are followed by either *da* or its formal version, *desu*, when used as predicates. When modifying a noun, the *na*-ending basic form is used, while when used as a predicate, *na* is deleted and *da* co-occurs. The stem of [Adj-*na*] is reached by taking away *na* from thc basic form of the *na*-type adjective. Conjugation of nominal adjectives follows that of the verb *da*, including past tense. (For conjugation of [Adj-*na*], see the list provided in Entry 38.)

Adjectives in casual speech. Adjectives are used as predicate in casual speech in simplified forms. *Ookii* is used instead of *ookii desu*, and *kantan* is used instead of *kantan desu*.

(a) ああ、この問題？ **簡単、簡単**。
*Aa kono mondai? **Kantan, kantan**.*
(Oh, this question? It's easy, really easy.)

List of *Na*-type Adjectives

暖かな	*atatakana*	warm
あわれな	*awarena*	pitiful
偉大な	*idaina*	great
いじわるな	*ijiwaruna*	mean
いやな	*iyana*	distasteful
簡単な	*kantanna*	simple*1
かすかな	*kasukana*	faint
危険な	*kikenna*	dangerous
きらいな	*kiraina*	disliking
きれいな	*kireina*	pretty, clean
高価な	*kookana*	expensive
がんこな	*gankona*	stubborn
静かな	*shizukana*	quiet

好きな	*sukina*	preferred, favorite
ぜいたくな	*zeitakuna*	extravagant
上手な	*joozuna*	skillful
ていねいな	*teineina*	polite
派手な	*hadena*	showy
不便な	*hubenna*	inconvenient
平凡な	*heibonna*	commonplace
便利な	*benrina*	convenient, useful
にぎやかな	*nigiyakana*	bustling
ゆかいな	*yukaina*	pleasant, funny
冷静な	*reiseina*	cool (in disposition)

*1. Simple here means easy to solve, not in the sense of simple life which is translated with another nominal adjective, as *shissona seikatsu*.

■ Examples

(1) **A:** この問題、簡単だね。
Kono mondai, kantan da ne.
(This question is simple, isn't it?)

B: そう？
Soo?
(Is it?)

A: 超簡単な問題。
Choo kantanna mondai.
(It's a very simple question.)

B: そうかなあ。
Soo ka naa.
(Really so?)

(2) 田中さんは会社でいろいろな仕事をする。
Tanaka-san wa kaisha de iroirona shigoto o suru.
(Mr. Tanaka performs various kinds of tasks at his company.)

(3) あの人の人生はあまり平凡ではなかった。
Ano hito no jinsei wa amari heibon dewa-nakatta.
(That person's life was not so ordinary.)

危険なこともたくさんあった。
Kikenna koto mo takusan atta.
([lit., There were many dangerous things.] He faced many dangers.)

(4) **A:** 今日一日中、子供たちは静かでしたよ。
Kyoo ichinichijuu, kodomo-tachi wa shizuka deshita yo.
(The children were quiet all day long today.)

B: そうですか。きのうは静かじゃありませんでしたが……
*Soo desu ka. Kinoo wa shizuka ja-arimasen-deshita ga ...**2
(Really? They weren't quiet yesterday ...)

*2. The conjunction *ga* used at the end of an utterance makes the expression less abrupt, and therefore encourages a softer and more comfortable interaction. See Entry 57 for further explanation.

■ Additional Information

- Some grammarians treat [Adj-*na*] as a nominal or a noun, and it is sometimes called "*na* nominal." Although [Adj-*na*] behaves in part like a nominal, it cannot become the sentential topic, subject, or object by itself. Due to this and other reasons I prefer to categorize it as an adjective. Note, however, that dictionaries normally list [Adj-*na*] without *na*.
- When faced with a phrase, such as *byooki no hito* 'a sick person' and *kenkoona hito* 'a healthy person,' you may wonder how you handle the choice between *no* or *na*. There is no way to predict which one is correct; you must learn case by case as to which is a noun and which is [Adj-*na*].

  In this case *byooki* is a noun and *kenkoo* is a *na*-type adjective, and therefore, when modifying the noun *hito, byooki* requires the linker *no* while *genki* requires the *genkina* form. It might be helpful to know that only *na*-type adjectives can be modified by adverbs; *kenkoona* can be modified to form *motto kenkoona*. (**Motto byooki no* is a wrong structure.) But of course, to use the modifier correctly you must first know whether a phrase is a noun or a *na*-type adjective.

38. Modifying (2)—More about Adjectives

■ Target Expressions

a new house, not-new house

新しい家、新しくない家
atarashii ie, atarashikunai ie

■ Grammatical Explanation

Negative forms of adjectives. Here we summarize the use of the two types of adjectives. As shown below, when immediately preceding nouns, both adjectives take the basic form; the *i*-ending form for the [Adj-*i*] and *na*-ending form for the [Adj-*na*]. Unlike English adjectives, Japanese adjectives themselves can take negative and past tense forms. For example, *wakakatta sensei* '(lit., was-young teacher) the teacher who was young' and *wakakunai hito* '(lit., not-young person) a person who is not young,' and so on.

Adjective Pre-nominal Forms

[Adj-*i*]	[Adj-*na*]
新しい家 *atarashii ie* (new house)	簡単な問題 *kantanna mondai* (simple question)
新しくない家 *atarashikunai ie* (not-new house)	簡単ではない問題 *kantan dewa-nai mondai* (not-simple question)
新しかった家 *atarashikatta ie* (house that was new)	簡単だった問題 *kantan datta mondai* (question that was simple)
新しくなかった家 *atarashikunakatta ie* (house that was not new)	簡単ではなかった問題 *kantan dewa-nakatta mondai* (question that was not simple)

Adjective Forms Used as Predicates

	[Adj-*i*]	[Adj-*na*]
INF	この家は新しい。 *Kono ie wa atarashii.*	この問題は簡単だ。 *Kono mondai wa kantan da.*
FO	この家は新しいです。 *Kono ie wa atarashii-desu.* (This house is new.)	この問題は簡単です。 *Kono mondai wa kantan desu.* (This question is simple.)
INF	この家は新しくない。 *Kono ie wa atarashikunai.*	この問題は簡単ではない。 *Kono mondai wa kantan dewa-nai.* (この問題は簡単じゃない。) *(Kono mondai wa kantan ja-nai.)*

FO	この家は新しくないです。 *Kono ie wa atarashikunai-desu.* この家は新しく(は)ありません。 *Kono ie wa atarashiku(wa-)arimasen.* (This house is not new.)	この問題は簡単ではないです。 *Kono mondai wa kantan dewa-nai-desu.* この問題は簡単ではありません。 *Kono mondai wa kantan dewa-arimasen.* (この問題は簡単じゃありません。) *(Kono mondai wa kantan ja-arimasen.)* (This question is not simple.)
INF	この家は新しかった。 *Kono ie wa atarashikatta.*	この問題は簡単だった。 *Kono mondai wa kantan datta.*
FO	この家は新しかったです。 *Kono ie wa atarashikatta-desu.* (This house was new.)	この問題は簡単でした。 *Kono mondai wa kantan deshita.* (This question was simple.)
INF	この家は新しくなかった。 *Kono ie wa atarashiku-nakatta.*	この問題は簡単ではなかった。 *Kono mondai wa kantan dewa-nakatta.* (この問題は簡単じゃなかった。) *(Kono mondai wa kantan ja-nakatta.)*
FO	この家は新しく(は)なかったです。 *Kono ie wa atarashiku(wa-) nakatta-desu.* この家は新しく(は)ありませんでした。 *Kono ie wa atarashiku(wa-) arimasen-deshita.* (This house was not new.)	この問題は簡単ではなかったです。 *Kono mondai wa kantan dewa-nakatta desu.* この問題は簡単ではありませんでした。 *Kono mondai wa kantan dewa-arimasen-deshita.* (この問題は簡単じゃありませんでした。) *(Kono mondai wa kantan ja-arimasen-deshita.)* (This question was not simple.)

INF = Informal style, FO = Formal style

Using multiple adjectives. When multiple adjectives are used, all but the last one take the gerundive form. The gerundive form of the *i*-type adjective is made by replacing the final *-i* with *-kute*; the gerundive form of the *na*-type adjective is reached by replacing *na* with *de*, which is the gerundive form of *da*.

It is also possible to use multiple negative forms. In such cases, since the negative ending *-nai* is an *i*-type adjective, the gerundive form *-nakute* is used for both *i*-type and nominal adjectives. For example, *benri dewa-nakute, yasukunakute, shizuka dewa-nai apaato* 'not-convenient, not-cheap, not-quiet apartment.'

■ Examples

(1) **A:** 田中さんはどんな人ですか。
Tanaka-san wa donna hito desu ka.
(What [kind of] person is Ms. Tanaka?)

B: 田中さんねえ……そうですねえ……いじわるな人ですね。
Tanaka-san nee ... soo desu nee ... ijiwaruna hito desu ne.
(Ms. Tanaka ... well ... she's a mean person.)

(2) **A:** きのうの試験はどうでしたか。
Kinoo no shiken wa doo deshita ka.
(How was yesterday's exam?)

B: それが……簡単ではない問題がたくさんあってねえ……
Sorega ... kantan dewa-nai mondai ga takusan atte nee ...
(Uhh ... there were many difficult questions ...)

(3) おいしくて安くて新鮮な魚ない?
Oishikute yasukute shinsenna sakana nai?
(Do you have any delicious, inexpensive, and fresh fish?)

(4) 友だちの佐野さんは毎日便利でにぎやかなスーパーで買物をする。
Tomodachi no Sano-san wa mainichi benri de nigiyakana suupaa de kaimono o suru.
(My friend, Ms. Sano, shops every day at a convenient and bustling supermarket.)

■ Additional Information

Using adjectives in different tenses can create a semantic difference worth noting. Examine the pair of sentences below, for example.

(a) 男は**はげしい**雨の中を急いで歩いた。
*Otoko wa **hageshii** ame no naka o isoide aruita.*
(The man hurried through the pouring rain.)

(b) 男は**はげしかった**雨の中を急いで歩いた。
*Otoko wa **hageshikatta** ame no naka o isoide aruita.*
(The man hurried through the rain that came pouring down then.)

Expression (a) implies that it was a pouring rain, and not a quiet, soft rain. Expression (b), however, implies that the rain may have been light at times, but when the man hurried through, the rain came pouring down at that very moment.

39. Speech Style (2)—Masculine and Feminine Speech

■ Target Expressions

I had sushi.

Masculine speech: おれ、すし食った。
Ore, sushi kutta.

Feminine speech: 私、おすし食べた。
Watashi, osushi tabeta.

■ Strategic Explanation

Masculine and feminine speech. Although the differences between masculine and feminine speech style in formal Japanese are few, in casual Japanese, there are a number of differences.

It is best to study with tutors and instructors representing both genders when studying Japanese. When you have access to Japanese drama and documentaries or actual interaction of Japanese male and female speakers, pay attention to the different manner of communication between male and female speakers.

Certain vocabulary items are typically used in masculine speech. For example, *kuu* 'to eat' instead of *taberu, meshi* 'meal' instead of *gohan,* and *umai* 'delicious' instead of *oishii. Umai meshi kuitee naa* 'I want to eat some delicious meal' would be marked as masculine speech, while *oishii gohan tabetai naa* would not.

Pronouns as *ore* and *omae* for 'I' and 'you' are used in masculine speech, while *watashi* and *anata* are preferred in feminine speech.

Blunt versus gentle style. The difference between masculine and feminine speech style under discussion here should be understood in the broader category of more or less blunt versus more or less gentle style. Masculine speech is representatively blunt and feminine speech more gentle in casual conversational interaction. Over all, feminine speech tends to take on more extensive polite expressions in both formal and informal situations. However, female speakers may sometimes choose to use a rather blunt style when the blunt style is effective, and male speakers may choose the gentle style when the gentle quality is favorably evaluated.

Using respectful prefixes. With certain words, the respectful prefixes *o-* and *go-* are more readily used in feminine speech. As a rule, *o-* is added to words which originated in Japan, while *go-* is added to words of Chinese origin. Although the basic function of these respectful prefixes is to show politeness and/or to show respect to the addressee, and therefore may be used by both genders, for some words the prefix *o-* is used predominantly in feminine speech. Since respectful prefixes are attached to nouns associated with one's social superior in formal situations, one must not use them in reference to actions related to oneself or to one's *uchi* members.

Examples of Respectful Prefixes (1)
Used in Masculine and Feminine Speech

ご卒業	***go**sotsugyoo*	graduation
ご結婚	***go**kekkon*	marriage
ご旅行	***go**ryokoo*	travel
お名前	***o**namae*	name
お話	***o**hanashi*	talk

Examples of Respectful Prefixes (2)
Used Predominantly in Feminine Speech

おすし	***o**sushi*	*sushi*
お友だち	***o**tomodachi*	friend
お勉強	***o**benkyoo*	study

It is best for beginners not to overuse respectful prefixes. Not all nouns are readily prefixed with these affixes, so one should exercise restraint and caution when using them.

Exclamatory interjections. Some exclamatory interjections are restricted to feminine speech. These include *ara* and *maa,* both expressing surprise. Among younger female speakers, instead of *ara* and *maa,* other exclamatory interjections such as *ett!* 'what!' and *uso* 'you must be kidding' are used.

Politeness and pitch. There is a noticeable pitch difference between masculine and feminine speech. Listen carefully for features pointed out here when you have an opportunity to encounter both male and female speakers of Japanese.

40. Requesting (2)—Requesting to Do or Not to Do

Target Expressions

Please open the window.

窓を開けてください。
Mado o akete-kudasai.

Don't smoke, please.

タバコをすわないでください。
Tabako o suwanaide-kudasai.

[V*te* + -*kudasai*]

Grammatical Explanation

Requesting (not) to do. Earlier we learned the phrase *kudasai* for requesting the transfer of items. Here we extend that use by replacing the object noun phrases with the gerundive forms of verbs. The gerundive form of the verb takes -*te* (or -*de*) endings, and therefore it is sometimes called the -*te* form, which is transcribed as [V*te*] throughout this book. Deriving -*te* forms is simple. Replace the final -*ta* of the informal past tense of the verb with -*te*, and -*da* with -*de*. (Use the "*Ta*" song [given in Entry 22] if you need to refresh your memory in obtaining [Vinformal past] forms.) For making a negative request, add -*de* to the negative informal non-past form. In informal familiar style, -*kudasai* may be deleted altogether. Some sample gerundive forms are given below.

Verbs		Gerundive *te*-form	Negative	Gerundive negative
行く *iku*	to go	行って *itte*	行かない *ikanai*	行かないで *ikanaide*
泳ぐ *oyogu*	to swim	泳いで *oyoide*	泳がない *oyoganai*	泳がないで *oyoganaide*
食べる *taberu*	to eat	食べて *tabete*	食べない *tabenai*	食べないで *tabenaide*
する *suru*	to do	して *shite*	しない *shinai*	しないで *shinaide*
来る *kuru*	to come	来て *kite*	来ない *konai*	来ないで *konaide*

■ Examples

(1) 電話してください。
Denwa-shite-kudasai.
(Please call.)

(2) 忘れないでください。
Wasurenaide-kudasai.
(Please don't forget.)

(3) 急いで！
Isoide!
(Hurry!)

(4) 教えてね。
Oshiete ne.
(Tell me, will you?)

■ Additional Information

The negative gerundive may also be formed by the negative expression of *nai*, i.e., *nakute*. For example, *iwanakute*, instead of *iwanaide*. There are some restrictions in using these forms. See Entry 76 for differences between *-naide* and *-nakute*. The [V*te* + *-kudasai*] structure requires *-naide* endings.

■ Warning

One important point to be noted is that the [V*te* + *-kudasai*] structure is not normally used toward one's social superiors. Since this form clearly spells out the request without much consideration given to the person requested, even when it is delivered politely, it conveys the feeling of a mild command. The [V*te* + *-kudasai*] expresses a request or command made politely or casually toward social equals or subordinates. In fact, some notices and announcements which prohibit smoking are expressed in a formal style as in: *(o)tabako wa goenryo kudasai* 'please refrain from smoking.' If one wants to request something from one's social superior, interrogative sentences with respectful forms, that is, [V*te* + *-itadakemasu ka*], [V*te* + *-itadake-masu-deshoo ka*], and [V*te* + *-itadakemasen-deshoo ka*] are preferred. (This will be discussed later again.)

Part III:
CORE

Oklahoma's Road to Nowhere

41. Appealing to the Listener (2)—Tagged Auxiliary Verbs

■ Target Expression

You saw Kazuko today, didn't you?

今日、和子さんに会ったでしょう？
Kyoo, Kazuko-san ni atta-deshoo?

■ Grammatical Explanation

Using *daro(o)* and *desho(o)*. Auxiliary verb forms, *-daro(o)* and *-desho(o)*, when pronounced with rising intonation, may be added immediately following verbs and adjectives to appeal to the listener. When *-daro(o)*/*-desho(o)* are tagged, similarly to the interactional particle *ne*, a meaning of 'isn't it right?' or 'don't you agree?' is added. It is a question requesting confirmation and/or agreement.

Pre-Aux forms. The form immediately preceding *-daro(o)* is what I call "pre-auxiliary form." There are several cases where [pre-Aux] forms precede items including [AuxV] and auxiliary adjective [AuxAdj] forms, and therefore it is useful to learn this set of forms.

Pre-Aux Forms

Verbs:			
non-past:	affirmative	泳ぐ	*oyogu*
	negative	泳がない	*oyoganai*
past:	affirmative	泳いだ	*oyoida*
	negative	泳がなかった	*oyoganakatta*
Existential verbs:			
non-past:	affirmative	ある、いる	*aru, iru*
	negative	ない、いない	*nai, inai*
past:	affirmative	あった、いた	*atta, ita*
	negative	なかった、いなかった	*nakatta, inakatta*
Be-verb:			
non-past:	affirmative	(deleted totally)	
	negative	ではない、じゃない	*dewa-nai, ja-nai*
past:	affirmative	だった	*datta*
	negative	ではなかった、 じゃなかった	*dewa-nakatta,* *ja-nakatta*

[*Adj-i*]:			
non-past:	affirmative	赤い	*akai*
	negative	赤くない	*akakunai*
past:	affirmative	赤かった	*akakatta*
	negative	赤くなかった	*akakunakatta*
[*Adj-na*]:			
non-past:	affirmative	簡単	*kantan*
	negative	簡単ではない、 簡単じゃない	*kantandewa-nai,* *kantanja-nai*
past:	affirmative	簡単だった	*kantandatta*
	negative	簡単ではなかった、 簡単じゃなかった	*kantandewa-nakatta,* *kantanja-nakatta*

Daro?, desho?,* and *jan? Although *-daroo* and *-deshoo* were introduced earlier as expressions of uncertainty, they are introduced here again since they function differently when used as tagged [AuxV]. Note that *-daro(o)/desho(o)* discussed here are always pronounced with rising intonation. *-Deshoo* is normally used as formal expression, and *-daroo* in blunt masculine style; these are used primarily in spoken discourse.

The shorter versions *-desho* and *-daro* are used among *uchi* members in casual situations only. These expressions encourage friendliness and closeness among speakers and listeners. In extremely colloquial situations *-jan* is used for the same purpose. Since *-deshoo*, *-daroo*, and *-jan* request confirmation or agreement, the listener normally sends feedback responses such as *un* or *aa*.

■ Examples

(1) **A:** ほら、今日、田中さんに会ったでしょ？
Hora, kyoo, Tanaka-san ni atta-desho?
(See, I saw Ms. Tanaka today, right?)

B: うん。
Un.
(Uh huh.)

A: あの時ね、もう九時半だったでしょ？
Ano toki ne, moo ku-ji han datta-desho?
(At that time, it was already 9:30, wasn't it?)

B: うん。
Un.
(Yeah.)

(2) もうたくさん食べただろ？ [masculine speech]
Moo takusan tabeta-daro?
(You already ate enough, didn't you?)

(3) あのそばに美術館あるじゃん？
Ano soba ni bijutsukan aru-jan?
(The art museum is near there, right?)

■ Additional Information

- In casual conversation, especially among familiar members, instead of *-desho*, *-ssho* is added to [V/Adj pre-Aux] form. Instead of *wakaru-desho*, *wakaru-ssho* is used, for example.

(a) 田中さんに会った**っしょ**。
*Tanaka-san ni atta**-ssho**.*
(So you saw Tanaka, right?)

(b) その気持ちわかる**っしょ**。
*Sono kimochi wakaru**-ssho**.*
(You understand that feeling, right?)

- *-Jan* may be used in very casual utterances that do not necessarily ask for the listener's response. This *-jan* is used without a rising intonation.

(c) **A:** あいつ、アメリカ行くよ。
Aitsu, Amerika iku yo.
(He is going to Amerika.)

B: スゲー**じゃん**。 [blunt style]
*Sugee**-jan**.*
(Really amazing.)

(d) そう言ってる**じゃん**。
*Soo itte-ru**-jan.***
(Don't you see, I'm telling you so.)

■ Warning

The use of *-daroo* and *-deshoo* (and *-jan*) should be avoided when speaking to one's social superior. This is because these phrases ask for confirmation of something that your superior is assumed to already know. Using these phrases gives the impression that you are challenging the depth and the extent of your superior's knowledge; it carries a condescending tone.

42. Inquiring (2)—Negative Questions

■ Target Expression

Didn't Mr. Yamada come to the company yesterday?

山田さんはきのう会社に来ませんでしたか。

Yamada-san wa kinoo kaisha ni kimasen-deshita ka.

■ Grammatical Explanation

Negative questions with *ka.* Placing the question marker *ka* immediately after a negative verb-ending creates a negative question. Negative questions are also produced by slightly raising the last syllable of formal or informal negative statements; *ikimasen-deshita?* and *ikanakatta?*, for example.

Negative questions with *-desho(o)/-daro(o)* and *ne.* In addition to this type of negative question, there are two other possibilities for expressing questions which strongly assume negation. One is the utterance with the tagged [AuxV] form *-desho(o)/-daro(o)* added after the negative verb-ending. For example, 'you didn't go to a concert yesterday, did you?' can be expressed in Japanese *kinoo ongakukai ni ikanakatta-desho?* The other is adding *ne* for confirmation; *ikimasen-deshita ne* 'you didn't go, did you?'

Negative question as invitation. One point of interest regarding the negative question is that present tense negative questions addressed directly to the listener may be used when inviting someone or making a request.

(a) **A:** 夕食いっしょにしませんか。
Yuushoku isshoni shimasen ka.
(Won't you have dinner with me?)

B: いいですねえ。
Ii-desu nee.
(That will be nice.)

(b) **A:** ランチ行かない？
Ranchi ikanai?
(Want to go out for lunch?)

B: うん、行く。
Un, iku.
(Yes, I'll go.)

■ Examples

(1) ユキ、私のコーヒーカップ使わなかった？
Yuki, watashi no koohii kappu tsukawanakatta?
(Yuki, didn't you use my coffee cup?)

(2) 山田さん来なかったでしょ？
Yamada-san konakatta-desho?
(Mr. Yamada didn't come, did he?)

(3) **A:** みんな会議に出席しましたか。
Minna kaigi ni shusseki-shimashita ka.[*1]
(Did everyone attend the meeting?)

B: いいえ。
Iie.
(No.)

A: 誰がいませんでしたか。
Dare ga imasen-deshita ka.
(Who wasn't there?)

B: 小山さんが出席しませんでしたが……
Koyama-san ga shusseki-shimasen-deshita ga . . .
(Ms. Koyama didn't attend.)

*1. The verb *shusseki-suru* 'to attend' takes *ni* as a direct object marker.

■ Additional Information

Negative expressions *nai* and *nakunai* are used in questions that appeal indirectly to the partner. For example, *omoshirokunai?* 'isn't it interesting?' may be changed to *omoshirokunakunai?* 'isn't it not interesting?' Both utterances are based on the premise that the speaker basically thinks it is interesting. *Nakunai* is considered more indirect and effectively softens the utterance.

(a) ちょっと高くない？
Chotto takakunai?
(Isn't this a bit expensive?)

(b) **A:** これ、ちょっとおもしろくなくない？
Kore, chotto omoshirokunakunai?
(Isn't this sort of interesting?)

B: うん、そうだね。
Un, sooda ne.
(Yeah, it is.)

43. Responding to Questions (2)—Answering Negative Questions

■ Target Expressions

Didn't Mr. Yamada come to the company yesterday?

山田さんはきのう会社に来ませんでしたか。
Yamada-san wa kinoo kaisha ni kimasen-deshita ka.

No, he didn't.

ええ、来ませんでしたが……
Ee, kimasen-deshita ga ...

■ Strategic Explanation

Responding to negative questions. When answering a negative question, what is assumed by the questioner plays a major role. If the assumption is negative, answering yes or no depends on whether that negative assumption is agreeable (yes) or not (no). Thus in the target expression, unlike English, the listener responds that the questioner's assumption is correct by *ee* 'yes,' although the content of the answer itself is negative as shown above in *kimasen-deshita ga ....*

Negative questions may also be used for politeness and indirectness. For example, *jikan arimasen ka* instead of *jikan arimasu ka* is a politer way of asking for the same information (i.e., if the partner has time to spare). In this case even though the construction is negative, the speaker's assumption is not. The answer takes *ee, arimasu* or *iie, arimasen.*

Responding to invitation and request. When negative questions are used for offering invitations and making requests, the assumption is positive. As a result, the use of *ee/iie* is similar to the use for affirmative questions; that is, *ee* (*hai* or *un*) indicates agreement to the positiveness, whereas *iie* is used for a negative answer.

Avoiding *ee* and *iie*. If you get confused about the usage of *ee* (*hai* or *un*) and *iie* when answering (negative) questions, one way to avoid any misunderstandings is to avoid saying *ee* or *iie* altogether. Simply answer with a verb, either in the affirmative or negative form. For example, when asked *ikimasen-deshita ka?*, by answering with *ikimashita yo* or *ikimasen-deshita yo*, you will communicate clearly.

■ Examples

(1) **A:** 妹に会わなかったでしょ？
Imooto ni awanakatta-desho?
(You didn't see my younger sister, did you?)

B: うん、会わなかったよ。
Un, awanakatta yo.
(No, I didn't see [her].)

(2) A: きのう酒井さんといっしょに新宿へ行きませんでしたね。
Kinoo Sakai-san to isshoni Shinjuku e ikimasen-deshita ne.
(You didn't go to Shinjuku yesterday with Mr. Sakai, right?)

B: ええ、行きませんでした。
Ee, ikimasen-deshita.
(No, I didn't go.)

(3) A: マンガの本はありませんか。
Manga no hon wa arimasen ka.
(Are there comic books?)

B: はい、ありますよ。
Hai, arimasu yo.
(Sure, there are.)

(4) A: あとでショッピングに行かない？
Atode shoppingu ni ikanai?
(Won't you go shopping later?)

B: 今日はちょっと…… *1
Kyoo wa chotto . . .
(Not, today . . .)

(5) A: そろそろ帰りませんか。
Sorosoro kaerimasen ka.
(Shall we go home now?)

B: はい。
Hai.
(Yes.)

*1. When responding to an invitation, if the answer is negative, an expression such as *kyoo wa chotto* '(lit., today a bit . . .) perhaps not today . . .' is useful. There is no need to elaborate why you cannot accept the invitation. Just let your speech trail off after saying *chotto* . . . .

44. Inviting and Suggesting (2) —Inviting and Suggesting to Do Something Together

■ Target Expressions

Shall we eat?

食べましょうか。
Tabemashoo ka.

Let's eat.

食べましょう。
Tabemashoo.

[Vstem + *-mashoo (ka)*]
[V + *(y)oo (ka)*]

■ Strategic Explanation

Using volitional forms. When inviting and suggesting to do something, use non-past negative verb forms; for example, *tabemasen (ka)?* 'shall we eat?' There is an additional form, the "volitional" form, used for invitation and suggestion. Volitional forms are available for verbs that describe humanly controllable action only. Invitation expressed by volitional forms is direct, and should not be used toward social superiors. For the purpose of inviting social superiors, *ikaga deshoo ka* and other respectful strategies are required. In order to reach volitional forms, the following operation is necessary.

Volitional Forms

Formal:	All verbs	change *-masu* of formal non-past form to *-mashoo* (i.e., [Vstem + *-mashoo*])
Informal:	*U*-verbs	change the last vowel *-u* to *-oo*
	RU-verbs	change the final *-ru* to *-yoo*
	Irregular verbs	*suru* takes *shiyoo*
		kuru takes *koyoo*

For existential verbs, only *iru,* meaning 'to stay,' takes the form *iyoo* and *imashoo.* Inviting and suggesting by using volitional forms is similar to the English expression of *let's* ... or *let's not* ... Volitional forms may also be used with the interrogative particle *ka.*

Negative invitation and suggestion. Use *naide-iyoo, naide-imashoo, naide-okoo* and *naide-okimashoo* for the negative invitation and suggestion; for example, *ikanaide-imashoo* 'let's not go,' *tabenaide-iyoo* 'let's not eat,' *kakanaide-okoo* 'let's not write it (and leave it as is)' and *tabenaide-okimashoo* 'let's not eat it (and leave it as is).'

■ Examples

(1) **A:** どうですか、コーヒーでも飲みましょうか。
Doo desu ka, koohii demo nomimashoo ka.
(How about . . . shall we have coffee or something?)

B: ええ、デパートのカフェへ行きましょう。
Ee, depaato no kafe e ikimashoo.
(Yes, let's go to a coffee shop in the department store.)

(2) さあ、行きましょう。
Saa, ikimashoo.
(OK, let's go.)

(3) **A:** じゃあ、入ろうか。
Jaa, hairoo ka.
(Well, shall we enter?)

B: うん、そうしよう。
Un, soo shiyoo.
(Yes, let's do that.)

(4) 早く行こうよ。
Hayaku ikoo yo.
(Let's go now.)

(5) **A:** 手伝いましょうか。
Tetsudaimashoo ka.
(Shall I assist you?)

B: ええ、お願いします。
Ee, onegai-shimasu.
(Yes, please.)

(6) **A:** 今日は寒いですねえ。行かないでうちにいましょう。
Kyoo wa samui-desu nee. Ikanaide uchi ni imashoo.
(It's cold today, isn't it? Let's not go and stay home.)

B: ええ、そうしましょう。
Ee, soo shimashoo.
(Yes, let's do so.)

(7) **A:** 私が行きましょう。
Watashi ga ikimashoo.
(I will go.)

B: そうですか。お願いします。
Soo desu ka. Onegai-shimasu.
(All right. Please take care of it.)

■ Additional Information

- When the subject of the volitional forms is the first-person singular, it expresses the will and intention of the speaker. This expression normally appears in the form *-(y)oo to omotte-iru* (lit., thinking to do), for example, *ikoo to omotte-imasu* 'I think I will go.'
- Depending on the context, the first-person *ikoo* and *ikimashoo* may also function as a formal expression of the speaker's will, meaning 'I will go.'
- When volitional forms are used for interrogative purposes with the first person subject, they function as "consultative." For example, *ikoo ka?* or *ikimashoo ka?* 'shall I go?'

45. Responding to Invitations and Suggestions

■ Target Expression

Yes, let's do that.

ええ、そうしましょう。
Ee, soo shimashoo.

■ Strategic Explanation

When suggestions and invitations are offered, there are formulaic responses that will prove quite useful. When invited, for example, by the expression *ikimashoo* 'let's go,' the following responses are available.

1. *Positive response*:

(1a) ええ、いいですねえ。
Ee, ii-desu nee.
(Yes, that will be nice.)

(1b) ええ、そうしましょうか。
Ee, soo shimashoo ka.
(Yes, shall we do that then?)

(1c) はい、じゃあ、そうしましょう。
Hai, jaa, soo shimashoo.
(Yes, let's do so then.)

(1d) うん、そうしよう。
Un, soo shiyoo.
(Yes, let's do so.)

(1e) ええ、よろこんで。
Ee, yorokonde.
(Yes, with pleasure.)

(1f) ええ、ぜひ。
Ee, zehi.
(Yes, by all means.)

2. *Negative response*:

(2a) そうですねえ。ちょっと……
Soo desu nee. Chotto ...
(Let me see. Uhh ...)

(2b) 今夜はちょっと……
Kon'ya wa chotto . . .
(Tonight isn't the best time . . .)

3. *Undecided situation*:

(3a) そうですねえ……
Soo desu nee ...
(Well ...)

(3b) そうだなあ……
Soo da naa ...
(Well ...)

■ Examples

(1) **A:** 住所を書きましょうか。
Juusho o kakimashoo ka.
(Shall I write the address?)

B: ええ、お願いします。
Ee, onegai-shimasu.
(Yes, please.)

(2) **A:** お昼でもいっしょにどうですか。
Ohiru demo isshoni doo desu ka.
(How about having lunch together?)

B: ええ、よろこんで。
Ee, yorokonde.
(Yes, I'll be glad to.)

C: 私はちょっと……
Watashi wa chotto ...
(I'm tied up with something ...)

46. Verbal Predicate (5)—Transitive and Intransitive Verbs

■ Target Expressions

Please open the door.

ドアを開けてください。
Doa o akete-kudasai.

The library opens at eight.

図書館は八時に開きます。
Toshokan wa hachi-ji ni akimasu.

[Vt] [Vint]

■ Grammatical Explanation

Transitive and intransitive verbs. There are two basic ways an event may be described in language. The first is the type, "agent-operates-on-another-entity." For example, in the sentence *John eats an apple*, the agent (John) operates (eats) on another entity (an apple). The second is the type "agent-conducts-itself." For example, in the sentence *John sleeps*, the agent (John) conducts itself (sleeps). The verbs that prototypically co-occur with the first and the second type are transitive and intransitive, respectively.

Orientation toward intransitive description. Having said this, a more important point must be raised. In Japanese, there is a strong tendency to view and describe an event as something happening by itself—often beyond the control of an agent. In short, the language is skewed to favor intransitive description. The transitive/intransitive distinction in English, therefore, is not reflected fully in Japanese. For Japanese, to view the world as "agent-operates-on-another-entity" is not a required axis as observed in English.

Recall that Japanese is not under strict grammatical constraint as in English to create a sentence to fit this mold. The structure of the Japanese sentence is fluid and remains sensitive to the context in which it is used. This does not mean that Japanese do not describe events in the first type; in fact, transitive verbs, or the use of verbs as transitive verbs, occur substantially. Nonetheless, orientation toward intransitiveness is a strong general undercurrent in Japanese.

Four types of verb forms. In Japanese there are four types of transitive/intransitive verb forms as described below.

1. *Absolute intransitive verbs*:
   (Used solely as intransitive verbs)

死ぬ	*shinu*	to die
泣く	*naku*	to cry
歩く	*aruku*	to walk

2. *Transitive/intransitive pairs*:
   There are a number of transitive/intransitive verb pairs with similar roots, including those listed below.

3. *Absolute transitive verbs*:
   (Used solely as transitive verbs)

殺す	*korosu*	to kill
食べる	*taberu*	to eat
切る	*kiru*	to cut

4. *Verbs with both transitive and intransitive use*:
   (An identical verb, used either as transitive or intransitive)

開く	*hiraku*	to open, to be opened
閉じる	*tojiru*	to close, to be closed

List of Transitive/Intransitive Pairs

	[Vt]	[Vint]
-u/-aru	ふさ**ぐ** (to clog up) *husa**gu***	ふさ**がる** (to be clogged up) *husa**garu***
-eru/-aru	見つ**ける** (to find) *mitsu**keru***	見つ**かる** (to be found) *mitsu**karu***
-eru/-u	開**ける** (to open) *a**keru***	開**く** (to be opened) *a**ku***
-su/-ru	直**す** (to correct) *nao**su***	直**る** (to be corrected) *nao**ru***
-osu/-iru	起**こす** (to wake) *o**kosu***	起**きる** (to get up) *o**kiru***
-asu/-eru	さ**ます** (to cool) *sa**masu***	さ**める** (to become cool) *sa**meru***
-asu/-iru	閉**ざす** (to shut) *to**zasu***	閉**じる** (to be shut) *to**jiru***
-asu/-u	かわ**かす** (to dry) *kawa**kasu***	かわ**く** (to be dried up) *kawa**ku***
-esu/-ieru	消(け)**す** (to extinguish) *ke**su***	消(き)**える** (to be extinguished) *ki**eru***

Note that these changes occur only among transitive/intransitive paired verbs. The changes described are not applicable to non-paired verbs.

Choosing transitive versus intransitive verbs. In order to understand the difference between transitive and intransitive verbs, let us imagine a situation where an agent (Ms. Kanai) opened the door. This incident can be viewed in at least two ways.

(a) 金井さんがドアを開けました。
Kanai-san ga doa o akemashita.
(Ms. Kanai opened the door.)

The observer notices that someone (Ms. Kanai) acts toward another entity. The primary information derived from this view is that the agent performs an act on something or someone that experiences that act. The action is interpreted as dynamic, in that by performing an act, something (or someone) else becomes directly involved. In this view, Kanai's action makes a physical impact on an object, door, which changes the general state of the event.

(b) ドアが開きました。
Doa ga akimashita.
(The door opened.)

The observer describes the event focusing upon the door and what happened to the door. The observer may not have access to information as to who or what opened the door. Or, it could be that he or she simply wishes to concentrate on the door, although he or she knows who or what (in this case Ms. Kanai) opened the door. Imagine, for example, a situation where Ms. Kanai had several keys, and she is uncertain as to which one fits the door. After trying several, she finally succeeds. An observer may utter, *aa, doa ga aita!* defocusing on who or which key opened the door.

"Reactive" descriptions and transitive/intransitive verbs. An important issue closely related to transitive and intransitive verbs must be raised here. The predisposition not to mention the agent in Japanese is closely related to the way some Japanese sentence patterns follow. Earlier we defined subject in a broad sense—as an element of primary predicate focus. The person who directly experiences a phenomenon and who immediately reports this phenomenon is the experiencer and can be, but not necessarily, expressed with the [N + *ga*] structure.

It is important to identify the sentences which contain the source for the experiencer's reaction (sentences of "reactive" description) in light of transitive and intransitive verbs. Here are other verbal and adjectival predicates which are used for "reactive" description (see Appendix 5 for the full list of these predicates). Further explanation will be given in separate entries as indicated.

Remembering these types of sentences is important. This is because the *ga*-marked subjects in these structures do not correspond to the grammatical subjects in English, and therefore they sometimes cause confusion. The easiest way to master these special sentence structures is to memorize some representative sentences, and use them for future reference points.

1. *Natural phenomena*:

(1a) 雨が降っている。
Ame ga hutte-iru.
(It is raining.)

2. *Sense and perception*:

(2a) いいにおいがする。 (See Entry 128.)
Ii nioi ga suru.
(It smells good.)

3. *Emotional response*:

(3a) あの人が好きだ。 (See Entry 68.)
Ano hito ga suki da.
(I like him.)

(3b) 子供の頃がなつかしい。

Kodomo	*no*	*koro*	*ga*	*natsukashii.*
child	L	time	S	nostalgic

(I feel nostalgic about my childhood.)

4. *Spontaneous occurrence*:

(4a) 山が見える。 (See Entry 67.)
Yama ga mieru.
(The mountain is seen.)

5. *Physical condition*:

(5a) せきが出る。 (See Entry 66.)
Seki ga deru.
([lit., Coughs appear.] I cough.)

6. *Others*:

(6a) 日本語がわかります。 (See Entry 53.)
Nihongo ga wakarimasu.
([lit., Japanese is understood.] I understand Japanese.)

(6b) 海外旅行のためのお金がいります。
Kaigairyokoo no tame no okane ga irimasu.
([lit., Money for overseas travel is needed.] I need money for overseas travel.)

Note that some grammarians treat sentences such as *ano hito ga suki da* 'I like that person' in a different way from the way it is explained here. They view that *ano hito* is an object of the adjectival predicate *suki da*, although it is marked by *ga*. According to this view, *ga* is explained as marking subjects as well as objects in some special cases (as this one).

■ Examples

(1) 今朝、七時に起きました。
Kesa, shichi-ji ni okimashita.
(This morning, I got up at seven.)

あしたの朝は六時に起こしてください。
Ashita no asa wa roku-ji ni okoshite kudasai.
(Please wake me up at six tomorrow morning.)

(2) **A:** 間違いを直しましょうか。
Machigai o naoshimashoo ka.
(Shall I correct the mistake?)

B: 間違いはもう直りましたよ。
Machigai wa moo naorimashita yo.
(The mistake is already corrected.)

■ Additional Information

- Other ways to describe a door being opened include: (1) *Doa ga akerareta.* 'The door was opened.'; (2) *Doa ga aite-iru.* 'The door is open.'; and (3) *Doa ga akete-aru.* '(Someone opened the door, and as a result) the door is open.' These expressions will be discussed later under separate entries.
- Although in English an instrument can become the subject of the verb *open*, as in *this key opened the door*, in Japanese an inanimate object normally cannot perform dynamic action. *Kono kagi de doa o akemashita* 'with this key, (I) opened the door' must be used.
- The morphological changes listed above between transitive and its intransitive counterpart show an interesting feature; transitive verbs tend to have *-su* (as in *-asu, -osu, -su*) while intransitive verbs have *-aru, -eru, -iru,* and *-ru* endings. This is associated with the fact that in Japanese the causative takes the *-(s)aseru* ending, and the passive takes the *-(r)areru* ending, as we will learn later.

47. Common Apologies

■ Target Expression

I'm sorry.

すみません。
Sumimasen.

■ Strategic Explanation

Frequent apologies. Typically Japanese apologize far more frequently than Americans. Apologies convey that a person recognizes one's own responsibility and the failure to meet the expectations of others. This in turn relieves the blame on others, and therefore shows thoughtfulness and kindness toward others. Apology is considered a virtue in Japan. When one apologizes and shows regret, Japanese are often emotionally moved and are more willing to forgive.

While Japanese are ready to apologize frequently, Americans seem reluctant to admit their own failures, much less to apologize. Apologizing, since theoretically it admits one's failure, may not be the best route to take if the problem is to be resolved in a court of law. Admitting guilt is interpreted as a confession of wrongdoing.

For Japanese, apologizing, sometimes profusely, is a sign of humility and admittance of one's own weakness which deserves understanding and sympathy. This contrast in apology phenomena is clearly observable in service encounters. Japanese merchants and service providers are ready to apologize for the slightest inconveniences their customers may encounter.

Formulaic Phrases for Apology

すみません。	*Sumimasen.*	I'm sorry.
申しわけありません。	*Mooshiwake arimasen.*	I'm sorry. [polite]
ごめんなさい。	*Gomennasai.*	I'm sorry, please forgive me.
ごめん。	*Gomen.*	Sorry, excuse me. [casual style]
失礼。	*Shitsurei.*	Sorry, excuse me. [frequently used in masculine speech]

***Sumimasen* for gratitude.** We should be warned that *sumimasen* and *mooshiwake arimasen* are used for the purpose of expressing gratitude as well, which will be discussed later. Depending on circumstances, it is important to interpret some of these as expressions of gratitude, and not as apologies.

Non-verbal signs for apology. When apologizing, it is important that you give non-verbal signals along with your words. The more deeply felt your apology, the more slowly and deeply you bow. During the apology, one is normally expected to cast one's eyes downward, and to assume an apologetic and humble stance.

Taking the blame. There is a widely told episode (or different versions of a similar episode) involving the apologetic attitude of Japanese, which a foreigner in Japan failed to understand. A foreign worker said to his/her Japanese employer, *koppu ga kowaremashita* 'the glass broke.' This expression does not imply that the worker broke the glass. The expression *koppu o kowashimashita* 'I broke the glass,' however, implies that the blame is his or hers, since the transitive verb *kowasu* is used instead of the intransitive *kowareru*. The glass might have been old, and possibly it had a crack in it anyway. So, even though the worker may not have broken it, Japanese prefer to hear *koppu o kowashite-shimaimashita,* an expression that willingly takes the blame. This expression, normally coupled with an apology, something like *sumimasen, koppu o kowashite-shimaimashita,* is a formulaic strategy for apology. The use of transitive and intransitive verbs can convey different social meanings, indeed.

Expressing apology across societies. I should remind you that what deserves an apology differs from society to society. For example, during Tokyo's morning rush hour, it is practically impossible to apologize to everyone you bump into or whom you inadvertently touch. There are some occasions where allegedly polite Japanese do not apologize for what you think deserves an apology, and vice versa. Learning intricacies of these social rules is a part of the education we continue to receive by living in any society, whether you are a native or a non-native speaker.

As a student of Japanese, you may not feel comfortable to readily apologize for the smallest things for which theoretically you may not even be responsible for. There is no need to imitate Japanese behavior to the extent that you feel uncomfortable. It is useful, however, to know the different social meanings attached to the behavior of apology in Japan in contrast with your native country.

48. Adverbs (1)—Common Adverbs

■ Target Expression

Please get up early tomorrow.

あした早く起きてください。
Ashita hayaku okite-kudasai.

■ Grammatical Explanation

Forming adverbs. Just as adverbs may be formed by adding a suffix *-ly* to some adjectives in English (*happy–happily*), Japanese is equipped with two such processes. One is to generate adverbs from [Adj-*i*] by changing the final *-i* to *-ku*, that is, *oishii* (adjective) and *oishiku* (adverb). The other method is to form adverbs from [Adj-*na*] by changing the final *-na* to *-ni*, that is, *kireina* (adjective) and *kireini* (adverb).

Adjective–adverb Pairs

[Adj-*i*]				[Adv]	
新し**い**	*atarashi**i***	new	→	新し**く**	*atarashi**ku***
暖か**い**	*atataka**i***	warm	→	暖か**く**	*atataka**ku***
暑**い**	*atsu**i***	hot	→	暑**く**	*atsu**ku***
寒**い**	*samu**i***	cold	→	寒**く**	*samu**ku***
[Adj-*na*]				[Adv]	
簡単**な**	*kantan**na***	simple	→	簡単**に**	*kantan**ni***
便利**な**	*benri**na***	useful	→	便利**に**	*benri**ni***

Location of adverbs. Adverbs are placed according to the word-order preference studied earlier (Entry 18). Among adverbs, temporal and locative adverbs precede other adverbs.

Other Commonly Used Adverbs (Including adverbial quantifiers we learned earlier)

すぐ	*sugu*	right away, soon
もう	*moo*	already, more (when used with degree words as in *moo sukoshi* 'a little more')
あとで	*ato de*	later
いったい	*ittai*	in the world (emphatic as in *what in the world*)
いつも	*itsumo*	always
偶然	*guuzen*	unexpectedly, coincidentally
結構	*kekkoo*	more or less, to an expected degree
今度	*kondo*	this time, next time
さっき	*sakki*	a while ago
ついに	*tsuini*	finally, at last
ときどき	*tokidoki*	sometimes
たまに	*tamani*	occasionally
なかなか	*nakanaka*	with difficulty
ひんぱんに	*hinpanni*	frequently
間もなく	*mamonaku*	soon, in no time

もっと	*motto*	more (*motto muzukashii* 'more difficult')
最も	*mottomo*	most (*mottomo muzukashii* 'most difficult')
ゆっくり	*yukkuri*	slowly, leisurely
よく	*yoku*	frequently, well
ようやく	*yooyaku*	with toil

Adverbs with *to*. Some adverbs expressing manners of action optionally take *to*, as in *hakkiri/hakkiri to* 'clearly,' *yukkuri/yukkuri to* 'slowly,' and so forth.

■ Examples

(1) よく勉強しましたね。
Yoku benkyoo-shimashita ne.
(You studied well.)

(2) **A:** 電車はいつ来ますか。
Densha wa itsu kimasu ka.
(When will the train arrive?)

B: すぐ来ますよ。
Sugu kimasu yo.
(It should be here any moment.)

(3) **A:** この部分は新しく作りました。
Kono bubun wa atarashiku tsukurimashita.
(I newly made this section.)

B: ここは？
Koko wa?
(How about here?)

A: ああ、そこはあとでします。
Aa, soko wa atode shimasu.
(Oh, I'll do that later.)

■ Additional Information

- Some adverbs are used almost like nouns. For example, the adverb *itsumo* 'always' may be used like a noun as shown below:

(a) **いつも**の食べ物を注文しました。
***Itsumo** no tabemono o chuumon-shimashita.*
(I ordered the usual [food].)

(b) **A:** 父は毎朝六時頃散歩します。
Chichi wa maiasa roku-ji goro sanpo-shimasu.
(My father always takes a walk about six every morning.)

B: **いつも**ですか。
Itsumo *desu ka.*
(Always?)

A: ええ、**いつも**。
Ee, ***itsumo****.*
(Yes, always.)

- Among adverbs, perhaps *kekkoo* deserves our special attention. In conversation, *kekkoo* is not only used to mean 'more or less' but also is used to refuse an offer. For example, when your friend asks if you would like more tea, you may decline by saying *iie, kekkoo desu* 'no, thank you.' *Kekkoo* retains the meaning of 'to an expected degree' when a speaker uses it to convey acceptance, as in B's utterance in (c). In (d), however, *kekkoo* means more than expected. In casual conversation, *kekkoo* is often used as a conversation filler as well.

(c) A: お茶を入れましょうか。
Ocha o iremashoo ka.
(Should I make some tea for you?)

B: いいえ、水で**結構**です。
Iie, mizu de ***kekkoo*** *desu.*
(No, just water is fine.)

(d) このケーキ、**結構**おいしい。
Kono keeki, ***kekkoo*** *oishii.*
(This cake is delicious, more delicious than expected.)

- Some manner adverbs are combined with the verb *suru* to form verbs. For example, *yukkuri-suru* means 'to take it easy, to spend time leisurely.'

49. Offering and Accepting Assistance

■ Target Expressions

Shall I help you?

手伝いましょうか。
Tetsudaimashoo ka.

Yes, thanks.

すみません、お願いします。
Sumimasen, onegai-shimasu.

■ Strategic Explanation

Offering assistance. Earlier we have studied the consultative use of the volitional forms *-(y)oo (ka)* and the [Vstem + *mashoo (ka)*] construction. These expressions function to offer activity favorable or beneficial to the addressee. *Tetsudaimashoo ka* 'shall I help you?' for example, is used to offer assistance.

Enryo **and accepting assistance.** How should one accept assistance offered from others? The concept of *enryo*, a refusal of receiving another's favor for fear of the inconvenience it may cause, plays a major part in the process of accepting a favor or assistance. Naturally, if one does not wish to accept assistance for one reason or another, *iie, kekkoo desu* 'no, thank you,' said in a definite tone of voice will suffice. A less defiant refusal is to add expressions such as *iie daijoobu desu kara* 'I'll be fine, so . . .' Informal refusal *uun, ii yo*, or *iie, ii-desu* 'no that's OK' are also useful. Even when one does wish to accept assistance, Japanese tend to refuse it at first. Study the following interaction.

A: (お)荷物持ちましょうか。
(O)nimotsu mochimashoo ka.
(The luggage, shall I carry [it for you]?)

B: いいえ、大丈夫ですから……
Iie, daijoobu desu kara . . .
(No, thank you, I'll be fine . . .)

A: でも重いでしょう。
Demo omoi-deshoo.
(But it must be heavy.)

B: そうですか。どうもすみません。
Soo desu ka. Doomo sumimasen.
(Well. . . . Thanks.)

In this interaction speaker B first refuses assistance. Speaker A continues to show sympathy and B finally accepts it. For a Japanese, to accept assistance right away is felt to be a bit too imposing. After all, the other person is offering to go to some trouble, so one feels somewhat guilty for accepting the kindness right away; a too quick and ready acceptance would suggest that one has expected assistance as a natural consequence. It is almost like taking advantage of someone's goodwill without consideration for him or her. Sensing that assistance is indeed needed, however, speaker A insists on offering assistance, which is accepted in the second round.

Accepting assistance. When accepting an offer, *ee, onegai-shimasu* is used in formal situations and/or toward your social superior. The informal counterpart toward social equals or subordinates is *un, tanomu yo* (normally used in masculine speech), or *ee, jaa tanomu ne*.

By-passing *enryo*. Of course, depending on the situation as well as the interpersonal relationship between the participants, Japanese may accept the offer without expressing *enryo*, and without first refusing it. In fact, the tendency not to show *enryo* is prevalent among *uchi* members. *Enryo* is more frequently expressed when the offer comes from a social superior. Still, it is useful to know that accepting assistance may sometimes take more than a single turn exchange in Japan.

■ Examples

(1) A: 手伝いましょうか。
Tetsudaimashoo ka.
(Shall I help you?)

B: いいえ、大丈夫です。
Iie, daijoobu desu.
(No, it's OK.)

(2) A: 送ろうか。
Okuroo ka.
(Shall I take you home?)

B: じゃ、せっかくだからお願い。
Ja, sekkaku dakara onegai.[*1]
(Well, thanks, will you?)

(3) A: お電話しましょうか。
Odenwa-shimashoo ka.
(Shall I give you a call?)

B: ええ、お願いします。
Ee, onegai-shimasu.
(Yes, please.)

*1. The adverb *sekkaku* means 'especially, purposely' and 'kindly'; *sekkaku dakara* means 'since you are offering a special favor.' *Sekkaku* is also used to express the regret that the desired result was not achieved although a special, purposeful effort was made. This will be studied later in Entry 70.

50. Verbal Predicate (6)
—Verb Categories (Stative and Durative Verbs)

■ Grammatical Explanation

Four verb categories. Depending on whether or not a Japanese verb describes action or state, and whether or not the action or state is durative, the following verb categorization is made. Understanding the differences among categories is important and particularly useful, when the progressive forms of the verb are studied. Here we learn the verb categorization in preparation for the next entry. At this point we concern ourselves with four basic verb types as shown below:

Stative:	1. Stative	いる	*iru*	there exists
	2. Stative durative	似る	*niru*	to resemble
Active:	3. Active durative	歌う	*utau*	to sing
	4. Active non-durative	死ぬ	*shinu*	to die

Characteristics of verb categories. Stative verbs describe the state or condition of facts and objects. They do not represent concrete actions. Among stative verbs, the first type does not have progressive forms. The second type, stative durative, however, can take the progressive form. Active verbs are those that describe dynamic and concrete physical, often observable, action. Among them are durative and non-durative active verbs. An active durative verb refers to action that can be performed for a certain duration of time, such as singing, working, etc. An active non-durative verb describes an action or event that occurs in an instant, and cannot be performed for a duration of time. For example, *shinu* 'to die' occurs in an instant, and is a non-durative verb.

Partial List of Verbs in Four Categories

1. *Stative*:		
ある	*aru*	there exists
いる	*iru*	there exists
2. *Stative durative*:		
ちがう	*chigau*	to differ
似る	*niru*	to resemble
わかる	*wakaru*	to understand
3. *Active durative*:		
遊ぶ	*asobu*	to play
洗う	*arau*	to wash
食べる	*taberu*	to eat
走る	*hashiru*	to run

勉強する	*benkyoo-suru*	to study
待つ	*matsu*	to wait
笑う	*warau*	to laugh
4. *Active non-durative*:		
開く	*aku*	to open
結婚する	*kekkon-suru*	to get married
死ぬ	*shinu*	to die
止まる	*tomaru*	to stop
忘れる	*wasureru*	to forget

There are a few verbs that are both active durative and active non-durative, which include *kiru* 'to wear' and *kiku* 'to listen to/to hear about.' These verbs have two different meanings, one of which becomes significant in a specific context.

51. The Progressive Form —Action in Progress and State of Completed Action

■ Target Expressions

(He) is singing a song.

歌を歌っています。
Uta o utatte-imasu.

The train is stopped.

電車が止まっています。
Densha ga tomatte-imasu.

[V*te* + *-iru*]

■ Grammatical Explanation

[V*te*] as progressive form. Earlier we have studied the gerundive or the *-te* form of the verb in the context of [V*te* + *-kudasai*]. The gerundive form of the verb in essence refers to the realization of the action (as in the English *-ing* form), and although it alone cannot function grammatically as an independent verb, semantically it has the meaning of the verb. The [V*te*] form in Japanese is used in combination with several grammatical forms, one of the most important of which is the progressive form.

Meanings of progressive form. The *-te* form of the verb and the existential verb *iru*, [V*te* + *-iru*], constitutes progressive tense. By changing *iru/imasu* to *ita/imashita*, we have access to the past progressive tense.

The progressive tense structure has three related but distinct meanings.

1. For active durative verbs, the progressive tense expresses the progression of the action.

   (1a) スージーさんは今、カラオケで日本の歌を**歌っています**。
   Suujii-san wa ima, karaoke de Nihon no uta o ***utatte-imasu.***
   (Susie is now singing a Japanese song at a karaoke bar.)

2. For active non-durative verbs, it refers to the continuation of a present state resulting from the already completed action.

   (2a) **結婚しています**。
   Kekkon-shite-imasu.
   (I am married.)

   The verb *kekkon-suru* 'to get married' describes non-durative action (getting married is achieved in an instant); *kekkon-shite-iru* means 'be married, the result of getting married.'

   The negation of this type of progressive tense means an unachieved result, in a way similar to the negative statement in English perfect tense, as shown in (2b).

   (2b) 電車はまだ**来ていません**。
   Densha wa mada ***kite-imasen.***
   (The train hasn't arrived yet.)

3. For some active verbs, progressive tense refers to an action repeated for a certain duration of time.

   (3a) 大学に**通っています**。

Daigaku	*ni*	***kayotte-imasu.***
university	to	commute

   (I am commuting to the university.)

   This expression is used not to mean that the speaker is in the middle of commuting, such as riding in the train on his way to the university, but is used to refer to the habitual, repeated action of commuting.

   Similarly, the verb *sumu* 'to live' expresses habitual action and is always used in the form *sunde-iru* to mean the English equivalent of 'live'; for example, *Tookyoo ni sunde-imasu* 'I live in Tokyo.'

4. For a stative (non-durative) verb, there is no [V*te* + *-iru*] combination. For a stative durative verb, the [V*te* + *-iru*] structure describes the continued state. In case of the *be*-verb, *de-iru* is possible as in the example (4a).

   (4a) いい子**でいます**。
   Ii ko ***de-imasu***.
   (I continue to be a good child.)

Durative or non-durative interpretation. For the verb that has both active durative and non-durative interpretation, the meaning differs depending on how it is used in an utterance. See examples to follow in which (a) expresses the continuation of action, while (b) expresses the state of completed action.

(a) その時父はラジオの音楽を**聞いていた**。
Sono toki chichi wa rajio no ongaku o ***kiite-ita***.
(My father was listening to the music on the radio then.)

(b) 父はもうそのニュースを**聞いていた**。
Chichi wa moo sono nyuusu o ***kiite-ita***.
(My father had already heard that news.)

Negating [V*te* + *-iru*]. For negating the [V*te* + *-iru*] structure, two strategies are available: *utatte-imasen* and *utawanaide-imasu*. *Utatte-imasen* 'I'm not singing' is the straightforward negation of *utatte-imasu*, while *utawanaide-imasu* 'I remain not singing' describes the continuation of the state of not singing.

Shortened forms. In casual style, *i* of [V*te* + *-iru*] is deleted. Thus we have [V*te* + *-ru*], [V*te* + *-ta*], [V*te* + *-nai*], and [V*te* + *-nakatta*].

■ Examples

(1) 小山さんは東京に住んでいます。
Koyama-san wa Tookyoo ni sunde-imasu.
(Ms. Koyama lives in Tokyo.)

(2) **A:** どんな仕事をしていますか。
Donna shigoto o shite-imasu ka.
(What line of work are you in?)

B: 銀行関係の仕事をしています。
Ginkoo kankei no shigoto o shite-imasu.
(I work in a banking-related business.)

(3) **A:** 光君、今何してる?
Hikaru-kun, ima nani shite-ru?
(What's Hikaru doing now?)

B: ケータイで友だちと話してる。
Keetai de tomodachi to hanashite-ru.
(He's talking with his friend on the cell phone.)

(4) その頃父は慶応大学で教えていました。
Sono koro chichi wa Keioo Daigaku de oshiete-imashita.
(My father was teaching at Keio University around that time.)

(5) 三年前は結婚していませんでした。
San-nen mae wa kekkon-shite-imasen-deshita.
(Three years ago I wasn't married yet.)

(6) それ、私、聞いてないよ。
Sore, watashi, kiite-nai yo.
(I haven't heard that.)

■ Additional Information

There are two additional extended uses of the present progressive tense. First is to refer to an experience, as shown in (a).

(a) あの人はよく外国へ**行っている**。
*Ano hito wa yoku gaikoku e **itte-iru**.*
(He has traveled to foreign countries often.)

Second, the use of a certain group of verbs is restricted to the progressive tense only, and they merely describe the state or the quality of things.

(b) 目の前に高い山が**そびえていた**。
*Me no mae ni takai yama ga **sobiete-ita**.*
(In front of my eyes, the tall mountain rose.)

Other verbs that fall under this group include *sugureru* 'to excel,' *arihureru* 'to be common,' and a specific use of the verb *suru*, as in *kawaii kao o suru* 'to have a cute face.'

52. Adverbs (2)—Onomatopoeic and Mimicry Words

■ Target Expression

It is raining quietly and steadily.

雨がしとしと降っています。
Ame ga shitoshito hutte-imasu.

■ Grammatical Explanation

***Giseigo* and *gitaigo*.** Japanese has a rich system of words describing sound or action directly and vividly. There are two categories; (1) *giseigo*, sound-imitating words, or onomatopoeic words, and (2) *gitaigo*, action-imitating words, or mimicry words. For example, the adverb *shitoshito* expresses the quiet and steady rhythm of the falling rain. English also has onomatopoeic words (for example, *pitter-patter* to describe the falling rain) but their use is limited. Although in English the use of onomatopoeic words may connote childishness, *giseigo* and *gitaigo* are frequently used by great writers of Japanese literature, and their use is not considered childish in the least.

Ways of describing laughter. Laughing may be described in English by different verbs; in Japanese both *giseigo* and *gitaigo* are attached as adverbs in order to describe the various ways to *warau* 'laugh.'

giseigo:	**げらげら**笑う	***geragera*** *warau*	to laugh boisterously
	くすくす笑う	***kusukusu*** *warau*	to giggle
	へらへら笑う	***herahera*** *warau*	to laugh condescendingly
gitaigo:	**にこにこ**する	***nikoniko*** *suru*	to smile
	にやにやする	***niyaniya*** *suru*	to grin

Frequently used *giseigo* and *gitaigo*. Other frequently used *giseigo* and *gitaigo* include:

がぶがぶ
gabugabu
水を**がぶがぶ**飲む。
Mizu o ***gabugabu*** *nomu.*
([He/She] drinks water thirstily in big gulps.)

きらきら
kirakira
星が**きらきら**輝いている。
Hoshi ga ***kirakira*** *kagayaite-iru.*
(The stars are shining and glittering.)

さらさら
sarasara
川の水が**さらさら**流れる。
Kawa no mizu ga ***sarasara*** *nagareru.*
(The river [water] flows smoothly.)

Giseigo and *gitaigo* are often four-mora words, formed with two two-mora pairs. There are a remarkable number of these words in the Japanese vocabulary. If you are interested in sound symbolism in Japanese, refer to *giseigo (giongo)* and *gitaigo* dictionaries available in bookstores or on the Internet.

■ Additional Information

- Onomatopoeic words are used by speakers to enhance the situational effect. *Jaan* is used when something dramatic is going to happen. The speaker may dramatically reveal a gift and say "*Jaan!*" similar to English "Ta-da!" *Gaan* is a sound that you may hear when someone hits your head with a fist or something hard. This is uttered when the speaker is in shock. Imagine a situation where you are told that you failed an important exam. You might respond by *gaan, shokku!* 'ouch, what a shock!' These speech effects are used most frequently in comic books, and they are creeping into young people's casual speech.
- Onomatopoeic words can become verbs as shown below.

ピンポンする	*pinpon-suru*	to ring the door bell [from the sound of the door bell]
チンする	*chin-suru*	to cook in the microwave [from the sound it makes when it's done]

53. Expressions Meaning "I Don't Know"

■ Target Expressions

Do you understand?

わかりますか。
Wakarimasu ka.

I don't understand.

わかりません。
Wakarimasen.

Do you know?

知っていますか。
Shitte-imasu ka.

I don't know.

知りません。
Shirimasen.

■ Strategic Explanation

Although the target expressions listed above seem too specific to warrant an independent entry in this book, I decided to do precisely that. This is because when learning a foreign language, it is useful to be able to express whether or not you understand the point being made. It is frustrating when you cannot convey that you do not understand, and worse, it is embarrassing when you do this incorrectly. Here are some tips.

***Shiru* versus *wakaru*.** The basic distinction between *shiru* 'to know' and *wakaru* 'to be understood' is the following. *Wakaru* refers to an understanding of various aspects related to an object whose existence is already recognized. *Shiru* denotes recognition of an object and a familiarization with it. *Wakaru* is a verb for "reactive" description, which takes the form, *Nihongo ga wakarimasu* '(lit., Japanese is understood) I understand Japanese.' Thus, the question form is, *Nihongo ga wakarimasu ka?* The answer to this question takes the form *hai, wakarimasu* or *iie, wakarimasen*. On the other hand *shiru* is a transitive verb which takes object maker *o*. When asking *do you know Mrs. Tanaka?* always use the *shitte-iru* form; thus *Tanaka-san o shitte-imasu ka?* The answer to this question takes either *hai, shitte-imasu* or *iie, shirimasen*.

■ Examples

(1) **A:** この言葉の意味わかる？
Kono kotoba no imi wakaru?
(Do you understand the meaning of this word?)

B: うん、わかるよ。
Un, wakaru yo.
(Yeah, I do.)

(2) **A:** ニューヨーク支店の酒井さんを知っていますか。
Nyuuyooku shiten no Sakai-san o shitte-imasu ka.
(Do you know Mr. Sakai at the New York office?)

B: いいえ、知りませんが……
Iie, shirimasen ga . . .
(No. I don't know him, I'm afraid.)

■ Additional Information

Shitte-ru and *wakatte-ru* are used in conversation responses, as shown below.

(a) **A:** あの人、結婚したよ。
Ano hito, kekkon-shita yo.
(She got married.)

B: 知ってる。
Shitte-ru.
(I know.)

(b) **A:** イタリアンのレストランって、私そんなお金ないよ。
Itarian no resutoran tte, watashi sonna okane nai yo.
(You mention an Italian restaurant, but I don't have that kind of money.)

B: わかってる。
Wakatte-ru.
(I know.)

The choice between *shitte-ru* and *wakatte-ru* depends on the particular emphasis, i.e, whether it conveys knowledge (*shitte-ru*) or it involves understanding (*wakatte-ru*).

54. Structure of the Japanese Sentence (2) —Proposition and Modality

■ Target Expression

(Regrettably) I lost my passport.

パスポートをなくしてしまいました。
Pasupooto o nakushite-shimaimashita.

[V*te* + *-shimau*]

■ Grammatical Explanation

Proposition and modality. As for Japanese sentence construction, we have learned earlier about the structural axis of topic-comment and subject-predicate. We look once more at the internal structure of the sentence, but with a different focus. A sentence (or an utterance) can be considered a combination consisting of "proposition"—logical propositional information (that is, who does what to whom, and so forth)—and "modality"—the expression of personal and emotional commitment the speaker makes toward that proposition. In fact, we already studied various strategies for expressing modality in Japanese, such as negation, suggestion, and invitation.

Aspect and mood. Among modality, we can see two related but distinct types, "aspect" and "mood." Aspect means specific focus placed on different parts of action described by the verb, in relation to its tense and manner. For example, if one focuses on the fact that the action is in progress, [V*te* + *-iru*] is used for the active durative verb. The progressive form is one good example of aspect. By mood, we mean psychological and emotional judgments one makes toward the statement, such as speculation and suggestion.

Structures and strategies for modality. For the expression of modality, the [V + (Aux)V] construction, [AuxV], auxiliary adjectives [AuxAdj], and the [N + *da*] structure, among other strategies, are used. I list here important devices for expressing aspects and mood in Japanese. We will study the meaning and use of these expressions later, under separate headings as indicated in parentheses.

Aspects: **[V*te* + V] construction**

V*te-iru*	(Entry 51)
V*te-aru*	(Entry 95)
V*te-shimau*	(Entry 54)
V*te-oku*	(Entry 95)
V*te-iku*	(Entry 55)
V*te-kuru*	(Entry 55)

[Vstem + AuxV] construction

(All these expressions appear in Entry 121.)

Vstem-*hajimeru*
Vstem-*dasu*
Vstem-*kakeru*
Vstem-*kaesu*
Vstem-*sugiru*
Vstem-*naosu*

[N + *da*] construction

tokoro da	(Entry 129)

Mood: **[AuxV] and [AuxAdj]**

kamoshirenai	(Entry 99)
nakereba naranai	(Entry 107)
chigainai	(Entry 108)
-daroo/-deshoo	(Entry 99)
rashii	(Entry 91)
soona	(Entry 87)
mitaina	(Entry 89)
yoona	(Entry 89)

[N + *da*] construction

koto da	(Entry 120)	([Nominalizer + *da*] structure)
hazu da	(Entry 104)	
beki da	(Entry 106)	
mono da	(Entry 120)	
wake da	(Entry 74)	
no da	(Entry 74)	([Nominalizer + *da*] structure)

V*te* + *-shimau*. At this point we concentrate on only one of the aspects, namely, [V*te* + *-shimau*]. The verb *shimau* means 'to put away,' and 'to store.' When using the [V*te* + *-shimau*] combination, it indicates "completion" and "finality." The speaker emphasizes that the event is completed, expressing a sense of fatalism in that what is done once cannot be undone. It focuses on the completion of action and event, meaning 'end up doing' and 'finish doing.'

Sense of regret. Because [V*te* + *-shimau*] emphasizes the aspect of an event or incident being totally completed (and irreversible), it is often used when one wishes to express a sense of regret.

(a) ねこが死ん**でしまった**。
*Neko ga shin**de-shimatta**.*
(The cat died [and we cannot change this reality . . .].)

Sense of completion. There are cases where the [V*te* + *-shimau*] construction does not imply a sense of regret; for example, *sono hon wa moo yonde-shimatta* 'as for that book, I've read it already,' or *shukudai wa moo shite-shimatta yo* 'as for my homework, I've finished it already.' These expressions simply point out the sense of completion.

■ Examples

(1) 電車に遅れてしまった。
Densha ni okurete-shimatta.
(I missed the train.)

(2) 妹がケーキを全部食べてしまいました。
Imooto ga keeki o zenbu tabete-shimaimashita.
(My sister ate the whole cake.)

■ Additional Information

A colloquial version of [V*te* + *-shimau*] is created by replacing *te-shimau* with *-chau* (and *de-shimau* with *-jau*).

Te-shimau and *-chau* sometimes indicate joy over unexpected good fortune. In example (a), *atatchatta* is a contracted version of *atatte-shimatta*, the verb *ataru* meaning 'win (a lottery).' Sentence (a) expresses the speaker's joy.

(a) 宝くじに**あたっちゃった**。

Takarakuji	*ni*	***atatchatta*.**
lottery	at	won

(I won the lottery.)

55. Actions Involving Directions—Come and Go

■ Target Expression

I borrowed the book (and came back).

本を借りてきました。
Hon o karite-kimashita.

[V*te* + -*iku*] [V*te* + -*kuru*]

■ Grammatical Explanation

Marking with directionality. When the action described is associated with movement between two points of space or time, that is, when it involves direction, the verbs of coming and going are attached to the [V*te*] form. These directional markers are obligatory; without them they sound incomplete. Since [V*te* + -*iku*] and [V*te* + -*kuru*] emphasize direction of the verb, they express an aspect of the verb. Although *iku* and *kuru* are independent verbs, when used in combination with [V*te*] forms, they add aspectual meaning to the preceding verb, and this fact is indicated by a hyphen. For the verb *hashiru* 'to run' we obtain the following:

hashitte-iku when the speaker views the action of running from the location close-to-self toward the location away-from-self
hashitte-kuru when the speaker views the action from the location away-from-self to the location close-to-self

Meanings of [V*te* + -*iku*] and [V*te* + -*kuru*]. Based on this primary meaning, there are extended uses of [V*te* + -*iku*] and [V*te* + -*kuru*] to express the following aspects.

[V*te* + -*iku*]
1. Process of disappearance:

(1a) 飛行機は空のかなたへ消え**ていきました**。
*Hikooki wa sora no kanata e kie**te-ikimashita**.*
(The airplane disappeared into the distance of the sky.)

2. Process of change within others:

(2a) その男はだんだん貧しくなっ**ていった**。
*Sono otoko wa dandan mazushikunat**te-itta**.*
(The man became increasingly poorer.)

3. Continuation of process into the future:

(3a) これからもがんばっ**ていきましょう**。
*Korekara mo ganbat**te-ikimashoo**.*
(Let's continue to keep on doing our best.)

[V*te* + *-kuru*]
4. Process of appearance:

(4a) いい考えがうかん**できた**。
*Ii kangae ga ukan**de-kita**.*
([lit., Good ideas appeared.] I hit upon some good ideas.)

5. Process of change that takes place in self and those close to self:

(5a) 気持ちが悪くなっ**てきた**。
*Kimochi ga waruku nat**te-kita**.*
(I began to feel ill.)

6. Beginning of process:

(6a) 冷たい風が吹い**てきた**。
*Tsumetai kaze ga hui**te-kita**.*
(A cold wind began to blow.)

(6b) あの人の気持ちがわかっ**てきた**。
*Ano hito no kimochi ga wakat**te-kita**.*
(I began to understand his or her feelings.)
(Compare this with the English expression *come to understand*.)

7. Continuation of process to a certain point of past or up to the present:

(7a) 今までがんばっ**てきました**。
*Ima made ganbat**te-kimashita**.*
(I've done my best up until now.)

■ Examples

(1) 東京では九月には涼しい日が多くなる。
Tookyoo de wa kugatsu ni wa suzushii hi ga ooku naru.
(In Tokyo in September the days become cooler.)

十月には渡り鳥が南の国へ帰っていく。
Juugatsu ni wa wataridori ga minami no kuni e kaette-iku.
(In October migratory birds go back to southern countries.)

十一月には朝晩かなり寒くなってくる。
Juuichigatsu ni wa asaban kanari samuku natte-kuru.
(In November mornings and evenings become rather cold.)

(2) 今九時三分前です。
Ima ku-ji san-pun mae desu.
(It is three minutes to nine now.)

すぐ日本語の授業が始まります。
Sugu Nihongo no jugyoo ga hajimarimasu.
(Soon the Japanese language class starts.)

友だちのミックが教室に入ってきました。
Tomodachi no Mikku ga kyooshitsu ni haitte-kimashita.
(Mick, a friend, came into the classroom.)

ミックは新しい辞書を持ってきました。
Mikku wa atarashii jisho o motte-kimashita.
(Mick brought [with him] a new dictionary.)

ミックの友だちのチョーさんも入ってきました。
Mikku no tomodachi no Choo-san mo haitte-kimashita.
(Mick's friend, Mr. Cho, also came [into the room].)

チョーさんは今朝日本語の新聞を買ってきました。
Choo-san wa kesa Nihongo no shinbun o katte-kimashita.
(This morning Mr. Cho bought and brought [with him] a Japanese newspaper.)

56. Conjunctions (1)—Common Conjunctions

■ Target Expressions

Although I read the book, I didn't understand it.

本を読んだけれどもわかりませんでした。
Hon o yonda keredomo wakarimasen-deshita.
本読んだけどわからなかった。
Hon yonda kedo wakaranakatta.

[V*te*] [Adj *te*]
[*soshite*] [*keredomo*]

■ Grammatical Explanation

Connecting clauses. So far we have focused primarily on simple sentences containing one main verb. Now we proceed to complex sentences with multiple clauses. Here are ways to connect clauses in Japanese.

1. By the gerundive [V/Adj *te*] form:
   It is possible to end each clause by [V/Adj *te*] in order to continue with consequent clauses. This structure connects different clauses with the basic meaning of 'and.' In certain extended interpretations, however, a meaning of cause may be added depending on the context in which it appears.

   (1a) すしを**食べて**、酒を**飲んで**、楽しいパーティーだった。

Sushi	*o*	***tabete,***	*sake*	*o*	***nonde,***	*tanoshii*	*paatii*	*datta.*
sushi	O	eat	*sake*	O	drink	enjoyable	party	was

   (We ate *sushi*, drank *sake*, and it was an enjoyable party.)

   (1b) 田中さんは日本人**で**、ブラウンさんはアメリカ人です。
   *Tanaka-san wa Nihon-jin **de**, Buraun-san wa Amerika-jin desu.*
   (Mrs. Tanaka is Japanese, and Mrs. Brown is American.)

   (1c) 朝ねぼうを**して**、遅れてしまった。
   *Asaneboo o **shite**, okurete-shimatta.*
   (I overslept, and so I was late.)

2. By using a number of conjunctions:

   soshite 'and'/*sorekara* 'then':

   (2a) 夕ごはんを食べました。**そして/それから**寝ました。
   *Yuugohan o tabemashita. **Soshite/Sorekara** nemashita.*
   (I ate supper. And then went to bed.)

   keredomo/keredo/shikashi/demo 'but':

   (2b) 妹のアパートへ行きました。**けれども/しかし/でも**いませんでした。
   *Imooto no apaato e ikimashita. **Keredomo/Shikashi/Demo** imasen-deshita.*
   (I went to my younger sister's apartment. But she wasn't there.)

   dakara/desukara (polite version of *dakara*)/*sorede/de* 'and so':

   (2c) あした会議があります。**だから/ですから/それで**その準備をしています。

Ashita	*kaigi*	*ga*	*arimasu.*	***Dakara/Desukara/Sorede***
tomorrow	meeting	S	there is	therefore

sono	*junbi*	*o*	*shite-imasu.*
that	preparation	O	do

   (There is a meeting tomorrow. Therefore/So I am preparing for it.)

   kedo/ga 'although':

   (2d) この本は何度も読みました**けど/が**よくわかりません。
   *Kono hon wa nando-mo yomimashita **kedo/ga** yoku wakarimasen.*
   (I read this book many times, but I cannot understand it well.)

noni 'in spite of':

(2e) あの人は雨が降っている**のに**ジョギングをしている。
*Ano hito wa ame ga hutte-iru **noni** jogingu o shite-iru.*
(In spite of the rain, he is jogging.)

node 'since':

(2f) あした友だちに会う**ので**楽しみです。
*Ashita tomodachi ni au **node** tanoshimi desu.*
(Since I will see my friend tomorrow, I look forward to it [lit., it is a pleasure].)

Where to place conjunctions. Regarding where the conjunctions appear in relation to the clauses, the following should be noted. First, *soshite, sorekara, shikashi, demo, dakara, desukara, sorede,* and *de* appear utterance-initially, connecting the preceding statement with the one starting with the conjunction. On the other hand, *kedo, ga, noni,* and *node* must appear immediately following a clause; they cannot start a new utterance. *Keredomo* and *tokoroga* can appear in either position.

Using *noni* and *node*. When using *noni* and *node*, if preceded by *da*, you must replace *da* with *na*. For example, *Nihon-jin na noni Eigo ga joozu desu* 'despite being Japanese, he or she is good at English' and *ii jisho na node kaimashita* 'since this is a good dictionary, I bought it.'

Formal and informal forms when connecting clauses. When conjunctions connect two clauses, the predicate in the subordinate clause is normally, but not exclusively, in the informal form. As a basic rule the style of the sentence is expressed by the ending of the main verb. When a formal ending is used in a subordinate clause along with the formal ending in the main clause, the utterance is considered to be highly formal.

■ Examples

(1) **A:** ではそのレポートはあした持ってきます。
Dewa sono repooto wa ashita motte-kimasu.
(Well then, I will bring that report tomorrow.)

B: あしたは忙しいのであさって持ってきてくださいませんか。
Ashita wa isogashii node asatte motte-kite-kudasaimasen ka.
(Since I am busy tomorrow, could you bring it the day after tomorrow?)

A: 三時頃はいかがですか。
San-ji goro wa ikaga desu ka.
(How about around three o'clock?)

(2) ターナーさんは日本に五年間住んでいました。ですから日本語はペラペラです。
Taanaa-san wa Nihon ni go-nenkan sunde-imashita. Desukara Nihongo wa perapera desu.
(Mr. Turner lived in Japan for five years. Therefore he is fluent in Japanese.)

(3) いっしょうけんめい働いたのに結局会社はつぶれてしまった。
Isshookenmei hataraita noni kekkyoku kaisha wa tsuburete-shimatta.
(Despite the fact that I worked hard, in the end, the company went bankrupt.)

■ Additional Information

Another way of connecting clauses to make multiple-clause sentences are to use the stem of the verb, [Vstem]. Conjoining clauses with [Vstem] are frequently used in written Japanese and formal speech, but limited in casual speech.

(a) 六時に**起き**、六時半に家を出た。
*Roku-ji ni **oki**, roku-ji han ni ie o deta.*
(I got up at six and left home at six-thirty.)

57. Conjunctions (2)—Conjunctions for Interactional Appeal

■ Target Expression

Excuse me, but . . .

すみませんが……
Sumimasen ga . . .

■ Strategic Explanation

Using conjunctions for interactional purposes. Some Japanese conjunctions do not necessarily connect clauses logically. As in the use of the English *but* in the expression *excuse me, but . . .* , Japanese conjunctions often function to convey meanings useful in facilitating interaction. In spoken Japanese some conjunctions are added at utterance-final positions with the deleted main clause being either implied or suggested. Since ending an utterance with a conjunction implies continuation, the listener has a feeling that the thought is unfinished. The feeling of incompleteness expresses a less imposing, and therefore more considerate attitude. For example, by saying *soo wa omoimasen ga . . .* 'I don't think so (but) . . . ,' the speaker softens his or her opposing statement, and thereby minimizes disruption and ensures the maintenance of interpersonal harmony.

Imagine a situation where you hear an announcement at a department store requesting you to come to the reception desk. When you see the receptionist, you might say, *Watanabe* (your name) *desu ga* 'I'm Watanabe.' The *ga* added at the end implies that something is to continue. It conveys the speaker's desire to solicit the addressee's response, and therefore it expresses receptiveness.

Using conjunctions for topics and prefixes. Conjunctions *ga, kedo,* and *keredo* are also used to introduce a topic of conversation. For example, *haru no ryokoo desu ga* 'it's about the spring trip, but.' An expression *yoku wakarimasen ga* 'I don't understand well (I'm not sure) but' is frequently used as a prefix to stating one's opinion. By appealing to the listener with a statement that disclaims authority, the speaker leaves room for further discussion and negotiation. Especially when one's opinion opposes another's, prefixing of this kind is considered useful and tactful.

■ Examples

(1) よくわかりませんが……
Yoku wakarimasen ga . . .
(I don't understand it well, but . . .)

(2) **A:** すみませんが、これを横浜工場へ届けてくださいませんか。
Sumimasen ga, kore o Yokohama koojoo e todokete-kudasai-masen ka.
(Sorry to bother you, but could you please deliver this to the Yokohama plant?)

B: はい。十時頃になりますが……
Hai. Juu-ji goro ni narimasu ga . . .
(Sure. It will be about ten o'clock . . .)

A: いいですよ。お願いします。
Ii-desu yo. Onegai-shimasu.
(Fine. Please take care of it.)

(3) よくわかりませんが、それはあちらの間違いじゃないでしょうか。
Yoku wakarimasen ga, sore wa achira no machigai ja-nai-deshoo ka.
(I'm not sure, but isn't it their mistake?)

(4) ところで、来月の旅行のことだけど……
Tokorode, raigetsu no ryokoo no koto da kedo . . .
(By the way, it's about the trip planned for next month . . .)

■ Additional Information

- Among conjunctions used for interaction, *dakara* warrants special mention. As shown in B's second utterance in (a), *dakara* is used for emphasis, reminding the listener that the speaker has already alluded to it.

  (a) A: 忘れたの？
  Wasureta no?
  (You forgot?)

  B: うん、ちょっと忘れたの。
  Un, chotto wasureta no.
  (Don't you see, I just forgot.)

  A: ほんと？
  Honto?
  (Really?)

  B: **だから**そう言ってるでしょ。
  ***Dakara** soo itteru desho.*
  (Don't you get it, I'm telling you so.)

- The *te*-form of *da*, i.e., *de*, is used as a conjunction as well, especially in casual conversation. *De* is more casual than *sorede*, and is used to connect the speaker and the listener in the conversational interaction.

  (b) A: **で**？
  ***De**?*
  (Then?)

  B: **で**、すぐ帰ってきた。
  ***De**, sugu kaette-kita.*
  (Then, I came back right away.)

- In general there is a tendency to use conjunctions more freely in Japanese than in English. In written discourse, conjunctions and conjunctive phrases such as *shitagatte* 'therefore,' *sarani* 'furthermore,' *mata* 'additionally,' *ijoo nobeta yoo ni* 'as stated above,' and *yuu made mo naku* 'needless to mention' are frequently inserted merely to connect clauses. These conjunctions may not imply a logical connection, such as statement/conclusion; they are often used to signal general connectedness between statements.
- The use of the conjunction *ga* in the example below may be best called a transition word rather than a conjunction connecting opposing statements.

  (c) 佐々木さんとはよく会議で会います**が**、なかなかやり手ですね。
  *Sasaki-san to wa yoku kaigi de aimasu **ga**, nakanaka yarite desu ne.*
  (I see Sasaki often at meetings; [but] she is quite an achiever.)

■ Warning

It is absolutely crucial to pronounce utterance-final *ga* and *kedo* for interactional appeal in a falling tone, gradually fading and trailing. If the conjunction receives a rising tone, the listener is likely to wait for you to continue. In order to signal that you are yielding your turn, make sure to pronounce *ga* and *kedo* in a falling tone.

58. Getting Attention from Friends and Strangers

■ Target Expression

Uh, excuse me . . .

あのう、すみませんが……
Anoo, sumimasen ga . . .

■ Strategic Explanation

When you want to attract your friends' attention, you can simply use their names, as in *nee, Maki-san* 'say, Maki.' *Nee* functions as an attention-getting phrase among in-group members.

Attention-getting expressions. When you don't know the name, or cannot recall the name of the person, the following phrases are useful.

(a) あのう、すみません(が)……
Anoo, sumimasen (ga) . . .
(Uh, excuse me [but] . . .)

(b) あのう、失礼ですが……
Anoo, shitsurei desu ga . . .
(Uh, sorry to be rude . . .)

(c) あのう……
Anoo . . .
(Uhhh . . .)

(d) ねえ……
Nee . . .
(Say . . .)

The phrase *anoo* is pronounced hesitantly. The hesitation marker *anoo* is useful to express your unwillingness (with even a sense of guilt) to bother strangers for your need. Thus, hesitation shows a respect for and consideration toward others. In casual situations, the interactional particle *nee* (often used in feminine speech) or an adverb *chotto* may be used as a pre-announcement of address terms toward familiar partners as in *nee okaasan* 'say, mom.'

Sumimasen* and *gomenkudasai. If you need to catch the attention of someone far away from you, use *sumimaseeen!* 'excuse me!' in a loud voice. When you are visiting someone's home, you can call attention to the fact that you are there by saying *gomenkudasai* 'hello.'

■ Warning

As in the case of *ne(e)*, the expression *ano ne* is used between *uchi* members only. *Ano ne* has an intimate, friendly, and somewhat condescending tone, and therefore should be avoided toward your superiors.

59. Family Terms

■ Target Expressions

my mother, my younger brother

母、弟
haha, otooto

(someone else's) mother, (someone else's) younger brother

お母さん、弟さん
okaasan, otootosan

■ Strategic Explanation

My mother or his mother. One important feature in Japanese family terms shows a striking contrast with English. Japanese provides two distinct sets of terms depending on whether you are referring to the family among *uchi* or *soto* group members. This system reflects the fact that Japanese make a clear distinction between the members of *uchi* versus *soto*; and this is particularly so when they make reference to family members.

Family Terms

	Referential terms:		Address terms:	
	one's own	*someone's*	*one's own*	*someone's*
grandfather	祖父 *sohu*	おじいさん *ojiisan*	おじいさん *ojiisan*	おじいさん *ojiisan*
grandmother	祖母 *sobo*	おばあさん *obaasan*	おばあさん *obaasan*	おばあさん *obaasan*
father	父 *chichi*	お父さん *otoosan*	(お)父さん/パパ *(o)toosan/papa*	お父さん *otoosan*
mother	母 *haha*	お母さん *okaasan*	(お)母さん/ママ *(o)kaasan/mama*	お母さん *okaasan*
elder brother	兄 *ani*	お兄さん *oniisan*	(お)兄さん *(o)niisan*	FN[*1]さん FN + *-san*
elder sister	姉 *ane*	お姉さん *oneesan*	(お)姉さん *(o)neesan*	FNさん FN + *-san*
younger brother	弟 *otooto*	弟さん *otootosan*	FN	FNさん FN + *-san*
younger sister	妹 *imooto*	妹さん *imootosan*	FN	FNさん FN + *-san*
uncle	おじ *oji*	おじさん *ojisan*	おじさん *ojisan*	おじさん *ojisan*
aunt	おば *oba*	おばさん *obasan*	おばさん *obasan*	おばさん *obasan*
daughter	娘 *musume*	おじょうさん *ojoosan*	FN	FN さん FN + *-san*
son	息子 *musuko*	息子さん *musukosan*	FN	FN さん FN + *-san*
wife	妻/家内 *tsuma/kanai*	奥さん *okusan*	おまえ/FN *omae*/FN	奥さん *okusan*
husband	主人 *shujin*	ご主人(さま) *goshujin(sama)*	あなた *anata*	ご主人さま *goshujinsama* (LN[*1] + *-san*)
child	子供 *kodomo*	子供さん *kodomosan*		
sibling	兄弟 *kyoodai*	ご兄弟 *gokyoodai*		
family	家族 *kazoku*	ご家族 *gokazoku*		

*1. FN/LN are abbreviations of first name/last name.

■ Additional Information

The use of family terms is extended to the fictive use as well. In this use, a husband may be called *otoosan* by his wife. Here the wife views her husband as a "father" from the child's point of view. Obviously, the husband is not the wife's biological father. In fact the husband calls himself "father" when facing a child. This is also observed in the United States, but its use is much more limited.

Similar referential terms are used by children, or adults taking the children's point of view, to identify man and woman by using *oniisan*, *ojisan* and *ojiisan*, or *oneesan*, *obasan* and *obaasan*, respectively, depending on the age of the person. A younger male resembles a "brother," a middle-aged man is like an "uncle," an older man is described as "grandfather," even when there is no biological link. You can imagine the unpleasant shock a woman might feel when she is called *obasan*, instead of *oneesan*, and *obaasan* instead of *obasan*, by neighborhood children. Compare this with English; although uncle and aunt are used for family friends who are about the age of the child's uncle and aunt, when a person addresses someone unfamiliar, general address terms such as *Mr.* and *Miss* are used regardless of the age.

60. Description of Possession

■ Target Expression

Do you have the ticket?

切符を持っていますか。
Kippu o motte-imasu ka.

[N + *o* + *motte-iru*]

■ Grammatical Explanation

Motte-iru. Earlier we have studied that *aru* and *iru* can be used to express possession. Another strategy is to use the verb *motsu* 'to possess.' The verb *motsu* is used in the present progressive tense, and it expresses the state of possessing or the state of being in possession of something. To be noted is that when what is possessed is animate, *motte-iru* cannot be used; *iru* must be chosen.

■ Examples

(1) マンガ本は何冊ぐらい持っていますか。
Mangabon wa nan-satsu gurai motte-imasu ka.
(About how many comic books do you possess?)

(2) 今日はお金をたくさん持っています。
Kyoo wa okane o takusan motte-imasu.
(I have a lot of money [on me] today.)

(3) 友だちがたくさんいる。
Tomodachi ga takusan iru.
(I have many friends.)

(4) 和也には兄弟がいない。
Kazuya ni wa kyoodai ga inai.
(Kazuya has no siblings.)

61. Expressing Gratitude

■ Target Expression

Thank you very much.

どうもありがとうございます。
Doomo arigatoo gozaimasu.

■ Strategic Explanation

Saying thank you. Expressing gratitude is important in many societies, but some of the regulatory rules of saying thank you in Japanese differ from those in other countries. But first, let us learn the formulaic phrases expressing gratitude.

ありがとう。	*Arigatoo.*	Thanks.
ありがとうございます。	*Arigatoo gozaimasu.*	Thank you. [polite]
ありがとうございました。	*Arigatoo gozaimashita.*	Thank you for … [often after the favor is done]
サンキュ(ー)。	*Sankyu(u).*	Thank you. [particularly among young speakers]
サンキュ(ー)でした。	*Sankyu(u)-deshita.*	Thank you. [somewhat polite]
どうも(どうも)。	*Doomo (doomo).*	Thanks.
どうもすみません。	*Doomo sumimasen.*	Thank you for your trouble.
どうもすみませんでした。	*Doomo sumimasen-deshita.*	Thank you for doing … [after the favor is done]

Sumimasen(-deshita) is an expression of apology, but is often used as an expression of gratitude. By apologizing for bothering someone on one's behalf, appreciation is indirectly expressed.

Osewa ni narimashita. An expression *osewa ni narimashita* 'lit., thanks for taking care of me' is used when one parts from someone whose care he or she has been under. For example, when parting the host family (for good), this expression is used to mean 'thank you for taking care of me.' It is advisable to bow as these words are uttered.

Responding to someone's "thank you." When you are thanked, the response should be:

(a) いいえ、どういたしまして。
Iie, doo itashimashite.
(You are welcome, it's my pleasure.)

Or, you can simply say *iie* or *iya iya* to deny that what you did for the other person deserves such an expression of gratitude.

Saying thank you for prior favors. In Japan it is customary for a person who received a favor earlier to express gratitude again the next time they meet. Let's assume that your teacher invited you to his or her home and served dinner a week ago. What follows is a typical interaction when you run into him or her again.

(b) **A:** ああ、鈴木先生、おはようございます。
Aa, Suzuki sensei, ohayoo gozaimasu.
(Ah, Professor Suzuki, good morning.)

B: ああ、おはよう。
Aa, ohayoo.
(Good morning.)

A: 先生、**この間はどうもありがとうございました**。
Sensei, ***kono aida wa doomo arigatoo gozaimashita.***
(Thank you very much for [your favor] the other day.)

B: いや、いや。
Iya, iya.
(You are quite welcome.)

It is important to follow the ritual of mentioning the favor given by the other at a previous occasion. Among friends, a shortened expression *kono aida wa doomo* 'thanks for the other day' suffices. Repeated thanks express the depth of your appreciation.

***Sumimasen* and *doomo*.** If a person learned only one or two phrases in Japanese, he or she couldn't do better than *sumimasen* and *doomo*. Both *sumimasen* and *doomo* can express apology, gratitude, leave-taking, and other things. See the following interaction.

(c) A: **すみませーん。** [At the door, requesting attention.]
Sumimaseeen.
(Excuse me!)

B: あ、**どうもどうも。** [Answering to A casually.]
A, ***doomo doomo.***
(Oh, hi.)

A: これお願いします。 [A hands B a community bulletin.]
Kore onegai-shimasu.
(Here is [the bulletin] for you.)

B: ああ、**すみません**ねえ。 [B thanks A for distributing the bulletin.]
Aa, ***sumimasen*** *nee.*
(Oh, thanks.)

A: いいえ。じゃあ**どうも。** [A performs informal leave-taking.]
Iie, jaa ***doomo****.*
(Don't mention it. See you.)

B: **どうも。** [B responds to A's leave-taking.]
Doomo.
(I'll see you.)

■ Additional Information

At work, the boss sometimes shows gratitude toward the workers by saying *goku-roosan* or *gokuroosama* (*desu / deshita*). The word *kuroo* means 'toil' and 'hardship.' The phrase *gokuroosan* and *gokuroosama* are used to express appreciation for the effort put in by a subordinate who is expected to perform certain duties for the direct or indirect benefit of the speaker. A housewife may say *gokuroosama* to a delivery man; a husband, spotting a newspaper delivery man, may say *gokuroosan* to express his acknowledgment and appreciation of his service. This phrase is not to be used when addressing your social superior.

62. Stating Purpose

■ Target Expressions

I'm going (in order) to see Ms. Kato.

加藤さんに会いに行きます。
Katoo-san ni ai ni ikimasu.

I'm saving money (in order) to travel.

旅行するために(お)金をためている。
Ryokoo-suru tame ni (o)kane o tamete-iru.

[Vstem + *ni* + *iku/kuru*]
[Vbasic + *tame ni*] [N + *no tame ni*]

■ Grammatical Explanation

Two ways to convey purpose. In expressing purpose, two patterns are used. First, add *iku* 'to go' and *kuru* 'to come' (and other directional verbs such as *kaeru* 'to return' and *hairu* 'to enter') to [Vstem (that is, take off *-masu* from the *-masu* form of the verb) + *ni*]. For example, *tabe ni ikimasu* 'go (in order) to eat.'

Second, for all verbs, add *tame ni* after the [Vbasic] form. When [*tame ni*] is preceded by *da*, however, *da* changes to *no*. (*Tame* itself is a noun meaning 'benefit,' 'purpose,' and 'cause.') For example, *kuruma o kau tame ni (o)kane o tameru* '(I) save money in order to buy a car.' When the phrase *tame ni* is used for the directional verbs, including *iku* and *kuru*, it carries the effect of a somewhat dramatized narrative style.

Noun followed by *ni* or *no tame ni*. When the purpose is described in the noun form, the same restriction applies. *Ni* can be attached immediately after the nouns if the relevant verb is directional as in *kaimono ni ikimasu* 'go for shopping.' The expression of purpose takes the [N + *no tame ni*] structure when it co-occurs with verbs other than directional as in *kazoku no tame ni hataraku* 'to work for (the sake of) the family.'

■ Examples

(1) すみませんが、二時に田中さんに会いに行ってくださいませんか。
Sumimasen ga ni-ji ni Tanaka-san ni ai ni itte-kudasai-masen ka.
(Could you please go see Mr. Tanaka at two o'clock?)

(2) 日本語を勉強するために新しい教科書を買いました。

Nihongo	*o*	*benkyoo-suru*	*tame ni*	*atarashii*	*kyookasho*	*o*	*kaimashita.*
Japanese	O	study	for	new	textbook	O	bought

(I bought a new textbook in order to study Japanese.)

(3) **A:** 妹（のため）にこれ買っていこうか。
Imooto (no tame) ni kore katte-ikoo ka.
(Shall we buy this for our younger sister?)

B: うん、そうしようよ。
Un, soo shiyoo yo.
(Yeah, let's.)

(4) 自由のために戦おう。
Jiyuu no tame ni tatakaoo.
(Let us fight for the sake of freedom.)

(5) **A:** 日本へは何をしに行きますか。

Nihon	*e*	*wa*	*nani*	*o*	*shi*	*ni*	*ikimasu*	*ka.*
Japan	to	T	what	O	do	in order to	go	Q

([lit., In order to do what do you go to Japan?] For what purpose are you going to Japan?)

B: 勉強しに行きます。
Benkyoo-shi ni ikimasu.
(I'm going in order to study.)

■ Additional Information

- The expression of purpose may precede adjectival predicates. In both [Adj-*i*] and [Adj-*na*], *ni* is used. This combination takes either [N + *ni*] or [Vbasic + *no ni*]. This *no* is a nominalizer which will be discussed in Entry 105. Thus, we have *seiyoo ni ii* 'good for a rest,' and *seiyoo-suru no ni ii* 'good for resting.'

(a) スポーツはストレス解消**に**いいですね。
Supootsu wa sutoresu kaishoo ***ni*** *ii-desu ne.*
(Sports are good for relieving stress.)

(b) この部屋は本を読む**のに**いいですねえ。
Kono heya wa hon o yomu ***no ni*** *ii-desu nee.*
(This room is good for reading books.)

(c) これは小さいものを見る**のに**便利ですよ。
Kore wa chiisai mono o miru ***no ni*** *benri desu yo.*
(This is useful for looking at small items.)

- There is a similar expression *yooni* which is equivalent to the English *so that*. This use of *yooni* takes the [Vinformal non-past] form, excluding the *be*-verb.

(d) 忘れない**ように**メモをしてください。
Wasurenai ***yooni*** *memo o shite-kudasai.*
(Please take notes so that you won't forget.)

(e) 早くレポートを仕上げる**ように**がんばります。
*Hayaku repooto o shiageru **yooni** ganbarimasu.*
soon report O finish so that do my best
(I'll do my best so that I'll complete the report soon.)

■ Warning

The structure [*(no) tame ni*] also expresses cause. For example, *jiko no tame ni densha ga okuremashita* 'because of an accident, the train was late.' When [*tame ni*] expresses cause, unlike when it expresses purpose, it is preceded by the [V/Adj pre-nominal] form. [Adj pre-nominal] and [Vpre-nominal] forms are introduced in Entries 38 and 74, respectively. To determine the meaning of [*(no) tame ni*], as to whether it implies purpose or cause, it is necessary to examine the context in which it appears (this is pointed out again in Entry 77).

63. Physical Condition (1)—Hunger and Thirst

■ Target Expression

Boy, am I hungry!

おなかがすいたなあ。
Onaka ga suita naa.

■ Grammatical Explanation

I'm hungry. When expressing one's physical condition in Japanese, the actual conditions of the parts of the body are described. For example, *onaka ga suita* 'lit., (my) stomach got empty.' When describing that you are hungry now, the past tense of the verb is used as shown in the target sentence. *Onaka ga sukimasu* is possible; but this expression simply describes a universally applicable, neutral statement, as in *hataraku to onaka ga sukimasu* 'when you work, you get hungry.' Since the condition of one's stomach being empty continues when expressing 'I am hungry,' the present progressive tense form, that is, *onaka ga suite-imasu* 'lit., I am in the state of being hungry' is also used.

In masculine speech, *hara ga suita/hetta*, instead of *onaka ga suita*, may be used, although this expression is blunt and is permissible only when used among *uchi* members in very casual situations.

I'm thirsty. Another frequently used expression is *nodo ga kawakimashita* '(lit., my throat got dry) I'm thirsty.' In casual situation, *aa nodo kawaita* 'ah, am I thirsty' is useful.

Reactive description. Expressions introduced here take predicates for "reactive" description; *onaka* and *nodo* are the elements of primary predicate focus followed by *ga*, unless of course they are topicalized, in which case they are marked by *wa* (or other topic markers). The experiencer may also appear in this structure as in *watashi wa onaka ga suita* 'I am hungry.'

■ Examples

(1) **A:** のどかわいちゃったよ。
Nodo kawaichatta yo.
(I am thirsty.)

B: 私も。
Watashi mo.
(Me, too.)

A: 何か冷たいものでも飲みに行かない？
Nani-ka tsumetai mono demo nomi ni ikanai?
(Want to go out for some cold drinks or something?)

B: いいですねえ。そうしましょう。
Ii-desu nee. Soo shimashoo.
(That's a good idea. Let's do so.)

(2) **A:** ああ、腹へったなあ。 [masculine speech]
Aa, hara hetta naa.
(Boy, I'm hungry.)

B: おれも。めっちゃ腹へった。 [masculine speech]
Ore mo. Metcha hara hetta.
(Me, too. I'm starved.)

(3) **A:** おなかすいてない？
Onaka suitenai?
(Aren't you hungry?)

B: うん、ちょっとね。
Un, chotto ne.
(Yes, a little.)

■ Warning

- The direct expressions of physical condition introduced in this entry are used only by the person who experiences these conditions. Only the first-person subject can be used for affirmative and negative statements, and only the second-person subject in interrogative sentences. In Japanese a grammatical distinction is required when expressing what one can or cannot directly experience.

- In describing someone else's physical condition, you must express something like 'it seems, or it appears, that he is hungry,' that is, *kono ko wa onaka ga suiteiru yoo da* 'this child seems to be hungry.' The [*yoona*] expression will be learned later. It is important to remember that expressions such as **ano hito wa onaka ga suita* is not normally used. Of course a writer of a novel, being omniscient, may express the third-person's personal experience and feelings directly.

64. Comparative and Superlative Forms

■ Target Expression

This cell phone is newer than that one.

このケータイの方があれより新しいですよ。

Kono keetai no hoo ga are yori atarashii-desu yo.

[N + *no hoo ga* N + *yori*]

[V/Adj informal non-past + *hoo ga* V/Adj informal non-past + *yori*]

[*(no naka) de ichiban*]

■ Grammatical Explanation

Comparative and superlative forms in English call for *-er* and *-est* endings in adjectives or for the addition of the adverbs *more* and *most*. Japanese adjectives do not change forms when used in comparative and superlative expressions. Instead, for comparative and superlative purposes specific sentence patterns are used.

Comparing two items. When comparing two items, the expression [N + *no hoo*], [Vinformal non-past + *hoo*] or [Adj informal non-past + *hoo*] is used in order to point out one in comparison to the other (the word *hoo* is a noun, and it literally means 'direction').

(a) **日本の方**が小さい。
__Nihon no hoo__ ga chiisai.
(Japan is smaller.)

(b) 車で**行く方**が簡単だよ。
Kuruma de __iku hoo__ ga kantan da yo.
(It is easier to go by car.)

(c) **近い方**がいいです。
__Chikai hoo__ ga ii-desu.
(Being near is better.)

Using *yori* when comparing. When making a statement about one item in contrast to the other, *yori* is added to the item with which it is being contrasted.

(d) 日本は**フランスより**小さいです。
*Nihon wa **Huransu yori** chiisai-desu.*
(Japan is smaller than France.)

(e) 電車で行く方が**バスで行くより**速い。
*Densha de iku hoo ga **basu de iku yori** hayai.*
(Going by train is faster than going by bus.)

Superlative forms. For the superlatives, *ichiban* 'lit., number one' or *mottomo* 'most' is added to the adjectives and adverbs. The particle *de* is used to indicate the limit within which the comparison is made. When the limitation is defined in terms of members of a group, [*no naka de*] is used instead of *de*.

(f) この建物は京都**で一番/最も**古い。
*Kono tatemono wa Kyooto **de ichiban/mottomo** hurui.*
(This building is the oldest in Kyoto.)

(g) ペット**の中で**はインコが**一番**かわいいよ。

Petto	***no naka de***	*wa*	*inko*	*ga*	***ichiban***	*kawaii*	*yo.*
pet	among	T	parakeet	S	most	endearing	IP

(Among [all] pets, parakeets are the most endearing.)

***Hoo ga ii* for suggestions.** As an extension of the comparative form, another important use should be mentioned here. The structure [Vinformal (excluding negative past form) + *hoo ga ii*] is equivalent to the English pattern *had better*. For example, *hayaku iku/itta hoo ga ii-desu yo* '(lit., going early is better) you had better go early.' *Itta hoo ga ii* is considered slightly more polite than *iku hoo ga ii*. This [*hoo ga ii*] construction is used to express suggestions and advice, and we will return to this later under Entry 118.

About the same. When the compared items are thought to be equal, [*to onaji yooni/kurai ni*] is used. For example, *Sachiko mo Hiroko to onaji yooni wakai* 'Sachiko is just about as young as Hiroko.' When you need to negate the comparative statement, *hodo* '(not) to the degree' is used, as in *Sachiko wa Hiroko hodo wakakunai* 'Sachiko is not so young as Hiroko.'

Comparative questions. To form a comparative question, use the pattern [A *to* B *to dochira (no hoo) ga* Adj/Adv + V]. A and B must be nouns; when using verbs and adjectives, the nominalizer *no* must be inserted before *to*.

(h) この魚**と**あの魚**とどちら（の方）が**おいしいでしょうか。
*Kono sakana **to** ano sakana **to dochira (no hoo) ga** oishii-deshoo ka.*
(Which is more delicious, this fish or that fish?)

(i) 電車で行くの**と**バスで行くの**とどちらが**速いでしょうか。
*Densha de iku no **to** basu de iku no **to dochira ga** hayai-deshoo ka.*
(Which is quicker, going by train or going by bus?)

In casual speech, *dotchi* instead of *dochira* is used.

(j) A: たかしちゃん**と**まきちゃん**とどっちが**早く起きる？
*Takashi-chan **to** Maki-chan **to dotchi ga** hayaku okiru?*
(Who gets up earlier, Takashi or Maki?)

B: まきちゃんだよ。
Maki-chan da yo.
(Maki.)

Superlative questions. For superlative questions, the pattern [question words + grammatical particle + *ichiban*] is used: *kazoku no naka de dare ga ichiban yoku terebi o mimasu ka* 'among family members, who watches television the most?'

■ Examples

(1) 電車の方が便利だよ。
Densha no hoo ga benri da yo.
(Trains are more convenient.)

(2) 今はニューヨークの方が東京より寒いでしょう。
Ima wa Nyuuyooku no hoo ga Tookyoo yori samui-deshoo.
(Now New York is probably colder than Tokyo.)

(3) A: このクラスの学生の中で誰が一番早く来ましたか。
Kono kurasu no gakusei no naka de dare ga ichiban hayaku kimashita ka.
(Who came the earliest among all the students in this class?)

B: キャシーです。
Kyashii desu.
(Cathy did.)

(4) 早く寝た方がいいよ。
Hayaku neta hoo ga ii yo.
(You had better go to bed early.)

(5) どれが一番好き？
Dore ga ichiban suki?
(Which one do you like most?)

Additional Information

The phrase *no hoo* is often used in conversation as a softening device. For example, you might ask for coffee by saying (a). Simply by adding *no hoo*, the utterance becomes less specific, indirect, and therefore more polite.

(a) コーヒー**の方**お願いします。
Koohii ***no hoo*** *onegaishimasu.*
(Coffee, please.)

65. Expressing Desire

Target Expessions

I want money.

お金が欲しいなあ。
Okane ga hoshii naa.

I want to eat a bit more!

もうちょっと食べたい！
Moo chotto tabetai!

[*hoshii*] [Vstem + *tai* (*desu*)]
[*hoshigatte-iru*] [Vstem + *tagatte-iru*]

Grammatical Explanation

Expressing desire with nouns and verbs. Two patterns are used for expressing desire. If what one desires takes a grammatical noun, *hoshii* 'to want, to desire' is used. If what one wants involves action and it is expressed by a verb, [Vstem + *tai*] is used, except when the verb is *da*, in which case *dearu* or *de-iru* are used. The verbs used in this pattern are limited to those expressing controllable action only. *Hoshii* is an [Adj-*i*]; *-tai* is an [AuxAdj] and both conjugate as [Adj-*i*].

Tai **and** ***tagaru.*** Interesting observations must be noted in regard to the way Japanese express desire. Since desire is internal, a feeling unobservable to others, [*hoshii*] and [*-tai*] forms are used only for the first person, and in question forms for the second person.

For describing a third-person's desire, *-gatte-iru* (a present progressive form of *-garu*, a marker to indicate expression of emotion) must be added. When followed by *-gatte-iru*, the final *i* of *hoshii* and *-tai* is deleted (that is, [Adj stem]), thus we have *hoshigatte-iru* 'to want' and *tabetagatte-iru* 'to want to eat.'

This distinction is required in Japanese grammar because an epistemological distinction is made between what a person directly experiences or feels and information a person has only indirect access to. (When accompanied by other expressions meaning 'it seems,' 'it appears,' and 'they say,' it is possible to use both *hoshii* and *-tai* for the third-person subject. These expressions make the direct statement semantically indirect, and therefore do not violate the rule of "not expressing others' personal experience and feelings directly.")

Expressions of desire with particles. When expressing desire, Japanese describe the object of desire as a source that causes one to respond to it. Going back to our broader notion of subject, that is, the element of primary predicate focus, the source that causes desire is considered the information of central focus. When *hoshii* is used, the source is marked by the subject marker *ga*, unless it constitutes a topic, in which case it is marked by *wa* (or other topic markers). When the [*-tai*] expression is used, the source is marked either by *o* or *ga*, or *wa* in case of a topic. When [*hoshigatte-iru*] and [Vstem + *tagatte-iru*] are used, the source is marked by *o* (not *ga*).

In English translation, the source or the object of one's desire constitutes a grammatical object. In Japanese, desire is expressed somewhat passively—something one desires simply exists there and one responds to it. *Hoshii* and *tai* are predicates for "reactive" description and the experiencer may also appear in the form of [N + *ga*]. For example, *dare ga nomimono ga hoshii?* 'who wants something to drink?' *watashi ga (nomimono ga) hoshii* 'I want something to drink.' If the experiencer becomes the topic, an expression such as *(watashi wa) nomimono ga hoshii* is possible.

■ Examples

(1) 私は英語で話がしたい。
Watashi wa eigo de hanashi ga shitai.
(I wish to speak in English.)

だから、イギリス人かアメリカ人の友だちが欲しい。
Dakara, Igirisu-jin ka Amerika-jin no tomodachi ga hoshii.
(That's why I want a British or American friend.)

英語の本も読みたい。
Eigo no hon mo yomitai.
(I want to read English books also.)

だから、いい電子辞書も欲しい。
Dakara, ii denshi jisho mo hoshii.
(So I also want a good electronic dictionary.)

妹は中国語の本を欲しがっている。
Imooto wa Chuugokugo no hon o hoshigatte-iru.
(My younger sister wants Chinese books.)

そして、勉強するために北京へ行きたがっている。
Soshite, benkyoo-suru tame ni Pekin e ikitagatte-iru.
(And she wants to go to Beijing to study.)

■ Additional Information

Hoshii is also used in the structure [(N *ni*) V*te* + *hoshii*] to express a desire to have someone (marked by the particle *ni*) do something. This use normally occurs in the first-person declarative and the second-person interrogative.

(a) これ山田さん**に**読ん**でほしい**んですけど。
*Kore Yamada-san **ni** yon**de hoshii** n desu kedo.*[*1]
(I want Yamada to read this.)

(b) じゃ、高橋**に**すぐ行っ**てほしい**んですか。
*Ja, Takahashi **ni** sugu it**te hoshii** n desu ka.*
(Then you want Takahashi to go right away?)

*1. The *n* in the *n desu* expression is used for the purpose of making a request less blunt. We will study this use of *n(o)* later.

■ Warning

- Although in English the expression *do you want to* and *don't you want to* are informal invitations, as in *do/don't you want to go out tonight?*, the Japanese question with the [-*tai*] expression does not connote this invitational meaning. *Kon'ya dekaketai?* is a straightforward question asking if one wants to go out; it is not meant to be an invitation. To express an invitation, as we studied earlier, the non-past negative form is used; *kon'ya dekakenai?* 'won't you go out tonight?'
- Note also that the [-*tai*] expression is not normally used when addressing one's superior.

66. Physical Condition (2)—Health Problems

■ Target Expression

I have a headache.

頭が痛い。
Atama ga itai.

■ Grammatical Explanation

Describing physical conditions. When describing your physical condition, the actual condition of specific organs and body parts or their symptoms are stated. Many of these expressions take predicates for "reactive" description with the element of primary predicate focus marked with *ga*. Contrast the Japanese sentence structure presented here with the English equivalent of [I have . . .] and [I feel . . .] structures.

頭が痛い	*atama ga itai*	to have a headache
おなかが痛い	*onaka ga itai*	to have a stomachache
かぜをひく	*kaze o hiku*	to catch a cold (to express 'I have a cold,' *kaze o hiita* or *kaze o hiiteiru*.)
腰が痛い	*koshi ga itai*	to have a lower back pain
せきが出る	*seki ga deru*	to have a cough
疲れる	*tsukareru*	to be tired (to express 'I got tired' and 'I am tired,' *tsukareta* or *tsukarete-iru*.)
熱がある	*netsu ga aru*	to have a fever
のどが痛い	*nodo ga itai*	to have a sore throat
歯が痛い	*ha ga itai*	to have a toothache
腹痛がする	*hukutsuu ga suru*	to have a stomach pain (more formal than *onaka ga itai*)
病気になる	*byooki ni naru*	to become sick
目がまわる	*me ga mawaru*	to feel giddy
めまいがする	*memai ga suru*	to feel dizzy

You should be reminded here again that expressions referring to personal experiences cannot directly describe a third-person's physical condition. Adding expressions such as *-garu* or *yoona* is necessary.

■ Additional Information

There is no expression equivalent to *bless you* (said to the person who sneezes) in Japanese. Normally nothing is said. According to Japanese folklore, if you sneeze, someone is gossiping about you.

67. Verbal Predicate (7)—Spontaneous Verbs

■ Target Expression

Music is heard. (I hear music.)

音楽が聞こえます。
Ongaku ga kikoemasu.

[*kikoeru*] [*mieru*]

■ Grammatical Explanation

Non-agent orientation. As we discussed earlier regarding transitive and intransitive verbs (Entry 46), when describing an event, Japanese often prefer to express "something spontaneously happened," without focusing on "who made something happen" (refer to characteristic 10: Non-agent orientation). For example, you hear some music in the air. Rather than saying "I" hear music, the expression preferred is *ongaku ga kikoeru* '(lit., the music is audible) the music is heard.'

Spontaneous verb forms. In order to accommodate the Japanese preference for describing events spontaneously and passively, some verbs have "spontaneous" forms. Spontaneous verb forms are best understood as a special case of intransitive verbs. In English the [*be* + Vpast-participle] or [*be* + Adj] structure is used for this purpose, as in *the music is heard*. Verb spontaneous forms (for verbs that have spontaneous forms only) are derived by changing the final *-u* to *-eru* (exception: *kiku* becomes *kikoeru*). The following are frequently used examples.

Transitive Verbs			Spontaneous Intransitive Verbs		
聞く	*kiku*	→	聞こえる	*kikoeru*	to be heard
切る	*kiru*	→	切れる	*kireru*	to be cut
見る	*miru*	→	見える	*mieru*	to be seen
ぬく	*nuku*	→	ぬける	*nukeru*	to come off, to come out
焼く	*yaku*	→	焼ける	*yakeru*	to be burned, to be grilled
割る	*waru*	→	割れる	*wareru*	to be broken

The expression with structural equivalence to the English *I listen to music* is *ongaku o kikimasu*, which is possible in Japanese. *Ongaku o kiku*, however, means that a person listening to music has an intention to listen.

■ Examples

(1) 今日は富士山が見えますよ。
Kyoo wa Hujisan ga miemasu yo.
(Today Mt. Fuji is seen.)

(2) 火事でビルの七階が焼けました。
Kaji de biru no nana-kai ga yakemashita.
(Due to a fire, the seventh floor of the building was burned.)

■ Additional Information

- Although spontaneous verb forms take intransitive verb forms, there are some differences between them. When using spontaneous verbs, an event is described as spontaneously and naturally taking place. While with intransitive verbs the agent or the actor of the action is identified or assumed, with spontaneous verbs, information regarding the agent of the event is kept out of consciousness.
- The spontaneous form *mieru* may also be used as a respectful form of *kuru* 'to come.' For example, in describing the teacher coming to visit you, *sensei ga miemashita* 'the teacher came,' instead of *sensei ga kimashita*. We will discuss respectful forms in Entry 86.

68. Personal Preference

■ Target Expression

Do you like classical music?

クラシック音楽は好きですか。
Kurashikku ongaku wa suki desu ka.

[*sukina*] [*kiraina*]

■ Grammatical Explanation

What you like and don't like. Personal preference or dislike are expressed by the *na*-type adjective *sukina* 'favorite' and *kiraina* 'dislike.' Again, what one likes takes *ga*; the source of one's preference is the element of primary predicate focus. The way to understand this structure may be to put the target sentence into a different English expression, that is, *classical music is preferred*. For expressing dislike for something, a *na*-type adjective *kiraina* 'disliked' is used, co-occurring with [N + *ga*]. *Sukina* and *kiraina* follow the conjugation of [Adj-*na*], that is, it follows *da* conjugation. For emphatic purposes, the prefix *dai-* may be added to both *sukina* and *kiraina*. For example, *chokoreeto ga daisuki desu* 'I like chocolate a lot.'

***Sukina* and *kiraina* as reactive description.** *Sukina* and *kiraina* are predicates for "reactive" description. In the target sentence, the noun *kurashikku ongaku* is what is preferred, which is the element of primary predicate focus. Recall that any noun phrase can become a topic, and if so chosen, *wa* (or other topic markers) replaces *ga* in the process. Since the target sentence is a question about classical music, it is chosen to be the topic; thus, it is marked by *wa*.

***Sukina* and *kiraina* for modification.** Also to be noted is that *sukina* and *kiraina* (including *daisukina* and *daikiraina*) can modify nouns, and so can their negative counterparts, *suki de(wa)-nai* and *kirai de(wa)-nai*; for example, *sukina hito* 'my favorite person,' and *suki de(wa)-nai tabemono* '(lit., disliked food) food I do not like.'

■ Examples

(1) **A:** 音楽はどんなのを聞きますか。
Ongaku wa donna no o kikimasu ka.
(What kind of music do you listen to?)

B: 私はジャズが好き。
Watashi wa jazu ga suki.
(As for myself, I like jazz.)

(2) **A:** 食べものは何が好きですか。
Tabemono wa nani ga suki desu ka.
(As for food, what do you like?)

B: さしみが好きです。
Sashimi ga suki desu.
(I like *sashimi*.)

(3) 今でもあの人が好き。
Ima de mo ano hito ga suki.
(Even now I like [love] him.)

(4) **A:** アメリカのビール、好き?
Amerika no biiru, suki?
(Do you like American beer?)

B: ええ、もちろん。
Ee, mochiron.
(Yes, of course.)

(5) **A:** あのう、何かきらいな食べもの(が)ありますか。
Anoo, nani-ka kiraina tabemono (ga) arimasu ka.
(Do you have any food that you dislike?)

B: いいえ、何も（ありません）。
Iie, nani mo (arimasen).
(No, I don't.)

■ Additional Information

For the expression with structural equivalence to the English *I like/dislike to do something,* use [Vinformal non-past + *no* + *ga* + *sukina*/*kiraina*] structure. For example, *kurashikku ongaku o kiku no ga suki* 'I like to listen to classical music.' The use of this *no*, called "nominalizer," will be discussed further in Entry 105.

69. Listener Responses in Conversation

■ Target Expressions

yeah, uh-huh, I see

はい、うん、なるほど
hai, un, naruhodo

■ Strategic Explanation

Responding as a listener. As listeners, Japanese display a great deal of feedback. Frequent head nods and much encouraging chatter are sent from a Japanese conversation partner. The brief utterances such as *un* 'uh-huh,' *huun* 'I see' and other nonverbal signs such as nods called *aizuchi* (listener response or back-channel expressions) occur frequently. This listener activity is thought to be good manners. In general, Japanese speakers send many more frequent listener responses. Japanese speakers may feel uneasy when speaking to an American who just listens quietly, even if he or she listens attentively.

When to send *aizuchi*. In casual conversation it is important to send *aizuchi* when the speaker pauses and at the point where the speaker uses particles and tag-like auxiliary verbs. The speaker's request for listener response is frequently expressed by (1) final particles such as *ne*, (2) auxiliary tags such as *-desho?*, and (3) brief questions such as *soo omowanai?* 'don't you think so?' Some listener responses occur concurrently with speakers' head nods which often indicate the end of the utterance.

Different types of listener responses.

1. *Expressing confirmation*:

そうですか。	*Soo desu ka.*	I see.
そうですね。	*Soo desu ne.*	That's right.
やっぱり。	*Yappari.*	That's what I thought.
なるほど。	*Naruhodo.*	I see. [used when resolving doubt]

2. *Showing one's attention*:

うん。	*Un.*	Uh-huh. [casual style]
ふーん。	*Huun.*	I see.
そう。	*Soo.*	Right.
はい。/ええ。	*Hai./Ee.*	Yeah. Yes.

3. *Expressing reservation or doubt*:

さあ。	*Saa.*	Well ...
(まあ) たぶん。	*(Maa) tabun.*	Perhaps ...
そうですかねえ……	*Soo desu ka nee ...*	Well, I am not sure ...
そう？	*Soo?*	Really?
そうかなあ……	*Soo ka naa ...*	I wonder ...

4. *Showing surprise*:

ええ？	*Ee?*	What?
ほんと？	*Honto?*	Really?
うそ！	*Uso!*	You're kidding. [casual style]
まさか！	*Masaka!*	It can't be. Nonsense!
まじ？	*Maji?*	Seriously? [casual style]

5. *Offering sympathy*:

困りましたねえ。	*Komarimashita nee.*	It's a problem, isn't it?
弱ったなあ。	*Yowatta naa.*	Oh, boy, what trouble!
残念だねえ。	*Zannen da nee.*	Sorry to hear that. That's too bad.
かわいそうに。	*Kawaisooni.*	Poor thing. That's pitiful.
気の毒に。	*Kinodokuni.*	I'm sorry to hear that.

■ Additional Information

- In Japanese casual conversation, non-verbal signs like nodding are frequently used as listener responses. Non-verbal communication is very important in any culture. We will study only limited aspects of non-verbal signs in this book.
- One point of importance relating to non-verbal signs should be noted. Under normal circumstances, Japanese do not constantly look directly into the eyes of the person they are talking to. Sustained eye-contact (which is normally avoided) can be an expression of confrontation or suspicion. Avoid looking constantly

into the eyes of your Japanese listener. As a listener, you should also avoid too much eye contact. Especially if the speaker is your social superior, staring into your superior's eyes consistently is considered rude. Look toward the speaker and cast your eyes in the general area of the speaker's neck and shoulders as you look into your partner's eyes from time to time. Contrast this with American culture where gazing steadfastly into the eyes of one's partners is by and large thought to be positive behavior. In fact, averting your eyes in American culture somehow makes you a suspicious person, sometimes to the extent that saying someone is shifty-eyed is to practically say that the person is a crook.

- You might be interested in knowing that the Japanese word for social superior is *meue* (lit., above eye level) while social inferiors are called *meshita* (lit., below eye level). The right to gaze freely is granted to social superiors; continuous gaze is more permissible from higher to lower eye level, i.e., from superiors to subordinates but not vice versa.
- *Maji* is used frequently in casual conversation. *Maji* and *maji de* are used independently, or as adverbs as shown below.

(a) **A:** マジ？
Maji?
(Seriously?)
B: マジ。
Maji.
(Yes, seriously.)

(b) **A:** まじですか。
Maji desu ka.
(Are you serious?)
B: まじで。
Maji de.
(Yes, I am.)

(c) ほんと、マジ、ごめん。
Honto, maji, gomen.
(Really, I'm really sorry.)

(d) マジむずかしい。
Maji muzukashii.
([Honestly,] it's really difficult.)

70. Adverbs (3)—Sentential Adverbs

■ Target Expression

> *You won't be in time anyway.*
>
> **どうせ間に合わないだろう。**
>
> ***Doose maniawanai daroo.***

■ Grammatical Explanation

Expressing attitude. Some Japanese adverbs do not directly modify the verb. Instead, they express the speaker's attitude toward what is being talked about. These are similar to English sentential adverbs, such as *regrettably* as in *regrettably, the concert was canceled due to the illness of the performer*. These adverbs convey an emotional or evaluative attitude toward the statement.

Marking cohesive elements. Another type of sentential adverb functions primarily as a cohesive element in discourse. For example, *tsumari* 'in order words' signals that what is coming is a paraphrase of what was just said.

For sentential adverbs that mark discourse cohesion, the discourse context in which they occur has a direct bearing on their meaning. Cohesive devices such as *tatoeba* 'for example' and *tsugini* 'next' are useful when you connect a group of utterances, especially when you take a long speaking turn expressing complex thoughts and opinions.

Some Sentential Adverbs

いったい	*ittai*	how, what, why on earth (in the world)
せっかく	*sekkaku*	with much trouble and effort
どうせ	*doose*	anyway, after all
やっと	*yatto*	at last, with difficulty
すなわち	*sunawachi*	in other words
たとえば	*tatoeba*	for example
次に	*tsugini*	next
とにかく	*tonikaku*	at any rate

***Sekkaku* and its meaning.** As an example, let's concentrate on the use of *sekkaku* and *doose*. *Sekkaku* is frequently attached when you express the feeling that although you've made a special effort, you didn't achieve what you wanted.

(a) **せっかく**行ったのに留守でした。

Sekkaku	*itta*	*noni*	*rusu*	*deshita.*
purposefully	went	despite	absence	was

(Although I went there for the [explicit] purpose of seeing them, they weren't in.)

As an extension to this basic meaning, *sekkaku* is used to express the feeling that a subsequent action ought to follow because it is performed with some degree of purpose or sacrifice.

(b) **せっかく**アメリカまで行くのだから、ニューヨークへも行きたいです。
Sekkaku *Amerika made iku no da kara*[*1], *Nyuuyooku e mo ikitai-desu.*
(Since I am going purposefully [all the way] to America, I want to get to New York, too.)

*1. The *no* in *no da kara* will be studied later (Entry 105).

Doose **and its meaning.** The sentential adverb *doose* expresses the speaker's emotional attitude—resignation to an unfavorable yet unavoidable fate or fact.

(c) **どうせ**間に合わないだろう。
Doose *maniawanai daroo.*
(I probably won't be in time anyway.)

More specifically, *doose* in (c) is a device to directly express the speaker's attitude, i.e., 'well, I won't be in time anyway, although I wish it were otherwise, but, anyway, I cannot change the fact.'

71. Verbs of Giving and Receiving

■ Target Expression

Mr. Turner gave me this map.

ターナーさんがこの地図をくださいました。
Taanaa-san ga kono chizu o kudasaimashita.

[*kureru*] [*ageru*] [*morau*]

■ Grammatical Explanation

Kureru, ageru, **and** ***morau.*** Japanese verbs of giving and receiving involve elements not necessarily significant in English. First, depending on who receives, two different types of verbs of giving are used. If you are the receiver, or someone in your *uchi* group is the receiver, the verb chosen for expressing 'to give' is *kureru*; Someone 'gives' *kureru* something to self or the member of self's group. On the other hand, if you or a member of your group is not the receiver, for the expression 'to give' something to someone, *ageru* is used. Simply put, if someone else gives you an object, use *kureru*. When you give something to someone, use *ageru*. For the verb of receiving, *morau* is used regardless of whether you receive, or someone else receives.

Different forms of *kureru, ageru,* and *morau.* Second, depending on the relative social status of the participants and the person who is mentioned in the description of the giving/receiving event, different verb forms are chosen. For each *kureru*, *ageru*, and *morau*, the following additional expressions are available.

Verbs of Giving and Receiving

Verbs		Social status of the giver and receiver
kureru (someone gives to self)		
くださる	*kudasaru*	giver is higher
くれる	*kureru*	giver is equal
くれる	*kureru*	giver is lower
ageru (self or other gives to someone)		
さしあげる	*sashiageru*	giver is lower
あげる	*ageru*	giver is equal
やる	*yaru*	giver is higher
morau (self or other receives from someone)		
いただく	*itadaku*	receiver is lower
もらう	*morau*	receiver is equal
もらう	*morau*	receiver is higher

Giving/receiving and social relationship. To recapitulate, consider that the transferance of an object or service can be described in two ways. First, we can say that A gives it to B. Second, the same incident can be reported from the receiver's point of view, in which case the main verb to describe this incident is that B receives something from A. But in Japanese, there is an additional dimension. Recall the tendency of Japanese to identify with *uchi* members. If the object or service is transferred from a *soto* member to an *uchi* member (including self), that incident must be described as giving-to-me. Your empathy as you describe this incident is with the *uchi* member, the receiver. It is not grammatically correct to say someone *ageru* something to me or to the *uchi* member. Instead, the other verb, *kureru*, must be used.

If the transaction occurs between self and other members of the *uchi* group, use *kureru* to describe when someone else gives you something, and use *ageru* when you are giving something to another. If the transaction occurs between *uchi* members other than self, *ageru* is chosen for expressing 'to give.'

Case markers for giving and receiving. For describing the giver (G), receiver (R), and the things exchanged (T), the following case markers are used:

[G *ga* R *ni* T *o kudasaru/kureru*]
[G *ga* R *ni* T *o sashiageru/ageru/yaru*]
[R *ga* G *ni/kara* T *o itadaku/morau*]

Choosing between *ni* and *kara*. The particle *ni* is preferred when the receiver has direct personal contact with the giver, whereas the particle *kara* is preferred when the source is somewhat impersonal. Thus, *daigaku kara shoogakukin o morau* 'to receive a scholarship from the university' versus *chichi ni okane o morau* 'to receive money from one's father.'

■ Examples

(1) 先生がこの本をくださいました。

Sensei	*ga*	*kono*	*hon*	*o*	*kudasaimashita.*
teacher	S	this	book	O	gave-to-me

(The teacher gave this book to me.)

(2) 妹は先生にこれをいただきました。

Imooto	*wa*	*sensei*	*ni*	*kore*	*o*	*itadakimashita.*
younger sister	T	teacher	from	this	O	received

(My sister received this from the teacher.)

(3) 花に水をやってくださいね。
Hana ni mizu o yatte-kudasai ne.
(Please give some water to the flowers.)

(4) 弟は妹にプレゼントをもらった。
Otooto wa imooto ni purezento o moratta.
(My younger brother received a present from my sister.)

■ Additional Information

There is another verb, *ataeru* 'to give' in Japanese. *Ataeru* is used only when the giver has a higher social status than the receiver. When a giver is of a significantly higher social status, *sazukeru* 'award, confer' is used. Both *ataeru* and *sazukeru* are primarily used in written Japanese.

(a) 妹はむだ使いするのに母はいつも金を**与える**。

Imooto	*wa*	*mudazukai*	*o*	*suru*	*noni*	*haha*	*wa*	*itsumo*
sister	T	wasteful spending	O	do	despite	mother	T	always

kane	*o*	***ataeru.***
money	O	give

(Although my younger sister wastes money, my mother always gives her some.)

72. Action-accompanying Expressions (1) —When Giving and Receiving Gifts

■ Target Expression

Here's a little something for you, it's not much but …

つまらないものですが……

Tsumaranai mono desu ga …

■ Strategic Explanation

When giving a gift. Expressions such as *here's something for you* or *I thought you might like this* are used when giving a gift in America. In Japan, in formal situations, particularly toward one's superiors, expressions to minimize the value of the gift are often used. For example, in formal gift-giving, as one presents the formal gift in both hands (using both hands conveys politeness and sincerity), one might say, *makoto ni tsumaranai mono desu ga* … 'lit., this isn't of much value, but …'

When receiving a gift. The potential gift receiver may refuse it initially as a part of a ritual by saying *konna koto o shite-itadaite* … 'lit., I don't deserve such a favor …' or *ii n desu yo, sonnani ki o tsukatte-itadakanakute* … 'it isn't necessary to be so kind and considerate …' However, to really refuse a gift is considered an ultimate insult in Japan. The second time around the potential receiver may answer, *jaa sekkaku desu kara* 'lit., well since you went to all the trouble of giving me this gift, I will thankfully receive this ….'

Casual gift giving. Between good friends and in familiar personal relationships, this ritual is frequently ignored, especially when what is presented is a personal and small gift. It is useful nonetheless to be aware of the ritual of formally giving and receiving a gift in Japan. It should also be mentioned that when visiting a friend or family, it is polite to bring some small gift (*(o)miyage*). Perishable items such as sweets, fruits, or beverages are recommended. This is not considered a personal gift (*okurimono*); it just expresses consideration and appreciation to the host or hostess.

■ Examples

(1) **A:** つまらないものですが……
Tsumaranai mono desu ga ...
(This is just something for you.)

B: すみませんねえ、気をつかっていただいて……
Sumimasen nee, ki o tsukatte-itadaite ...
(Thank you for your kindness and consideration ...

A: いいえ、ほんの少しですから。
Iie, honno sukoshi desu kara.
(Oh, it is just a small amount.)

B: ではありがたく頂戴いたします。どうもすみません。
Dewa arigataku choodai-itashimasu. Doomo sumimasen.
(Well then, I accept your kindness. Thank you very much.)

(2) **A:** これ、プレゼント。
Kore, purezento.
(This is for you.)

B: わあ、開けていい？
Waa, akete ii?
(Wow, can I open it?)

A: もちろん。
Mochiron.
(Of course.)

B: かわいーい！ サンキュ！ [feminine speech]
Kawaiii! Sankyu!
(How cute! Thanks!)

■ Additional Information

Twice a year Japanese ritually give formal gifts to people whose care or guidance they are under. For example, students (actually parents of students) give gifts to *juku* 'private cram school' teachers. Service industry agents frequently send gifts to clients and patrons. The summer gift-giving is called *ochuugen*, and the winter gift-giving is called *oseibo*.

73. Giving and Receiving Favorable Actions

■ Target Expressions

My friend kindly helped me.

友だちが手伝ってくれました。
Tomodachi ga tetsudatte-kuremashita.

I had my teacher write a letter of recommendation.

先生に推薦状を書いていただきました。
Sensei ni suisenjoo o kaite-itadakimashita.

[V*te* + *-kureru*]
[V*te* + *-ageru*]
[V*te* + *-morau*]

■ Grammatical Explanation

Te-ageru. When favorable actions are performed for the benefit of someone (and occasionally for bringing damage to someone), it is customary to express the benefit by using the various levels of verbs of giving and receiving we studied earlier. The [V*te*] form precedes the verbs of giving and receiving: thus, we have *kaite-ageru* 'give the favorable action of writing,' that is, 'to write something for someone's benefit.' Among verbs, the *be*-verb *da* must be changed to *de-iru*; for example, *tomodachi de-ite-ageru* 'to be friends with someone for his or her benefit.'

Te-morau* and *te-kureru. If the action is performed for yourself or for *uchi* members, and you express the action from the recipient's point of view, *kaite-morau* 'receive the favorable action of writing,' that is, 'have someone write something for me' is useful. If the action is performed for yourself or *uchi* members and if you are describing the action from the point of view of the person who is doing the giving, *kaite-kureru* 'give (to self) the favorable action of writing,' that is, '(she kindly) wrote this for me' is appropriate. Describing events in terms of favors given for the benefit of others is obligatory in Japanese. Expressions without the [V*te* + *-kureru*] structure, for example, **tomodachi ga tetsudaimashita,* instead of *tomodachi ga tetsudatte-kuremashita,* are awkward; the appropriate verb choice for giving and receiving is a must.

Different forms of *te-ageru, te-morau,* and *te-kureru.* The specific verb of giving and receiving chosen for this structure depends on the relative social status of the giver and the receiver. The appropriate verb should be chosen depending on the social status of participants and referents involved from the group we learned earlier. For example, if the action of writing is performed by a superior, and the event is described as 'receiving,' the verb selected is *itadaku*, which is the case demonstrated in the second of the target expressions. Note also that in sentences using the verb *morau*, the indirect object, that is, the person who performs the action, is marked by *ni*.

Characteristics of [V*te* + *-ageru*], [V*te* + *-kureru*], and [V*te* + *-morau*]. Characteristics of the three relationships of giving and receiving, [V*te* + *-ageru*], [V*te* + *-kureru*], and [V*te* + *-morau*] along with extended uses are given below.

1. [V*te* + *-ageru*]:
   Describes self-performed, other-influencing action; conveys doing a favor, occasionally disfavor, strong will, and sometimes as an extended use, a feeling of self-abandonment.

   (1a) この本、読ん**であげる**ね。 [favor]
   *Kono hon, yon**de-ageru** ne.*
   (I will read this book [for you].)

   (1b) 弟がうるさいのでなぐっ**てやった**。 [disfavor]
   *Otooto ga urusai node nagu**tte-yatta**.*
   (I hit my younger brother since he is bothersome.)

   (1c) いつかきっとピアノのコンクールで一等をとっ**てやる**。 [strong will]
   *Itsuka kitto piano no konkuuru de ittoo o to**tte-yaru**.*
   (Sometime I will win the first-prize in the piano contest.)

   (1d) 結婚を許してくれない。死ん**でやる**! [self-abandonment]
   *Kekkon o yurushite-kurenai. Shin**de-yaru**!*
   (They don't approve of my marriage. I'm going to die!)

2. [V*te* + *-kureru*]:
   Describes other-performed, self-benefiting, occasionally disfavorable and damaging action; expresses the feeling of thankfulness or occasionally regret.

   (2a) 友だちが本を貸し**てくれた**。 [favor]
   *Tomodachi ga hon o kashi**te-kureta**.*
   (My friend [kindly] loaned me a book.)

3. [V*te* + *-morau*]:
   Describes self-benefiting action; expresses that the action was performed by another, but beneficial to self, and such action is often requested by self.

   (3a) 友だちに傘を貸し**てもらった**。 [favor]
   *Tomodachi ni kasa o kashi**te-moratta**.*
   (I had my friend loan me an umbrella.)

■ Examples

(1) **A:** この推薦状は？
Kono suisenjoo wa?
(How about this letter of recommendation?)

B: ああ、それは山下先生が書いてくださいました。
Aa, sore wa Yamashita-sensei ga kaite-kudasaimashita.
(Oh, that one ... Professor Yamashita wrote it for me.)

(2) **A:** 弟さんの誕生日のパーティーはどうでしたか。
Otootosan no tanjoobi no paatii wa doo deshita ka.
(How was your younger brother's birthday party?)

B: 弟は父におもちゃを買ってもらって結構喜んでいました。
Otooto wa chichi ni omocha o katte-moratte kekkoo yorokonde-imashita.
(My younger brother had my father buy him toys, and he was quite pleased.)

(3) **A:** これ誰がしてくれた？
Kore dare ga shite-kureta?
(Who did this [for me]?)

B: ゆうちゃん。
Yuu-chan.
(Yuu [did].)

(4) **A:** 田中さんにそのニュース知らせてあげた？
Tanaka-san ni sono nyuusu shirasete-ageta?
(Did you [kindly] notify Tanaka of the news?)

B: うん、メッチャ喜んでたよ。 [casual style]
Un, metcha yorokondeta yo.
(Yes, she was really pleased.)

■ Additional Information

- When the verbs of giving and receiving accompany verbs, they imply that the action that took place is, in some way, involved with the recipient's interest. In asking a question 'who did this?,' if no personal interest is involved, a speaker would ask *kore dare ga shita no?* However, if there is either a positive or negative influence to personal interest, *kore dare ga shite-kureta no?* is preferred. Depending on the context, this latter expression can imply gratitude or reprimand.
- Because of the implication of personal interest, special care is required when using [V*te* + *-ageru*] expression. When used in a question like *kore katte-agemashoo ka?* 'shall I buy this for you?,' the listener may resent it. This expression gives an impression that since the listener is helpless and is perhaps incapable of performing the action, he or she must receive charity from the other. A thoughtful Japanese will use instead *kore kaimashoo ka?* 'shall I buy this?'

- The [V*te* + *-morau*] structure is often used as an expression of request.

(a) これをコピーし**てもらいたい**んですけど……
*Kore o kopii-shi**te-moraitai** n desu kedo ...*
(I would like you to make a copy of this ...)

(b) それは山田さんか木下さんに教え**てもらって**ください。
*Sore wa Yamada-san ka Kinoshita-san ni oshie**te-moratte**-kudasai.*
(Please have either Mr. Yamada or Mr. Kinoshita teach that to you.)

(c) 推薦状を書い**ていただけません**でしょうか。
*Suisenjoo o kai**te-itadakemasen**-deshoo ka.**1
(Would it be possible for you to write a letter of recommendation?)

*1. *Itadakemasu* is the formal version of *itadakeru*, which is a potential form of *itadaku*.

Note that in (b), the person who is requested to perform the action is marked by an indirect object marker *ni*. We have studied a similar use of *ni* with another request expression in Entry 65, namely, [V*te* + *hoshii*].

- *Te-morau* frequently appears in *te-moratte ii desu ka* as an expression of request. This form is widely used as a polite request, but should not be used toward your social superiors (*te-itadakemasen-deshoo ka* should be used instead).

(d) これ、貸し**てもらっていいですか**。
*Kore, kashi**te-moratte ii desu ka**.*
(Is it OK if I borrow this?)

(e) ここに書い**てもらっていいですか**。
*Koko ni kai**te-moratte ii desu ka**.*
(Could you write it here?)

74. Predicate with Explanatory Mode—*No da, N da,* and *Wake da*

■ Target Expression

(What took you so long?)
(It's that) I went to the bank.

銀行へ行ってきたんです。
Ginkoo e itte-kita n desu.

[V/Adj pre-nominal + *no*/*wake* + *da*]

Grammatical Explanation

Offering explanations, etc. Predicates with explanatory mode are expressed by two similar forms; (1) placing *no*, or its colloquial version *n*, and (2) placing *wake* 'reason' before the *be*-verb *da*. When adding *no/n* or *wake*, use [Adj pre-nominal] forms, directly preceding *no* and *wake*. (See [Adj pre-nominal] forms given in Entry 38.) When [V] precedes *no* and *wake*, use [Vpre-nominal] forms, which are given below, except when *no* is preceded by [N + *da*] structure. In that case, use only [N + *na no*] construction. In using the *wake da* expression, when it is preceded by the [N + *da*] structure, use [N + *no wake da*] or [N + *to yuu wake da*].

Verb Pre-nominal Forms

Verbs:		
informal non-past	泳ぐ	*oyogu*
informal past	泳いだ	*oyoida*
negative informal non-past	泳がない	*oyoganai*
negative informal past	泳がなかった	*oyoganakatta*
Existential verbs:		
informal non-past	いる、ある	*iru, aru*
informal past	いた、あった	*ita, atta*
negative informal non-past	いない、ない	*inai, nai*
negative informal past	いなかった、なかった	*inakatta, nakatta*
Be-verb:		
informal non-past	の	*no* (instead of *da*)
informal past	だった	*datta*
negative informal non-past	ではない	*dewa-nai*
negative informal past	ではなかった	*dewa-nakatta*

Extended predicate. Since there is already a main verb, adding these phrases "extends" the predicate, and therefore the [*no da*] and [*wake da*] structures are called "extended predicates." Although the extended predicate may sound redundant when translated into English, i.e., 'it is (the case) that,' or 'it is for the reason that,' this structure is used quite commonly in Japanese and needs to be learned with care.

Basic functions of *n(o) da*. The basic function of [*n(o) da*] is to appeal to the assumed common understanding or knowledge shared between the speaker and the listener. When such common knowledge does not exist, [*n(o) da*] is used to describe the information as if the knowledge were shared; it encourages emotional rapport since it assumes that they share the same information.

Three functions of *n(o) da.* There are at least three related but distinct functions of extended predicates as listed below.

1. To signal that what precedes *no da* offers the reason or cause related to the issue at hand.

(1a) A: 最近戸田さんをあまり見かけませんが……
Saikin Toda-san o amari mikakemasen ga . . .
(I haven't seen Ms. Toda recently . . .)

B: ああ、戸田さんは病気だった**んです**よ。
Aa, Toda-san wa byooki datta ***n desu*** *yo.*
(Oh, Ms. Toda has been ill.)

2. To emphasize what precedes *no da.*

(2a) A: どうしたんですか。 [idiomatic]
Doo shita n desu ka.
(What happened to you?)

B: スーパーへ行ったんですが、(お)さしみはもう売り切れだった**んです**。
Suupaa e itta n desu ga, (o)sashimi wa moo urikire datta ***n desu.***
(I went to the supermarket, but *sashimi* was sold out.)

3. To present the request in a milder tone.

(3a) 今日少し早く帰りたい**んです**けど……
Kyoo sukoshi hayaku kaeritai ***n desu*** *kedo . . .*
(I would like to leave a little earlier today . . .)

Functions of *wake da.* *Wake da* is used in the manner similar to the first use of *no da* described above (*wake* is a noun, meaning 'reason'). When a speaker intends to explain a reason, cause, or circumstance which leads to the known result or conclusion, *wake da* is used. *Wake da* is often used to explain something one might have wondered about, and may be best described by the English expression *that means* . . . or *no wonder* . . . .

(a) あそこは工事中ですか。それで車が通れない**わけです**ね。
Asoko wa koojichuu desu ka. Sore de kuruma ga toorenai ***wake desu*** *ne.*
(Oh, that place is under construction. That's why it is closed to automobiles.)

Extended functions. It should be noted that *no da* and *wake da* are often used even when the reason and cause are not strongly implied and/or when strong emphasis is not evident. This additional use occurs when the speaker or writer wishes to point out some facts, and when he or she wishes the listener to realize the special, important meaning that statement carries.

Extended predicates in conversation. Let us examine the dialogue example below to understand how extended predicates are used to express emphasis and reason for the previous statement.

(b) A: どうして人がたくさん集まっている**んです**か。
*Dooshite hito ga takusan atsumatte-iru **n desu** ka.*
(Why are there so many people gathered?)

B: 人気のある歌手が来る**んです**。
*Ninki no aru kashu ga kuru **n desu**.*

A: ああ、それで女の人がたくさんいる**わけです**ね。
*Aa, sore de onna no hito ga takusan iru **wake desu** ne.*
(Oh, I see, no wonder there are many women here.)

In this dialogue, A first uses *n desu* to catch attention, B uses *n desu* to provide reason for the question, and A uses *wake desu* to convey a reason for the known result.

■ Additional Information

- The extended predicate may be shortened by eliminating *da/desu*, leaving only *no*. With rising intonation placed at *no*, for example, *ashita iku no?* 'are you going tomorrow?' is a shortened version of *ashita iku no desu ka?*, and functions as a question.
- The extended predicate in the pattern *soo na n da* is used to convey an understanding of what the speaker is trying to get across, meaning, 'I see what you mean.' It is frequently used as a listener response.

(a) A: これ買ったの？
Kore katta no?
(Did you buy this?)

B: 弟にもらった。
Otooto ni moratta.
(I got it from my younger brother.)

A: **そうなんだ**。
Soo na n da.
(I see.)

75. Expressions of Potential and Ability

■ Target Expressions

Can you speak French?

フランス語を話すことができますか。
Huransugo o hanasu koto ga dekimasu ka.
フランス語が話せますか。
Huransugo ga hanasemasu ka.
フランス語 話せる?
Huransugo hanaseru?
フランス語できる?
Huransugo dekiru?

[N + *ga dekiru*]
[Vbasic + *koto ga dekiru*]
potential [V + *-eru*/*-rareru*]

■ Grammatical Explanation

Koto ga dekiru. The expression of ability is achieved by two different methods. First, the [*koto ga dekiru*] pattern is attached immediately after the [Vbasic] form. *Koto* 'thing(s)' functions as a nominalizer and *dekiru* literally means 'can do.' Thus, *hanasu koto ga dekiru* '(I) can speak.' For the *be*-verb *da, de-iru* is used when co-occurring with [*koto ga dekiru*]. *Dekiru,* which is a potential form of the irregular verb *suru,* may be used with a noun as in:

(a) 飛行機の操縦が**できます**。
Hikooki *no* *soojuu* *ga* ***dekimasu.***
airplane L control S can do
(I can fly [lit., control] an airplane.)

Potential verb forms. Second, potential and ability are expressed by potential verb endings which are formed as shown below.

U-verbs: replace the final *-u* with *-eru*.

書く	*kak**u***	to write	→	書ける	*kak**eru***
遊ぶ	*asob**u***	to play	→	遊べる	*asob**eru***

(Exception: *yuu* 'to say' changes into *ieru*. Remember to consider *yuu* as *iu* for conjugation purposes.)

RU-verbs: replace the final *-ru* with *-rareru*.

食べる	*tabe**ru***	to eat	→	食べられる	*tabe**rareru***
起きる	*oki**ru***	to get up	→	起きられる	*oki**rareru***

As an alternative to this change, the final *-ru* of the potential form may be replaced by *-reru*. These expressions are called *ranuki kotoba* (*ra*-deleted phrases) and are more frequently used by the younger generation.

食べる	*tabe**ru***	to eat	→	食べれる	*tabe**reru***
起きる	*oki**ru***	to get up	→	起きれる	*oki**reru***

Irregular verbs:

来る	***kuru***	to come	→	来られる、来れる	***korareru**, **koreru***
する	***suru***	to do	→	できる	***dekiru***

Potential form of *iru*. Among existential verbs, *iru* meaning 'to stay' has the potential form *irareru* 'can stay.' The verb *da* does not have a potential form; instead, *de-iru* is used with its potential form *de-irareru* 'can be.'

Potential verb forms and *ga*. When using the potential expression *dekiru*, which is a verb for "reactive" description, the *ga* marked noun, the thing a person can do, is the element of the primary predicate focus. For example, as shown in the target expression, *Huransugo ga hanaseru* means that someone is good at speaking French, and *Huransugo ga dekiru* means that someone has a full capacity to function in the French language.

For the [*koto ga dekiru*] structure, the particle *o* marks what a person can do within the clause preceding *koto*. Still, the *koto* clause itself is marked by *ga* as in *Nihongo o hanasu koto ga dekiru* 'I can speak Japanese.'

Potential verb forms and *o*. When the potential verb reflects the speaker's volition, what one can do may be optionally marked by *o*. In this case what one can perform is considered a grammatical object rather than the *ga*-marked element of primary predicate focus.

■ Examples

(1) A: ジムさんは車の運転ができますか。

Jimu-san	*wa*	*kuruma*	*no*	*unten*	*ga*	*dekimasu*	*ka.*
Jim	T	car	L	driving	S	can do	Q

(Jim, can you drive the car?)

B: ええ。

Ee.

(Yes.)

(2) **A:** ゆうべよく眠れた？
Yuube yoku nemureta?
(Could you sleep well last night?)

B: うん、よく眠れたよ。
Un, yoku nemureta yo.
(Yes, I could sleep well.)

(3) **A:** 弟さんはゴルフもテニスもできますね。
Otootosan wa goruhu mo tenisu mo dekimasu ne.
(Your younger brother can play both golf and tennis, can't he?)

B: ええ、スポーツはなんでもできるんですよ。
Ee, supootsu wa nan demo dekiru n desu yo.
(Yes. He does well in all sports.)

(4) **A:** 中川さんって、結婚した？
Nakagawa-san tte, kekkon-shita?
(Did Mr. Nakagawa get married?)

B: いいえ、まだです。
Iie, mada desu.
(No, not yet.)

A: でもずっと独身でいることはできないよね？
Demo zutto dokushin de-iru koto wa dekinai yo ne?
(But he won't be able to remain a bachelor indefinitely, will he?)

B: どうでしょうかねえ。
Doo deshoo ka nee.
(I wonder about that.)

■ Additional Information

- Some potential forms are also used for passive and respectful forms as will be explained later, and, therefore, it is extremely important to learn their conjugation at this point.
- For some verbs, potential forms and the spontaneous forms are identical; for example, *kireru* 'to be able to cut,' *mieru* 'to be able to see,' *wareru* 'to be able to break,' and so forth. When potential forms are used, normally the persons who are capable of the stated action are specified or at least assumed. When spontaneous verbs are used, the actor is not stated and is not in the consciousness of the speaker. In using potential forms, the speaker's intention to perform the act must be presumed. Therefore as shown in (a) when the matter is beyond the speaker's control, the spontaneous verb form is used. Since (b) indicates intention, the spontaneous form is not appropriate.

(a) 相手の声が小さくて**聞こえない**。
*Aite no koe ga chiisakute **kikoenai**.*
(My companion's voice is so small and it isn't heard.)

(b) *相手の声が小さくて聞けない。
Aite no koe ga chiisakute kikenai.

- Another difference between spontaneous and potential forms lies in the fact that while spontaneous verbs can occur in the [V*te* + *-iru*] form, i.e., *kirete-imasu* 'is in the state of having been cut,' the potential form cannot. Since the potential form of the verb describes the state rather than the action, it seems natural that it is less likely to take the [V*te* + *-iru*] form.

■ Warning

Although we have translated Japanese potential expressions into English *can* in this entry, you must avoid expressing the English *can* into Japanese potential forms unless you have given it careful scrutiny. This is because the English *can* is used not only for potential expressions but for many other purposes, including permission and possibility. The English expression such as *it can happen* cannot be translated into Japanese potential forms studied here. In using Japanese potential expressions, the action described must be supported by the agent's willingness to perform the act.

76. The Use of the Gerundive Forms

■ Target Expression

I didn't have time and (so) I couldn't read it.

時間がなくて読めませんでした。
Jikan ga nakute yomemasen-deshita.

[V/Adj *te*]

■ Grammatical Explanation

Using gerundive forms. We have already learned the gerundive [V*te*] form in three contexts; (1) to form an expression of request [V*te* + *-kudasai*], (2) to form the progressive form [V*te* + *-iru*], and (3) to conjoin clauses. In this section we will learn additional uses of the gerundive forms of the verb and the adjectives. We restrict our study here, however, to those cases where [V/Adj *te*] occurs independently without another verbal suffix.

Verb and Adjective Gerundive Forms

	basic form	*te*-form	informal non-past negative	negative *te*-form
U-verbs:				
to go	行く *iku*	行って *itte*	行かない *ikanai*	行かないで/行かなくて *ikanaide/ikanakute*[*1]
to drink	飲む *nomu*	飲んで *nonde*	飲まない *nomanai*	飲まないで/飲まなくて *nomanaide/nomanakute*
RU-verbs:				
to eat	食べる *taberu*	食べて *tabete*	食べない *tabenai*	食べないで/食べなくて *tabenaide/tabenakute*
Existential verbs:				
there is/are	ある *aru*	あって *atte*	ない *nai*	なくて *nakute*
there is/are	いる *iru*	いて *ite*	いない *inai*	いなくて *inakute*
Irregular verbs:				
to come	来る *kuru*	来て *kite*	来ない *konai*	来ないで/来なくて *konaide/konakute*
to do	する *suru*	して *shite*	しない *shinai*	しないで/しなくて *shinaide/shinakute*
Be-verb:				
to be	だ *da*	で *de*	ではない *dewanai*	ではなくて *dewanakute*
[*Adj-i*]:				
expensive	高い *takai*	高くて *takakute*	高くない *takakunai*	高くなくて *takakunakute*
[*Adj-na*]:				
convenient	便利な *benrina*	便利で *benri de*	便利で(は)ない *benri de (wa) nai*	便利で(は)なくて *benri de (wa) nakute*

As stated earlier, the [V*te*] forms are created by changing the final -*ta* and -*da* of [Vinformal past] to -*te* and -*de*, respectively.

*1. The -*nakute* ending is optional for the verb negative gerundive form.

Basic meanings of gerundive forms. What the gerundive form fundamentally conveys is that the said action or the state is realized. This points to the similarity between the Japanese *te*-form and the English verb *-ing* (gerundive) form. Since grammatically a gerundive form is frequently combined with another verb and adjective, it gives the impression that something else is to be mentioned. This is why adding the conjunction *and* in its English translation is useful, particularly when the [V/Adj *te*] form appears independently at the end of a clause. The semantic relationship between the two clauses connected by the gerundive form depends on the specific context in which the utterance is made.

Functions of gerundive forms.

1. *Enumeration 'and'*:

(1a) 今朝早く起きてジョギングをしました。
Kesa hayaku okite jogingu o shimashita.
(I got up early and jogged.)

(1b) 傘を持たないで会社へ行きました。
Kasa o motanaide kaisha e ikimashita.
(Not bringing an umbrella, he went to the office.)

(1c) この梨、安くておいしいですね。
Kono nashi, yasukute oishii-desu ne.
(This pear is inexpensive and delicious, isn't it?)

2. *Specifying cause and reason, 'as; since'*:

(2a) 時間がなくて読めませんでした。
Jikan ga nakute yomemasen-deshita.
(There wasn't time and that's why I couldn't read it.)

(2b) ここはとても不便であまり人気がありません。
Koko wa totemo huben de amari ninki ga arimasen.
(This place is very inconvenient and [so] it's not too popular.)

(2c) こんな家具は高くてなかなか買えない。
Konna kagu wa takakute nakanaka kaenai.
(Such furniture is expensive and so I cannot buy it easily [too expensive to buy].)

3. *Ending statements to soften the impact*:

(3a) 遅くなりまして……
Osoku narimashite ...
([lit., It has become late] Sorry, I'm late ...)

(3b) よく皆様お元気で…… [idiomatic]
Yoku minasama ogenki de . . .
(It's nice to know that everyone is well . . .)

Choosing between *-naide* and *-nakute*. The difference between two gerundive negative forms, i.e., *-naide* and *-nakute*, is that the [*-naide*] clause is more closely connected to the main clause than the [*-nakute*] clause. The [*-nakute*] clause tends to be separate from the main clause. This affects the use of these gerundive negative forms as explained below.

(a) 勉強**しないで**/*しなくてテストを受けます。
*Benkyoo-**shinaide**/*-shinakute tesuto o ukemasu.*
(I take exams without studying.)

(b) 勉強**しないで/しなくて**困ります。
*Benkyoo-**shinaide**/-**shinakute** komarimasu.*
(He doesn't study, which is troublesome.)

(c) あの人はアメリカ人じゃ**なくて**/*ないでイギリス人でしょう。
*Ano hito wa Amerika-jin ja-**nakute**/*-naide Igirisu-jin deshoo.*
(He is probably not an American, but British.)

Benkyoo-shinaide in (a) serves as an adverbial clause associated with the main clause. In this context *-nakute* is not acceptable. In (b), however, either *benkyoo-shinakute* or *benkyoo-shinaide* is acceptable. This is because the two clauses are semantically connected (the first clause offers the reason for the second), and the first clause is not considered to be an adverbial phrase. In (c), since two clauses are independent, only *-nakute* negation is acceptable.

■ Additional Information

The verb and adjective gerundive forms may be followed by the particle *mo*, which is similar to English *even though* and *even when* (See Entry 97 for details).

(a) いっしょうけんめい勉強して**も**よくわかりません。
*Isshookenmei benkyoo-shite **mo** yoku wakarimasen.*
(Even though I study hard, I don't understand well.)

(b) 高くて**も**買おう。
*Takakute **mo** kaoo.*
(Even though it is expensive, let's buy [it].)

(c) 静かで**も**駅から遠くて不便だね。
*Shizuka de **mo** eki kara tookute huben da ne.*
(Even though it is quiet, it is far from the station and is inconvenient, isn't it?)

77. Conjunctions (3)—Cause-effect Conjunctions

■ Target Expression

Because I got up late, I took a taxi.

遅く起きたからタクシーで行きました。
Osoku okita kara takushii de ikimashita.

[*kara*] [*node*]

■ Grammatical Explanation

Connecting clauses with *kara* and *node*. Conjunctions [*kara*] and [*node*] are frequently used to express cause or reason and its resulting effect as shown in the target expression. Be warned that the order of the conjunction and the clause within a sentence is the reverse of what it is in English. Just like particles, these conjunctions are attached to the clause-final position whose clause is conjoined with another. It may be helpful to think of *kara* as *that's why* and *node* as *and so* in English; this way the correct order is easily understood. *Kara* and *node* are attached to both formal and informal forms of the verbs. There is one exception: when *node* is preceded by *da*, it changes into *na*, producing [*na node*] structure. In casual speech, *nde* is used instead of *node*.

Conjunctions and formal/informal forms. Normally the formality markers in Japanese appear at the utterance- and sentence-final position. Therefore in *kara* and *node* clauses, informal endings are used more frequently. When formal endings are used preceding *kara* and *node*, the main verb ending must also be formal, and as a result the degree of formality increases. When *kara* is used in the [*kara da*] pattern, what precedes *kara* must be in the informal form.

Differences between *kara* and *node*. While the [*kara*] conjunction focuses more readily on the reason/cause, the [*node*] conjunction focuses more strongly on the resulting effect. This is why the [*kara*] clause is used independently, while [*node*] is less likely to be so used. An independent [*kara*] clause can also be used as an answer to a question, as shown in B's utterances in (1) and (2).

Semantically, the [*kara*] clause provides a personally interpreted cause or reason for the personal opinions expressed in the main clause. For this reason, sentences expressing personal judgment such as speculation, opinion, intension, command, suggestion, question, request, and so forth must take the [*kara*] conjunction. The [*node*] conjunction, on the other hand, presents the cause more objectively without projecting the speaker's personal opinion.

■ Examples

(1) A: なぜ来なかったんですか。
Naze konakatta n desu ka.
(Why didn't you come?)

B: 急に用事ができたからです。
Kyuuni yooji ga dekita kara desu.
(It's because suddenly I had an errand to attend to.)

(2) A: どうして遅れたの？
Dooshite okureta no?
(Why were you late?)

B: 目覚まし時計が鳴らなかったから。
Mezamashidokei ga naranakatta kara.
(Because the alarm clock didn't go off.)

(3) あした母が六時頃来ますから、それまでに帰ってきてください。
Ashita haha ga roku-ji goro kimasu kara, sore made ni kaette-kite-kudasai.
(Since my mother is coming tomorrow about six o'clock, please be back by then.)

(4) 今朝会議があるから、山田さんは早く来るんじゃない？
Kesa kaigi ga aru kara, Yamada-san wa hayaku kuru n janai?
(There is a meeting this morning and so [I think] Mr. Yamada will come early.)

(5) 朝からずっと仕事をしたので、おなかがすきました。
Asa kara zutto shigoto o shita node, onaka ga sukimashita.
(Since I worked straight through the morning, I got hungry.)

(6) 天気がよかったんで富士山が見えた。
Tenki ga yokatta nde Hujisan ga mieta.
(Since the weather was good, we could see Mt. Fuji.)

■ Additional Information

Recall here another strategy for expressing cause or reason, namely, the phrase [*tame ni*]. For this use, the form preceding [*tame ni*] is the [V/Adj pre-nominal].

(a) 雨が降った**ために**ハイキングに行けませんでした。
*Ame ga hutta **tame ni** haikingu ni ikemasen-deshita.*
(Because it rained, we couldn't go hiking.)

(b) 交通事故の**ために**渋滞が続いています。
*Kootsuujiko no **tame ni** juutai ga tsuzuite-imasu.*
(Due to the traffic accident, there is an extensive traffic jam.)

(c) この道具は便利な**ために**よく売れます。
*Kono doogu wa benrina **tame ni** yoku uremasu.*
(This tool sells well because it is useful.)

78. Requesting (3)—More about Requests and Special Requests

■ Target Expressions

Please, please, come right away!

たのむからすぐ来て！
Tanomu kara sugu kite!
お願いだからすぐ来て！
Onegai da kara sugu kite!

■ Strategic Explanation

Making requests. We have studied several ways to make requests in Japanese. Here we review those expressions. The following strategies are listed in the order of the request made most directly followed by those that are less direct.

電話しなさい。 (Entry 79)
Denwa-shinasai.

すみませんが、電話してください。 (Entry 40)
Sumimasen ga, denwa-shite-kudasai.

電話してほしいんですけど。 (Entry 65)
Denwa-shite hoshii n desu kedo.

電話してもらいたいんですが…… (Entry 73)
Denwa-shite-moraitai n desu ga . . .

電話してもらっていいですか。 (Entry 73)
Denwa-shite-moratte ii desu ka.

お電話していただけませんでしょうか。 (Entry 73)
Odenwa-shite-itadakemasen-deshoo ka.

すみませんが、お電話していただけませんでしょうか。 (Entries 58, 73, and 80)
Sumimasen ga, odenwa-shite-itadakemasen-deshoo ka.

Making an urgent plea. When one needs to make an urgent and desperate plea, some phrases may be added before the [V*te* (*kudasai*)] pattern already introduced. Toward social equals or subordinates only, use *onegai da kara* 'I'm pleading with you' and *tanomu kara* 'please, I beg of you.' Toward your social superior, *murina onegai da to wa omoimasu ga* '(lit., although I think it is an unreasonable request to grant …)' is attached to appeal to the addressee by expressing your respect and sympathy toward him or her.

Responding to requests. When responding to requests, the following representative expressions are available.

1. *Granting request*:

(a) はい、承知しました。
Hai, shoochi-shimashita.
(Yes, certainly.)

(b) はい、わかりました。
Hai, wakarimashita.
(Yes, I'll take care of it.)

(c) はい。
Hai.
(Yes, I will.)

(d) オッケー。 [casual style]
Okkee.
(OK.)

2. *Refusing request*:

(e) そう言われましてもねえ……
Soo iwaremashite mo nee …
(Well, my apologies, but I cannot …)

(f) それが、ちょっとねえ……
Sore ga, chotto nee …
(Well, it's a bit of a problem …)

(g) ごめん。ちょっとむずかしいなあ、それは……
Gomen. Chotto muzukashii naa, sore wa …
(Sorry. It's a bit too difficult, I'm afraid …)

■ Examples

(1) **A:** お願いだから、車貸してくれない？
Onegai da kara, kuruma kashite-kurenai?
(Please, kindly lend me [allow me to use] your car.)

B: いいよ。
Ii yo.
(Sure.)

(2) **A:** たのむから今日中に仕上げてくださいよ。
Tanomu kara kyoojuu ni shiagete-kudasai yo.
(Please, [I beg of you] please finish it by the end of the day.)

B: それが……ちょっとむずかしいんですが。
Sore ga ... chotto muzukashii n desu ga.
(Well, ... that might be a problem.)

(3) **A:** 無理なお願いだとは思いますが、よろしくお願いします。
Murina onegai da to wa omoimasu ga, yoroshiku onegai-shimasu.
(Although this request is unreasonable, please give favorable consideration to it.)

B: はい、承知しました。
Hai, shoochi shimashita.
(Yes, certainly.)

■ Additional Information

Sometimes even when an explicit request is not made, if you share the problem, your friend may come to your rescue. See, for example, the following exchange:

(a) **A:** 今日さいふを忘れてきちゃった[*1]。どうしよう。

Kyoo	*saihu*	*o*	*wasurete-kichatta.*	*Doo shiyoo.*
today	wallet	O	forgot	what should I do

(I forgot my wallet today. What should I do?)

B: お金貸してあげるよ。
Okane kashite-ageru yo.
(I'll loan you some money.)

*1. Recall that *kichatta* is a colloquial version of *kite-shimatta* (as explained in Entry 54.)

79. Orders and Commands

Target Expression

Study!

勉強しなさい！
Benkyoo-shinasai!

[Vstem + *nasai*]

Grammatical Explanation

Giving orders. Order-giving expressions, [Vstem + *nasai*], and the abrupt command form of the verb introduced here are used strictly by one who is socially superior to the addressee. The reverse, a command from one who is socially subordinate, is considered extremely rude. One may give two levels of commands to social subordinates. [Vstem + *nasai*] form is used in both masculine and feminine speech, and the abrupt command form is used predominantly in masculine speech. [Vstem + *nasai*] form may be used toward children or subordinates. In general, however, even when a social superior gives a command, if addressed to an adult, the [V*te* + *-kudasai*] pattern is recommended. It shows consideration for others and is more pleasantly accepted.

Controllable actions only. Both types of order-giving expressions co-occur only with verbs that refer to controllable action. If the person receiving a command is unable to control the outcome, giving a command does not make sense. For the [N + *da*] structure, use [N + *dearinasai*].

(a) 早く行き**なさい**。
*Hayaku iki**nasai**.*
(Go right away.)

(b) 本当の自分であり**なさい**。
*Hontoo no jibun deari**nasai**.*
(Be your true self.)

Abrupt command forms. The abrupt command form is restricted in use and is considered rude unless the situation is absolutely appropriate.

Abrupt Command Forms

U-verbs: replace last *-u* with *-e*					
書く	*kak**u***	to write	→	書け	*kak**e***
買う	*ka**u***	to buy	→	買え	*ka**e***
行く	*ik**u***	to go	→	行け	*ik**e***

RU-verbs: replace last *-ru* with *-ro*

食べる	*tabe**ru***	to eat	→	食べろ	*tabe**ro***
起きる	*oki**ru***	to get up	→	起きろ	*oki**ro***

Be-verb:

だ	***da***	to be	→	でいろ	***de-iro***
である	***dearu***	to be	→	であれ	***deare***

Irregular verbs:

来る	***kuru***	to come	→	来い	***koi***
する	***suru***	to do	→	しろ	***shiro***

For existential verbs, only *iro* (command form of *iru*) is used.

The negative abrupt command forms are formed by adding *na* to the [Vbasic] form.

書く	*kaku*	don't write	→	書く**な**	*kaku**na***
起きる	*okiru*	don't get up	→	起きる**な**	*okiru**na***
来る	*kuru*	don't come	→	来る**な**	*kuru**na***

■ Examples

(1) 早く起きて勉強しなさい。
Hayaku okite benkyoo-shinasai.
(Get up early and study.)

(2) **A:** 気をつけなさいよ。
Kiotsukenasai yo.
(Be careful.)

B: はい。
Hai.
(Yes. I will.)

(3) ここ通るな。 [as used on a sign post]
Koko tooruna.
(Don't trespass here.)

■ Additional Information

- An abbreviated form of [Vstem + *nasai*], that is, [Vstem + *na*] may also be used as a command. Thus instead of saying *tabenasai* 'eat!,' *tabena* may be used, the latter of which is colloquial, more informal, and even more abrupt than [Vstem + *nasai*].

  The negative abrupt command forms are frequently used as a warning sign, such as *koko wataruna* 'don't cross here.'

- Abrupt command forms may be used rhetorically. For example, *Uso tsuke!* (lit., tell lies) means 'Don't tell lies,' and *Baka ie!* (lit., say something foolish) means 'Don't be so foolish.' These are used mostly in blunt masculine speech.

80. Managing Conversation (1)—Openers and Fillers

■ Target Expression

Well . . .

まあ、あの……
Maa, ano . . .

■ Strategic Explanation

Conversation openers. Conversational utterances are filled with fragments that do not carry meaning in a strict sense. When assuming the speaking turn, speakers often start with openers, that is, brief expressions claiming the turn and alerting others that the speaker is about to say something. This happens in English also; the conjunction *so* in the expression *so, what's up?*, for example.

Openers:

1. Marking a new topic:

(それ) で	*(Sore) de*	So
で今日は……	*De kyoo wa . . .*	So, today . . .

2. Signaling that what you are going to say is off the topic:

ところで	*Tokorode*	By the way
話ちがうけど	*Hanashi chigau kedo*	(Not) to change the subject

3. Adding to the current topic:

そう言えばねえ……	*Soo ieba nee . . .*	Speaking of . . .
言いかえれば/言いかえると	*Iikaereba/Iikaeruto*	In other words
たとえば	*Tatoeba*	For example
具体的に言うと	*Gutaiteki ni yuu to*	More concretely

4. Introducing the main important topic:

実は……	*Jitsu wa . . .*	To discuss the serious matter/Seriously, though

5. Qualifying the utterance:

ぶっちゃけ	*Butchake*	To be totally frank [casual speech]
もしかして	*Moshika shite*	I'm not sure, but is it possible . . .

Conversation fillers. Speaker's turns are also interposed by fillers, which are equivalent to *uhh* and *like* in English conversation, as in *uhh, you know, he's like, he is really crazy*. Conversational fillers may just simply fill in the pause, or they may signal the speaker's hesitation or trouble spots. These openers and fillers are useful because they allow the speaker to hold on to the speaking turn.

Openers and Fillers:

1. Hesitation sounds that can be used as openers and fillers:

あのう……	*Anoo ...*	Well ...
まあ、そうですね……	*Maa, soo desu ne ...*	Oh, I guess so ...
ええと……	*Eeto ...*	Well, let's see ...
ええ……	*Ee ...*	Uhh ...
まあ……	*Maa ...*	Well, say ...
まあ、それで……	*Maa, sorede ...*	So, then ...
なんか……	*Nan-ka ...*	Uhh ...

2. Expressions used to fill otherwise awkward pauses:

何と言いましょうか……	*Nan to iimashoo ka ...*	What should I say ...
むずかしい質問ですね……	*Muzukashii shitsumon desu ne ...*	That's a difficult question to answer ...

Mixing different openers and fillers. When using openers and fillers, avoid overusing any one expression. It is acceptable to combine several short fillers to fill the time, for example, *anoo ... maa ... eeto ....* You will find native speakers using these fillers quite frequently.

Inhaling hissing sound. Japanese male adult speech (especially when formal) is characterized by an inhaling hissing sound. The inhaling hissing sound functions as an opener and a filler. Observe male speech when you have access to native speakers. There is no need to imitate it, however, unless you are a male and you want to.

■ Additional Information

Te yuu ka and its casual versions, *te ka* and *tsuu ka*, are used for multiple purposes. As an opener, *te yuu ka* warns the listener that what follows is something that might be unexpected or oppositional. It also signals that what follows is something truthful, something that has been kept hidden but is now being revealed. When *te yuu ka* appears at the end, it marks the content as something iffy, uncertain, or something that the speaker hesitantly presents. Note that *te yuu ka* is pronounced as *tte yuu ka* when it follows words other than those ending with *n*.

(a) A: お昼、ラーメン？
Ohiru, raamen?
(For lunch, how about *raamen* noodles?)

B: **ていうか**、カレーはどう？
Te yuu ka*, karee wa doo?*
(Uh, how about curry with rice?)

(b) A: カナさんて、どうかなあ。
Kana-san te, doo ka naa.
(I wonder about Kana.)

B: **てか**、きらいなんでしょ？
Te ka*, kirai na n desho?*
(To tell the truth, you don't like her, right?)

(c) A: あの人、まだ来てない**っていうか**。
Ano hito, mada kitenai ***tte yuu ka****.*
(She isn't coming, I'm afraid.)

B: 今日も来ないんじゃない？
Kyoo mo konai n ja-nai?
(She won't come today again, right?)

81. Conjunctions (4)—Enumerative Actions or States

■ Target Expressions

I went to London, Paris, and Amsterdam.

ロンドンと、パリと、アムステルダムへ行った。
Rondon to, Pari to, Amusuterudamu e itta.

I went to London and also went to Paris; this summer was really fun.

ロンドンへ（も）行ったし、パリへ（も）行ったし、
今年の夏は楽しかった。
Rondon e (mo) ittashi, Pari e (mo) ittashi,
kotoshi no natsu wa tanoshikatta.

[V/Adj + *shi*]
[. . . *tari*, . . . *tari* . . . *suru/da*]

■ Grammatical Explanation

Enumeration of actions and states. There are several ways in which enumeration of actions and states are described. Naturally one can express enumeration by connecting nouns with the particle *to* as shown in the first example of the target expression. Here, instead of connecting nouns, we focus on three ways to connect verbs or clauses.

1. [V/Adj *te*]

   One can enumerate simply by changing verbs into [V/Adj *te*] forms. In the [V*te*] pattern, if the verb is not stative, the actions occur in the order of the statement.

   (1a) ロンドンへ**行って**、パリへ行きました。
   *Rondon e **itte**, Pari e ikimashita.*
   (I went to London and [then] Paris.)

   (1b) このビルは**新しくて**、**広くて**、きれいだね。
   *Kono biru wa **atarashikute**, **hirokute**, kirei da ne.*
   (This building is new, spacious, and beautiful.)

2. [V/Adj + *shi*] (Adjectives must be in predicate forms.)

   This pattern is used when enumerative actions or states combined together lead to certain results or expectations. For example, you express that you had a real good summer this year partly because you went on a European tour. If you want to list the cities you visited, you might say:

   (2a) ロンドンへ(も)行った**し**、パリへ(も)行った**し**、今年の夏は楽しかった。
   *Rondon e (mo) itta**shi**, Pari e (mo) itta**shi**, kotoshi no natsu wa tanoshikatta.*
   (I went to London and also went to Paris; this summer was really fun.)

   In this enumeration strategy, actions and states occur in random alternatives. They are not necessarily chronologically ordered. Other examples include:

   (2b) 雪が降っている**し**大変寒いので、今日の講演は中止です。

Yuki	*ga*	*hutte-iru**shi***	*taihen*	*samui*	*node,*
snow	S	is falling and	very	cold	since

kyoo	*no*	*kooen*	*wa*	*chuushi*	*desu.*
today	L	lecture	T	cancellation	is

   (Since it is snowing and it is very cold, today's public lecture is canceled.)

   (2c) この辺は寒い**し**、暗い**し**、危険だ**し**、あまりいい所ではありませんね。
   *Kono hen wa samui**shi**, kurai**shi**, kiken da**shi**, amari ii tokoro dewa-arimasen ne.*
   (This area is cold, dark, and dangerous, and it's not really a nice place, is it?)

(2d) 仕事もしない**し**、勉強もしない**し**、どうしたんですか。
*Shigoto mo shinai**shi**, benkyoo mo shinai**shi**, dooshita n desu ka.*[*1]
(You don't work, and you don't study; what happened to you?)

*1. *Dooshita n desu ka?* is an idiomatic expression meaning 'what happened (to you)?, what's wrong with you?'

3. [*... tari, ... tari ... suru/da*] (*Tari* is produced by [V/Adj informal past + *ri*].) This pattern is used normally with two *tari*'s (although more than two is possible), with the second one normally followed by *suru* or *da*. As in the case of the [*shi*] enumeration, the actions and states expressed in this enumeration are not necessarily chronologically ordered.

(3a) ロンドンへ行っ**たり**、パリへ行っ**たりしました**。
*Rondon e it**tari**, Pari e it**tari shimashita**.*
(I went to London, and I also went to Paris.)

(3b) 日曜日は出かけ**たり**出かけなかっ**たりです**。
*Nichiyoobi wa dekake**tari** dekakenakat**tari desu**.*
(On Sundays, I sometimes go out, sometimes not.)

(3c) 学生は日本人だっ**たり**、アメリカ人だっ**たり**。
*Gakusei wa Nihon-jin dat**tari**, Amerika-jin dat**tari**.*
(Students are Japanese and also Americans.)

(3d) ここにある帽子は私には小さかっ**たり**大きかっ**たりして**、いいのがみつかりません。

Koko ni aru	*booshi*	*wa*	*watashi*	*ni*	*wa*	*chiisakat**tari***
here at there is	hat	T	me	for	T	small

*ookikat**tari***	***shite**,*	*ii*	*no*	*ga*	*mitsukarimasen.*
large	do	good	one	S	cannot be found

(These hats [that are] here are [too] small or [too] large and I can't find an appropriate one.)

(3e) 新聞を読ん**だりして**、ゆっくりしていた。

Shinbun	*o*	*yon**dari***	***shite**,*	*yukkuri-shite-ita.*
newspaper	*O*	*read*	*do*	*relax*

(I read the newspaper [among other things], and I relaxed.)

■ Additional Information

- The enumerative endings [V/Adj *te*] and [V/Adj + *shi*] are used for softly offering the cause or reason in conversation. They often appear at the utterance-final position, leaving the impression that the statement is incomplete, and therefore, implying a less imposing attitude of the speaker.

(a) 買わなかった。高く**て**。
*Kawanakatta. Takaku**te**.*
(I didn't buy it. It was expensive.)

(b) 今週はちょっと忙しいんですよ。出張がある**し**……
*Konshuu wa chotto isogashii n desu yo. Shutchoo ga aru**shi** . . .*
(This week I'm a bit busy. There is a business trip and . . .)

- [V/Adj + *shi*] also appears in the context where there is no need for offering cause or reason. By leaving sentences incomplete, an indirect and soft atmosphere is achieved.

(c) もうそろそろ出かける**し**。
*Moo sorosoro dekakeru**shi**.*
(I guess I'm leaving soon.)

(d) よくわかんない**し**。
*Yoku wakannai**shi**.*
(I don't quite understand it.)

■ Warning

The enumerative particles [*to*], [*ya*], and [*mo*], which we learned in Entries 17 and 29, are used to connect nouns and noun phrases only. When combining clauses, one of the above strategies must be chosen. It is also useful to remember that there is a similarity in the way enumeration is presented between [*to*] and [V/Adj *te*]; between [*ya*] and [... *tari*]; between [*mo*] and [V/Adj + *shi*].

82. Managing Conversation (2)—Repair for Trouble Spots

■ Target Expressions

Uh?

ええ?　はあ?
Ee? Haa?

■ Strategic Explanation

Asking for clarification. A repair in conversation is especially useful for language learners. You may need, at least in the beginning, to ask for clarification. *Ee?* and *haa?*, with rising intonation, indicate that you did not hear what was just said. These expressions give the impression that the enunciation on the part of the speaker was not clear, and therefore the speaker is to blame. Unless it is obvious that the problem is of physical sound quality, these short expressions are to be avoided.

Politer strategies are (1) to repeat the part you understand and trail off, with a facial expression of confusion, and (2) to ask the meaning of a specific word if you can repeat it. Imagine that you cannot understand the word *jinjika* 'personnel division' in the following utterance.

A: ではあした八時に人事課に来てください。
Dewa ashita hachi-ji ni jinjika ni kite-kudasai.

Possible repair strategies:

B: **(a)** あした八時に……？
Ashita hachi-ji ni . . . ?
(Tomorrow at eight o'clock . . . ?)

(b) 人事課っていうのは？
Jinjika tte yuu no wa?
([What is] *jinjika*?)

(c) 人事課って？
Jinjika tte?
(*Jinjika*?)

(d) すみません、人事課っていう言葉の意味がわからないんですが……
Sumimasen, jinjika tte yuu kotoba no imi ga wakaranai n desu ga . . .
(Sorry, but I don't understand the meaning of the word *jinjika*.)

Asking to repeat. As a last resort, if you can't identify what you can't understand, request the partner to speak slowly, or to repeat it one more time.

(e) すみません、もう少しゆっくりお願いします。
Sumimasen, moo sukoshi yukkuri onegai-shimasu.
(Sorry, but could you speak a little more slowly?)

(f) すみません、もう一度お願いします。
Sumimasen, moo ichido onegai-shimasu.
(Sorry, but could you repeat it one more time?)

These repair strategies are not often used by native speakers, and they often mark the speaker as a "foreigner." These repair remedies are good to know; the worst course of action is to ignore the problem and to be left in the dark.

When it's hard finding the right words. When you have difficulty producing Japanese utterances, use fillers discussed in Entry 80. Here are some more examples.

(g) つまり、あのう……
Tsumari, anoo ...
(In other words, uh ...)

(h) ええ、まあ……
Ee, maa ...
(Well, uhh, so ...)

Correcting wrong statements. When you make a wrong statement and wish to correct it, you should use a negation *dewa-nakute*.

(i) きのう……**ではなくて**、おととい会いました。
*Kinoo ... **dewa-nakute**, ototoi aimashita.*
(Yesterday, no ... rather, the day before yesterday I saw him.)

■ Additional Information

Hai? 'Uh, what?' with rising intonation, indicates displeasure at what you are hearing, and so it demands clarification. Your friend may request something unexpected, unfair, and surprising. And this may upset you. *Hai?* would force your friend to repeat (or hopefully reconsider) the request or comment. This expression carries a sense of blame, so it should not be used to your superiors.

83. Modifying (3)—Clausal Modifiers

■ Target Expressions

The book my father wrote is selling well.

父が書いた本はよく売れています。
Chichi ga kaita hon wa yoku urete-imasu.

I forgot my promise to see my friend.

友だちに会う約束を忘れてしまいました。
Tomodachi ni au yakusoku o wasurete-shimaimashita.

[clausal modifier + N]

■ Grammatical Explanation

Modifying with clauses. Characteristic 6, the modifier precedes the modified, applies when modification is achieved by a modifying subordinate clause. The clausal modification is widely used in English (in fact more common in English than in Japanese) in expressions such as *the book (that) my father wrote*, in which *my father wrote* modifies the noun *the book*. Unlike English, the Japanese clausal modification reverses the order of elements; the clausal modifier precedes the noun modified, and the modifying clause takes [V/Adj pre-nominal] forms.

When the predicate of the modifying clause ends with [N + *da*], it takes the pre-nominal form *no* preceding nouns, for example, *hurusato ga Yamanashi no tomodachi* 'a friend whose hometown is Yamanashi.' The [N + *da*] structure may also take [N + *dearu*] 'to be' preceding the noun.

If the sentence requires a formal style, it is expressed by the verb of the main clause. There are no relative pronouns in Japanese—such as the English *who, which,* and *that* (in, for example, *the book [that] my father wrote*).

Avoiding *wa* in modifying clauses. Since the modifying clause is a subordinate clause, and since topic identifies the topic of the whole sentence, topic marker *wa* must be avoided unless *wa* conveys strong contrast. Instead of *wa,* whatever appropriate case marker is used within the modifying subordinate clause.

Changing *ga* to *no*. The subject marker *ga* in the modifying clause is optionally changed into *no*. For example, *Katoo-san no kaita hon* 'the book Mrs. Kato wrote' and *Nihongo no hanaseru hito* 'a person who can speak Japanese.' This applies to the particle *ga* in reactive predicates as well; for example, *umi no mieru machi ni sunde-iru* 'he lives in the town from where one can see the ocean.'

Basic and extended types. There are two types of clausal modifiers. The first, the basic type, is the kind where the modified noun constitutes a part of the propositional content of the modifying clause. For example, in the first target sentence, the relationship between *chichi ga kaita* and *hon* is such that they constitute a proposition [*chichi ga hon o kaita*].

The second, the extended type, is the case where the modified noun is semantically associated with the modifying clause, but the noun itself does not constitute an item within the relevant propositional content. See, for example, in the second target expression, the relevant proposition is [*watashi ga tomodachi ni au*], and *yakusoku* is not an essential element within the proposition.

Out of these two types, only the first type functions similarly to so-called English clausal modifiers with relative pronouns. In order to understand the clausal modification of the second type, it is necessary to adopt an extended meaning of clausal modification. Sometimes in order to make sense in English it is necessary to add appropriate phrases. Here we focus on the first basic type; the second type is discussed in Entry 114.

Verb tense in subordinate clauses. Before proceeding too far, we must pay attention to the verb tense within the modifying clause in relation to the tense of the main verb. For the active verb, [Vnon-past] in the subordinate clause refers to the action not yet completed. When the verb in the modifying clause is [Vpast], it refers to action completed before the time of speech as in (c) or the tense defined by the main verb as in (d). The past tense in the subordinate clause used here is best characterized as "perfective" or "previous" tense.

(a) 今夜**食べる**ものを**買いましょう**。
Kon'ya ***taberu*** *mono o* ***kaimashoo.***
(Let's buy things that we will eat tonight.)

(b) 今夜**食べる**ものを**買いました**。
Kon'ya ***taberu*** *mono o* ***kaimashita.***
(We bought things that we would eat tonight.)

(c) 今夜**食べた**ものはもう二度と**買わないでしょう**。

Kon'ya	***tabeta***	*mono*	*wa*	*moo nido to*	***kawanai-deshoo.***
tonight	ate	thing	T	never	will not buy

(I will never buy the [kind of] food I ate tonight.)

(d) 買い物を**した**人は早く**もどってきました**。

Kaimono	*o*	***shita***	*hito*	*wa*	*hayaku*	***modotte-kimashita.***
shopping	O	did	person	T	early	return

(Those who had shopped returned early.)

Note that if the semantic focus is placed on the perfective nature of the past tense, [Vpast] may be used even when the action referred to is not yet completed, as shown in (e).

(e) 買い物を**した**人は早くバスに**もどってください**。
Kaimono o ***shita*** *hito wa hayaku basu ni* ***modotte-kudasai.***
(Those who shopped [already], please return to the bus.)

Interpreting tense in modifying clauses. When the verb within the modifying clause is stative, existential, *be*-verb, adjectival, or [V*te* + -*iru*], the [V/Adj non-past] form is interpreted as the same tense as the main verb, and the [V/Adj past] form is interpreted only as occurring in the past.

(f) 子供たちは木がたくさん**ある**公園で**遊ぶ**。
Kodomo-tachi wa ki ga takusan ***aru*** *kooen de* ***asobu.***
(Children play in the park where there are many trees.)

(g) 子供たちは木がたくさん**ある**公園で**遊んだ**。
Kodomo-tachi wa ki ga takusan ***aru*** *kooen de* ***asonda.***
(Children played in the park where there were [and are] many trees.)

(h) 子供たちは木がたくさん**あった**公園で**遊ぶ**。
Kodomo-tachi wa ki ga takusan ***atta*** *kooen de* ***asobu.***
(Children play in the park where there were [but are not now] many trees.)

(i) 子供たちは木がたくさん**あった**公園で**遊んだ**。
*Kodomo-tachi wa ki ga takusan **atta** kooen de **asonda**.*
(Children played in the park where there were [but are not now] many trees.)

(j) あのめがねを**かけている**人はどこへ**行くんだろう**。
*Ano megane o **kakete-iru** hito wa doko e **iku n daroo**.*
(Where is the person wearing glasses going?)

(k) あのめがねを**かけている**人はどこへ**行きました**か。
*Ano megane o **kakete-iru** hito wa doko e **ikimashita** ka.*
(Where did the person wearing glasses go?)

■ Examples

(1) 先週読んだ本おもしろかったよ。
Senshuu yonda hon omoshirokatta yo.
(The book I read last week was interesting.)

(2) 小さかった木が大きくなりました。
Chiisakatta ki ga ookiku narimashita.
(The tree that was small became large.)

(3) **A:** ねえ、毎日使うものだから買いましょうよ。
Nee, mainichi tsukau mono da kara kaimashoo yo.
(Because it is something that we use every day, let's buy it.)

B: そうしようか。
Soo shiyoo ka.
(Let's do so.)

(4) 夫がアメリカ人である日本人女性が集まった。
Otto ga Amerika-jin dearu Nihon-jin josei ga atsumatta.
(Japanese women whose husbands are American gathered.)

(5) ハワイでは海の見えるホテルに泊まりました。
Hawai de wa umi no mieru hoteru ni tomarimashita.
(In Hawaii we stayed at a hotel with an ocean view.)

84. Conjunctions (5)—Temporal Conjunctions

■ Target Expressions

When I was a child, I played around here often.

子供の頃よくここで遊んだんですよ。
Kodomo no koro yoku koko de asonda n desu yo.

After I clean my room, I'll play tennis.

部屋のそうじをしてから、テニスをします。
Heya no sooji o shite kara, tenisu o shimasu.

While drinking beer, wouldn't you like to have a talk?

ビールでも飲みながら、話をしませんか。
Biiru demo nominagara, hanashi o shimasen ka.

[*toki*] [*koro*]
[V*te* + *kara*] [Vstem + *nagara*]

■ Grammatical Explanation

***Toki* and *koro* clauses.** When connecting clauses with temporal phrases, nouns such as *toki* 'time' and *koro* 'approximate time' are used. What precedes *toki* and *koro* is a modifying clause ending with the [V/Adj pre-nominal] form. (Refer to Entry 83 for tense relations between the modifying and main clauses. They operate the same way.)

Interpreting tense in *toki* sentences. If the tense of the verb in the [*toki*] clause is non-past, the actions described are interpreted as happening simultaneously with the tense of the main clause verb as in (a) and (c). If the tense of the verb in the [*toki*] clause is past, the action referred to is already completed as in (b) and (d). If the verb in the subordinate clause involves duration, [Vpast] can be interpreted as being concurrent with the main clause verb as in (e).

(a) 買い物を**する時**、注意しましょう。
*Kaimono o **suru toki**, chuui-shimashoo.*
(Let's be careful when [before] you shop.)

(b) 買い物を**した時**、注意しましょう。
*Kaimono o **shita toki**, chuui-shimashoo.*
(After we've bought [something], let's be careful.)

(c) 日本へ**行く時**、新しいカメラを買います。
*Nihon e **iku toki**, atarashii kamera o kaimasu.*
(When I go to Japan [i.e., before I go], I will buy a new camera.)

(d) 日本へ**行った時**、新しいカメラを買います。
*Nihon e **itta toki**, atarashii kamera o kaimasu.*
(When I get to Japan, [i.e., after arriving in Japan], I will buy a camera [in Japan].)

(e) 日本に**住んでいた時**、新しいカメラを**買いました**。
*Nihon ni **sunde-ita toki**, atarashii kamera o **kaimashita**.*
(When [i.e., while] I was living in Japan, I bought a new camera.)

Connecting sequential events. Additionally, as strategies for connecting sequential events, the following connecting devices are available.

1. [V*te* + *kara*] 'after doing …':
The verb must indicate action or change in state. The *be*-verb and adjectival predicates as they are cannot co-occur.

(1a) 食事を**してから**行きましょう。
*Shokuji o **shite kara** ikimashoo.*
(Let's go after eating supper.)

2. [Vinformal past (affirmative only) + *ato de*] 'after doing …':
This expression is used primarily with active verbs.

(2a) 晩ごはんを**食べたあとで**散歩しましょう。
*Bangohan o **tabeta ato de** sanpo-shimashoo.*
(Let's go for a walk after eating supper.)

3. [Vbasic + *mae ni*] 'before (doing) …':
This expression is used primarily with active verbs.

(3a) 暗く**なる前に**帰ってきなさい。
*Kuraku **naru mae ni** kaette-kinasai.*
(Come back before it gets dark.)

Connecting concurrent events. For connecting concurrent events, the following strategies are used.

4. [V/Adj pre-nominal + *aida ni*]:
This expression normally requires verbs that describe continuing action or state.

(4a) あの人を**待っている間に**ケータイ小説を読みます。
*Ano hito o **matte-iru aida ni** keetai shoosetsu o yomimasu.*
(While waiting for him, I read a cell-phone novel.)

(4b) **涼しい間に**勉強しよう。
Suzushii aida ni *benkyoo-shiyoo.*
(While it's cool, I will study.)

(4c) 子供が**寝ている間に**DVDを見よう。
Kodomo ga ***nete-iru aida ni*** *dii-bui-dii o miyoo.*
(I'll watch a DVD while the kid is sleeping.)

5. [Vstem + *nagara*]:
The [*nagara*] expression is used when the same agent performs two actions simultaneously. For this reason the verb in the [*nagara*] clause must designate an action which lasts over a period of time. Non-durative verbs cannot be used within a [*nagara*] clause.

(5a) あの人を**待ちながら**いろいろ考えた。
Ano hito o ***machinagara*** *iroiro kangaeta.*
(While waiting for him, I thought about various things.)

(5b) テレビ**見ながら**勉強できる？
Terebi ***minagara*** *benkyoo dekiru?*
(Can you study while watching TV?)

■ Examples

(1) あそこは父が元気だった頃よくいっしょに行きました。
Asoko wa chichi ga genki datta koro yoku issho ni ikimashita.
(When my father was well, we went there together often.)

(2) サンフランシスコに住んでいた時、日本人の観光客をよく見かけましたが……
Sanhuranshisuko ni sunde-ita toki, Nihon-jin no kankookyaku o yoku mikakemashita ga . . .
(When I lived in San Francisco, I saw many Japanese tourists.)

(3) 祭りの頃ふるさとへ帰ります。
Matsuri no koro hurusato e kaerimasu.
(About the time of the festival, I will return to my hometown.)

(4) 勉強してから遊びなさい！
Benkyoo-shitc kara asobinasai!
(Play after you study.)

(5) ものを食べながら歩かないでください。
Mono o tabenagara arukanaide-kudasai.
(Please do not walk while eating.)

■ Additional Information

- Conjunctions *ato de* and *mae ni* may also be preceded by [N + *no*].

  (a) 昼休み**のあとで**会いましょう。

Hiruyasumi	***no***	***ato de***	*aimashoo.*
lunch break	L	later	let's meet

  (Let's meet after the lunch break.)

  (b) 昼休み**の前に**この仕事をしてしまおう。
  Hiruyasumi ***no mae ni*** *kono shigoto o shite-shimaoo.*
  (Let's get this work done before the lunch break.)

- The [*nagara*] expression can also be used to mean 'despite,' especially when the verb is stative. Note also that *da* changes to *dearu* when it procedes *nagara*, resulting in the expression, *dearinagara*.

  (c) あの人は大学生**でありながら**漢字をあまり知らない。
  Ano hito wa daigakusei ***dearinagara*** *kanji o amari shiranai.*
  (Despite the fact that he is a university student, he doesn't know *kanji* well.)

  In some cases two readings are possible; the correct interpretation is based on the discourse context in which it is placed.

  (d) 何度も**失敗しながら**それでも最後まで仕上げた。

Nando mo	***shippai-shinagara***	*soredemo*	*saigo*	*made*	*shiageta.*
many times	fail	even then	end	till	finished

  Reading 1: (In spite of the fact that I made mistakes many times, still, I finished it [stuck with it] to the end.)
  Reading 2: (While I was making many mistakes, I finished it [stuck with it] to the end.)

85. Leave-taking and Parting

■ Target Expressions

Good-bye.

じゃあ、また。さようなら。
Jaa, mata. Sayoonara.

■ Strategic Explanation

Meaning of *sayo(o)nara*. Although *sayo(o)nara* is best known as a greeting for farewell, it is important to know that among *uchi* members, one says *sayo(o)nara* only when the separation is long; saying *sayo(o)nara* implies that they may never see each other again. It would be quite upsetting for Japanese parents to hear their son or daughter leave the house saying *sayo(o)nara* in the morning. The parents would think their child is running away from home or even ready to commit suicide! If you stay with a Japanese family, for example, the only time you should use *sayo(o)nara* to family members is when leaving them for good.

Leave-taking expressions. The *uchi* group applies to company employees as well. When leaving one's office, *jaa osakini* (*shitsurei-shimasu*) 'excuse me for leaving before you' is normally used for leave-taking. School children do use *sayo(o)nara* to teachers at the end of the day, however, even when they will meet the teacher the next day.

Parting phrases in different social situations. It is useful to know a variety of Japanese parting phrases to be used in different social situations.

1. When leaving the house:

行ってまいります。	*Itte-mairimasu.*	lit., I will go and return. [formal]
行ってきます。	*Itte-kimasu.*	lit., I will go and return. [less formal]

2. When saying good-bye to someone you meet every day or frequently:

じゃ(あ)、また。	*Ja(a), mata.*	See you again.
じゃ(あ)、あとで。	*Ja(a), ato de.*	Well then, see you later.
じゃ(あ)、あした。	*Ja(a), ashita.*	See you tomorrow.
バイバイ。	*Bai bai.*	Bye-bye. [used especially among young speakers]
それではまた。	*Soredewa mata.*	Well then, see you again.
では後ほど。	*Dewa nochi hodo.*	Well then, see you later. [polite form]

3. When leaving the office before others:
   お先に(失礼[します])。*Osakini (shitsurei[-shimasu]).*
   lit., Excuse me for leaving early.

4. When someone is leaving for a long time:

さよ(う)なら。	*Sayo(o)nara.*	Good-bye.
お元気で。	*Ogenki de.*	Take care of yourself.

5. Students and teachers greeting at the end of the day:

先生さよ(う)なら。	*Sensei sayo(o)nara.*	Good-bye, teacher.
さよ(う)なら。	*Sayo(o)nara.*	Good-bye.

6. When asking to send one's regards:
   奥さんによろしく。*Okusan ni yoroshiku.* Please give my regards to your wife.

■ Additional Information

- When visiting a Japanese family, it is common that the family encourages the guest to stay longer. A typical phrase is *mada ii ja-nai-desu ka* 'it's still early, (please stay longer).' Leave-taking is a ritual in which the guest indicates that he or she is leaving while the host attempts to discourage the guest's parting. One should not take the host's kind words at face value, however. It is important not to overextend your stay. Particularly when your visit extends into mealtime, the host or the hostess may feel obliged to serve you a meal. Mealtime visits should be avoided in general, unless invited beforehand. Regardless of how hard (it seems) the host tries to encourage you to stay, you should take various facts into consideration and express your interest in leaving. *Jaa sorosoro shitsurei shimasu node* ... 'well, I should be leaving soon ...' is useful when expressing your intention to leave.
- When a co-worker leaves the office by saying *osakini (shitsurei[-shimasu])*, the remaining co-workers will respond with *otsukare sama (deshita)* 'lit., Thank you for your effort.' If your superior leaves by saying *osakini*, you should respond *aa doomo* and not with *otsukare sama*, unless the superior is considered a member of your immediate work group. When a family member leaves home saying *itte kimasu* (or *itte mairimasu*), the remaining members respond with *itte (i)rasshai* 'lit., go and return.'

■ Warning

A non-verbal sign for parting is waving sideways with one's palm facing the partner. The hand gesture of flapping your fingers with the palm facing the partner—a gesture accompanying a greeting of farewell in America—is a sign asking someone to come toward you in Japan.

86. Speech Style (3)—Honorifics: Respectful and Humble Forms

■ Target Expression

The company president has come.

社長さんがいらっしゃいました。
Shachoo-san ga irasshaimashita.

[*o* + Vstem + *ninaru*]
[*o* + Vstem + *suru*]
respectful [V + *-reru*/*-rareru*]

■ Strategic Explanation

Respectful and humble forms. Earlier we learned the styles of formal and informal speech. Formalness indicated by the *desu* and *masu* style, as we have been using, is basically an expression of politeness. Honorifics as stated in characteristic 5 is another aspect of Japanese speech style which generates politeness. Honorifics describe two different strategies. Beyond being formal or informal, the verb can be expressed in its respectful and humble forms.

Respectful forms are used when addressing, or talking about, someone whose social status is relatively higher than yours. In the same situation of relative social status, humble forms of the verb may be used in reference to one's own action and state; by humbling the speaker's action, social differentiation is achieved. The use of respectful and humble forms is not optional; appropriate forms must be chosen in each social situation, except when social equals interact, or when the *uchi* relationship is firmly established.

Two types of respectful forms. There are two distinct respectful forms, (1) by using the verb respectful form, and (2) by using the pattern [*o* + Vstem + *ninaru*], with the latter considered to be slightly more formal. The prefix *o* is normally attached to Japanese words, while *go* is attached to vocabulary of Chinese origin.

Verb Respectful Forms

U-verbs: replace *-u* by *-areru*

書く	*kak**u***	to write	→	書かれる	*kak**areru***
思う	*omo**u***	to think	→	思われる	*omow**areru***

Note that *-u* + *-areru* produces *-wareru*. When the verb ends with a mora consisting of *u* as in *kau* and *utau*, the respectful form takes *kawareru* and *utawareru*, respectively.

食べる	*tabe**ru***	to eat	→	食べられる	*tabe**rareru***
起きる	*oki**ru***	to get up	→	起きられる	*oki**rareru***

In fact, in both *U*- and *RU*-verbs, the change is identical; the final *-u* becomes *-areru*. For *RU*-verbs, the respectful forms introduced here are identical to potential forms introduced in Entry 75. Among verb potential forms, the alternative potential forms (for example, *okireru* instead of *okirareru*) are not used as respectful forms.

Humble forms. Humble forms are generated by the pattern [*o* + Vstem + *suru*]. If you are telling your boss that you will deliver (*todokeru*) the file later, you should say *otodokeshimasu*. All humble and respectful forms introduced here can be used either in informal or formal style, depending on the situation, although it is often the case that formal style is used.

Special honorific forms. Verbs listed below have special respectful and humble forms. As shown, some do not go through [*o* + Vstem + *suru*] nor [*o* + Vstem + *ninaru*] structures; these forms must be learned one by one.

Special Verb Honorific Forms

		Respectful	Humble
会う *au*	to meet	お会いになる *oaininaru*	お目にかかる *omenikakaru*
いる *iru*	to exist, to be	いらっしゃる、 おいでになる *irassharu, oideninaru*	おる *oru*
行く/来る *iku/kuru*	to go/to come	いらっしゃる、 おいでになる *irassharu, oideninaru*	参る、うかがう *mairu, ukagau*
思う *omou*	to think	お思いになる *oomoininaru*	存じる *zonjiru*
借りる *kariru*	to borrow	お借りになる *okarininaru*	拝借する *haishakusuru*
する *suru*	to do	なさる *nasaru*	いたす *itasu*
食べる/飲む *taberu/nomu*	to eat/to drink	めしあがる *meshiagaru*	いただく *itadaku*
だ *da*	to be	でいらっしゃる *de-irassharu*	—
見る *miru*	to see	ごらんになる *goranninaru*	拝見する *haikensuru*
言う *yuu*	to say	おっしゃる *ossharu*	申す、申し上げる *moosu, mooshiageru*

Additionally, a special form *de-gozaru* (normally used as *de-gozaimasu*) represents a neutrally polite style. *De-gozaimasu* usage is chosen more because of style rather than social status.

It is also possible to change *suru* into its humble form, *itasu*, creating an even more humble form *otodokeitashimasu*, for example. When the progressive form [V*te* + *-iru*] is used, it is possible to use respectful and humble forms of [V*te* + *-iru*]; that is, [V*te* + *-irassharu*] and [V*te* + *-oru*], respectively, as in *sensei wa ima (o)tegami o yonde-irasshaimasu*, for example.

Conjugating *-aru* ending verbs. As a special class of verbs among verbs listed above, the following special verbs, which are *-aru* ending verbs, conjugate as shown below.

[Vbasic]	formal non-past	informal past	formal past
いらっしゃる *irassharu*	いらっしゃいます *irasshaimasu*	いらっしゃった *irasshatta*	いらっしゃいました *irasshaimashita*
おっしゃる *ossharu*	おっしゃいます *osshaimasu*	おっしゃった *osshatta*	おっしゃいました *osshaimashita*
くださる *kudasaru*	くださいます *kudasaimasu*	くださった *kudasatta*	くださいました *kudasaimashita*
ござる *gozaru*	ございます *gozaimasu*	ござった *gozatta*	ございました *gozaimashita*

***Okaeri da* as a respectful form.** Another strategy for respectful expressions takes [*o* + Vstem + *da*]. For example, *kaeru* can take *okaeri desu*. This strategy carries a slightly lesser degree of respect than the [*o* + Vstem + *ninaru*] strategy.

■ Examples

(1) 先生はもうお帰りになりましたが…… [respectful/formal]
Sensei wa moo okaerininarimashita ga ...
(The professor has already [gone home] left ...)

(2) 先生はもう帰られましたが…… [respectful/formal]
Sensei wa moo kaeraremashita ga ...
(The professor has already left ...)

(3) すぐお電話おかけしますので…… [humble/formal]
Sugu odenwa okakeshimasu node ...
(I will call right away.)

(4) 先生いらっしゃいますか。 [respectful/formal]
Sensei irasshaimasu ka.
(Is the professor in?)

(5) 会議で小出部長にお会いになりましたか。 [respectful/formal]
Kaigi de Koide buchoo ni oaininarimashita ka.
(Did you see manager Koide at the meeting?)

(6) お手紙拝見いたしました。 [super humble/formal]
Otegami haiken-itashimashita.
(I read your letter.)

(7) それでは少しお聞きしますが…… [humble/formal]
Soredewa sukoshi okikishimasu ga . . .
(Now I would like to ask you something . . .)

(8) あしたいらっしゃる？ [respectful/informal]
Ashita irassharu?
(Are you going tomorrow?)

■ Additional Information

The term "politeness" is a general term that encompasses various aspects of interaction. The humble and respectful forms of the honorific system, which are our focus here, are only a part of the overall "politeness" phenomenon. To be polite in human interaction involves social etiquette, euphemism, and conversational strategies—including things such as what to talk about, how and how not to ask questions, and how non-verbal and paralinguistic (intonation, for example) features are incorporated in your interaction.

87. Eye-witness Conjecture—*Soona*

■ Target Expression

That cake looks delicious.

そのケーキおいしそうだなあ。
Sono keeki oishisoo da naa.

[V/Adj stem + *soona*]

■ Grammatical Explanation

Conjecture with *soona*. The auxiliary adjective [*soona*] is attached to [Vstem] and [Adj stem], and functions to add the meaning of 'looks (as if) . . .' and 'appears as if . . .' (The [Adj stem] is obtained by: for [Adj-*i*], delete the final -*i*, for [Adj-*na*], delete the final -*na*). *Soona* cannot co-occur with [N + *da*] structure except when it is negative; *gakusei ja nasasoo da* 'he doesn't seem to be a student.'

When using [*soona*], the speaker conjectures the likelihood of a future event or the current condition of something, based on what the speaker personally perceives. When using [*soona*], the speaker conveys that as far as he or she is concerned, the information typically accompanying what one conjectures is immediately available and is directly observed. For example, you are looking at a beautiful and delicious-looking cake at a pastry shop. You conjecture based on that directly perceived information that it looks good, *oishisoo da naa!*

***Yosasoona* and *nasasoona*.** There are two exceptions to be noted when using the [*soona*] form; for the adjective *yoi* (or *ii*), *yosasoona* is used and similarly for the adjective *nai*, *nasasoona* is used.

(a) この映画は**よさそう**だよ。
*Kono eega wa **yosasoo** da yo.*
(This movie looks [as if it is] good.)

(b) 食べる物あまり**なさそう**ですね。
*Taberu mono amari **nasasoo** desu ne.*
(It appears [as if] there is not much food.)

Conjecturing future events. The [Vstem + *soona*] pattern is often used for conjecturing future events.

(c) 雨が**降りそう**だよ。
*Ame ga **hurisoo** da yo.*
(It looks as if it is going [it is likely] to rain.)

You might imagine the following situation where the expression above is appropriately used. You just stepped out of your house and realize that the sky is covered with dark rain clouds. You notice the wind kicking up, and the anticipation of summer rain is felt in the air. You call out to your brother with whom you are about to go out to play catch with, warning that the weather isn't cooperating. "Hey, it looks like rain is coming!" Again, this expression is used to mean 'I am personally under the impression that something is likely to be the case or to happen,' and that conclusion is based on the speaker's own sense perception (usually sight, occasionally smell).

Negating *soona*. Regarding the negation of [*soona*], the following is to be noted. [*Soona*] itself can be negated to mean 'doesn't look as if'; *oishisoo dewa-arimasen*. It is also possible to negate the adjective; *oishikunasasoo desu*, to mean 'looks as if it is not delicious.' When [*soona*] is preceded by a verb, however, only [*sooni nai*] or [*soomo nai*] negative forms are possible, with the latter conveying slightly stronger negation; *ame wa hurisoomo arimasen yo* 'it doesn't look (as if) it will rain at all.'

***Soona* as a modifier.** Since the [*soona*] expression itself conjugates as an [Adj-*na*], this structure can modify a noun directly.

(d) **おいしそうな**ケーキですね。
***Oishisoona** keeki desu ne.*
(It is a delicious-looking cake, isn't it?)

(e) **むずかしそうな**本ですね。
***Muzukashisoona** hon desu ne.*
(This is a difficult-looking book, isn't it?)

88. Connecting Clauses with *To*

■ Target Expression

When April comes, cherry blossoms bloom.

四月になると桜が咲きます。

Shigatsu ni naru to sakura ga sakimasu.

conjunction [*to*]

■ Grammatical Explanation

Using *to* to connect clauses. The conjunction [*to*] 'when' or 'whenever' (a different word from the particle [*to*] for joint action and enumerative expression) connects clauses in the following situations. The form preceding this [*to*] is [Vbasic].

1. When an action occurs, something else always or habitually occurs:

(1a) あの人は酒を少し飲む**と**陽気になります。

Ano	*hito*	*wa*	*sake*	*o*	*sukoshi*	*nomu*	***to***	*yookini*	*narimasu.*[*1]
that	person	T	*sake*	O	little	drink	when	cheerfully	become

(When [whenever] she drinks a little, she becomes cheerful.)

2. When an action is followed by something else which occurs as a natural and obvious consequence:

(2a) 3と5を足す**と**8になる。

San	*to*	*go*	*o*	*tasu*	***to***	*hachi*	*ni*	*naru.*[*1]
three	and	five	O	add	when	eight	to	become

(When you add three and five, it becomes eight.)

*1. The verb *naru* 'to become' takes [N + *ni*] to indicate the result of becoming; *Sensei ni naru* 'to become a teacher' and *otona ni naru* 'to become an adult.' When *naru* co-occurs with adjectives, both [Adj-*i*] and [Adj-*na*] take adverbial forms; *akaruku naru* 'to became light' and *benrini naru* 'to became convenient.'

3. When an action follows immediately after another action:
(This expression is normally followed by *sugu* 'immediately.')

(3a) 戸が開く**と**すぐ子犬が飛び出してきました。

To	*ga*	*aku*	***to***	*sugu*	*koinu*	*ga*	*tobidashite-kimashita.*
door	S	open	when	right away	puppy	S	jumped out

(When the door opened, a puppy jumped out right away.)

Warning

As shown in sentence (3a) above, in Japanese there is no grammatical "tense agreement" as observed in English. In English when the tense of the main verb is past, the tense of the subordinate clause must agree with this past tense. In Japanese the tense of the *to* clause, which cannot take the past tense, is interpreted on the basis of the tense of the main verb. In (3a), although the verb *aku* is in the nonpast form, since the main verb is in past tense form, *tobidashite-kimashita* 'jumped out,' the time that the door opened is interpreted as past tense as reflected in the English translation.

89. Pointing Out Resemblance and Likelihood—*Yoona*

Target Expressions

He speaks like a Japanese.

あの人は日本人のようにしゃべるね。
Ano hito wa Nihon-jin no yooni shaberu ne.

It seems (to me) that it began to rain.

雨が降ってきたようですね。
Ame ga hutte-kita yoo desu ne.

[*yoona*]

Grammatical Explanation

Resemblance/likelihood and *yoona*. When pointing out resemblance and expressing the likelihood, the [Adj-*na*] *yoona* is used. (The word *yoo* means 'manner' and 'appearance.') [*Yoona*] may be used as an adjective in the form of [*yoona*] and as an adverb in the form of [*yooni*]. [*Yoona*] cannot be used independently; it must be preceded by modifiers such as demonstratives, [N + *no*] structure, adjectives, and clausal modifiers. The verb and adjective forms immediately preceding [*yoona*] is [V/Adj pre-nominal].

Two meanings of *yoona*. The [*yoona*] pattern is used in two distinctive ways. First, it is used to mean in English 'it resembles' to express that something is approximately X although it is not quite X. We will call this use the "resemblance" [*yoona*]. The "resemblance" *yoona* co-occurs only with the noun; *ano ko wa otoko no ko no yoo da* 'that child resembles a boy,' for example, is used when describing a tomboy.

Second, it is used to mean in English 'it appears (to me)' or 'it seems (to me)' when the speaker expresses a personal judgment as to the likelihood of a state or event. We will call this use of [*yoona*] the "likelihood" *yoona*.

Negating *yoona*. For negation of the [*yoona*] expression, in the case of "resemblance" use, it is possible to negate both the noun and *yoona* itself, as shown in (a) and (b). In case of "likelihood" *yoona*, however, negation of *yoona* itself is not normally used, as illustrated by (c) and (d).

(a) 男の子**ではない**ようだ。 *Otoko no ko **dewa nai** yoo da.*

(b) 男の子のよう**ではない**。 *Otoko no ko no yoo **dewa-nai**.*

(c) 雨は**降っていない**ようだ。 *Ame wa **hutte-inai** yoo da.*

(d) *雨は降るよう**ではない**。 **Ame wa huru yoo **dewa-nai**.*

***Yoona* versus *soona*.** By now you might be wondering about the difference between the "likelihood" [*yoona*] and [*soona*] which we learned two entries earlier. The difference between these two can be found by contrasting these forms in the following situation.

You see a fork sticking partly off the table, in a precarious position. Here you must use *ochisoo da* 'looks (as if) it's going to fall' in order to describe the fork. You have direct visual evidence to make this statement.

Imagine another situation. You are in your dorm room with poor soundproofing. You aren't quite sure if your next-door resident left his room or not. You do hear some noise, however, which seems to come from his room, although you are not sure. Considering the fact that he is sometimes in his room at nine in the morning, you say, *mada iru yoo da* 'it is likely that he is still there.' When using *yoona*, the evidence consists of a combination of various facts (including some that are gained through sense perception), and the speaker does not have access to decisive direct evidence to conjecture as in the case of [*soona*]. What is involved in using [*yoona*] is that the speaker uses information available to reach a conclusion, after going through a certain reasoning process.

Unlike [*soona*], "likelihood" *yoona* can be used to point out the likelihood of a past event or state. While it is not possible to conjecture a past event when using [*soona*], it is possible with the [*yoona*] expression, as shown in example (3) to follow. The [*yoona*] pattern is different from the [*soona*] structure in that the [*yoona*] expression describes approximately the way things are. [*Soona*] on the other hand is used primarily for predicting something in the future or for describing states relevant to the future.

Using *yooni*. The adverbial form of [*yoona*], that is [*yooni*], has many useful functions. First, [N + *no yooni*] and [clause + *yooni*] are equivalent to the English conjunction *as*.

(e) ご存じ**のように**……
*Gozonji **no yooni**...*
(As you know ...)

(f) 先生が**おっしゃったように**この本はとてもむずかしかったです。
*Sensei ga **osshatta yooni** kono hon wa totemo muzukashikatta-desu.*
(As you told me, professor, this book was quite difficult.)

Additionally, [*yooni*] expresses purpose, as in:

(g) 早く**終わるように**急いで仕事をしましょう。
*Hayaku **owaru yooni** isoide shigoto o shimashoo.*
(Let's do the work in a hurry so that it will be over soon.)

Other idiomatic uses include *yooni yuu* 'to tell to' and *yooni naru* 'to become,' which we will revisit.

Preference for *yoona*. The [*yoona*] expression is favored by Japanese even when the meaning of 'it appears' and 'it seems' is only weakly traced. For example, it is customary to say *kono yoona baai* 'in this case,' not **kono baai*. Instead of saying *sonna koto*, using *sono yoona koto* makes the statement more formal and somewhat softer, indirect, and less impactful.

■ Examples

(1) ここはどこ？
Koko wa doko?
(Where am I?)

みんなサラリーマンのような服装をしている。
Minna sarariiman no yoona hukusoo o shite-iru.
(Everybody is dressed like a businessman.)

しかし子供のような日本語でしゃべっている。
Shikashi kodomo no yoona Nihongo de shabette-iru.
(But they are all speaking childish Japanese.)

まわりは静かで、あまり店もないようだ。
Mawari wa shizuka de, amari mise mo nai yoo da.
(The surroundings are quiet and there seem to be no stores.)

駅だけあって人が大勢いる。
Eki dake atte hito ga oozei iru.
(There is only a station where there are a lot of people.)

みんな電車を待っているようだ。
Minna densha o matte-iru yoo da.
(They all seem to be waiting for a train.)

これは夢の中に出てきた風景。
Kore wa yume no naka ni dete-kita huukei.
(This is a scene which appeared in a dream.)

ふしぎな風景だ。
Hushigina huukei da.
(It's a strange scene.)

(2) まあ山中先生のような先生はあまりいませんよね。
Maa Yamanaka-sensei no yoona sensei wa amari imasen yo ne.
(Well, there aren't too many teachers like Ms. Yamanaka.)

(3) 会議はもう終わったようだね。
Kaigi wa moo owatta yoo da ne.
(The meeting seems like it ended.)

■ Additional Information

- A colloquial expression [*mitaina*] is also used similarly to "likelihood" [*yoona*]. [*Mitaina*] is preceded by a noun or [V/Adj pre-Aux] forms.

(a) ねえ、あの人ほんとにばか**みたい**。
*Nee, ano hito hontoni baka **mitai**.*
(He's really like a fool.)

(b) ほら、急げよ、映画はもう終わった**みたい**だから。 [blunt style]
*Hora, isoge yo, eiga wa moo owatta **mitai** da kara.*[*1]
(Come on, hurry, the movie seems to have ended.)

*1. *Isoge* is an abrupt command form briefly discussed in Entry 79.

- The phrase *mitaina* functions at utterance-final position as a device to qualify what precedes. As shown below, *mitaina* functions like a quotation marker, only to qualify the quoted portion as being something similar (and not exact). *Mitaina* makes it possible to express one's feelings without fully committing to it.

(c) あした会社休む、**みたいな**。
*Ashita kaisha yasumu, **mitaina**.*
(It's like, I'm going to skip my work tomorrow, maybe.)

(d) **A:** はっきり言いなさいよ、彼に。
Hakkiri iinasai yo, kare ni.
(Tell that to him clearly!)

B: えっ。あなたが好きです、**みたいな**？
*Ett. Anata ga suki desu, **mitaina**?*
(What? Like, I love you?)

90. Language of Emotion (1)—Pleasure, Sadness, and Anger

■ Target Expressions

Wow, am I glad!

やあ、うれしいよ、ほんとに！
Yaa, ureshii yo, hontoni!
わあ、うれしい！
Waa, ureshii!

■ Grammatical Explanation

Expressing emotion with adjectives. Although there may be an impression held by Westerners that Japanese do not show emotion, among familiar *uchi* members in informal and intimate situations, Japanese show their emotions quite readily. When expressing one's own emotions, descriptive terms of [Adj-*i*] and [Adj-*na*] are used as shown below. Since emotion is frequently expressed straightforwardly without regard to the speech style, informal expressions are widely used.

(a) うれしいなあ！
Ureshii naa!
(Great!)

(b) 幸せ！
Shiawase!
(I am happy!)

(c) 残念ですねえ。
Zannen desu nee.
(I'm sorry to hear that.)

(d) めっちゃ悲しい。 [casual style]
Metcha kanashii.
(I'm really sad.)

When emotion is expressed in written style, it is often accompanied by the phrase *omou* 'to think,' as in *kanashiku omou* '(lit., to think) to feel sad.'

Referring to someone else's emotion. When describing someone else's emotion, a different strategy must be used. This is because these personal emotions are only indirectly describable. The only way to have access to someone's internal feelings is to observe an outward sign that someone is actually feeling the emotion. When such a sign is evident, the [*soona*] expression or the [Adj stem + *gatte-iru*] structure is used.

(e) ラリーさんは奥さんをなくして**寂しそうだ**。
Rarii-san wa okusan o nakushite ***sabishisoo da.***
Larry T wife O lose seems lonely
(Larry seems lonely since his wife passed away.)

(f) ラリーさんはとても**寂しがっています**よ。
Rarii-san wa totemo ***sabishigatte-imasu*** *yo.*
([lit., Larry shows that he is very lonely] Larry is very lonely.)

Expressing anger. Although so far we have focused on adjectives that express emotion, there are many other ways to express one's emotion. Anger is often expressed in such a way, as shown below.

腹が立つ	*hara ga tatsu*	to get angry, to be furious
頭に来る	*atama ni kuru*	to get mad, to lose one's cool
ムカつく	*mukatsuku*	to get disgustedly mad

(g) あいつまた一時間も遅刻。**ムカつく**！ [blunt style]
Aitsu mata ichijikan mo chikoku. ***Mukatsuku!***
(He's an hour late again. I'm totally disgusted!)

(h) **頭に来る**なあ。また値上げだって。
Atama ni kuru *naa. Mata neage datte.*
(I'm mad [and upset]. They are raising the price again.)

Cursing words. At the point of extreme anger, Japanese people use curse words. Needless to say, these expressions should be used very sparingly. They are blunt, and rarely observed in feminine speech.

(i) くそ。
Kuso.
(Shit.)

(j) くそ、ビールもうないや。
Kuso, biiru moo nai ya.
(Shit, the beer's all gone.)

(k) ちくしょう。
Chikushoo.
([lit., beasts] Hell!/Damn!/Fuck!)

■ Additional Information

- Direct expressions of a psychological state and emotion may be used when describing someone else's emotion in a narrative. For example, when a writer chooses an expression *Saeko wa kanashikatta* 'Saeko was sad,' the writer assumes an omniscient viewpoint; the writer has access to Saeko's internal feelings.

- I should also mention that there is a group of verbs to express active emotional experience. For example, *kanashimu* 'to grieve' as in *gakusei wa tomo no shi o kanashinda* 'the student grieved over his or her friend's death.'
- For those of you who are interested in learning more about how to express feelings and emotion in Japanese, refer to *Jooi no Gengogaku: Bakooshooron to Nihongo Hyoogen no Patosu* (Maynard 2000) and *Expressive Japanese: A Reference Guide to Sharing Emotion and Empathy* (Maynard 2005). The latter introduces emotion expressions in detail, including emotion adjectives and other expressive strategies, such as (a), which uses no emotion words yet conveys strong feelings.

(a) **A:** やったあ！ 大学、合格した。
Yattaa! Daigaku, gookaku-shita.
(Wow, I did it! I passed the university entrance exam.)

B: やったね。おめでとう。
Yatta ne. Omedetoo.
(You did it. Congratulations.)

91. Non-self-committing Speculation—*Rashii*

■ Target Expression

The person who newly joined the company seems to be from Kyoto.

今度入社した人は京都の出身らしい。
Kondo nyuusha-shita hito wa Kyooto no shusshin rashii.

[*rashii*]

■ Grammatical Explanation

Speculating with *rashii*. A structure using the *i*-type auxiliary adjective *rashii* 'it seems' expresses speculation based on information, primarily obtained from sources other than self. *Rashii* follows [V/Adj pre-Aux] forms. The [*rashii*] pattern is used when there is speculation based on a definite source or reason, but most likely to have come from someone else as hearsay. [*Rashii*] is not used when your speculation is merely based on a purely personal impression or interpretation. When using *rashii*, the speaker conveys a likeliness of it being so, but little commitment is made as to whether the speaker himself or herself believes the certainty of it. This is partly because speculation is based on secondhand information.

Rashii* versus *yoona. When using *rashii*, unlike *yoona*, the speaker distances himself or herself from the statement made; the speaker conveys that he or she is not totally committed to nor is totally responsible for the statement made. This speaker's attitude may be best described in English as 'it seems … and it apparently is the case, according to what I hear, although I'm not going to bet on it.'

Negating *rashii*. The negation is achieved by negating the verb preceding *rashii*, and not by negating *rashii* itself. For example, *ano hito wa Kyooto no shusshin janai rashii* 'it seems that he is not from Kyoto.'

Sensei-rashii hito. Another use of *rashii* should not be forgotten, although it does not express speculation nor estimation. This *rashii* expresses an appropriate quality of action and state when it appears as [N + *rashii*]. For example, a teacher who behaves as a teacher should is *sensei rashii* 'teacher-like.' When using *rashii* in this sense, the speaker has made an evaluative judgment that X exhibits the kind of standard quality and characteristics necessary to be X. For this use of *rashii*, a negative *rashikunai* 'of inappropriate quality' is used.

■ Examples

(1) **A:** 秘密で、佐々木さん結婚したらしいよ。
Himitsu de, Sasaki-san kekkon-shita rashii yo.
([lit., Being a secret] Secretly, Ms. Sasaki seems to have gotten married.)

B: えっ、うそ。マジ？
Ett, uso. Maji?
(You must be kidding. Really?)

(2) **A:** トムは先月アメリカへ帰ったらしいですよ。
Tomu wa sengetsu Amerika e kaetta rashii-desu yo.
(It seems that Tom went back to the States last month.)

B: まじッスか。知りませんでした。
Maji ssu ka. Shirimasen-deshita.
(Is that right? I didn't know that.)

(3) **A:** となりの木村さんはきのうから留守らしいね。
Tonari no Kimura-san wa kinoo kara rusu rashii ne.
(Ms. Kimura, the next door neighbor, seems to have been gone since yesterday.)

B: うん、そうみたい。
Un, soo mitai.
(Yes, so it seems.)

(4) この子は朝から何も食べてないらしい。
Kono ko wa asa kara nani-mo tabete-nai rashii.
(It seems that this child hasn't eaten anything since morning.)

(5) 疲れたらしく、子供は寝てしまいました。
Tsukareta rashiku, kodomo wa nete-shimaimashita.
(Seeming to be tired, the child is now asleep.)

(6) あの人は少しも先生らしくないね。
Ano hito wa sukoshimo sensei rashikunai ne.
(That person is not teacer-like at all, is he?)

(7) かなちゃんは本当に女の子らしいですねえ。
Kana-chan wa hontooni onna no ko rashii-desu nee.
(Kana is really girl-like, isn't she?)

(8) 学生らしくきちんと行動してください。
Gakusei rashiku kichinto koodoo-shite-kudasai.
(Please behave appropriately by doing what students are expected to do.)

■ Additional Information

Here is a summary of differences among the three expressions [*soona*] (Entry 87), [*yoona*] (Entry 89), and [*rashii*], all of which share similar meanings represented by the English *seem* or *appear to*.

[*soona*]: [Adj-*na*] 'it looks (as if)' 'it appears as if'
Expresses the speaker's conjecture regarding the present state and the future event based on the speaker's own perceptual evidence.

[*yoona*]: [Adj-*na*] 'resemble' 'looks like (to me)'
Expresses "resemblance" and "likelihood" of facts, including past events, based on indirectly obtained evidence. The speculation is reached after reasoning; [*mitaina*] is similar to [*yoona*] except that it is more colloquial.

[*rashii*]: [Adj-*i*] 'it seems, (it apparently is the case)'
Expresses speculation based on evidence often witnessed or obtained by others; the deductive and speculative thought process is conducted based on secondhand information. Weak or no personal commitment to the statement.

Good sentences to memorize for these expressions are:

(a) 雨が降り**そう**です。
*Ame ga huri**soo** desu.*
(It appears to rain.)

(b) おいし**そうな**ケーキですね。
*Oishi**soona** keeki desu ne.*
(It's a delicious-looking cake.)

(c) メリーは男の子の**よう**だ。
*Merii wa otoko no ko no **yoo** da.*
(Mary resembles [behaves like] a boy.)

(d) 会議はもう終わった**よう**ですよ。
*Kaigi wa moo owatta **yoo** desu yo.*
(The meeting seems to have ended.)

(e) 茜は外国で結婚した**らしい**よ。
*Akane wa gaikoku de kekkon-shita **rashii** yo.*
(Akane seems to have gotten married abroad.)

(f) 男**らしい**男って誰かな。
*Otoko **rashii** otoko tte dare ka na.*
(I wonder who a manly man may be.)

92. Conditional (1)—*Ba*-form

■ Target Expressions

If you read that letter, you'll understand.

その手紙を読めばわかりますよ。
Sono tegami o yomeba wakarimasu yo.

If it's fresh fish, it will be delicious.

新鮮な魚なら(ば)おいしいでしょう。
Shinsenna sakana nara(ba) oishii-deshoo.

conditional [-*ba*]
[V/Adj pre-Aux + *nara(ba)*]

■ Grammatical Explanation

***Ba* conditional.** The conditional *ba*-form is used to express condition, that is, something is required in order for the event or state of something else to occur. The [-*ba*] conditional is the most general straightforward conditional expression in Japanese. In the [-*ba*] pattern, the condition specified in the [-*ba*] clause must be satisfied first; then on that condition, the event described in the main clause is expected to occur.

Conditional [-*Ba*] Form

U-, RU-, existential and irregular verbs: Replace the final *-u* with *-eba*.

行く	ik**u**	to go	→	行けば	ik**eba**
食べる	taber**u**	to eat	→	食べれば	taber**eba**
いる	ir**u**	to exist, to be	→	いれば	ir**eba**
来る	kur**u**	to come	→	来れば	kur**eba**

[*Adj-i*]: Replace the final *-i* with *-kereba*.

高い	taka**i**	expensive	→	高ければ	taka**kereba**
涼しい	suzushi**i**	cool	→	涼しければ	suzushi**kereba**

Note that the negation of verbs, takes the *-nai* form, which conjugates like [Adj-*i*]; *ikanai*, for example, takes *ikanakereba*.

[*Adj-na*]: Replace *da* with *nara(ba)*. The *ba* of *nara(ba)* is frequently deleted.

便利だ	benri **da**	convenient	→	便利なら(ば)	benri **nara(ba)**

Be-verb: Replace the verb with *nara(ba)*. The *ba* of *nara(ba)* is frequently deleted.

日本人だ	Nihon-jin **da**	Japanese	→	日本人なら(ば)	Nihon-jin **nara(ba)**
五千円だ	go-sen-en **da**	five thousand yen	→	五千円なら(ば)	go-sen-en **nara(ba)**

The negative conditional also has the meaning of 'unless' in situations as shown below:

(a) 早く起き**なければ**五時の電車に間に合いませんよ。

Hayaku	*oki**nakereba***	*go-ji*	*no*	*densha ni*	*maniamasen*	*yo.*
early	do not get up	five o'clock	L	train	be in time	IP

(Unless you get up early, you will be late for the five-o'clock train.)

***Nara(ba)* conditional.** Beyond the *ba*-form, condition is expressed by [V/Adj pre-Aux + *nara(ba)*]. The [*nara(ba)*] condition preceded by [V/Adj] is used when the information given as condition originates not in the speaker, but is suggested by someone else, often by the addressee. For example, when the addressee says or shows signs to indicate that he or she is going to pay for the drinks, the appropriate conditional expression is something like *kimi ga harau nara isshoni iku yo* 'if (you say that) you are going to pay for it, I will go with you.' In these situations, the addressee has expressed or at least has hinted at the idea. While the *ba*-form conditional originates in the speaker, the [*nara(ba)*] conditional is preferred when the condition is suggested by the addressee. It should be pointed out that *naraba* is used in written or formal style more frequently. In casual conversation *nara* is often preferred.

Meaning of [N + *nara*]. When *nara* is preceded by [N], it has both straightforward and condition-originating-in-the-addressee readings.

(b) (お)金持ち**なら**何でも買えるね。
*(O)kanemochi **nara** nan de mo kaeru ne.*
(If you are rich, you can buy anything.)

(c) (お)金持ち**なら**少し(お)金貸して。
*(O)kanemochi **nara** sukoshi (o)kane kashite.*
(If [you say that] you are rich, loan me some.)

■ Examples

(1) これを読めばわかりますよ。
Kore o yomeba wakarimasu yo.
(If you read this you will understand.)

(2) 大阪を八時に出れば、東京に十一時には着きます。
Oosaka o hachi-ji ni dereba, Tookyoo ni juu ichi-ji ni wa tsukimasu.
(If you leave Osaka at eight o'clock, you will arrive at Tokyo by eleven.)

(3) 君が来なければ、パーティー、盛り上がらないよ。
Kimi ga konakereba, paatii, moriagaranai yo.
(If you don't come, the party won't be fun.)

(4) 学生なら学生らしく行動して。
Gakusei nara gakusei rashiku koodoo-shite.
(If you are a student, behave like a student should.)

(5) 五千円なら買うけど……
Go-sen-en nara kau kedo . . .
(If it is five thousand yen, I will buy it.)

(6) そうしたいならばそうしましょう。
Soo shitai naraba soo shimashoo.
(If you want to do so, let's do so.)

(7) 山田さんがそう言うなら、それが正しいんじゃない？
Yamada-san ga soo yuu nara, sore ga tadashii n ja-nai?
(If Yamada-san says so, won't that be correct?)

(8) 君が正しいと思うなら、そうするよ。
Kimi ga tadashii to omou nara, soo suru yo.
(If you think it right, I will do it.)

■ Additional Information

- The conditional phrase *nara* may also be used to introduce topics as shown below. Unlike the topic marker *wa* which introduces the topic originating from the speaker, *nara* introduces topics which have often been suggested by the addressee. The speaker picks up the topic suggested by the addressee and continues by offering his or her personal opinions on the topic.

(a) A: 京都大学に行こうと思っています。
Kyooto daigaku ni ikoo to omotte-imasu.
(I'm thinking about going to Kyoto University.)

B: あの大学**なら**いい勉強ができますよ。
Ano daigaku ***nara*** *ii benkyoo ga dekimasu yo.*
([lit., If that university] As for that university, you can study well.)

(b) A: 田代さんどうしてるでしょうかねえ……
Tashiro-san doo shite-ru deshoo ka nee . . .
(How is Ms. Tashiro doing, I wonder . . .)

B: 田代さん**なら**元気ですよ。
Tashiro-san ***nara*** *genki desu yo.*
(Oh, Ms. Tashiro, she's fine.)

- The [*-ba*] conditional is also used in the structure [V + *-ba yokatta*]—with *yokatta* being informal past tense of the [Adj-*i*] *yoi* (or *ii*) 'good'—meaning 'I should have done so . . .'

(c) パーティーに行け**ばよかった**。
*Paatii ni ike**ba yokatta**.*
(I should have gone to the party.)

(d) 電話しなけれ**ばよかった**。
*Denwa-shinakere**ba yokatta**.*
(I should not have called.)

93. Conditional (2)—*Tara*

■ Target Expression

If and when you have read this letter, please call right away.

この手紙を読んだらすぐ電話してください。

Kono tegami o yondara sugu denwa-shite-kudasai.

[-*tara*]

■ Grammatical Explanation

***Tara* conditional.** The conditional [-*tara*] has both a temporal and conditional function. [-*Tara*] is formed by [V/Adj informal past + -*ra*] structure. For negation, use *tabenakattara* 'if you haven't eaten,' which is the product of the same process by changing *nai* to past informal *nakatta*.

Using *tara* conditional. The [-*tara*] conditional offers several interpretations depending on the type and the tense of the verb.

1. When the situation expressed in the [-*tara*] clause is certain to happen, temporal interpretation 'when ...' is appropriate.

   (1a) 六時になっ**たら**帰りましょう。
   *Rokuji ni nat**tara** kaerimashoo.*
   (When it becomes six o'clock, let's go back.)

2. When the situation expressed in the [-*tara*] clause is uncertain, use a conditional interpretation.

   (2a) 時間があっ**たら**飲みに行きましょう。
   *Jikan ga at**tara** nomi ni ikimashoo.*
   (If there's time, let's go out drinking.)

3. When the main clause is in past tense, temporal reading is appropriate.

   (3a) 駅につい**たら**すぐ山本先生がいらっしゃいました。
   *Eki ni tsui**tara** sugu Yamamoto-sensei ga irasshaimashita.*
   (When I arrived at the station, soon Professor Yamamoto came.)

4. When the verb in the [-*tara*] clause is stative, or [-*tara*] occurs with an adjective, only the conditional reading is appropriate.

   (4a) 買いたい本があっ**たら**、買いましょう。
   *Kaitai hon ga at**tara**, kaimashoo.*
   (If there are books you'd like to buy, let's buy some.)

(4b) 高かっ**たら**買わないでください。
*Takakat**tara** kawanaide-kudasai.*
(If it is expensive, please do not buy it.)

When the stative verb is used in the [-*tara*] clause, the main verb is normally non-past.

5. When the action referred to in the main clause is in the past tense, that action must be uncontrollable by the speaker.

(5a) *うちへ帰っ**たら**勉強した。
*Uchi e kaet**tara** benkyoo-shita.*

(5b) うちへ帰っ**たら**すぐ友だちが来た。
*Uchi e kaet**tara** sugu tomodachi ga kita.*
(When I returned home a friend came right away.)

***Tara* and main verb.** When using the [-*tara*] clause, two events are always interpreted in the chronological order in which they appear; the [-*tara*] clause event occurs prior to the main clause event, as shown in (5b) above. However, if the main verb is stative, the two events may occur simultaneously as in (a).

(a) うちへ帰っ**たら**母がいた。
*Uchi e kaet**tara** haha ga ita.*
(When I returned home, my mother was there.)

Expressing desire with *tara*. The [-*tara*] clause can be used independently to express desire. For example, *okane ga attara naa/nee* 'I wish I had money …' It describes a situation contrary to facts. We will discuss the subjunctive expressions later under a separate entry.

***Tara* versus *ba* conditional.** The difference between the [-*tara*] conditional and the [-*ba*] conditional is found in the degree to which the speaker assumes the condition will be realized. Compare the following sentences.

(b) 春子さんが**帰ってきたら**これをわたしてください。

Haruko-san	*ga*	***kaette-kitara***	*kore*	*o*	*watashite-kudasai.*
Ms. Haruko	S	return	this	O	please hand

(If and when Haruko returns, please hand this to her.)

(c) 春子さんが**帰ってくれば**この問題の答えはわかるんですが……
*Haruko-san ga **kaette-kureba** kono mondai no kotae wa wakaru n desu ga …*
(If Haruko should return, this problem would be solved.)

In (b) the speaker feels that the condition (of Haruko returning) is likely to be met. In (c), the speaker is less committed as to the possibility of the condition to be met, and communicates that 'if Haruko returns at all,' expressing a greater sense of doubt.

■ Examples

(1) ジャクソンさんに会ったらよろしく言ってください。
Jakuson-san ni attara yoroshiku itte-kudasai.
(If and when you see Mr. Jackson, please give my regards.)

(2) ビルを出たらすぐケータイが鳴った。
Biru o detara sugu keetai ga natta.
(When I came out of the building, immediately the cell phone rang.)

(3) A: お金がたまったらアフリカ旅行をしたいなあ。
Okane ga tamattara Ahurika ryokoo o shitai naa.
(If and when I have saved [enough] money, I want to make a trip to Africa.)

B: 私もアフリカへ行きたい。
Watashi mo Ahurika e ikitai.
(I want to go to Africa, too.)

(4) すみませんが、ココアがなかったらカフェオレをお願いします。
Sumimasen ga, kokoa ga nakattara kafeore o onegaishimasu.
(If there is no cocoa, I will take café au lait, please.)

(5) A: シカゴにいらっしゃったらぜひお寄りください。
Shikago ni irasshattara zehi oyori-kudasai.
(If and when you come to Chicago, please stop by.)

B: ありがとうございます。
Arigatoo gozaimasu.
(Thank you.)

■ Additional Information

The [*-tara*] conditional has an idiomatic use, i.e., *-tara doo desu ka* as an expression of mild invitation and suggestion. In its colloquial version, *desu ka* may be deleted, as in (b), which can further be shortened to *hayaku netara?*

(a) 頭が痛いなら帰っ**たらどうですか**。
*Atama ga itai nara kaet**tara doo desu ka**.*
(If you have a headache, [lit., How about returning home] why don't you go home?)

(b) 今夜は早く寝**たらどう**？
*Kon'ya wa hayaku ne**tara doo**?*
(How about going to bed early tonight?)

94. Greetings (2)—Formulaic Expressions for Special Occasions

■ Target Expression

Take care of yourself.

お大事に。
Odaiji ni.

■ Strategic Explanation

A number of formulaic phrases are used for greetings at special occasions in Japan. Greetings with the appropriate phrase is important for smooth social interaction. The following expressions are useful.

1. *New year's celebration*:

At the end of the year, the latter half of December, to those who you will not meet before New Year's Day:

(1a) それではよいお年を（お迎えください）。
Soredewa yoi otoshi o (omukae kudasai).
(I wish you'll have a good new year.)

During New Year's days (Jan. 1 to 3), and through early January, when you meet someone for the first time in the New Year:

(1b) A: 明けましておめでとうございます。今年もよろしくお願いします。
Akemashite omedetoo gozaimasu. Kotoshi mo yoroshiku onegai-shimasu.
(Happy New Year. [lit., Please treat me kindly.])

B: おめでとうございます。こちらこそよろしくお願いします。
Omedetoo gozaimasu. Kochira koso yoroshiku onegai-shimasu.
(Happy New Year. Same here.)

Note that among youth the greetings are shortened as *Ake ome* (from *Akemashite omedetoo*) and *Koto yoro* (from *Kotoshi mo yoroshiku*). These are used in very casual communication among youth only.

2. *Celebration*:

(2a) A: おめでとう(ございます)。
Omedetoo (gozaimasu).
(Congratulations.)

B: ありがとうございます。
Arigatoo gozaimasu.
(Thank you.)

(2b) (ご)結婚おめでとうございます。
(Go)kekkon omedetoo gozaimasu.
(Congratulations on your wedding.)

(2c) 誕生日おめでとう。
Tanjoobi omedetoo.
(Happy birthday.)

3. *Seeing someone after a long absence*:

(3a) A: ごぶさたしております。
Gobusata-shite-orimasu.
(lit., I haven't seen/written you for a long time.)

B: こちらこそ。
Kochira koso.
(Same here.)

(3b) お久しぶりです。
Ohisashiburi desu.
(Long time no see.)

(3c) A: よう、久しぶり！
Yoo, hisashiburi!
(Hey, how have you been?)

B: 久しぶりねえ。
Hisashiburi nee.
(Long time no see.)

4. *Showing sympathy*:

(4a) A: 大変ですねえ。
Taihen desu nee.
([lit., It's terrible, isn't it?] It's tough; I sympathize with you.)

B: ええ……
Ee . . .
(Yes . . .)

(4b) それはいけませんねえ。
Sore wa ikemasen nee.
(That's too bad.)

(4c) それは残念ですねえ。
Sore wa zannen desu nee.
([lit., It is regrettable.] I'm sorry to hear that.)

5. *To a sick person*:

(5a) おかぜはいかがですか。
Okaze wa ikaga desu ka.
(How is your cold?)

(5b) A: かぜはどう？
Kaze wa doo?
(How is your cold?)

B: もう大丈夫。
Moo daijoobu.
(I'm OK now.)

(5c) 具合はどう？
Guai wa doo?
([lit., How is your condition?] How are you feeling?)

(5d) A: お大事に。
Odaiji ni.
(Please take care.)

B: ありがとうございます。
Arigatoo gozaimasu.
(Thank you.)

6. *At a store*:
When a store attendant welcomes a customer or a guest:

(6a) いらっしゃいませ。
Irasshaimase.
(Welcome [to our place].)

When the customer leaves:

(6b) Store clerk: どうもありがとうございました。またどうぞ。
Doomo arigatoo gozaimashita. Mata doozo.
(Thank you very much. Please come again)

Customer: どうも。
Doomo.
(Bye.)

7. *General greetings in very familiar situations among* uchi *members* (not to be used when addressing your superior):

(7a) A: よう！
Yoo!
(Hi!)

B: ああ、おはよう！
Aa, ohayoo!
(Oh, Good morning!)

(7b) A: どう？ 最近は。
Doo? Saikin wa.
(How are you doing these days?)

B: うん、まあまあだね。
Un, maa maa da ne.
(So-so.)

(7c) A: 元気？
Genki?
(How have you been?)

B: うん、なんとか……
Un, nantoka . . .
(Oh, I've been fine . . .)

95. Describing State (4)—Current State in Reference to Past and Future

■ Target Expressions

The window is open.

窓が開けてあります。
Mado ga akete-arimasu.

I bought drinks (in preparation) for the party.

パーティーのための飲みもの、買っておきましたよ。
Paatii no tame no nomimono, katte-okimashita yo.

[V*te* + *-aru*] [V*te* + *-oku*]

■ Grammatical Explanation

Using [V*te* + *-aru*] structure. In Japanese, there are preferred methods for describing states in relation to the relevant past and present events. Here we concern ourselves with two such expressions. The first is the use of [V*te* + *-aru*] with transitive verbs, especially those that describe volitional action. The pattern [V*te* + *-aru*] indicates a state created as a result of someone's specific action described by the active verb. For example, when describing the window being open, if you wish to convey that someone opened it, *mado ga akete-aru* 'the window (was opened by someone and as a result it) is open' should be used. In other words, this pattern is used when the speaker is conscious of someone having caused the particular state being described.

More specifically, there are two situations where [V*te* + *-aru*] is ideally used; first, to focus on the existing result of an action implying that someone performed the action, and second, to focus on the fact that the preparation and/or efforts are made and the resulting state exists. Stative verbs and the *be*-verb are not used in this structure. This pattern cannot be used with the verb that the result of action is not observable or the result is not accumulative. For example, **shinjite-aru* (*shinjiru* 'to believe in') and **utatte-aru* (*utau* 'to sing') are not normally used.

Contrasting [V*te* + *-iru*] and [V*te* + *-aru*]. Recall that we learned the [V*te* + *-iru*] structure earlier. Here we contrast the usage of [V*te* + *-aru*] and [V*te* + *-iru*].

	Transitive	Intransitive
V*te-iru*	state/action in progress **(a)** 窓を開け**ている**。 *Mado o ake**te-iru**.*	state/action in progress or state resulting from an action **(b)** 窓が開い**ている**。 *Mado ga ai**te-iru**.*
V*te-aru*	state resulting from an action **(c)** 窓が開け**てある**。 *Mado ga ake**te-aru**.*	(not used)

Each of the three sentences appearing above is best used in the following circumstances.

1. When describing the very action of someone opening the window:

   (a) 窓を開け**ている**。
   *Mado o ake**te-iru**.*
   ([Someone] is opening the window.)

2. When describing the fact that the window is open, without concern as to who opened it or how it became open:

   (b) 窓が開い**ている**。
   *Mado ga ai**te-iru**.*
   (The window is open.)

3. When describing a cause/effect relationship where someone or something opened the window, and as a result the window is open:

   (c) 窓が開け**てある**。
   *Mado ga ake**te-aru**.*
   (The window is opened.)

Using [V*te* + -*oku*] structure. Let us examine another useful structure shown in the second target expression, the [V*te* + -*oku*] structure. [V*te* + -*oku*] structure describes a state achieved intentionally for some future purpose. The verbs used in this pattern are only those that describe volitional action. What you cannot control cannot be done intentionally in preparation for future use. As a colloquial version, *te-oku* changes to *toku* by dropping *te* and combining *t* and the initial *o* of *oku*.

(d) あしたは入学試験の日だから、よく眠っ**ておき**なさい。
*Ashita wa nyuugakushiken no hi da kara, yoku nemut**te-oki**nasai.*
(Tomorrow is the day for the entrance exam, so sleep well [for that].)

(e) 連絡し**といた**から。
*Renrakushi-**toita** kara.*
(I already contacted them, so.)

■ Examples

(1) **A:** テレビ消して！
Terebi keshite!
(Turn off the TV.)

B: テレビは消してありますよ。
Terebi wa keshite-arimasu yo.
(The TV is off.)

A: 本当？
Hontoo?
(Really?)

B: ええ、さっき消しましたから。
Ee, sakki keshimashita kara.
(Yes, I turned it off a while ago.)

A: ああ、ほんとだ！ 消えてる！
Aa, honto da! Kiete-ru!
(Ah, really. It is off.)

(2) **A:** あやかちゃんは？
Ayaka-chan wa?
(Where's Ayaka?)

B: さっきお皿、洗ってたよ。
Sakki osara, aratteta yo.
(She was washing dishes a while ago.)

A: ほんとだ。全部きれいに洗ってある。
Honto da. Zenbu kireini aratte-aru.
(Sure enough, all the dishes are washed clean.)

(3) 試験がある(の)ならよく勉強しておきなさいよ。
Shiken ga aru (no) nara yoku benkyoo shite-okinasai yo.
(If there's an exam, study well [in preparation for it].)

(4) 海外旅行をする前によく英語の練習をしておきました。
Kaigairyokoo o suru mae ni yoku eigo no renshuu o shite-okimashita.
(Before we traveled abroad, we practiced English [in preparation for it].)

(5) A: あしたの会議で発表するレポートは書いてありますか。
Ashita no kaigi de happyoo-suru repooto wa kaite-arimasu ka.
(Is the report to be presented at tomorrow's meeting written?)

B: 先週書いておいたから大丈夫です。
Senshuu kaite-oita kara daijoobu desu.
(I wrote it last week, so it should be fine.)

96. Compliments and Compliment Responses

■ Target Expressions

Your Japanese is very good.

日本語(お)上手ですね。
Nihongo (o)joozu desu ne.

Oh, no, I still have a lot to learn.

いいえ、まだまだです。
Iie, mada mada desu.

■ Strategic Explanation

Complimenting. Often in American culture, people comment on your clothing or other visual signs (such as hairstyle) and offer compliments like *I like your sweater*. These compliments express friendliness and are used to "break the ice" in conversation. In Japan, however, it is less common to call attention to another person's wardrobe or hairstyle in order to "break the ice" or to start a conversation. Among close friends compliments on clothing are made, but usually only when it is somehow relevant to the topic of the talk. More often than not, a person's skill or intelligence becomes the object of compliments in Japanese conversation. Japanese people love to comment on foreigners' ability to speak Japanese. (Remember these are compliments; so one should take them with a grain of salt.) But even so, how should one respond to these well-meaning compliments?

Responding to compliments. The typical response to a compliment in Japanese is to deny it. Instead of saying "Thank you" which is common in American English, something in the order of *iie, soo de mo nai n desu, maa maa desu* (lit., no, not so [nice], but I guess it's fine) is commonly voiced. The word *maa* means 'a little' or 'more or less.' It often appears in a pair as *maa maa* (*desu*) 'it's OK, more or less.' An English equivalent to the straight interpretation of *maa maa* is the American gesture of holding out a hand in front of you with palm facing down and flapping it several times. I have seen this in answer to questions like 'how do you like the new project?' In Japanese, *maa maa* can be used even when everything is going very well if you want to humbly minimize your glorious success.

In response to compliments, usually something negative about the item being complimented is added in one's response. At first you may think this strategy "spoils" the good feeling, but compliment response in Japanese is part of the public humility face that a Japanese person often likes to wear, and so it should be learned with care. The incorrect thanking response actually "spoils" the compliment-giving sentiment.

Willingly accepting compliments. As you may guess, Japanese speakers do readily accept compliments from family members or close friends. Simple responses such as *ee, maa* 'yeah, I guess' may suffice in such cases. Some people even boast a little! But in the company of those people with whom you have to show modesty and reserve, it is best not to accept a compliment unconditionally. As shown in the target expressions, it is recommended that you show modesty by expressing in some way that you still have a lot to achieve. Saying something like *ee, sensei no okage desu* 'with the help from the teacher ...' is also favorably accepted.

■ Examples

(1) **A:** 料理、すごく上手だね。
Ryoori, sugoku joozu da ne.
(You are a really good cook, aren't you?)

B: いいえ、まだまだ。
Iie, mada mada.
(No, not yet, at all.)

(2) **A:** 静かでいいですねえ。
Shizuka de ii-desu nee.
(It's quiet and nice, isn't it?)

B: ええ、まあ。でもせまいんですよ。
Ee, maa. Demo semai n desu yo.
(I guess. But it's so small.)

(3) **A:** 日本語お上手ですねえ。
Nihongo ojoozu desu nee.
(Your Japanese is very good.)

B: そうですか、みなさんのおかげです。
Soo desu ka, minasan no okage desu.
(Really? Well, thanks to you all …)

97. Particles (4)—*Mo* Revisited

■ Target Expression

It took FIVE hours (surprisingly).

五時間もかかったんだよ。
Go-jikan mo kakatta n da yo.

■ Grammatical Explanation

Multiple functions of *mo*. We studied the topic-marking particle *mo* earlier. *Mo* also appeared in combination with interrogative words such as *dare-mo*, meaning 'no one' in negative statements. *Mo* has additional functions; we will study and review here how *mo* is used for a variety of purposes.

1. A general meaning of 'in addition' or 'also' and for the purpose of enumeration (*Mo* connects nominals; for connecting clauses, use the nominalizers *no* or *koto*, which will be studied in Entry 105.):

(1a) 私**も**行きたいなあ。
Watashi ***mo*** *ikitai naa.*
(I want to go, too.)

(1b) (お)正月には兄**も**妹**も**ふるさとに帰ってきます。
(O)shoogatsu ni wa ani ***mo*** *imooto* ***mo*** *hurusato ni kaette-kimasu.*
(For New Year's, both my elder brother and younger sister will return to our home town.)

(1c) 勉強**も**スポーツ**も**大切です。
Benkyoo ***mo*** *supootsu* ***mo*** *taisetsu desu.*
(Study and sports are both important.)

2. Pointing out the coming and passing of seasons or things in general:

(2a) 晩秋**も**過ぎ、いよいよ初冬の気配ですが……
*Banshuu **mo** sugi, iyoiyo shotoo no kehai desu ga . . .*
(Late fall is over and it is already the beginning of winter . . .)

3. Equivalent to 'even':

(3a) 猿**も**木から落ちる。 [proverb]
*Saru **mo** ki kara ochiru.*
(Even monkeys fall from trees.)

(3b) その子はむずかしい本**も**読めます。
*Sono ko wa muzukashii hon **mo** yomemasu.*
(That child can read even difficult books.)

4. With quantity, meaning 'about':

(4a) 五十人**も**集まればいいんだけど……
*Go-juu-nin **mo** atsumareba ii n da kedo . . .*
(If fifty people gather, that would be fine . . .)

5. With quantity, implying surprise over the unexpected quantity (unlike the case of 4 above, this use receives phonological prominence on quantifiers when pronounced):

(5a) 五時間**も**かかるんですよ。
*Go-jikan **mo** kakaru n desu yo.*
(It takes five hours.)

6. *Mo* used after interrogative words (see Appendix 6):

With affirmative: 'every'

(6a) どこ**も**一杯。
*Doko-**mo** ippai.*
(Every place is filled [with people].)

With negative: 'not anything,' 'nothing'

(6b) 何**も**ありません。
*Nani-**mo** arimasen.*
(There isn't anything.)

■ Additional Information

- *Mo* can also be added to [V/Adj *te*], forming [V/Adj *te* + *mo*], to convey the meaning of 'even though.'

  (a) 勉強し**ても**わからない。
  *Benkyoo-shi**te mo** wakaranai.*
  (Even though I study, I don't understand.)

  (b) これはむずかしくて先生**でも**わからない。
  *Kore wa muzukashikute sensei **de mo** wakaranai.*
  (This is difficult and even the teacher cannot understand.)

- The [V/Adj *te* + *mo*] is used in expressions such as:

  (c) 雨が降っ**ても**降らなく**ても**行きますから……
  *Ame ga hut**te mo** huranaku**te mo** ikimasu kara ...*
  ([Regardless of] whether it rains or not, I will go.)

- [V/Adj *te* + *mo*] also appears in expressions of permission, which will be discussed in Entry 110.

98. Word Order (2)—Postposing

■ Target Expression

Did you see Yuki's new car?

見た? ユキの新しい車。
Mita? Yuki no atarashii kuruma.

■ Grammatical Explanation

Reasons for postposing. Although we studied that Japanese is a verb-final language (as described in characteristic 1), in spoken discourse, there are cases where verbs precede some postposed elements. Postposed sentences may be used as the result of (1) adding something afterward, perhaps realizing there is a need to provide additional information in the postposed phrase, and (2) focusing on the postposed element, when the postposed phrase is pronounced with phonological prominence. Note that sentence-final intonation occurs at the point where a normally ordered sentence ends. In the target expression, *mita?* is marked with slightly rising intonation, but not at the end of *atarashii kuruma*.

■ Examples

(1) それで新宿行ったんだよ、鈴木と。
Sorede Shinjuku itta n da yo, Suzuki to.
(So I went to Shinjuku, with Suzuki.)

(2) **A:** お見えになったんですか、お母さま。
Omie ni natta n desu ka, okaasama.
(Did she come, your mom?)

B: はい、そうなんです。
Hai, soo na n desu.
(Yeah, she did.)

(3) **A:** あいつ好きなのかな、ナオちゃんのこと。
Aitsu suki na no kana, Nao-chan no koto.
(Does he like her, I mean Nao?)

B: わかんないよ、そんなこと。
Wakannai yo, sonna koto.
(I don't know, about such a thing.)

99. Guessing with Doubt—*Daroo* and *Kamoshirenai*

■ Target Expressions

It will probably rain tomorrow.

あしたは雨が降るだろう。
Ashita wa ame ga huru-daroo.

あしたは雨でしょう。
Ashita wa ame deshoo.

He may be a Japanese.

日本人かもしれません。
Nihon-jin kamoshiremasen.

[V/Adj pre-Aux + *kamoshirenai*]

■ Grammatical Explanation

Guessing with *daroo*. As we have learned earlier, when conveying doubt, the [-*daroo*] expression and its formal counterpart [-*deshoo*] are used, sometimes together with the adverb *tabun* 'perhaps.' Although we learned -*daroo* only in the context of future uncertainty, it should be noted that the speaker's uncertainty and imprecision regarding present and past events and states is also expressed by adding *-daroo*. [*-Daroo*] is also used to soften the statement when one wishes to avoid making a definite statement. If your sense of doubt is stronger [*-daroo ka*] is used. [*-Daroo*] follows [V/Adj pre-Aux] form. Since *-daroo* is the tentative equivalent of *da*, when the *be*-verb appears, *daroo* is used in the place of *da*. *Daroo* can be shortened to *daro* in casual (masculine) speech.

(a) **A:** あの人、アメリカ人？
Ano hito, Amerika-jin?
(Is he or she possibly an American?)

B: そう**だろ**。
Soo ***daro****.*
(Perhaps.)

Guessing with *kamo(shirenai).* Another [AuxAdj], *kamoshirenai*, is often used to indicate that the speaker is guessing. [*Kamoshirenai*] is preceded by [V/Adj pre-Aux] forms, meaning X may be true, or, maybe X. It is used when one doesn't know all the facts, yet may conclude a reasonable likelihood that it is so. *Kamoshirenai* and its formal version *kamoshiremasen* express speculation similar to the English expression of *might (may) be*. The phrase *moshika suruto* 'if it is' or *moshika shitara* 'if it should be' may be added to express even greater uncertainty, although one feels that there is some possibility of it. In casual speech, *kamo*, a shortened version of *kamoshirenai*, is frequently used.

(b) **A:** あしたのパーティー、もしかすると行けない**かも**。
Ashita no paatii, moshika suruto ikenai ***kamo****.*
(I may not be able to go to tomorrow's party.)

B: 私も。
Watashi mo.
(Me either.)

(c) さいふは電車の中で落としたの**かもしれません**。
Saihu wa densha no naka de otoshita no ***kamoshiremasen****.*[*1]
(I may have dropped my wallet in the train.)

(d) 今人気のあるロックバンドだから込んでる**かも**。
Ima ninki no aru rokku bando da kara konde-ru ***kamo****.*[*2]
(Since it's a popular rock band, it may be crowded.)

*1. The particle *no* in *no kamoshiremasen* is an example of extended predicate. In this case instead of *no da*, *no kamoshirenai* is used.

*2. If you are wondering about the *no* in this phrase, recall that the subject marker *ga* is optionally interchanged with *no* within the modifying clause.

***Kashira* and *ka na*.** In feminine speech only, an expression using [*kashira*] is optional. [*Kashira*] is preceded by [V/Adj pre-Aux] forms. A similar expression used by both genders is the use of the question marker *ka* followed by another particle *na(a)*. This pattern is close to the English phrase 'I wonder ...'

(e) A: これいくらかしら。 [feminine speech]
Kore ikura kashira.
(I wonder how much this is.)

B: 超高そうだね。
Choo takasoo da ne.
(It looks very expensive.)

(f) A: キムさんはいつ頃日本へ来たのかなあ。
Kimu-san wa itsugoro Nihon e kita no ka naa.
(I wonder when Mr. Kim came to Japan.)

B: さあ、いつ頃かなあ。
Saa, itsu goro ka naa.
(I wonder when ...)

■ Additional Information

-Deshoo is frequently used in questions, as in *itsu deshoo (ka)* 'when is it?' instead of *itsu desu ka*. *Itsu deshoo (ka)* is considered a slightly more friendly expression, as discussed earlier in Entry 23.

100. Language of Emotion (2)—Interjections and Exclamations

■ Target Expressions

What! No kidding! You must be kidding!

えっ、なに！ まさか！ うっそー！
Ett, nani! Masaka! Ussoo!

■ Strategic Explanation

Exclaiming. Exclaiming in a foreign language requires a solid understanding of the target culture, and often is achieved only after considerable experience. After all, without thinking, in situations where we are most vulnerable and excited, our native language seems to appear from nowhere. And of course, if the appropriate expression does not come to your mind instantly, what you will say will sound as if you were reading a memorized statement, a far cry from what exclamatory expressions are meant to convey. Always using the same interjection also reveals a poor command of the language, something one should try hard to avoid.

Interjections and exclamations appear, being what they are, almost always in direct informal style. When you have the opportunity to hear Japanese people exclaiming in films, television programs, on the Internet, or in real situations, observe them closely. Listen to how they say it, and note their facial expressions. You'll want to imitate their manner as well as their tone. Unless delivered just so, these interjections can make people feel uncomfortable.

Frequently used interjections. Following is a list of frequently used interjections.

1. *Surprise*:

(1a) あ; ああ	*A; Aa*	Oh.
(1b) あれー; おや; まあ	*Aree; Oya; Maa*	Oh my!, Why!, Gee whiz! [feminine speech]

2. *Surprised at the content of the statement*:

(2a) え？	*E?*	What?
(2b) まさか！	*Masaka!*	No kidding!
(2c) うっそー！	*Ussoo!*	You must be kidding!
(2d) へえ！	*Hee!*	Really!

3. *Doubt*:

(3a) はてな？	*Hate na?*	I wonder …
(3b) うそ！	*Uso!*	(lit., lie) I don't believe it!
(3c) まじ(で)？	*Maji (de)?*	Seriously?

4. *Resolving doubt*:

(4a) へえ。	*Hee.*	Is that right!
(4b) なるほど。	*Naruhodo.*	I see.

5. *Distress*:

(5a) あーあ。	*Aaa.*	Whew!
(5b) やれやれ。	*Yare yare.*	Oh, boy!

If you are interested in these and other exclamatory expressions, take a look at Japanese comic books. They contain many exclamatory phrases and onomatopoeic words that might interest you.

Restricting interjections and exclamations. Interjections and exclamations are used sparingly, if at all, in formal situations. Until you are comfortable, it is best to keep these phrases to a minimum.

■ Examples

(1) **A:** 今日ボーナスが出たんだ！
Kyoo boonasu ga deta n da!
(I got my bonus today!)

B: へえ、よかったね。
Hee, yokatta ne.
(Wow, that's great.)

(2) **A:** これ何？
Kore nani?
(What's this?)

B: ふろしきですよ。こう使うんです。
Huroshiki desu yo. Koo tsukau n desu.
(It's *huroshiki*. You use it this way.)

A: ああ、なるほど。便利なんですね。
Aa, naruhodo. Benrina n desu ne.
(Ah, I see. It's convenient, isn't it?)

(3) 雨は降るし、車は故障するし……ああ、やれやれ、何てことだ！
Ame wa hurushi, kuruma wa koshoo-surushi ... aa, yare yare, nante koto da!
(It's raining, and the car breaks down on me ... oh boy, what a disaster!)

■ Additional Information

- Two additional expressions associated with emotion should be mentioned. The first is the so-called exclamatory sentence. Exclamatory sentences in Japanese are not frequently uttered in isolation, but are followed by verbs such as *omou* 'to think,' and are used generally in written language to express the extremity of emotion. It takes the phrase *nante* or *nanto* followed by [Adj pre-nominal (+ N + *na*) + *n(o) daroo/deshoo*] or, *nante/nanto* followed by [Adv + Vinformal + *koto ka*], the latter of which is used primarily in written discourse.

(a) 何ていい人なんだろうと思った！
Nante ii hito na n daroo to omotta!
(I thought what a nice person he is!)

(b) あの子は何と美しくなったことか！
Ano ko wa nanto utsukushiku natta koto ka!
(How beautiful that child has become!)

- The second is forming sentences equivalent to the English *I cannot help* ... or *I am dying to* ... which takes [Vstem + *takute* + *tamaranai/tamarimasen*]. *-Takute* is a gerund of *-tai*, an expression of desire that we learned earlier. *Tamaranai,* which is always in negative form, means 'cannot bear' or 'cannot stand.' For example, *uchi ni kaeritakute tamarimasen* 'I am dying to return home.' Its colloquial version is *uchi ni kaeritakute tamannai.*

Part IV:
EXPANSION

Oregon's Forgotten Beach

101. Responding to Questions (3) —Avoiding "No": Expressions of Doubt and Opposition

■ Target Expression

That is so, but . . .

それはそうですが……

Sore wa soo desu ga . . .

■ Strategic Explanation

Mildly expressing doubt. Japanese are known to go to great lengths in their avoidance of saying "no." Although this characterization is not entirely accurate, there is no question that Japanese speakers have a marked preference for avoiding direct confrontation. Naturally if you are an American and are asked whether you are British, a straightforward "no" is appropriate. When the question involves suggestion or request, however, or if the speaker's statement seeks recognition and agreement, even when an American might say "no" straightforwardly, a Japanese may only mildly suggest it. Not saying "no" directly to a person's face is motivated by the feeling that such a direct act of denial lacks consideration and courtesy. Saying "no" in the face of those to whom you are supposed to show respect, therefore, is not a recommendable strategy.

When "no" is used. Among family members where the *amae* relationship is established, however, the direct "no" is often heard. In this warm and forgiving relationship, self-assertion and selfishness are perhaps unconditionally accepted. In such an environment, saying "no" with no accommodation to the other person's feelings, which sometimes is taken as a sign of immaturity and selfishness, is allowed. In casual conversation, expressions of doubt, such as *soo ka naa* 'I wonder about it,' are frequently used to express disagreement as a buffer to any real confrontation.

Avoiding flat "no." In formal meetings, particularly if one is speaking in Japanese, a flat "no" is almost never the best strategy to express disagreement (especially toward your social superiors). Naturally, disagreeing with one's superior in any culture requires tact, but it is fair to say that for Americans, being able to say "no" and being able to express oneself clearly is important. It is precisely this quality that Americans consider trustworthy and reliable. Ironically, this quality of frankness may not be taken so positively in Japanese circles.

Strategies for expressing opposition and doubt. The statement above does not mean that you should never say "no" in Japanese. I am sure there will be times you have to say "no." The important thing is to remember that disagreeing and refusing take different levels of expressions and different kinds of strategies in Japanese.

1. *Expressions implying negative answers:*

(1a) まあ、考えておきます。
Maa, kangaete-okimasu.
(I will think about it.)

(1b) まあ、また様子を見てということで。
Maa, mata yoosu o mite to yuu koto de.
(Well, we will see what happens ...)

When using these expressions, the speaker does not really intend to literally think about the request at a later date.

2. *Using clausal fillers:*
Use clausal fillers (1) to agree with the speaker first, and then to suggest disagreement, (2) to agree with certain points the speaker has made and disagree with others, or (3) to lessen the impact of the straightforward disagreement.

(2a) 原則的には賛成ですけど……三番についておうかがいします。

Gensokuteki ni	*wa*	*sansei desu*	*kedo...*	*san-ban*	*ni tsuite*	*oukagaishimasu.*
in principle	T	agreement	but	number 3	about	inquire

(I agree with you in principle, but concerning number 3, I would like to ask some questions.)

(2b) まあそれはちょっと……、私にはそうは思えないんですが……
Maa sore wa chotto ... , watashi ni wa soo wa omoenai n desu ga ...
(Well, that's a bit [difficult] ... , I [personally] can't think so.)

(2c) そうかなあ、そんなことないんじゃない？
Soo ka naa, sonna koto nai n ja-nai?
(I wonder about that, isn't it the case that it isn't so?)

(2d) そうかも。でも、私はそうは思わない。
Soo kamo. Demo, watashi wa soo wa omowanai.
(Maybe. But I [personally] do not think so ...)

These expressions of doubt are preceded by clausal fillers. This strategy is useful in warning the listener that what follows may be against the listener's opinion. This further warns that the disagreeing opinion is a personal preference and is not necessarily an opinion against the listener's position. Also the first-person pronoun which is normally deleted may be used to express 'I personally.'

3. *Expressing disagreement and doubt:*

(3a) そうですかねえ。
Soo desu ka nee.
(lit., I wonder if it is so.)

Strategies similar to English. Some of the strategies introduced above must certainly be familiar to the reader; these are not uniquely Japanese. In fact there are many indirect, suggestive ways to say "no" in English. I have heard English expressions such as *I don't feel too warm toward that idea, you know* or *It's interesting, but frankly I don't feel quite so enthusiastic about it*. Even still, Japanese avoidance of confrontation and opposition in all aspects of life is overall much stronger than it is for Americans, especially in formal situations.

Using particles. Another general strategy useful for disagreement in Japanese is to increase the frequency of response-seeking interactional particles. *Nee*, for example, serves to bond the participants of conversation and helps create empathy and rapport even while expressing disagreement.

102. Particles (5)—*Ka* Revisited

■ Target Expression

I don't know whether she is a student, but ...

学生かどうか知らないけど……
Gakusei ka doo ka shiranai kedo ...

■ Grammatical Explanation

Functions of *ka*. The question marker *ka* is used in various structures, and needs special summing-up. *Ka* is used for signaling questions, and in combination with negation it functions as an expression of invitation. Beyond these two basic functions, there are roughly four different places you will find *ka*.

1. *After interrogative words:*
Adds the meaning of 'any' or 'some.' (See Appendix 6 for the list.)

(1a) **誰か**いますか。
Dare-ka *imasu ka.*
(Is anyone there?)

(1b) A: **何か**冷たい飲みものでもいかがですか。
Nani-ka *tsumetai nomimono demo ikaga desu ka.*
(How about something cold to drink?)

B: すみません。
Sumimasen.
(Thank you.)

A: ジュースか**何か**。
Juusu ka ***nani-ka****.*
(Juice or something?)

B: では、オレンジジュースお願いします。
Dewa, orenji juusu onegaishimasu.
(Then, I would like some orange juice.)

2. *In subordinate questions:*
When questions using question words become subordinate clauses, they are followed by *ka*. For yes/no questions, *ka* and *ka doo ka* 'whether or not' are used. It is also possible to form alternate questions in negation as in B's utterance in (2b). When *da* appears immediately preceding *ka*, delete it; there is no combination **da ka*.

(2a) A: 注文していただいている**かどうか**もう一度お調べいたしましょう。
Chuumon-shie-itadaite-iru ***ka doo ka*** *moo ichido oshirabe-itashimashoo.*
(I will examine whether [or not] we have received your orders.)

B: そうですか。じゃあ、すみませんがお願いします。
Soo desu ka. Jaa sumimasen ga onegai shimasu.
(Oh, thanks. I'd appreciate it.)

(2b) A: 来週の旅行、いらっしゃいますか。
Raishuu no ryokoo, irasshaimasu ka.
(Are you going on a trip next week?)

B: まだ行く**か**行かない**か**決めてないんです……
Mada iku ***ka*** *ikanai* ***ka*** *kimete-nai n desu . . .*
(I haven't decided yet whether we go or not.)

3. *For expressing uncertainty and doubt:*

(3a) そうでしょう**か**。
Soo deshoo ***ka****.*
(I wonder if it is so.)

(3b) A: 準備なさっておいた方がよろしいんじゃないでしょう**か**。
Junbi-nasatte-oita hoo ga yoroshii n ja-nai deshoo ***ka****.*
(Wouldn't it be better to prepare [for the future] beforehand?)

B: そうかもしれませんねえ。
Soo kamoshiremasen nee.
(I guess so.)

(3c) A: 準備しておいた方がいいんじゃない**か**と思いますが……
Junbi-shite-oita hoo ga ii n ja-nai ***ka*** *to omoimasu ga . . .*
(I think it would be better to prepare [for the future] beforehand.)

B: そうでしょう**か**……
Soo deshoo ***ka*** *. . .*
(I wonder about that . . .)

4. *Presenting alternatives:*

(4a) A: 会議があるんですよ。
Kaigi ga aru n desu yo.
(There's a meeting.)

B: どこで ?
Doko de?
(Where?)

A: 東京**か**横浜で。
Tookyoo ***ka*** *Yokohama de.*
(Either in Tokyo or Yokohama.)

B: そうですか。いつ ?
Soo desu ka. Itsu?
(Is that so? When?)

A: 来週の火曜日**か**水曜日。
Raishuu no kayoobi ***ka*** *suiyoobi.*
(Either next Tuesday or Wednesday.)

(4b) A: 上田さん**か**林さんに来てもらって。
Ueda-san ***ka*** *Hayashi-san ni kite-moratte.*
(Have either Ms. Ueda or Ms. Hayashi come [here].)

B: 上田さんも林さんもどこかへ行って留守ですが……
Ueda-san mo Hayashi-san mo doko-ka e itte rusu desu ga . . .
(Both Ms. Ueda and Ms. Hayashi are out somewhere . . .)

(4c) 生きる**か**死ぬ**か**、それが問題だ。
Ikiru ***ka*** *shinu* ***ka****, sore ga mondai da.*
(To live or to die, that is the question.)

103. Expressing One's Intentions—*Tsumori*

■ Target Expression

I intend to finish this job by tomorrow.

あすまでにこの仕事を仕上げるつもりですから。

Asu made ni kono shigoto o shiageru tsumori desu kara.

[Vinformal non-past + *tsumori*]

■ Grammatical Explanation

Expressing intentions with *tsumori*. Since the word *tsumori* 'intention' behaves like a noun, it might be best to think of this structure as a clausal explanation of the noun. There are two distinct [*tsumori*] structures. The first type appears following [Vinformal non-past] and it expresses intentions or personal expectations. For this type of [*tsumori*], only verbs referring to controllable action can be used. You cannot intend to do things that you cannot possibly control.

[*Tsumori*] cannot be used alone; it has to be modified either by a demonstrative or a clause. It is usually followed by the copula *da*, but occasionally it occurs in the [*tsumori ga aru*] or [*tsumori wa nai*] structure. When negating, use [*tsumori dewa-nai*], as in *iku tsumori dewa-nai*. Or, use the negative form of the [Vinformal non-past] preceding [*tsumori*], as in *ikanai tsumori*.

(a) **A:** 来年日本へ行くつもりですか。
Rainen Nihon e iku tsumori desu ka.
(Do you intend to go to Japan next year?)

B: ええ、そのつもりですが……
Ee, sono tsumori desu ga . . .
(Yes, I intend to.)

***Tsumori* meaning 'I think.'** The second use of [*tsumori*] occurs when it appears following [V/Adj pre-nominal] forms, excluding [Vnon-past]. In this use, *da* is possible and takes the [pre-nominal] form including non-past tense. This *tsumori* is associated with *impression* or *to think, to mean to be*, or *to pretend to be*. For negating purposes, normally negation of the verb preceding *tsumori* is used.

(b) いっしょうけんめい勉強したつもりですが……
Isshookenmei benkyooshita tsumori desu ga . . .
(I think I studied hard, but . . .)

■ Examples

(1) 今度の日曜日会社へ来るつもり。
Kondo no nichiyoobi kaisha e kuru tsumori.
(I intend to come to the office this coming Sunday.)

(2) **A:** もうあの人とは旅行しないつもり。
Moo ano hito to wa ryokoo-shinai tsumori.
(I intend not to travel with him any more.)

B: どうして？
Dooshite?
(Why not?)

(3) **A:** あした帰るつもりでおりますが……
Ashita kaeru tsumori de-orimasu ga . . .
(I intend to return tomorrow.)

B: ああ、そうですか。じゃあ、みなさんによろしく。
Aa, soo desu ka. Jaa, minasan ni yoroshiku.
(Oh, I see. Please give my regards to everyone.)

(4) あの人ピアノが上手なつもりなんだよ。
Ano hito piano ga joozuna tsumori na n da yo.
(She/he thinks she/he is good at playing the piano.)

■ Additional Information

Similar expressions of personal intentions are available by using nouns *yotei* and *keikaku*, both meaning 'plan.' The [Vinformal non-past + *yotei/keikaku + da/ga aru*] structure expresses 'plan to do . . .' For example, *ashita wa hayaku kaeru yotei desu* 'I plan to return early,' or *Oosaka e iku keikaku wa arimasen yo* 'there isn't a plan to go to Osaka.' Grammatically, when using these patterns, think of them as extended [clausal modifier + N] structures.

104. Pointing Out Facts as a Natural Course of Events—*Hazu*

■ Target Expression

(Is Professor Yamada coming to his office today?)
Yes, he is supposed to come.

ええ、いらっしゃるはずですが……
Ee, irassharu hazu desu ga . . .

[V/Adj pre-nominal + *hazu*]

■ Grammatical Explanation

Using *hazu*. As in the pattern of *tsumori* and *yotei/keikaku*, [*hazu*] is also a noun normally modified by demonstratives or clauses. It is preceded by [V/Adj pre-nominal] forms. When using [*hazu*], the speaker expects and anticipates events and facts as a natural outcome, based on the objective conditions and situation that the speaker has direct access to. The speaker has every reason to believe that things will turn out just as expected—equivalent to the English expression *what ought naturally to be true* or *what one would normally expect*. It is often translated into the English 'is expected to,' 'is supposed to,' or 'should' for convenience.

Negating *hazu*. For negation, *Aoki-san wa konai hazu da* 'it is expected that Mr. Aoki will not come,' and its formal version, *konai hazu desu* are used. Negation of *hazu* itself is also used, as in *Aoki-san wa kuru hazu ga nai* 'there is no likelihood that Mr. Aoki will come.' *Kuru hazu ga nai* is a strong negative assertion indicating no possibility of Aoki coming in, whereas the [*konai hazu da*] negation implies a slight possibility that Aoki might come.

***Hazu* versus *beki*.** The [*hazu*] structure is different from the pattern using *beki*, which is also translated into the English as 'should.' In the case of *beki*, 'should' is used in a sense of obligation, literally 'ought to.' We will study *beki* in Entry 106. As in the case of *can*, the English *should* has many distinctive meanings, and therefore we must avoid equating *hazu* merely with *should*.

■ Examples

(1) 母は四時半までにもどってくるはずです。
Haha wa yo-ji han made ni modotte-kuru hazu desu.
(My mother is supposed to be back by 4:30.)

(2) **A:** あのう、この間お願いした小包みですが……
Anoo, kono aida onegai-shita kozutsumi desu ga ...
(Excuse me, about the package I requested the other day ...)

B: その小包みはもう届いているはずですが……
Sono kozutsumi wa moo todoite-iru hazu desu ga ...
(That package should have arrived by now ...)

A: いや、それがまだ届いていないんですよ。
Iya, sore ga mada todoite-inai n desu yo.
(Not really, it has not arrived yet.)

B: そんなはずはありませんがねえ……
Sonna hazu wa arimasen ga nee ...
(It shouldn't be so ...)

(3) 出費の合計は約五万円のはずですが……
Shuppi no gookei wa yaku go-man-en no hazu desu ga ...
(The total of the expense is expected to be approximately fifty thousand yen.)

(4) 丈夫なはずだけどねえ、このロープは。
Joobuna hazu da kedo nee, kono roopu wa.
(This rope, you know, is expected to be durable.)

(5) このプリンターはこわれないはずですけど。
Kono purintaa wa kowarenai hazu desu kedo.
(This printer is not expected to be broken.)

■ Additional Information

Hazu is also used to mean 'no wonder' or 'it makes sense.' See the example below, paying attention to the semantic context.

(a) これは上級の問題ですからむずかしい**はず**です。

Kore	*wa*	*jookyuu*	*no*	*mondai*	*desu*	*kara*	*muzukashii* ***hazu*** *desu.*
this	T	upper class	L	question	is	since	difficult

(Since this is a question for the advanced level, no wonder it is difficult.)

105. Nominalization of a Clause—*Koto* and *No*

■ Target Expression

It is difficult to keep promises.

約束を守ることはむずかしいです。
Yakusoku o mamoru koto wa muzukashii-desu.

[*koto*] [*no*]

■ Grammatical Explanation

Nominalizing with *koto* and *no*. The two devices, *koto* 'fact(s), intangible things' and *no* 'thing(s), one(s),' are nominalizers which make clauses into noun phrases. In English there are ways to make a clause into a grammatical noun: by using *that* in forming a that-clause (*that I keep promises*), by attaching *to* (*to keep promises*) and by making a verb into a gerundive form (*keeping promises*).

***No* versus *koto*.** [*No*] is used for nominalizing concrete actions or events, whereas [*koto*] nominalizes the clause that refers to actions or events in more abstract, indirect, or general ways. The [*no*] clause is used to express facts directly and immediately as perceived, while the [*koto*] clause is used to express a formal and more distant feeling, pointing out facts reached after giving the matter some thought. Simply put, *utau no* refers to a specific case of someone 'singing,' while *utau koto* refers to the general meaning of 'singing.' If the main verb requires concrete immediate action, such as *mieru* 'to be seen,' or *kikoeru* 'to be heard,' the nominalizer *no* is required. *Koto* is often used with verbs connoting a deductive or abstract thinking process.

Forms that precedes *koto* and *no*. *Koto* and *no* are preceded by [V/Adj pre-nominal] forms, except when the verb immediately preceding is [N + *da*]. In such a case, instead of taking the pre-nominal form *no*, it takes [N *da to yuu*] before *koto*, and it takes [N *na*] before *no*. By making clauses into grammatical nouns, you can insert a clause in place of a noun. Mastering the nominalizers *koto* and *no* opens various possibilities. For example, you can expand the use of *sukina* as shown below.

(a) テレビでプロ野球を見る**の**が好きだ。
*Terebi de puro yakyuu o miru **no** ga suki da.*
(I like to watch professional baseball on television.)

Recall the expression of potential, [*koto ga dekiru*]. In that structure, *koto* is in fact a nominalizer. So is *no* in the extended predicate [*no da*] expression.

■ Examples

(1) 安田さんが手を振っているのが見えます。
Yasuda-san ga te o hutte-iru no ga miemasu.
(I can see Yasuda waving.)

(2) 夜遅かったのでスミスさんに電話するのはやめました。
Yoru osokatta node Sumisu-san ni denwa-suru no wa yamemashita.
(I did not call Mr. Smith because it was late at night.)

(3) 言うことは簡単。でも、実際にすることはむずかしい。
Yuu koto wa kantan. Demo jissai ni suru koto wa muzukashii.
(It is easy to say something, but it is difficult to actually do something.)

(4) コロンブスがアメリカを発見したことは誰でも知っている。
Koronbusu ga Amerika o hakken-shita koto wa dare de mo shitte-iru.
(Everyone knows that Columbus discovered America.)

(5) 勉強するのもしないのも君の自由さ。
Benkyoo-suru no mo shinai no mo kimi no jiyuu sa.
(Whether you study or not is up to you.)

■ Additional Information

- *Koto* may be used as a regular noun, meaning '(intangible) thing(s)' or 'fact(s).'

  (a) 先生がおっしゃったことは今でも覚えております。
  Sensei ga osshatta koto wa ima demo oboete-orimasu.
  (I still remember what the teacher said.)

  (b) いやなことは忘れましょう。
  Iyana koto wa wasuremashoo.
  (Let's forget unpleasant things.)

- Adding *koto* to nouns can make the noun more abstract, making the statement less blatant. For example, instead of saying *Taroo-san ga suki* 'I like Taro,' *Taroo-san no koto ga suki* 'I like (things about) Taro' is generally preferred. This is because it points out facts in a more abstract, and therefore more indirect (and often thoughtful) way.

106. Social Responsibility—*Beki*

■ Target Expression

When young, you ought to work hard.

若い時はいっしょうけんめい働くべきだ。
Wakai toki wa isshookenmei hataraku beki da.

[Vbasic + *beki*]

■ Grammatical Explanation

Expressing responsibility with *beki*. *Beki* is used in the pattern [Vbasic + *beki* + *da*] and expresses social responsibility. When *beki* is preceded by [Adj-*na*] and the *be*-verb, instead of *da*, *dearu* is used. If it is preceded by [Adj-*i*], it takes the adverbial form of the adjective—*wakaku* instead of *wakai*—followed by *aru*. [*Beki*] is a pre-nominal form of literary *beshi*. It points out that such action is an obligation that should be followed as a rule, and as an action naturally expected of a person. [*Beki*] can modify nouns directly; for example, *kaku beki tegami* 'the letter that ought to (or, should) be written.' *Beki* sentences may be translated into English 'ought to,' 'be supposed to,' or 'should.'

Forms associated with *beki*. It is possible to form the past tense by [Vbasic + *beki* + *datta*], meaning 'ought to have' and 'should have.' For negation of *beki* sentences, negate [*beki*] to [*beki dewa-nai*] or [*beki dewa-nakatta*]. The phrase [*dewa*] as elsewhere may be shortened to [*ja*], as in [*beki ja-nai*].

■ Examples

(1) 忙しい日は朝早く起きるべきだ。
Isogashii hi wa asa hayaku okiru beki da.
(On busy days, you ought to get up early.)

(2) **A:** むずかしい問題は誰かに相談するべきでしょう？
Muzukashii mondai wa dare-ka ni soodan-suru beki deshoo?
(Shouldn't we consult someone about the difficult problems?)

B: でも誰に？
Demo dare ni?
(But whom?)

A: まず先生に相談するべきでしょうね。
Mazu sensei ni soodan-suru beki deshoo ne.
(First you should consult your teacher.)

(3) **A:** 読むべき本はたくさんあるけど、忙しくてちっとも読めないんです。
Yomu beki hon wa takusan aru kedo, isogashikute chittomo yomenai n desu.
(There are so many books I should read, but I can't read them because I'm too busy.)

B: そうですか。でも、学生なら毎日少しでも読むべきですよ。
Soo desu ka. Demo, gakusei nara mainichi sukoshi demo yomu beki desu yo.
(Is that so? But since you're a student, you should read a little bit every day.)

(4) もっと勉強しておくべきだった。
Motto benkyoo-shite-oku beki datta.
(I ought to have studied more thoroughly.)

(5) そんなことするべきじゃないよ。
Sonna koto suru beki ja-nai yo.
(You shouldn't do such a thing.)

(6) 人間はいつも正しくあるべきです。
Ningen wa itsumo tadashiku aru beki desu.
(A person should always be righteous.)

107. Social and Personal Obligation

■ Target Expression

I must get to Tokyo Station by eight o'clock.

八時までに東京駅へ行かなければなりません。

Hachi-ji made ni Tookyoo-eki e ikanakereba narimasen.

[*-nakereba naranai / ikenai*]

■ Grammatical Explanation

Expressing duty and obligation. Duty and obligation in Japanese are expressed indirectly by using the negative conditional *-ba*, that is, the [*-nakereba*] form, and negation of [V/Adj *te*], that is, the [*-nakute wa*] form. Literally these expressions mean 'if you do not do this, it is not good, or it bothers me,' and is normally translated into the English auxiliary verb 'must.'

***-Nakereba naranai* and *-nakereba ikenai*.** The expression *-nakereba naranai* (or *-nakute wa naranai*) describes absolute obiligation as described in a law; *kono tatemono ni hairu ni wa kyoka o enakereba naranai* 'you must obtain permission to enter this building.' It also describes logical truth; *wareware wa kanarazu shinanakereba naranai* 'without doubt we must die.' The [*-nakereba naranai*] pattern has an explanatory function in that it often implies that one must do certain things due to legal or personal obligations.

The [*-nakereba ikenai*] (or [*-nakute wa ikenai*]) structure is often used to offer advice, give orders, or to make a forceful request from one's social superiors. It is addressed directly to the listener.

***Beki* versus *nakereba naranai*.** The difference between [*beki*] and [*-nakereba naranai*] is that while [*beki*] points out one's social responsibility as an action expected from a person, [*-nakereba naranai*] provides a straightforward command with the purpose of controlling and restricting human behavior. For example, when conveying that one ought to (must) drive a car on the left side in Japan, *-nakereba naranai* is used.

■ Examples

(1) 新しい職場ですから、いっしょうけんめい働かなければなりません。
Atarashii shokuba desu kara, isshookenmei hatarakanakereba narimasen.
(Because it is a new job, I must work hard.)

(2) もう行かなければ(なりません)……
Moo ikanakereba (narimasen) ...
(I must be going now ...)

(3) **A:** かばんは小さくなければいけませんよ。
Kaban wa chiisakunakereba ikemasen yo.
(As for the bag, it must be small.)

B: じゃあ、どのくらいの大きさがいいんですか。
Jaa, dono kurai no ookisa ga ii n desu ka.
(Then how large should it be?)

(4) **A:** 大切な手紙だから字をきちんと書かなければいけませんよ。
Taisetsuna tegami da kara ji o kichinto kakanakereba ikemasen yo.
(Since this is an important letter, you must write the characters neatly.)

B: はい、わかりました。
Hai, wakarimashita.
(Yes, I will.)

(5) **A:** 今夜は早く寝なくてはいけませんよ。
Kon'ya wa hayaku nenakute wa ikemasen yo.
(You must go to bed early tonight.)

B: どうして？
Doo shite?
(Why?)

A: あした朝早く出かけなければなりませんから。
Ashita asa hayaku dekakenakereba narimasen kara.
(Tomorrow morning we must leave early.)

■ Additional Information

- Instead of *ikemasen* in the structure introduced in this entry, [*dame da*] and [*komaru*] may be used.

(a) 早く起きなければ**だめ**よ。
Hayaku okinakereba ***dame*** *yo.*
(You must get up early.)

(b) 二万円以下でなければ**困ります**。
Ni-man-en ika denakereba ***komarimasu****.*
(It must be under 20,000 yen.)

- [*-Nakereba*] and [*-nakute wa*] can be shortened to *-nakerya*/*nakya* and *-nakucha*, respectively, in casual fast speech.

(c) 勉強し**なきゃ**だめよ。
*Benkyoo-shi**nakya** dame yo.*
(You must study!)

108. Guessing with Confidence—*Ni Chigainai*

■ Target expression

He must be a Japanese.

日本人にちがいない。
Nihon-jin ni chigainai.

[V/Adj pre-Aux + *ni chigainai*]

■ Grammatical Explanation

Expressing certainty. When you are quite certain of your assumptions, [*ni chigainai*] is used. The [*ni chigainai*] expression is preceded by [V/Adj pre-Aux] forms. Here is a list of forms for your review. (See Entry 41 for negative forms.)

***Ni Chigainai* Form**

	pre-Aux	[V/Adj pre-Aux + *ni chigainai*]
Verbs:	行く *iku*	行くにちがいない *iku ni chigainai*
	行った *itta*	行ったにちがいない *itta ni chigainai*
Be-verb:	(deletion)	日本人にちがいない *Nihon-jin ni chigainai*
	だった *datta*	日本人だったにちがいない *Nihon-jin datta ni chigainai*
[*Adj-i*]:	楽しい *tanoshii*	楽しいにちがいない *tanoshii ni chigainai*
	楽しかった *tanoshikatta*	楽しかったにちがいない *tanoshikatta ni chigainai*
[*Adj-na*]:	便利 *benri*	便利にちがいない *benri ni chigainai*
	便利だった *benri datta*	便利だったにちがいない *benri datta ni chigainai*

***Ni chigainai* versus *daroo/kamoshirenai*.** The [*ni chigainai*] pattern shows confidence in your assumption more firmly than those guessing expressions we learned earlier, that is, [*-daroo*] and [*kamoshirenai*]. As reflected in the literal meaning of the phrase *chigainai* 'there is no mistake,' this expression is used when the speaker guesses about some facts based on his or her assumption, and holds it strongly with confidence. It conveys the sense of the English *must* supported by the speaker's strong commitment to his or her conjecture.

Ni chigainai **and self-convincing process.** When you use [*ni chigainai*], it is as if you are speaking in monologue and convincing yourself that what you are thinking or assuming must be true. For example, the target sentence, *Nihon-jin ni chigainai* is used almost self-convincingly. If you are describing your confident guesses directly addressed to others, you are more likely to use *ano hito kitto Nihon-jin da yo* 'he is certainly a Japanese' or *ano hito zettai Nihon-jin da to omou* 'I think for sure that he is a Japanese.' (*Kitto* and *zettai* are both adverbs meaning 'certainly' and 'for sure.') The [*ni chigainai*] expression, however, may appear independently in written Japanese.

Negating *ni chigainai*. For negation, negate the preceding verbs, as in *Nihon-jin dewa-nai ni chigainai* 'It must be the case that he is not a Japanese.'

■ Examples

(1) 八時だからスミスさんはもう出かけたにちがいない。
Hachi-ji da kara Sumisu-san wa moo dekaketa ni chigainai.
(Since it is eight o'clock, Mr. Smith must have left the house already.)

(2) 妹はきっとふるさとに帰ってくるにちがいない。
Imooto wa kitto hurusato ni kaette-kuru ni chigainai.
(My sister will certainly return to our hometown.)

(3) あの人はいい人だから、私の気持ちもわかってくれるにちがいありません。
Ano hito wa ii hito da kara, watashi no kimochi mo wakatte-kureru ni chigaiarimasen.
(Since she is a good person, I am sure that she understands my feelings.)

109. Passive Expressions—Direct and Indirect Passive

■ Target Expressions

I was chased by a strange man.

へんな男に追いかけられた。
Henna otoko ni oikakerareta.

I got caught in the rain.

雨に降られてねえ……
Ame ni hurarete nee . . .

passive [V + *-reru*/*-rareru*]

■ Grammatical Explanation

Forming passives with *reru* and *rareru*. Passive in Japanese is grammatically formed by the verb ending changes. The passive forms of *U*- and *RU*-verbs are identical to the respectful [V + -*reru*] and [V + -*rareru*] forms we studied in Entry 86. For existential verbs use *irareru* for the passive of *iru*. The *be*-verb *da* does not have a passive form. For irregular verbs, *suru* and *kuru* take *sareru* and *korareru*, respectively.

When there is a transitive/intransitive pair of verbs, only the transitive verb can be changed into the passive form. For example, for a pair such as *kowasu* 'to break something' and *kowareru* 'something breaks,' only *kowasareru* is possible.

Functions of passive structure. There are two primary motivations for using passive verb endings in Japanese. First, passives are used when the need for referring to the agent of the action is weak or nonexistent. This is similar to how English passives are used. In English, passives are used with or without the agent indicated by the *by* phrase, as in *America was discovered by Columbus* and *This house was built in the 1930s*. The Japanese equivalent for this expression would be: *Amerika wa Koronbusu niyotte hakken-sareta* and *kono tatemono wa sen kyuu-hyaku san-juu nendai ni taterareta*. (*Hakken-suru* means 'to discover' and *tateru*, 'to build.')

The second and more important function of the passive structure in Japanese is to indicate that the speaker is suffering from someone else's action or is experiencing something unpleasant. For this pattern, the subject noun of the passive sentence is always animate. Although in English only transitive verbs are used to form the passive, in Japanese both transitive and intransitive verbs may be used to form this passive. For example, the intransitive verb *shinu* 'to die' may be used in the passive form *shinareru* when you wish to express that you are suffering from and experiencing the negative results of someone's death. This feeling of negative consequences is often expressed in English by passive sentences with *on*, as in *I got rained on* or *my pet died on me*.

Direct and indirect passives. In terms of the grammatical structure of passive sentences, there are two types—direct and indirect. In direct passives the object of the related active sentence is the subject of the passive sentence. In indirect passives such correlation between the active and its passive counterpart does not exist. The passive sentence structure takes [N *ga*/*wa* + (N *ni*) + Vpassive].

The illustration below contrasts direct and indirect passive structures with the sentence structure we have learned so far. The term 'agent' refers to the actual performer of the action.

1. *Direct Passive:*

(1a) Active: 佐々木さんは山田さんをだました。
Sasaki-san wa Yamada-san o damashita.
(Ms. Sasaki deceived Ms. Yamada.)

(1b) Passive: 山田さん**は**佐々木さん**にだまされた**。

*Yamada-san **wa***	*Sasaki-san **ni***	***damasareta.***
Subject	Agent	Vpassive

(Ms. Yamada was deceived by Ms. Sasaki.)

2. *Indirect Passive:*

(2a) Active: 妹がお菓子を食べた。
Imooto ga okashi o tabeta.
(My younger sister ate sweets.)

(2b) Passive: わたし**は**妹**に**お菓子**を食べられた**。

*Watashi **wa***	*imooto **ni***	*okashi **o***	***taberareta.***
Person influenced	Agent	Object	Vpassive

(I got my sweets eaten up by my younger sister.)

(2c) Active: 雨が降った。
Ame ga hutta.
(It rained.)

(2d) Passive: わたし**は**雨**に降られた**。

*Watashi **wa***	*ame **ni***	***hurareta.***
Person influenced	Agent	Vpassive

(I was rained on.)

Characteristics of indirect passive. Note that in indirect passives, the person who becomes the subject/topic of the passive sentence is the person who is influenced by the event, and that person does not constitute a part of the related active sentence. In this sense the relation between the event described by the active sentence and the ensuing influence are only indirectly related; thus, the term "indirect passive" is appropriate.

It should be noted parenthetically that it is possible to have a positive influence when indirect passives are used, but overwhelmingly the implication is negative. In fact, when a positive indirectness is stressed, normally the verbs of giving and receiving are used.

(a) 先生に手紙を**書いていただいた**。
*Sensei ni tegami o **kaite-itadaita**.*
(I had the teacher write me a letter.)

Indicating source of action. In order to indicate the source of the action in passive sentences, most frequently [N + *ni*] is used. However, there are cases where [N + *kara*] and [N + *niyotte*] are preferred. When emphasizing the source from which something is made, *kara* is normally used.

(b) 酒は米**から**作られる。

Sake	wa	kome	**kara**	tsukurareru.
sake	T	rice	from	is made

(*Sake* is made from rice.)

In written Japanese *niyotte* is often preferred, as in *Amerika wa Koronbusu niyotte hakken-sareta* 'America was discovered by Columbus.'

■ Examples

(1) 六月のある日曜日京都へ行った。
Rokugatsu no aru nichiyoobi Kyooto e itta.
(On one Sunday in June, I went to Kyoto.)

駅からバスに乗って金閣寺へ行った。
Eki kara basu ni notte Kinkakuji e itta.
(I got on the bus at the station and went to the Golden Pavilion.)

木々のみどりに囲まれた金閣寺は美しかった。
Kigi no midori ni kakomareta Kinkakuji wa utsukushikatta.
(The Golden Pavilion was beautiful surrounded by green trees.)

外国から来た観光客に話しかけられたが、何と言っているのかわからなかった。
Gaikoku kara kita kankookyaku ni hanashikakerareta ga, nan to itte-iru no ka wakaranakatta.
(I was sporken to by a foreign tourist, but I didn't understand what he was saying.)

イタリア語かスペイン語だったと思う。
Itariago ka Supeingo datta to omou.
(I think it was either Italian or Spanish.)

帰りは雨に降られた。
Kaeri wa ame ni hurareta.
(While returning I got caught in the rain.)

ずぶぬれになったので、人にジロジロ見られて困った。
Zubunure ni natta node, hito ni jirojiro mirarete komatta.
(As I got drenched, I was stared at by people and that was uncomfortable.)

110. Requesting and Granting Permission

■ Target Expressions

May I enter the room?

部屋に入ってもいいですか。
Heya ni haitte mo ii-desu ka.

Yes, please.

ええ、どうぞ。
Ee, doozo.

[V/Adj *te* + *mo* + *ii*]

■ Grammatical Explanation

Requesting permission. The pattern [V/Adj *te* + *mo* + *ii*/*yoroshii* (*desu ka*)] is used for requesting permission to do something as shown in the Target Expressions. These requests can also be made with the [V/Adj negative gerundive] forms. However, in these expressions *-nakute* endings are more frequently used. The verb negative gerundive forms ending with *-naide* may be used in spoken language.

(a) 今日会社へ**行かなくてもいい**ですか。
Kyoo kaisha e ***ikanakute mo ii****-desu ka.*
(Is it all right not to go to the company today?)

Other forms similar to this pattern are:

[V/Adj *te* + *mo* + *daijoobu* (*desu ka*)] (Is it all right if . . . ?)
[V/Adj *te* + *mo* + *kamaimasen ka*] (It isn't bothersome if . . . , is it?)

In colloquial style, *mo* may be deleted. For example:

(b) 部屋に**入っていい**?
Heya ni ***haitte ii****?*
(Can I go into the room?)

Affirmative answers. The affirmative answers granting permission are:

ええ/はい、いい/よろしいです。 (Yes, it is fine.)
Ee/Hai, ii/yoroshii-desu.

ええ/はい、けっこうです。 (Yes, it is all right.)
Ee/Hai, kekkoo desu.

ええ/はい、かまいません。 (Yes, that's no problem at all.)
Ee/Hai, kamaimasen.

ええ/はい、どうぞ。 (Yes, please.)
Ee/Hai, doozo.

Negative answers. The negative answers to these questions are:

1. *Prohibition:* [V/Adj *te* + *wa* + *ikenai/komaru/dame da*]

(1a) A: 食べてもいいですか。
Tabete mo ii-desu ka.
(May I eat this?)

B: まだ(食べ**ては**)**だめです**よ。
*Mada (tabe**te wa**) **dame desu** yo.*
(No, not yet.)

These negative answers are translated into English 'you must not ... ,' which convey prohibition. These expressions are discussed again in Entry 111.

2. *Softer denial of permission:*
The prohibition expressed above is a strong refusal to grant permission. Softer strategies are to be used particularly to those socially equal to or superior to you.

(2a) A: 借りてもいいですか。
Karite mo ii-desu ka.
(May I borrow this?)

B: **いやあ、ちょっと**……
Iyaa, chotto ...
(Well ... I'm afraid not.)

(2b) A: 食べてもいいですか。
Tabete mo ii-desu ka.
(May I eat?)

B: すみませんねえ、**もう少し待ってください**。
*Sumimasen nee, **moo sukoshi matte-kudasai**.*
(I'm afraid not, please wait a little longer.)

■ Examples

(1) A: あのう、帰ってもいいですか。
Anoo, kaette mo ii desu ka.
(May I leave?)

B: ああ、それが……すみませんが、もう少し待ってくださいませんか。
Aa, sore ga ... sumimasen ga, moo sukoshi matte-kudasaimasen ka.
(Sorry, but could you wait a bit longer?)

(2) A: すみませんが、行かなくてもよろしいでしょうか。
Sumimasen ga, ikanakute mo yoroshii-deshoo ka.
(Is it all right if I don't go?)

B: ええ、かまいませんよ。
Ee, kamaimasen yo.
(Yes, that's all right.)

(3) 高くても大丈夫？
Takakute mo daijoobu?
([lit., Is it all right to be expensive?] Is the expensive one all right?)

(4) A: このワインでいいでしょうか。
Kono wain de ii-deshoo ka.
(Would this wine be all right?)

B: そうですねえ……カリフォルニアのワインはありませんか。
Soo desu nee ... Kariforunia no wain wa arimasen ka.
(Let's see ... do you have some wine from California?)

(5) A: これ買っていい？
Kore katte ii?
(Can I buy this?)

B: だめよ。
Dame yo.
(No, you may not.)

■ Additional Information

The expressions using [*de (mo) ii*] and [*de (mo) yoroshii*] imply that contrary to an ideal state, the best available choice is mentioned. Therefore, these expressions should be avoided when you answer an invitation. See, for example, in the following interaction, it is unwise to answer *ee, koocha de ii-desu* 'yes, tea will do.'

(a) A: 紅茶**で(も)いい**？
Koocha ***de (mo) ii****?*
(Would tea be fine?)

B: ええ、もちろん。すみません。
Ee, mochiron. Sumimasen.
(Of course. Thanks.)

■ Warning

Note the difference between *mo ii* and *de mo ii* when they co-occur with *dochira*. *Dochira mo ii*, meaning 'both are good,' while *dochira de mo ii* means 'either one is good' (refer to Appendix 6 for related forms).

111. Prohibition—*Te Wa Ikenai*

■ Target Expression

You must not say such a thing.

そんなことを言ってはいけませんよ。

Sonna koto o itte wa ikemasen yo.

[V/Adj *te* + *wa* + *ikenai*]

■ Grammatical Explanation

Strong negative command. To express prohibition, or strong negative command, [V/Adj *te* + *wa* + *ikenai*/*komaru*/*dame da* (and their formal counterparts *ikemasen*/*komarimasu*/*dame desu*) are used with slight connotative differences as listed below. All these are translated into the English 'must not' or 'should not.'

いけない	*ikenai*	it is wrong
困る	*komaru*	it is problematic
だめだ	*dame da*	it is bad

Avoiding command forms. When addressing your superiors, the command forms introduced here should be avoided. Instead, the negative request form *-naide-kudasaimasen ka*, or, a form with *itadaku* 'to receive,' *itadakemasen-deshoo ka* are recommended.

■ Examples

(1) スピーチをする時の注意：
Supiichi o suru toki no chuui:
(Points to be careful of when giving a speech:)

- あまり長く話してはいけない。
  Amari nagaku hanashite wa ikenai
  (You should not speak too long.)
- よく準備するべき。
  Yoku junbi-suru beki.
  (You should be well prepared.)
- 聴衆の顔を見ながら話さなくてはだめ。
  Chooshuu no kao o minagara hanasanakute wa dame.
  (You should look at the faces of your audience when you speak.)

(2) ここは病院ですから、大声をあげては困ります。
Koko wa byooin desu kara, oogoe o agete wa komarimasu.
(Since this is a hospital, you must not speak loudly [lit., speaking in a loud voice is problematic].)

(3) 飲酒運転をしてはいけません。
Inshuunten o shite wa ikemasen.
(You must not drive while intoxicated.)

■ Additional Information

In casual speech, *te wa* and *de wa* are contracted to *cha* and *ja*, respectively. For example, *kenka o shicha dame yo* 'you shouldn't fight' will be used in a familiar colloquial environment.

112. Reporting (1)—Direct and Indirect Quotations

■ Target Expression

Mr. Suzuki said, "I forgot that completely."

鈴木さんは「すっかり忘れていました」と言いました。
Suzuki-san wa "Sukkari wasurete-imashita" to iimashita.

[*to yuu*]

■ Grammatical Explanation

Direct quotation. The quoted portion of direct quotations in Japanese is normally either graphologically marked with quotation marks 「 」 (in written Japanese) or marked by intonation and voice quality. (There are cases where direct quotations are not marked by graphological marks in written Japanese, however.) Direct quotation reflects styles of the quoted person and carries features similar to spoken Japanese. After the quoted portion, the quotative particle *to* is attached followed by the verb *yuu* 'say.' In the colloquial style, *to* changes to *tte*, except when it is preceded by the syllabic *n*, in which case *to* changes to *te*. Recall that the verb *yuu* conjugates by replacing *yu* with *i*: *yuu* conjugates *iimasu*, *itta*, *itte*, and so forth.

Indirect quotation. In indirect quotations the quoted portion often takes [V/Adj informal] endings, and the [*to yuu*] expression follows. There is no verb tense agreement as observed in English. The non-past tense in the quoted clause refers to actions not yet complete, whereas the past tense indicates that the action has or had occurred.

(a) 高橋さんも**行く**って言いましたよ。
*Takahashi-san mo **iku** tte iimashita yo.*
(Takahashi also said that he will go.)

(b) 高橋さんも**行った**って言いましたよ。
*Takahashi-san mo **itta** tte iimashita yo.*
(Takahashi also said that he went.)

Yooni yuu. When the quoted speech is in command form, *yooni yuu* is also used for indirect quotation, for example, *yoku chuui-suru yooni iimashita* 'they said to be on alert' for the indirect quotation of *yoku chuui-shinasai.*

Using quotation when questioning. A quotative expression may be particularly useful when one is interested in finding out the equivalents of foreign words. For example, if you want to know how to say "manager" in Japanese, you can simply ask:

(c) **A:** 「manager」は日本語で何と言いますか。

"Manager"	*wa*	*Nihongo*	*de*	*nan*	*to*	*iimasu*	*ka.*
manager	T	Japanese	in	what	QT	say	Q

(How do you say "manager" in Japanese?)

B: 日本語では「部長」です。
Nihongo de wa "buchoo" desu.
(In Japanese, it is "*buchoo.*")

Functions of *to yuu.* Some extended uses of [*to yuu*] should also be pointed out.

1. The quotative expression [*to yuu*] may be used to connect clauses and nominalizers, *koto* and *no*, when it is preceded by *da*. The phrase [*to yuu*] must also precede other modified nouns if the relationship between the modifying clause and the modified noun is appositional and is related to the action of saying or reporting (this point will be discussed again in Entry 114). See the following examples.

(1a) 大学生だ**という**ことを忘れないでください。
Daigakusei da ***to yuu*** *koto o wasurenaide kudasai.*
(Don't forget the fact that you are college students.)

(1b) タカノ**という**レストランへ行きました。
Takano ***to yuu*** *resutoran e ikimashita.*
(We went to a restaurant called Takano.)

(1c) その男は無実だ**という**説もある。

Sono otoko	*wa*	*mujitsu*	*da*	***to***	***yuu***	*setsu*	*mo*	*aru.*
that man	T	innocent	be	QT	say	opinion	also	is

(There is an opinion that [states that] the man is innocent.)

(1d) 川井さんはもうアメリカへ行ってしまった**という**話でしたが……
Kawai-san wa moo Amerika e itte-shimatta ***to yuu*** *hanashi deshita ga . . .*
(The story was that Mr. Kawai had left for America already.)

2. The expression [*to yuu*] can also end an utterance to indicate hearsay.

(2a) 山奥のその村には今でも熊が出る**という**。

Yamaoku	*no*	*sono mura*	*ni*	*wa*	*ima*	*demo*	*kuma*	*ga*
deep in the mountains	L	that village	in	T	now	even	bear	S

deru	***to***	***yuu.***
appear	QT	say

(They say that in that village deep in the mountains, bears appear even now.)

3. An idiomatic use of [*to yuu*] should also be mentioned. As seen in the example below, when [N *to yuu* N] is used, it has a meaning of 'every N.'

(3a) 人間**という**人間はすべて幸せを求めている。

*Ningen **to yuu** ningen*	*wa*	*subete*	*shiawase*	*o*	*motomete-iru.*
every man	T	all	happiness	O	is seeking

(Every human being seeks happiness.)

■ Examples

(1) 「行ってきまーす」と言って、妹は出かけていきました。
"Itte kimaasu" to itte, imooto wa dekakete-ikimashita.
(Saying "Bye," my sister left the house.)

(2) 先生は「よく勉強しておきなさい」とおっしゃいました。
Sensei wa "Yoku benkyoo-shite-okinasai" to osshaimashita.
(The teacher said, "Study hard.")

(3) 山本さんはテニスの試合に負けて残念だと言っていました。
Yamamoto-san wa tenisu no shiai ni makete zannen da to itte-imashita.
(Mr. Yamamoto said he was sorry he lost the tennis match.)

(4) **A:** 中川っていうそば屋知ってる？
Nakagawa tte yuu sobaya shitte-ru?
(Do you know the *soba* shop called Nakagawa?)

B: はい、知っています。駅の近くですね。
Hai, shitte-imasu. Eki no chikaku desu ne.
(Yes, I do. It's near the station, isn't it?)

A: そこで会おう。
Soko de aoo.
(Yes. Let's meet there.)

(5) 父も駅まで行くと申しておりました。
Chichi mo eki made iku to mooshite-orimashita.
(My father said that he too would go as far as the station.)

(6) **A:** あの人が勤めていたのは何ていう会社でしたか。
Ano hito ga tsutomete-ita no wa nan te yuu kaisha deshita ka.
(What was the name of the company he worked for?)

B: さあ……、ああ、グローバルトレーディングとかいう会社じゃありませんか。
Saa . . . , aa, Guroobaru Toreedingu to ka yuu kaisha ja arimasen ka.
(Hmm . . ., oh, isn't it a company called "Global Trading" or something?)

(7) 先生はいつも「授業中おしゃべりをしてはいけません」とおっしゃいます。
Sensei wa itsumo "Jugyoochuu oshaberi o shite wa ikemasen" to osshaimasu.
(The teacher always says, "Don't chatter during the class.")

■ Additional Information

- The phrase *to yuu to*, *to iimasu to* and *to ieba* 'speaking of . . .' function to present a topic into conversation.

(a) サチ**っていうと**、もうアメリカから帰ってきたのかな。
*Sachi **tte yuuto**, moo Amerika kara kaette kita no ka na.*
(Speaking of Sachi, I wonder if she returned from the United States.)

- The quotative [*to*] may also appear with verbs of thought and reporting as indirect quotation. In these cases the form preceding the quotative particle is [V/Adj informal], and [*to*] marks the content of the thought and reporting.

(b) 早く日本へ帰ろう**と**決心した。

Hayaku	*Nihon*	*e*	*kaeroo*	***to***	*kesshin-shita.*
soon	Japan	to	will return	QT	decided

(I decided to return to Japan soon.)

(c) 来年は北海道旅行をしよう**と**思っています。
*Rainen wa Hokkaidoo ryokoo o shiyoo **to** omotte-imasu.*
(I'm thinking that I will make a trip to Hokkaido next year.)*1

*1. See volitional forms introduced in Entry 44 if you are not sure of the expression *shiyoo*.

- There are a number of verbs that involve reporting and thought process that may take the quotative [*to*] as listed below.

と教える *to oshieru* (to teach)

と思う *to omou* (to think)

と書く *to kaku* (to write)

その手紙には来月両親がアメリカへ来る**と書いてあった**。
*Sono tegami ni wa raigetsu ryooshin ga Amerika e kuru **to kaiteatta**.*

(In that letter it was written that my parents would come to the United States next month.)

と考える *to kangaeru* (to think, to consider)

新しい窓をつければ明るくなる**と考えた**。
*Atarashii mado o tsukereba akaruku naru **to kangaeta**.*
(I thought if I install the new window, it will be lighter.)

と聞く *to kiku* (to hear about)

小山先生はもうヨーロッパへいらっしゃった**と聞きましたが**……
*Koyama-sensei wa moo Yooroppa e irasshatta **to kikimashita** ga . . .*
(I heard that Professor Koyama had already left for Europe . . .)

と告白する *to kokuhaku-suru* (to confess)

犯人はその娘を殺した**と告白した**。
*Hannin wa sono musume o koroshita **to kokuhaku-shita**.*
(The criminal confessed to killing the young woman.)

と述べる *to noberu* (to state)

- These verbs can also take *to yuu koto o* instead of *to*, when the content of the report and thought is presented not verbatim but in the abstract. Compare the following:

(d) 元気でがんばるように**ということを**書いてやった。
*Genki de ganbaru yooni **to yuu koto o** kaite-yatta.*
(I wrote that [in essence] she should be well and do her best.)

(e) 元気でがんばるように**と**書いてやった。
*Genki de ganbaru yooni **to** kaite-yatta.*
(I wrote to her to keep well and to do her best.)

- When verbs of reporting and thought are preceded by *to* as above, the speaker is only mildly committed to presupposing that what is reported is a fact. If the verb expressing thought requires that the speaker believes it to be a fact, *to* cannot be used. For example, one can only forget (*wasureru*) or recall (*omoidasu*) what one believes to be fact; thus **to omoidasu* and **to wasureru* are not acceptable. Instead, use *koto* as in (f).

(f) 小山先生がヨーロッパへいらっしゃった（**という**）**ことを**忘れていました。
*Koyama sensei ga Yooroppa e irasshatta (**to yuu**) **koto o** wasurete-imashita.*
(I forgot that Professor Koyama went to Europe.)

113. Action-accompanying Expressions (2) —When Visiting Someone's Place

■ Target Expression

Please (come in).

さあ、どうぞ、どうぞ。
Saa, doozo, doozo.

■ Strategic Explanation

Formulaic phrases when visiting someone. The Japanese language seems to be filled with a great number of formulaic phrases that accompany specific actions. It becomes so much of a ritual to use expressions meaning 'I am leaving' when you are going out the door, or 'I am about to eat' before you pick up your chopsticks, that if you fail to say these words, you may well be thought to be rude. These ritualistic expressions may strike you as being obvious and even redundant. Nevertheless, one is expected to say them. The following expressions are some of the more common phrases you are likely to use when visiting a Japanese family. If you forget the use of these Japanese favorites, use *sumimasen* and *doomo* which have a wide range of applications.

1. *At the door:*

(1a) Guest: ごめんください。 *Gomenkudasai.*
([lit., Excuse me.] Hello.)

Host: いらっしゃい。 *Irasshai.*
(Welcome.)

2. *As you enter the room:*

(2a) Host: こちらへどうぞ。 *Kochira e doozo.*
(This way, please.)

Guest: おじゃまします。 *Ojama-shimasu.* [said with a slight bow]
(Excuse me.)
失礼します。 *Shitsurei-shimasu.* [said with a slight bow]
(Excuse me.)

3. *When your host begins to prepare drink and food:*

(3a) どうぞおかまいなく。 *Doozo okamainaku.*
(lit., Please don't go to any trouble.)

4. *When you present some gift:*

(4a) つまらないものですが…… *Tsumaranai mono desu ga . . .*
(Here's something for you.)

5. *When drinking or eating:*

(5a) Host: どうぞめしあがってください。 *Doozo meshiagatte-kudasai.*
(Please help yourself.)

Guest: (では) いただきます。 *(Dewa) itadakimasu.*
(lit., Thank you, I'll help myself.)

Itadakimasu may be said either when the guest accepts the offer or immediately before the guest eats or drinks.

(5b) Host: おかわりは？
Okawari wa?
(How about another serving?)

Guest: すみません。じゃあ少しお願いします。
Sumimasen. Jaa sukoshi onegai-shimasu.
(Thanks, a little, then.)

(5c) Host: もう少しいかがですか。
Moo sukoshi ikaga desu ka.
(How about some more?)

Guest: ええ、もうたくさんいただきましたから。
Ee, moo takusan itadakimashita kara.
(Thank you, but no thank you . . . I already had plenty.)

(5d) Guest: (when finished drinking or eating)
(どうも)ごちそうさまでした。
(Doomo) gochisoosama deshita.
(Thank you for the delicious food/drink.)

6. *When thinking about leaving:*

(6a) そろそろ失礼しますので……
Sorosoro shitsurei-shimasu node . . .
(It's about time, I should be leaving.)

7. *When you leave the host's home:*

(7a) おじゃましました。 *Ojama-shimashita.*
(Thanks for your hospitality.)

(7b) 失礼します。 *Shitsurei-shimasu.*
(Excuse me. Good-bye.)

114. Modifying (4)—Clausal Explanation

■ Target Expressions

The room was filled with the smell of meat being grilled.

部屋は肉を焼くにおいでいっぱいだった。
Heya wa niku o yaku nioi de ippai datta.

Did you hear the rumor that Ms. Kato got married?

加藤さんが結婚したっていううわさ聞いた?
Katoo-san ga kekkon-shita tte yuu uwasa kiita?

■ Grammatical Explanation

Explaining about a modified noun. We have studied clausal modifiers earlier in Entry 83. In this entry we concentrate on the second extended type. In this type, the modification clause provides general explanation about the noun which does not constitute an element necessary for the proposition. As seen in the first target expression, *niku o yaku nioi* 'lit., smell of grilling meat' is structurally different from *chichi ga kaita hon* 'the book my father wrote.' In the latter, *hon* constitutes the grammatical object, an essential element of the proposition, [*chichi ga hon o kaita*]. In the grilling-meat example, the smell is something that is closely associated with the process of grilling, but it is not a part of the proposition, [*niku o yaku*]. Since these modifiers are quite common in Japanese, it becomes necessary to interpret the meaning in an extended way. Recall the similar example in Entry 83; *tomodachi ni au yakusoku o wasurete-shimaimashita* 'I forgot the appointment to see my friend.'

Clausal explanation with *to yuu*. Although clausal explanation takes [V/Adj pre-nominal] forms, among extended types, there are some that obligatorily take the quotation phrase [*to yuu*], some that optionally take it, and some that normally do not. The clausal explanation that is semantically associated with reporting or that represents the reporter's view is followed by [*to yuu*]. For the clause that directly explains sensory information [*to yuu*] cannot be used.

■ Examples

(1) A: 山田先生からあした十一時に研究室に来るようにというお電話をいただきましたよ。
Yamada sensei kara ashita juu ichi-ji ni kenkyuushitsu ni kuru yooni to yuu odenwa o itadakimashita yo.
(I received a phone call from Professor Yamada telling you to go to his office at eleven o'clock tomorrow.)

B: そう、困ったなあ。あしたは十一時に川口と会う約束があるんだよ。
Soo, komatta naa. Ashita wa juu ichi-ji ni Kawaguchi to au yakusoku ga aru n da yo.
(Well, that's a problem. I have an appointment to see Kawaguchi at eleven tomorrow.)

(2) **A:** あれ、どこかでガラスを割る音がするよ。
Are, doko-ka de garasu o waru oto ga suru yo.
(Listen! I hear someone breaking glass.)

B: あれは誰かがビンを箱に入れている音でしょ。
Are wa dare-ka ga bin o hako ni irete-iru oto desho.
(That sound comes from someone putting glass bottles into a box.)

A: そうかなあ。
Soo ka naa.
(I wonder.)

(3) **A:** 本を買ったおつり、ここに置いとくね。
Hon o katta otsuri, koko ni oitoku ne.
(I'm leaving the change I got when I bought the book.)

B: ああ、ありがとう。
Aa, arigatoo.
(Oh, thanks.)

A: 本屋さんでちえ子さんが結婚したっていううわさを聞いたけど……
Hon'ya-san de Chieko-san ga kekkon-shita tte yuu uwasa o kiita kedo . . .
(I heard a rumor at the bookstore that Chieko got married.)

B: そんなのただのうわさだろ？ [masculine speech]
Sonna no tada no uwasa daro?
(That's just a rumor, isn't it?)

A: そうかなあ。
Soo ka naa.
(I doubt it.)

■ Additional Information

Here is a note regarding the tense of the explanatory clause in relation to the main clause. If the noun semantically calls for a future event, [Vnon-past] co-occurs as in (a); if the noun semantically calls for the past event, [Vpast] is used as in (b); if the noun involves relative tense, either [Vpast] or [Vnon-past] is chosen depending on the noun, as in (c) and (d).

(a) 友だちと**会う**約束をした。
*Tomodachi to **au** yakusoku o shita.*
(I promised to see my friend.)

(b) 楽しい旅行を**した**思い出は大切にしたい。

Tanoshii	*ryokoo*	*o*	***shita***	*omoide*	*wa*	*taisetsuni*	*shitai.*
enjoyable	trip	O	did	memories	T	want to	treasure

(I want to treasure the memories of having made enjoyable trips.)

(c) 買い物を**した**帰りにおじさんの家に寄ってきます。
*Kaimono o **shita** kaeri ni ojisan no uchi ni yotte-kimasu.*
(On the way back from shopping, I will visit my uncle's place.)

(d) 買い物を**する**前におじさんの家に寄っていきます。
*Kaimono o **suru** mae ni ojisan no uchi ni yotte-ikimasu.*
(Before [on the way to] going shopping, I will visit my uncle's place.)

115. Reporting (2)—Hearsay: *Soo Da*

■ Target Expression

They say Mr. Baker quit his job.

ベイカーさんは仕事をやめたそうですよ。
Beikaa-san wa shigoto o yameta soo desu yo.

[V/Adj informal + *soo da*]

■ Grammatical Explanation

Reporting hearsay with *soo da*. The pattern [V/Adj informal + *soo da*] is used to report hearsay. This expression is used when the speaker makes a general report regarding what he or she heard or obtained indirectly. Compare this with the reporting devices we have learned earlier, *to yuu* or *to kiku*, which report information where the speaker had direct access to the source. When using [*soo da*], the speaker's intention is merely to give a report that is often based on secondhand information. When using this expression of hearsay, you are not making any personal commitment as to the truth of the content of the sentence preceding *soo da*.

■ Examples

(1) **A:** スミスさん、きのう日本へ行ったそうですよ。
Sumisu-san, kinoo Nihon e itta soo desu yo.
(I hear that Mr. Smith left for Japan yesterday.)

B: そうですか。仕事で日本へ行くと言っていましたが。
Soo desu ka. Shigoto de Nihon e iku to itte-imashita ga.
(Is that so? He said he was going to Japan because of his job.)

A: アメリカ大使館の仕事だそうです。
Amerika taishikan no shigoto da soo desu.
(Yes, I hear it's a job at the American Embassy.)

(2) A: 新しい機械はすばらしいそうですねえ。
Atarashii kikai wa subarashii soo desu nee.
(They say that the new machine is just wonderful.)

B: ええ、そうなんですよ。ご覧になりますか。
Ee, soo na n desu yo. Goran ni narimasu ka.
(Yes, it is. Would you like to see it?)

■ Warning

The use of [*soo da*] for reportig is preceded by the [V/Adj informal] forms. Contrast this with the [*soona*] used to express conjecture, which takes [V/Adj stem] (as given in Entry 87). Compare the meaning of the following two sentences.

Used when you hear from some source about the likelihood of rain:

(a) 雨が**降るそうです**。
*Ame ga **huru soo desu**.*
(They say it will rain.)

Used when you see a rain cloud hanging low and you conjecture that it is likely to rain:

(b) 雨が**降りそうだ**。
*Ame ga **hurisoo da**.*
(It looks [as if] it is going to rain.)

116. Causative and Permissive Expressions

■ Target Expression

I made my brother go to the bookstore.

弟を本屋へ行かせました。
Otooto o hon'ya e ikasemashita.

[V + *-seru*/*-saseru*]

■ Grammatical Explanation

Using causatives. Causatives express the idea that someone or something causes, influences, or allows a third party to do something. Causative expressions normally do not co-occur with stative verbs, existential verbs, and the *be*-verb. Certain restrictions apply among some verbs; when there are transitive verbs that correspond with intransitive counterparts, transitive verbs are used instead of the causative forms.

Causatives as permissives. Causative forms are used as permissives when the causee performs an action willingly.

Causative and permissive forms. As in the case of respectful and passive forms, causatives and permissives are expressed by verb endings which are changed by the following rules.

U-verbs: change the final *-u* to *-aseru* (when the final *-u* is not preceded by a consonant, change *-u* to *-waseru*)

書く	*kak***u**	to write	→	書かせる	*kak***aseru**
買う	*ka***u**	to buy	→	買わせる	*ka***waseru**

RU-verbs: change *-ru* to *-saseru*

食べる	*tabe***ru**	to eat	→	食べさせる	*tabe***saseru**

Irregular verbs:

来る	***kuru***	to come	→	来させる	***kosaseru***
する	***suru***	to do	→	させる	***saseru***

As for existential verbs, use only *isaseru* (causative of *iru*) when it means 'to stay.' Causatives and permissives have shortened forms which are obtained by changing the final *-seru* to *-su*; for example, *kakaseru* to *kakasu*, *tabesaseru* to *tabesasu*, and *saseru* to *sasu*. The shortened causative forms tend to express more direct and forceful causation than the standard causative forms.

Particles in causatives and permissives. Particles used for the causative/permissive structure are: the causer takes *ga* (or a topic marker if it is a topic), the causee is marked by *o* or *ni*. For the selection of either *o* or *ni*, the following rules apply.

1. When the verb is transitive and the direct object marker *o* appears, the causee must be marked with *ni*.

    (1a) 弟**に**部屋をそうじさせた。
    *Otooto **ni** heya o sooji-saseta.*
    (I made my younger brother clean his room.)

2. When the verb expresses instant change and response, the causee takes *o*.

    (2a) お客さん**を**怒らせてしまった。
    *Okyakusan **o** okorasete-shimatta.*
    (I made the customer get angry.)

3. When the causative expression conveys the meaning that one is responsible for the event to happen or to have happened, only *o* is used.

   (3a) 息子**を**病気で死なせたんです。
   *Musuko **o** byooki de shinaseta n desu.*
   ([I am to blame that] I caused my son's death due to sickness.)

Using *ni* versus *o*. When these restrictions do not apply, use either *o* or *ni* to mark the causee. The choice of either particle is based on the following. As a general rule use *o* for either causative or permissive expressions, use *ni* for permissives. When *ni* is used, the causer acknowledges the causee's desire or will to perform the action, and the causee must be able to perform it. Thus, the verb used in this pattern must refer to a controllable action.

Although *o* can be used to express permissives similarly to *ni*, when the causee is marked by *o*, coercive causative meaning is emphasized. *Imooto o ikaseta* 'I made (or forced) my sister (to) go' is ambiguous between 'I forced my sister to go' and 'I let (permitted) my sister (to) go. The choice of meanings depends on the semantic context in which the utterance appears.

Using causative passives. The causative expression may be combined with the passive to form causative passive expressions. The causative ending *-seru* goes through a passive ending change following *RU*-verbs; thus *kakaseru* takes *kakaserareru* 'to be forced to write,' *tabesaseru* takes *tabesaserareru* 'to be forced to eat.' Irregular verbs *kuru* and *suru* take *kosaserareru* and *saserareru*, respectively. Shortened causative passive endings are available; *kakasu* changes according to the *U*-verb conjugation, resulting in *kakasareru*.

(a) 子供たちはきらいな食べものを**食べさせられた**。
*Kodomo-tachi wa kiraina tabemono o **tabesaserareta**.*
(Children were forced to eat the food they disliked.)

■ Examples

(1) 子供たちには三時まで好きなことをさせましょう。
Kodomo-tachi ni wa san-ji made sukina koto o sasemashoo.
(Let's let the children do whatever they like until three o'clock.)

(2) 切手が必要なら正人を買いに行かせますが。
Kitte ga hitsuyoo nara Masato o kai ni ikasemasu ga.
(If you need stamps, I will make Masato go buy them.)

(3) そんなことさせないで。
Sonna koto sasenai de.
そんなことさせるなよ。 [masculine speech]
Sonna koto saseru na yo.
(Don't make me do such a thing.)

(4) **A:** きのう銀行へ行ったんですが、長い間待たされましてねえ。
Kinoo ginkoo e itta n desu ga, nagai aida matasaremashite nee.
(I went to the bank yesterday, but I was made to wait for a long time.)

B: それは大変でしたねえ。込んでいたんですか。
Sore wa taihen deshita nee. Konde-ita n desu ka.
(That's too bad. Was it crowded?)

A: いいえ、会う約束をしておいた人が留守でね、急用で。ちょっとほかの仕事をさせられたらしいんです。
Iie, au yakusoku o shite-oita hito ga rusu de ne, kyuuyoo de. Chotto hoka no shigoto o saserareta rashii n desu.
(No, the person I was going to see was out due to an emergency. It seems that he was forced to tend to other matters.)

■ Additional Information

Causatives are used to declare one's intention while acknowledging the other's involvement in the decision. The result is a style that evokes great care, politeness, and humbleness, as shown in (a) and (b). These expressions signal awareness of the other's good will in letting the speaker take a certain action.

Note that causatives used for this purpose sometimes contain an extra *sa*. For example, *kikasasete* and *utawasasete*, although according to the conjugation rule, their causative forms are *kikaseru* and *utawaseru*. The insertion of this extra *sa* (called *saire kotoba 'sa*-inserted phrases') occurs frequently, although it is considered incorrect by some Japanese speakers. The insertion of the extra *sa* creates a greater degree of politeness.

(a) そんな理由でこの会を**開か(さ)せていただきました**。
Sonna riyuu de kono kai o ***hiraka(sa)sete-itadakimashita****.*
(For that reason, I went ahead and held this meeting.)

(b) **A:** 君の番だよ。一曲歌って。
Kimi no ban da yo. Ikkyoku utatte.
(It's your turn. Sing a song for us.)

B: そうですか。じゃ、**歌わ(さ)せていただきます**。
Soo desu ka. Ja, ***utawa(sa)sete-itadakimasu****.*
(All right. Well, then, let me sing you a song.)

117. Subjunctive Expressions

■ Target Expressions

If it were cheaper, I would have bought it.

もっと安ければ買ったのに。
Motto yasukereba katta noni.
もっと安かったら買ったんですけど。
Motto yasukattara katta n desu kedo.

■ Grammatical Explanation

Using conditionals as subjunctive expressions. When describing one's feelings of contradicting realities, the so-called subjunctive mood is used. In Japanese, conditional sentences with [-*ba*] and [-*tara*] are frequently used for this purpose. The main clause ends with disjunctive conjunctions such as *kedo* or *noni*. (For forming the *ba*-form see Entry 92; for the *tara*-form, see Entry 93.) The verbs and adjectival predicates in the main clause normally take [V/Adj past] forms.

■ Examples

(1) 天気がよければピクニックに行けたのに。
Tenki ga yokereba pikunikku ni iketa noni.
(If it was good weather, we could have gone for a picnic.)

(2) もう少し長生きをしてたら海外旅行もできたのに。
Moo sukoshi nagaiki o shite-tara kaigairyokoo mo dekita noni.
(If they lived a little longer, they would have been able to travel abroad.)

(3) お金があったら休みにはヨーロッパへ行けたんだけどねえ。
Okane ga attara yasumi ni wa Yooroppa e iketa n da kedo nee.
(If I had money, I could have gone to Europe for vacation.)

(4) もっとがんばればよかったのに。
Motto ganbareba yokatta noni.
(If I tried harder, it would have been better.)

■ Additional Information

A shortened version of subjunctives takes either the *ba*-form or *tara*-form followed by the final particle *nee* or *naa*. These expressions are normally used in casual situations.

(a) もっとお金が**あったらねえ**。
Motto okane ga ***attara nee****.*
(I wish I had more money ...)

(b) あの人があと三分早く**来ていたらなあ**。
Ano hito ga ato san-pun hayaku ***kite-itara naa.***
(I wish he came three minutes earlier ...)

118. Advising

■ Target Expressions

Wouldn't it be better for you to go by an earlier Bullet Train?
もっと早い新幹線で行った方がいいでしょう。
Motto hayai Shinkansen de itta hoo ga ii-deshoo.
もっと早い新幹線で行った方がいいんじゃない?
Motto hayai Shinkansen de itta hoo ga ii n ja-nai?
Since it is time already, wouldn't it be better to start?
もう時間だから始めたらどうでしょうか。
Moo jikan da kara hajimetara doo deshoo ka.

[Vpre-nominal + *hoo ga ii*]

■ Strategic Explanation

Advising and suggesting. Although we've learned structures introduced here earlier under the heading Comparative and Superlative forms (Entry 64), we will review the strategies for giving suggestions and advice in Japanese.

Hoo ga ii. The first is the [*hoo ga ii*] pattern studied under comparative forms. The [*hoo ga ii*] expression takes [Vpre-nominal], with the [Vinformal past] form considered slightly more indirect. For the *be*-verb *da*, use *de-iru*. For making a negative suggestion, use only the negative [informal non-past form + *hoo ga ii*]. When advising or making suggestions, use only the verbs that refer to controllable action.

***Tara* conditional.** The second is the [*tara*] conditional, followed by the deletable formulaic clause of [*doo da/daroo*], then followed by the question marker *ka*. It is important to remember in both cases that suggestions and advice given in these expressions are limited to those given to social subordinates or close friends.

Toward social superiors. When suggesting and advising one's social superiors or those with whom one is expected to be polite, a different expression must be used. For example, *motto hayai Shinkansen de irasshatta hoo ga yoroshii ka to omoimasu ga ...* 'I think it might be better if you took an earlier Bullet Train.'

Various expressions for giving advice and suggestions. Let us review a group of strategies used for giving advice and suggestions. The following are listed, starting with the most direct to the most indirect. As you can see, in general, the more elaborate the expression is, the more polite it becomes, which is also true in English.

1. 行け。 *Ike.* (Entry 79)
2. 行きなさい。 *Ikinasai.* (Entry 79)
3. 行く方がいい(です)。 *Iku hoo ga ii (desu).* (Entry 118)
4. 行った方がいい(です)。 *Itta hoo ga ii (desu).* (Entry 118)
5. 行った方がいいでしょう。 *Itta hoo ga ii-deshoo.* (Entry 118)
6. 行ったらどうですか。 *Ittara doo desu ka.* (Entry 93)
7. 行った方がよろしいかと思いますが……
   Itta hoo ga yoroshii ka to omoimasu ga ... (Entry 122)
8. いらっしゃったら？ *Irasshattara?* (Entry 93)
9. いらっしゃった方がよろしいんじゃないかと思いますが……
   Irasshatta hoo ga yoroshii n ja-nai ka to omoimasu ga ... (Entry 122)

119. Special Uses of *Dake*, *Bakari*, and *Hodo*

■ Target Expressions

As for kanji, it is important to be able not only to read it but to write it as well.

漢字は読めるだけ/ばかりでなく書けることも大切です。
Kanji wa yomeru dake/bakari de naku kakeru koto mo taisetsu desu.

I just arrived.

今来たばかりです。
Ima kita bakari desu.

■ Grammatical Explanation

Adverbial quantifiers listed here have basic usage as well as useful idiomatic expression, which we will study one by one.

Idiomatic use of *dake*. The form preceding *dake* is [V/Adj pre-nominal], except when [N + *da*] precedes *dake*, use [N + *dake*].

1. *dake* 'only; just':

   (1a) ちょっと声が聞きたかった**だけ**です。
   Chotto koe ga kikitakatta ***dake*** *desu.*
   (I just wanted to hear your voice.)

2. *dake de naku ... mo* 'not only but also ...':

   (2a) 日本人**だけでなく**アメリカ人**も**たくさん来ていました。
   Nihon-jin ***dake de naku*** *Amerika-jin* ***mo*** *takusan kite-imashita.*
   (Not only Japanese but many Americans were there.)

Idiomatic use of *bakari*.

1. *bakari* 'only':
   The form preceding this is [N], [Adj pre-nominal non-past] and [V*te*]. When [V*te*] precedes *bakari* to mean 'only [V],' it takes the [V*te bakari iru*] structure.

   (1a) 娘は甘いもの**ばかり**食べるんですよ。
   Musume wa amaimono ***bakari*** *taberu n desu yo.*
   (My daughter eats just sweets, you know.)

   (1b) 娘は**遊んでばかり**います。
   Musume wa ***asonde bakari*** *imasu.*
   ([lit., My daughter only plays.] All my daughter does is to play.)

2. *bakari de naku ... mo* 'not only but also ...':
   The form preceding this use is [N], [Vpre-Aux] and [Adj pre-nominal].

   (2a) 日本人**ばかりでなく**アメリカ人**も**たくさん来ていました。
   Nihon-jin ***bakari de naku*** *Amerika-jin* ***mo*** *takusan kite-imashita.*
   (Not only Japanese but many Americans came.)

3. [Vinformal past (affirmative only) + *bakari da*] 'just did ...':

   (3a) 今**始まったばかり**ですよ。
   Ima ***hajimatta bakari*** *desu yo.*
   (It just started.)

4. [quantifier + *bakari*] 'about':

   (4a) ロンドンには**二週間ばかり**いました。
   Rondon ni wa ***ni-shuukan bakari*** *imashita.*
   (I was in London for about two weeks.)

5. [Vbasic + *bakari da*] '... ready to':

   (5a) さて、準備はできましたよ、もう**食べるばかり**です。
   Sate, junbi wa dekimashita yo, moo ***taberu bakari*** *desu.*
   (Well, the preparation is complete, we are ready to eat.)

Idiomatic use of *hodo*. The form preceding *hodo* is [Vpre-nominal]. When the [N + *da*] precedes *hodo*, use [N + *to yuu hodo*].

1. *hodo* 'to the degree':

(1a) 今朝は暖かくて少し汗ばむ**ほど**でした。

Kesa	*wa*	*atatakakute*	*sukoshi*	*asebamu*	***hodo***	*deshita.*
this morning	T	warm	a little	sweat	degree	was

(It was warm this morning to the degree that I sweated a little.)

2. *hodo dewa nai* 'not so':

(2a) この問題はむずかしいが、むずかしくて全然わからない**ほどではない**。

Kono mondai	*wa*	*muzukashii*	*ga,*	*muzukashikute*	*zenzen*
this question	T	difficult	but	difficult	at all

wakaranai	***hodo***	***dewa nai.***
do not understand	degree	is not.

(This question is difficult, but not so difficult as to not being able to understand it at all.)

(2b) あの人はなまけものという**ほどではない**けど……

Ano hito wa namakemono to yuu ***hodo dewa nai*** *kedo . . .*

(He is not [lit., to the degree of being a lazy person] exactly a lazy person, but . . .)

3. [quantifier + *hodo*] 'about':

(3a) すみませんが、**二万円ほど**貸してくださいませんか。

Sumimasen ga, ***ni-man-yen hodo*** *kashite-kudasaimasen ka.*

(Could you please loan me twenty thousand yen or so?)

■ Additional Information

Recall that phrases expressing approximation of quantity, such as *hodo*, *kurai / gurai* and *bakari*, are closely associated with politeness, particularly when used with small numbers and when used in requests. By presenting the quantity in approximation, the speaker allows more leeway for the interactant to respond.

120. Special Uses of *Mono* and *Koto*

■ Target Expressions

I used to play around here a long time ago.

昔はここでよく遊んだものです。
Mukashi wa koko de yoku asonda mono desu.

We are moving soon, so ...

今度引っ越すことになりましたので……
Kondo hikkosu koto ni narimashita node ...

■ Grammatical Explanation

Here we focus on idiomatic uses of the noun *mono* and *koto*. *Mono* and *koto* are both nouns and mean 'thing(s)' and 'fact(s),' respectively. While *mono* refers to tangible things, *koto* is used to refer to intangible and abstract things or facts. The idiomatic uses of these nouns are frequent and warrant our special attention.

Idiomatic use of *mono*.

1. [V/Adj informal past + *mono da*]
   Reflecting on past experience with a sentimental, nostalgic feeling:

   (1a) 子供の頃はここでよく**遊んだものです**。

Kodomo	*no*	*koro*	*wa*	*koko*	*de*	*yoku*	***asonda mono desu.***
Child	L	time	T	here	at	often	played

   (In my childhood, [I remember] I used to play around here.)

2. [Adj + *mono*] (Adj must be in predicate forms.), [*da* + *mono*], [V/Adj pre-nominal + *n* + *da* + *mono*] (If *da* precedes *n*, *da* changes to *na*. In casual style, *mon* instead of *mono* is preferred.)
   Pointing out reason in colloquial speech:

   (2a) A: どうして食べないの？
   Dooshite tabenai no?
   (Why don't you eat?)

   B: おいしくない**もの**。
   Oishikunai ***mono****.*
   (Because it doesn't taste good.)

   (2b) A: どうして買ったの？
   Dooshite katta no?
   (Why did you buy it?)

B: 便利**だもの**。
Benri ***da mono****.*
(Because it is useful.)

(2c) A: どうしてそんなことしたの？
Dooshite sonna koto shita no?
(Why did you do such a thing?)

B: お兄さんがするように言った**んだもん**。
Oniisan ga suru yooni itta ***n da mon****.*
(Because my brother told me to.)

(2d) A: ひろしくんのおじさんってお金持ちなんだって？
Hiroshi-kun no ojisan tte okanemochi na n datte?
(Is it true that Hiroshi's uncle is rich?)

B: そう。会社の社長**なんだもん**。
Soo. Kaisha no shachoo ***na n da mon****.*
(Yes. Because he is a company president.)

3. [V/Adj pre-nominal + *mono da*] (Note that the [N + *da*] structure does not normally co-occur with this usage.)
Expressing surprise, empathy with a deep feeling:

(3a) この五年間いろいろなことが**あったものだ**なあと思う。
Kono go-nenkan iroirona koto ga ***atta mono da*** *naa to omou.*
(I feel overwhelmed when I think that so many things have happened in the past five years.)

(3b) アメリカは本当に**広いものだ**なあと思った。
Amerika wa hontooni ***hiroi mono da*** *naa to omotta.*
(I was overwhelmed by the vastness of the United States.)

4. [Vinformal + *mono*] (Note that the [N + *da*] structure does not normally co-occur with this usage.)
To add explanation in written style:

(4a) この建物は市民の寄付によって**建てられたもの**。

Kono	*tatemono*	*wa*	*shimin*	*no*	*kifu*	*niyotte*	***taterareta mono.***
this	building	T	citizen	L	donation	by	was built

(This building is the one built by the citizens' donation.)

5. [Vbasic + *mono da*] (Only controllable verbs are used for this structure.)
To convey mild, indirect command:

(5a) よそのうちへ行く時は何かおみやげを**持っていくものです**よ。
Yoso no uchi e iku toki wa nani-ka omiyage o ***motte-iku mono desu*** *yo.*
(When you visit someone else's house, you should bring some gift.)

Idiomatic use of *koto.*

1. [Vinformal non-past + *koto ni suru*] (Only controllable verbs are used for this structure.)
   Expression of decision 'to decide to do' or 'I will do':

   (1a) 新宿駅でタクシーに乗る**ことにします**。
   Shinjuku eki de takushii ni noru ***koto ni shimasu.***
   (I will take a taxi at Shinjuku Station.)

2. [V/Adj informal past + *koto ga aru*]
   To point out past experience, 'I have experienced it in the past':

   (2a) ヨーロッパへは何回も行った**ことがあります**。
   Yooroppa e wa nankai mo itta ***koto ga arimasu.***
   (I've been to Europe many times.)

   (2b) ケータイは一時たいへん高かった**ことがあります**。
   Keetai wa ichiji taihen takakatta ***koto ga arimasu.***
   (There was a time when cell phones were quite expensive.)

3. [V/Adj pre-nominal non-past + *koto ga aru*]
   To point out that an event or a state occurs sometimes or occasionally:

   (3a) 二日酔いするまで飲む**ことがあります**か。

Hutsukayoi-suru	*made*	***nomu koto ga arimasu***	*ka.*
have hangover	till	drink	Q

   (Do you sometimes drink to the extent that you have a hangover?)

   (3b) あのスーパーの方が安い**こともある**よ。
   Ano suupaa no hoo ga yasui ***koto mo aru*** *yo.*
   (There are some occasions when that supermarket is less expensive.)

4. [Vinformal non-past + *koto ni naru*] (For the [N + *da*] structure, use [N + *deiru koto ni naru*].)
   To mean 'it has been decided to':

   (4a) 今度九州へ行く**ことになりました**ので。
   Kondo Kyuushuu e iku ***koto ni narimashita*** *node.*
   (It has been decided that we will be going to Kyushu soon, so ...)

5. [Vbasic + *koto wa nai*] (For the [N + *da*] structure, use [N + *deiru koto wa nai*].)
   To mean 'there is no need to ...':

   (5a) 忙しいんなら行く**ことはない**よ。
   Isogashii n nara iku ***koto wa nai*** *yo.*[*1]
   (If you are busy, there is no need to go.)

*1. *N(o)* in this expression is a nominalizer used for the extended predicate *no da*. *Da* is then deleted before *nara(ba)*.

121. Useful Compounds (1)—Verb Compounds

■ Grammatical Explanation

We've studied several verb compounds already. Verb compounds consist of two verbs or a verb and [AuxV]. Compound verbs conjugate according to the category of the latter [V] or [AuxV]. In this section, we review and learn additional useful verb compounds in Japanese.

1. [V*te* + *-shimau*] (See Entry 54.)

2. [V*te* + *-oku*] (See Entry 95.)

3. [V*te* + *-miru*] 'try and see by doing something':
This expression is used when you attempt to perform an action as a trial for some other purpose.

(3a) A: これ**作ってみました**が。
*Kore **tsukutte-mimashita** ga.*
(I tried making this ...)

B: ああ、おいしそうですねえ。
Aa, oishisoo desu nee.
(Oh, that looks delicious.)

A: どうぞ**めしあがってみて**ください。
*Doozo **meshiagatte-mite**-kudasai.*
(Please try some.)

B: すみません。いただきます。
Sumimasen. Itadakimasu.
(Thank you.)

(3b) A: この本おもしろそうなので**読んでみて**ください。
*Kono hon omoshirosoona node **yonde-mite** kudasai.*
(Please read this book since it looks interesting.)

B: ああ、それはもう読みました。
Aa, sore wa moo yomimashita.
(Oh, I've aready read that one.)

A: どうでした？
Doo deshita?
(How was it?)

B: とてもいい本ですね。同じ著者の本をもっと**読んでみたく**なりました。
*Totemo ii hon desu ne. Onaji chosha no hon o motto **yonde-mitaku** narimashita.*
(It's a very good book. I've come to want to read other books by the same author.)

4. [Vstem + -*kakeru*] 'start doing something':

(4a) カレーを**食べかけた**ところへ、となりのミッチーがやってきた。
Karee o ***tabe-kaketa*** *tokoro e, tonari no Mitchii ga yatte-kita.*
(When I began eating curry and rice, Mitchy, my next-door neighbor, came for a visit.)

5. [Vstem + -*hajimeru*] [Vstem + -*dasu*] 'something begins to occur':
Dasu is preferred with verbs which indicate sudden and unexpected changes.

(5a) 四月なのに雪が**降り出した**んですよ。
Shigatsu na noni yuki ga ***huri-dashita*** *n desu yo.*
(Although it was April, the snow began to fall.)

(5b) A: もう**食べ始めて**もいいですか。
Moo ***tabe-hajimete*** *mo ii-desu ka.*
(Is it all right to start eating now?)

B: ええ、どうぞ。
Ee, doozo.
(Of course.)

6. [Vstem + -*naosu*] [Vstem + -*kaesu*] 'repeating something, especially to amend an earlier error':

(6a) こんな字では困ります。**書き直して**ください。
Konna ji de wa komarimasu. ***Kaki-naoshite*** *kudasai.*
(Such handwriting will not do. Please rewrite it.)

(6b) よくわからなかったので**聞き返した**んですが、まだわかりません。
Yoku wakaranakatta node ***kiki-kaeshita*** *n desu ga, mada wakarimasen.*
(Since I didn't understand well, I asked again, but I still don't understand it.)

7. [V/Adj stem + -*sugiru*] 'do or be in excess':

(7a) ゆうべ**飲みすぎて**、今朝は頭が痛いんです。
Yuube ***nomi-sugite****, kesa wa atama ga itai n desu.*
(I drank too much last night, and I have a headache this morning.)

Note that in all structures listed above, the *be*-verb *da* is excluded from the category [V].

122. Expressing Your Thoughts

■ Target Expressions

I think it's really wonderful.

本当にすばらしいと思います。

Hontooni subarashii to omoimasu.

I'm afraid that the deadline is next week.

締め切りは来週じゃないかと思いますが……

Shimekiri wa raishuu ja-nai ka to omoimasu ga . . .

[*to omou*]

■ Grammatical Explanation

Expressing one's thoughts. When expressing one's thoughts, the quotative *to* plus the verb *omou* or *omotte-iru* 'think' are frequently used. Although it is possible to express your feelings without [*to omou*], the [*to omou*] expression makes the communication less domineering. So it is used commonly to avoid making blunt assertions. What is quoted ends with the informal volitional form if the content of the quoted clause represents one's intention or one's speculation about a future event or state; for example, *ikoo to omotte-imasu* 'I'm thinking that I will go.' In expressing a thought other than one's volition or one's opinion toward the future, [V/Adj informal] forms are used preceding [*to omou*]; for example, *yuubinkyoku wa ano tatemono da to omoimasu ga* 'I think the post office is that building.' When the speaker is quite uncertain or when the speaker wishes to express hesitation, *ka* may be placed before the quotative *to*. The form preceding *ka* is [V/Adj pre-Aux].

Expressing "I don't think." When it is necessary to negate and mean 'I don't think . . . ,' unlike English, the negation is normally placed within the quoted clause. 'I don't think the post office is that building' is usually expressed as *yuubinkyoku wa ano tatemono dewa-nai to omoimasu ga* . . . It is possible to negate the verb *omou*, as in *yuubinkyoku wa ano tatemono da to (wa) omoimasen ga* . . . ; when this expression is used, it is closer to the English *I doubt that* . . . and expresses stronger doubt on the part of the speaker.

***To omou* as a humbling strategy.** As we have studied when we discussed the expression of advice (Entry 118), [*to omou*] is used to express one's opinion in a socially humble way. It is a frequently used strategy in Japanese conversation.

■ Examples

(1) **A:** 今日どうする？
Kyoo doo suru?
(What should we do today?)

B: 美術館にでも行こうかと思ってるんだけど。
Bijutsukan ni demo ikoo ka to omotte-ru n da kedo.
(I'm going to the museum, or somewhere.)

(2) **A:** 友だちに電話をしてみようと思いますが。
Tomodachi ni denwa o shite miyoo to omoimasu ga.
(I guess I'll give a call to my friend.)

B: そうですね。
Soo desu ne.
(Right.)

A: もしできれば、食事にでも誘いたいと思いますが。どうでしょう。
Moshi dekireba, shokuji ni demo sasoitai to omoimasu ga. Doo deshoo.
(If possible, I'd like to invite him for dinner. Shall we?)

B: いいですねえ。ぜひいっしょに行きましょう。
Ii desu nee. Zehi isshoni ikimashoo.
(Great. Let's go together.)

■ Additional Information

- When you oppose someone else's opinion, it is generally more polite in Japanese to mark the statement with [*to omou*]. In addition, by turning the content of the quoted clause into the negative, you will achieve a greater degree of hesitation and softness. The same opinion can be expressed in at least three different ways, depending on how indirect you wish to be. As you see, in general, the more auxiliary phrases added to an utterance, the politer it becomes. This applies to English as well, as shown below.

  Straightforward:

  これはちがいますよ。
  Kore wa chigaimasu yo.
  (This is wrong.)

  Polite:

  そうですねえ…これはちがう（か）と思いますが……
  Soo desu nee ... kore wa chigau (ka) to omoimasu ga ...
  (Well, let's see ... I think this is wrong, but ...)

- Additionally, there are other expressions you can use when you state your opinion, including *chigau n ja-nai ka na* 'isn't that wrong, I wonder.'

- When speaking in English with Japanese people, you might notice that Japanese insert *I think* quite frequently. This *I think* mirrors the style in their native Japanese; it should not be literally interpreted. As shown above, Japanese tend to end personal opinions with *to omoimasu* just to make the expression less imposing. In fact, even when the Japanese speaker is quite certain of the fact, *to omou* is still added. For example, *ano hito wa kitto kuru to omoimasu yo* '(I think) that he will come for sure'—a style considered to be more pleasant to the ears.

123. Useful Compounds (2)—Compounds with Adjectives and Nouns

■ Grammatical Explanation

Compound words in Japanese are created by combinations between verbs, adjectives, and nouns. The grammatical category of the compound word is based on the last word. We will learn only a few examples of compounds in this book. It is a good idea to look for evidence for compounds when you face Japanese words. Knowing the rules for compounds can help increase your Japanese vocabulary.

Verb-adjective compounds.

1. [Vstem + *yasui*] 'easy to do':

(1a) この車は**運転しやすい**ですか。
*Kono kuruma wa **unten-shi yasui** desu ka.*
(Is this car easy to drive?)

2. [Vstem + *nikui*] 'difficult to do':

(2a) これは**使いにくくて**だめですよ。
*Kore wa **tsukai nikukute** dame desu yo.*
(This is difficult to use and it is not good [at all].)

Nominal compounds. Many Japanese noun phrases are generated by adding verbs, adjectives, and, of course, nouns. Here are some useful noun compounds. The process specified below for these compounds is not generative in all cases. In short, these rules are applicable to select nouns; one should not create new ones. When you find compounds however, it is helpful to know how they are constructed.

1. Repetition of nouns for indicating plurality:

人**々**	*hito**bito***	people
日**々**	*hi**bi***	days

2. [Vstem + *mono*] 'thing':

買い**物**	*kai**mono***	shopping
食べ**物**	*tabe**mono***	food
読み**物**	*yomi**mono***	things to read

3. [N + *dai*] 'fare':

バス**代**	*basu**dai***	bus fare
本**代**	*hon**dai***	book expense

4. [N + *ryoo(kin)*] 'fare':

タクシー**料金**	*takushii**ryookin***	taxi fare
水道**料金**	*suidoo**ryookin***	water fee
入場**料**	*nyuujoo**ryoo***	admission fee

5. [Adj stem + *sa*]:
Sa nominalizes the [Adj]. This process creates nouns presenting the degree of the quality identified by the adjective.

深**さ**	*huka**sa***	depth
広**さ**	*hiro**sa***	size
高**さ**	*taka**sa***	height
暖か**さ**	*atataka**sa***	warmth
便利**さ**	*benri**sa***	convenience
涼し**さ**	*suzushi**sa***	coolness
美し**さ**	*utsukushi**sa***	beauty

6. [Adj stem + *mi*]:
Mi also nominalizes the [Adj-*i*]. This pattern tends to express more emotive feelings than -*sa* nominalization.

楽し**み**	*tanoshi**mi***	fun, pleasure
深**み**	*huka**mi***	depth

7. [Vstem + *kata*] 'the way of doing':

食べ**方**	*tabe**kata***	way (or manner) of eating
泳ぎ**方**	*oyogi**kata***	way (or style) of swimming

8. [N + *yoo*] 'for the use by':

子供**用**	*kodomo**yoo***	for use by children
練習**用**	*renshuu**yoo***	used for practice purposes
学校**用**	*gakkoo**yoo***	for consumption at school

9. [N + *muke*] 'bound for,' 'catered toward':

中国**向け**	*Chuugoku**muke***	bound for, or catered to China
若者**向け**	*wakamono**muke***	catered to young people

10. [N + *kei*] and [N + *teki*] 'like, characterized as' (both change nouns into [Adj-*na*]):

ビジュアル**系**	*bijuaru**kei***	visually pleasing and attractive, nice-looking
ジャニーズ**系**	*janiizu**kei***	pretty-boy-like ([lit., Johnny's-like boys] young male nice-looking talents belonging to the talent agency Johnny's Office Co. Ltd.)
健康**的**	*kenkoo**teki***	healthy
日本**的**	*Nihon**teki***	Japan-like

■ Examples

(1) 何か飲み物を買ってきます。
Nani-ka nomimono o katte-kimasu.
(I'm going to buy something to drink.)

(2) **A:** 水道料金、また上がったよ。
Suidooryookin, mata agatta yo.
(The water bill went up again.)

B: 本当？ いくらぐらい？
Hontoo? Ikura gurai?
(Really? How much did it go up?)

(3) さあ、この木の高さを計ろう。
Saa, kono ki no takasa o hakaroo.
(Let's measure the height of this tree.)

(4) この絵には深みがありますねえ、本当に。
Kono e ni wa hukami ga arimasu nee, hontooni.
(There is depth in this painting, indeed.)

(5) **A:** この傘、子供用よ。
Kono kasa, kodomoyoo yo.
(This umbrella is for children.)

B: ああ、だから小さいわけね。
Aa, dakara chiisai wake ne.
(Oh, I see, that's why it's small!)

124. The Meaning of Silence

■ Strategic Explanation

As we have seen throughout this book, values of human interaction are culturally and socially bound. The meaning of words cannot be defined without understanding the context of the society in which they are spoken. What it means when there is an absence of words also differs from culture to culture. We focus here on the silence in Japanese communication.

Appreciating silence. There is a Japanese tradition that views words as being unnecessary to reach a mutual understanding. In fact, it is widely held that words can destroy the creation of a deep mutual trust. Proverbs abound in Japanese to point out the uselessness of words as shown below. Japanese in general have a higher tolerance and appreciation for silence.

(a) 物言えば唇寒し秋の風。

Mono	*ieba*	*kuchibiru*	*samushi*	*aki*	*no*	*kaze.*
thing	if say	lip	cold	autumn	L	wind

([lit., If you utter words, your lips will feel cold.] It is safer not to speak.)

(b) 不言実行。

Hugen	*jikkoo.*
not-saying	doing

(Don't say it in words, show it by your deeds. Action before words.)

Often Japanese speakers negatively judge people (especially males) who (sometimes excessively) express their feelings in words. People who mumble and cannot effectively communicate with words are often considered honest, and trustworthy. Although being able to clearly express myself in words is a virtue, being a glib speaker is not so positively valued as it is in the United States.

Functions of silence. Silence may function in two ways. First toward your social superior, it means subordination. You are refraining from expressing your own view and you are paying attention to your superior's view. On the other hand, silence can also express strong defiance. Absence of response is taken as a sign of disagreement or defiance. Second, toward social subordinates, silence can express dominance. By offering no answer, for example, to your subordinates' request, you convey dominance and power. Comprehending the meaning of silence involves cultural and social interpretation. It is useful to know that the absence of speech is not a mere void to be filled, but it has these conflicting and yet socially significant meanings.

Paradoxical meanings of silence. As illustrated in English expressions *the silence was deafening* or *his silence spoke volumes*, the concept of "silence" is shaded by paradoxical subtleties that suggest silence is a powerful tool in communication. Knowing when to keep quiet and when to speak up is an art in any language. Your instincts will probably serve you well when you converse in Japanese. But do keep that in mind quite literally, especially if you are a man. Japanese people have a lot of heart for the "strong, silent" type. I should point out that the traditional view that values "strong, silent" men is changing, and being able to express oneself in words has become increasingly more important. Still, this tradition is very much a part of the establishment, and it is useful to know that Japanese society places a positive value on silence.

125. Managing Conversation (3) —Taking Turns and Designing Utterances

■ Target Expression

And so, I went to see them at the station, you know.

で、駅へ迎えに行ったんだよ。

De, eki e mukae ni itta n da yo.

■ Strategic Explanation

Conversational skills. Throughout this book I have explained many facts about the Japanese grammar and communication strategies. But as I have suggested in several entries, participating in face-to-face human interaction involves much more than being able to create utterances. One must know, to begin with, when to start talking. In other words, how do you find the correct timing to take speaking turns? Once you take a turn you must be able to design each utterance so that it fits comfortably within the on-going conversation. It is fair to assume that in our conversations we would want to express ourselves in ways in which our listeners feel positive about us. It is important to design our utterances to maximize such effect.

These and other conversational skills—both in English and Japanese—are skills we will be learning throughout our lives. Being sensitive and curious and keeping the humble attitude of learning anew is the key. If you are interested in learning more about the characteristics of Japanese conversation, refer to *Japanese Conversation: Self-contextualization through Structure and Interactional Management* (Maynard 1989) and *Kaiwa Bunseki* (Maynard 1993), as well as other articles in the

List of Author's Works at the end of this volume. Here are some useful clues for you to manage your Japanese conversations.

1. *Turn-taking rules:*

   (a) You should not take turns (or attempt to take turns) while the other person is speaking, unless there is an emergency. Although in some social and regional dialects of American English, overlapping of speaker turns may be considered a sign of enthusiasm, getting a word in edgewise is not a good idea in Japanese. Overtaking your superior's turns is especially rude.

   (b) If two speakers simultaneously start to take speaking turns, the socially subordinate partner should yield the turn by (1) stopping speech immediately, and/or (2) saying *doozo*.

   (c) When your partner stops apparently due to some speech production trouble, give sufficient time (four to five seconds is sufficient), but assist in some way to avoid potential embarrassment.

   (d) When your speaker turn is overtly assigned, as when you are asked a direct question, it is desirable to take the turn. You have various ways to avoid answering straightforwardly if you don't want to answer. Total silence is not considered polite under this circumstance, especially toward your superiors.

   (e) When your partner stops at a grammatically complete point, such as the end of a sentence structure—ideally with interactional particles—and looks at you, the floor is open to you; you may take the turn.

2. *How to start your turn:*

   (a) Before starting your turn, it is a good idea to send listener back-channel responses to the partner's previous utterance, if such responses are appropriate. Or, you can use echo questions; *raishuu desu ka* 'next week?' in response to a statement as *raishuu Maiami e iku yotei desu ga* 'I plan to go to Miami next week.'

   (b) Start your turn with openers and fillers as we have studied. This creates a buffer zone where two people meet interactionally. You can also use this moment to prepare your utterance.

3. *How to send turn-yielding signs:*

   (a) You can overtly yield your turn by asking a question.

   (b) Pause after you finish an utterance with listener-appealing devices, such as tag-like [AuxV] or interactional particles.

(c) Overtly solicit your partner's opinion.

(d) Make conclusive remarks if your turn is long and extensive.

(e) Make eye-contact with the listener at the end of your turn.

Importance of empathy. In conversation, the actual words used are designed to cater toward the specific needs of the communicators. In face-to-face communication, all aspects of modality play important roles. Often these interpersonal feelings provide the basis for which the propositional meanings are interpreted, and for that reason, it is important to design one's utterance to maximize empathy. In Japanese, as you have seen throughout this book, the beginning and the end of utterances are accompanied by openers, fillers, hedges, and final particles that appeal to interpersonal emotions.

Appealing to the listener. Let us summarize the various strategies for making Japanese utterances more appealing to the listener.

1. *At the beginning of the utterance:*

Openers (Entry 80)—to inform the listener that you are taking a speaking turn.
Conjunctions (Entry 56)—to signal connections and cohesion.

2. *In between the utterance:*

Interactional particles (Entry 35)—to check the listener's reaction.
Fillers (Entry 80)—to fill in between the utterances, to signal your intention to continue the turn, and to show hesitation for creating rapport.

3. *At the end of the utterance:*

Predicate with explanatory mode (Entry 74)—to connect what is said to the previous statements, to emphasize and to appeal to the listener's empathy.
Ending the statement with [V*te*] and other premature endings (Entry 81)—to soften the impact of statements.
Adding [*to omou*] (Entry 122)—to convey your opinion with considerateness to the listener.
Tagged [AuxV] (Entry 41)—to appeal to the listener's empathy.
Conjunctions (Entry 57)—to end the statement with after effect.
Interactional particles (Entry 35)—to solicit the listener's involvement.

A careful examination of utterances made during conversation will reveal that almost all utterances are designed with some of the devices listed above.

Useful conversation strategies. Beyond the utterance design strategies mentioned above, in general the following devices are useful to bring about similar effects.

(a) Frequent use of apology for sympathy-seeking.

(b) Frequent use of degree words, such as *chotto* 'a bit,' *daitai* 'more or less,' and *kekkoo* 'more or less.'

(c) Increased level of listener back-channel responses.

(d) Adding softening phrases, such as *to ieru to omoimasu* 'can be said ... ,' or *tabun ... ja-nai deshoo ka* 'perhaps, isn't that the case that ... ?'

■ Examples

(1) **A:** で、そのあとどうしたの？
De, sono ato doo shita no?
(So what did you do after that?)

B: でね、それから友だちのところへ行ったんだよ。
De ne, sorekara tomodachi no tokoro e itta n da yo.
(So, after that I went to my friend's place.)

(2) あのう、すみませんが、時間があったらこれを読んでおいていただけませんか。
Anoo, sumimasen ga, jikan ga attara kore o yonde-oite-itadakemasen ka.
(Uhh, excuse me, but if you have time, could you read this [for future purpose]?)

126. On the Verb *Naru*

■ Target Expressions

(It has been decided that) I will go to the United States soon.

今度アメリカへ行くことになりました。
Kondo Amerika e iku koto ni narimashita.

It's a nice warm day, isn't it? (lit., It's gotten warm, hasn't it?)

暖かくなりましたねえ。
Atatakaku narimashita nee.

■ Grammatical Explanation

As we noted earlier in reference to characteristic 10, Japanese tend to deemphasize the agent of the action, thereby avoiding the construction of a sentence that reads "subject-does-something-to-something (or someone)."

Using *naru*. Expressing something as "becoming" is a frequently used strategy. The verb *naru* 'to become' is used in [N + *ni naru*] and [Vbasic + *yooni naru*]. When accompanied by adjectives, they must take adverbial forms; thus, *ookiku naru* 'to become large' and *kireini naru* 'to become pretty.' Verb and adjective forms may precede *naru*; *benkyoo-shinaku naru* 'lit., to become not to study' and *kireidenaku naru* 'lit., to become not pretty.'

Idiomatic use of *naru*. The idiomatic use of *naru* is also frequent. For example, in the target sentence, instead of simply saying 'I will go to the United States soon,' *koto ni narimashita* '(lit., it has become) it has been decided' is added. The agent, or decision maker, is not specified in this structure. It only implies that the decision was made by someone else or was reached by some inevitable circumstances. This is how Japanese sometimes prefer to express themselves.

Using spontaneous verbs. The spontaneous verb is another good example of the agent-less tendency. Instead of saying 'I can see Mt. Fuji,' *Fuji-san ga mieru* is preferred. A group of predicates used for "reactive" description as explained throughout this book also represent this agent-less tendency. As evidenced in the proverb *naseba naru* 'lit., if you do, it will become,' the ultimate force of making things happen is not based on "doing," but simply the event "becomes." It emphasizes the view that the event is achieved independently of the agent involved in that event; what human beings can control is only to reach that mature point or time at which the action "becomes."

***Takaku suru* and *takaku naru*.** Naturally, Japanese is equipped with grammatical structures that clearly express agents of the action. The verb *suru* 'to do' (to be discussed in Entry 128), for example, co-occurs with [Adj] and creates *takaku suru* 'to make (it) expensive,' which complements the structure *takaku naru* 'to become expensive.' Even so, Japanese is skewed to favor *naru* expressions when compared with English.

***Haru ni naru* versus *spring has come*.** Nature's seasonal change, getting warm and spring arriving, for example, are best described with *naru* in Japanese. For example, *haru ni narimashita* 'lit., it has become spring.' Compare this with the English expression of *spring has come*. When learning a language, it is helpful to see how like events are expressed in different languages. The preference for agent-less sentence structure in Japanese offers one of the key insights into learning to think in Japanese.

Frequently used functions of *naru*. Functions of the verb *naru* follow.

1. *'To become'*:

(1a) あの人が病気に**なった**。
*Ano hito ga byooki ni **natta**.*
(He got sick.)

(1b) A: 山田さんのお嬢さんはエンジニアに**なりました**ねえ。
*Yamada-san no ojoosan wa enjinia ni **narimashita** nee.*
(Mr. Yamada's daughter became an engineer, you know.)

B: そうですか。医者に**なる**んだろうと思っていましたが。
*Soo desu ka. Isha ni **naru** n daroo to omotte-imashita ga.*
(Is that so? I thought she was going to be a doctor.)

(1c) A: 寒く**なりました**ねえ。
*Samuku **narimashita** nee.*
(Sure has gotten cold, hasn't it?)

B: ええ、本当に。
Ee, hontooni.
(Yes, indeed.)

(1d) 図書館の本を借りるのも簡単ではなく**なりました**ねえ。
*Toshokan no hon o kariru no mo kantan dewa-naku **narimashita** nee.*
(Borrowing books from the library has gotten to be complex [lit., not simple], hasn't it?)

(1e) 最近東京へは行かなく**なりました**。
*Saikin Tookyoo e wa ikanaku **narimashita**.*
(Recently [lit., it has become that] I don't go to Tokyo.)

(1f) あの人の気持ちがわからなく**なりました**。
*Ano hito no kimochi ga wakaranaku **narimashita**.*
([lit., It has become that] I don't understand his feeings [anymore].)

2. *'To begin, to develop into'*:
This use is often accompanied by *yooni*. While *koto ni naru* is often used when someone's decision is involved, *yooni naru* describes the shift or the change, focusing on the result itself, and meaning 'reach the point where.' This is similar to English *come to* as in *come to realize*.

(2a) 日本が好きに**なりました**。
*Nihon ga suki ni **narimashita**.*
(I've come to like Japan.)

(2b) 日本語が少し話せる**ようになった**。
*Nihongo ga sukoshi hanaseru **yooni natta**.*
(I've reached the point where I am able to speak Japanese a little.)

(2c) あの人の気持ちがわかる**ようになりました**。
*Ano hito no kimochi ga wakaru **yooni narimashita**.*
(I've come to understand his feelings.)

3. *'To result in':*

(3a) 結局、今日はいい天気に**なりました**ねえ。
*Kekkyoku, kyoo wa ii tenki ni **narimashita** nee.*
(After all, it turned out to be good weather today.)

4. *'To have been decided':*

(4a) 久美さんには、あした十一時に会うことに**なっています**が……
*Kumi-san ni wa ashita juu ichi-ji ni au koto ni **natte-imasu** ga . . .*
(It is decided that I am to see Kumi at eleven o'clock tomorrow.)

■ Additional Information

Especially at diners and not-so-exclusive restaurants (called *fami-resu* associated with the English phrase *family restaurant*), when the ordered item is brought out, *ni narimasu* is used as a set phrase. This expression conveys that what is being served is the very item that was ordered, although it may not be exactly what the customer is expecting.

(a) こちら和定食**になります**。
*Kochira wateishoku **ni narimasu**.*
(This is the Japanese-style set lunch.)

127. Connecting Sentences

■ Target Expressions

I ran to the station in a hurry. But I missed the train.

急いで駅に走っていった。けれども電車に遅れてしまった。
Isoide eki ni hashitte-itta. Keredomo densha ni okurete-shimatta.

Tulips bloomed in the garden. Daffodils also bloomed.

庭にチューリップが咲きました。水仙も咲きました。
Niwa ni chuurippu ga sakimashita. Suisen mo sakimashita.

■ Grammatical Explanation

Connecting sentences. In this entry we examine how Japanese sentences are connected to each other. First we focus on connecting strategies in Japanese. These include five different types of linguistic devices; (1) conjunctions, (2) demonstratives and pronouns, (3) particles, (4) repetition and lexical cohesion, and (5) response induced by the previous utterance. Second, in the Additional Information, we examine semantic relationships between two consecutive sentences which are categorized into seven types.

Obviously, in order to communicate, we must be able to create not an isolated sentence but also, if not more importantly, multiple sentences connected to each other. A group of sentences and utterances must be organized to make sense. We are not going into discourse organizational principles that characterize different genres of writing or speaking. Our limited discussion on sentence connection is meant to serve only as the beginning for your further study in Japanese. If you are interested in learning Japanese rhetorical and organizational principles, refer to *Danwa Bunseki no Kanoosei* (Maynard 1997), *Principles of Japanese Discourse: A Handbook* (Maynard 1998), and *Danwa Hyoogen Handobukku* (Maynard 2005).

Sentence-connecting devices. Here is a list of the five different types of linguistic devices to connect sentences.

1. *Conjunctions* (Entry 56):
   Conjunctions signal the relationship between statements whether, for example, it is a simple addition or a contradiction.

2. *Demonstratives and pronouns* (Entries 8 and 12):
   Demonstratives and pronouns are anaphoric devices, referring to something that has been identified earlier or that is acknowledged among participants. By connecting to previously mentioned information, these devices signal the direct relationship between what is currently happening and what had happened already.

3. *Particles for topic identification* (Entries 15 and 16):
   Topic-marking particles *wa*, *tte*, and *mo* are especially useful in this regard. By establishing and maintaining the topic across individual sentences, the group of sentences can become topically connected. (Obviously, the mere existence of common topics cannot create a connected discourse; co-occurring comments must be meaningfully associated with the topic to form a topical coherence.)

4. *Repetition and lexical cohesion:*
   Repeating what was mentioned already is a strong device to immediately connect what precedes with the consequent information. Sometimes, the word that is associated with the one previously mentioned (like *tulips* and *daffodils*) or the one that is a part of the one previously mentioned (like *window* is a part

of a *room*—a cultural knowledge shared by social members) is used to connect statements.

5. *Response induced by a previous utterance:*
Answering a question, for example, shows a direct connection defined within the question-answer adjacency pair.

■ Examples

(1) **(a)** ここは都会の高層ホテルの一室である。
Koko wa tokai no koosoo hoteru no isshitsu dearu.

(b) その窓からはビルと、その向こうに広がる海が見えた。
Sono mado kara wa biru to, sono mukoo ni hirogaru umi ga mieta.

(This is a room in a high-rise hotel in the city. From the window, one could see [tall] buildings and the ocean expanding beyond them.)

In (1b) we find two demonstratives appearing in *sono mado* and *sono mukoo*. Both of these demonstratives assist in cohesiveness; *sono mado* 'that window' is the window of *hoteru no isshitsu* 'a hotel room' given in (1a), and *sono mukoo* 'beyond those' is beyond the *biru* 'buildings.'

(2) **(a)** ある男がアパートを借りて住んでいた。
Aru otoko ga apaato o karite sunde-ita.

(b) 休日を除いてきちんと出勤していた。
Kyuujitsu o nozoite kichinto shukkin-shite-ita.

(c) 男はまだ独身。
Otoko wa mada dokushin.

(d) ときどき会社の帰りに同僚と酒を飲む。
Tokidoki kaisha no kaeri ni dooryoo to sake o nomu.

(e) しかし二日酔いになるほど飲んだことはなかった。
Shikashi hutsukayoi ni naru hodo nonda koto wa nakatta.

(A man rented and lived in an apartment. He went to work diligently except on his days off. The man was still single. Sometimes on his way home he goes out drinking *sake* with his colleagues. However, he never drank to the extent that he would have a hangover.)

In (2), we see how the particle *wa* assists in establishing *otoko* 'young man' as a topic in (2c). Non-specification of *otoko* in (2b), (2d), and (2e) also signals the topical connection. The conjunction *shikashi* in (2e) is an example of how this statement is related to (2d).

(3) **(a)** 弟は本屋に勤めている。
Otooto wa hon'ya ni tsutomete-iru.

(b) この付近で一番大きな本屋だ。
Kono hukin de ichiban ookina hon'ya da.

(c) きのう弟が勤めているところへ行って、私はたずねた。
Kinoo otooto ga tsutomete-iru tokoro e itte, watashi wa tazuneta.

(d) 「最近電話がないけど元気？」
"Saikin denwa ga nai kedo genki?"

(e) 「もちろんだよ」と弟は答えた。
"Mochiron da yo" to otooto wa kotaeta.

(My younger brother works at a bookstore. [It is] the largest bookstore around here. Yesterday I went to the place where my younger brother works and I asked him, "There haven't been any phone calls from you recently; are you OK?" "Of course," answered my brother.)

In (3b) we find a case of lexical cohesion achieved by the repetition of the word *hon'ya*. We also find in (3c) *otooto ga tsutomete-iru tokoro* 'the place where my brother works,' a rephrasing of the very *hon'ya* under discussion. In (3e) we find an answer to the question given in (3d), a case of question-response connection.

Each device examined here assists in comprehending how sentences are put together. It is true that comprehension involves much more than appreciation of these devices. Knowing these as cues, however, can be a great help when you are trying to comprehend texts in a foreign language.

■ Additional Information

Another aspect of connecting sentences is how these sentences are semantically connected. Here is a list of possible relationships between sentences.

1. *Expansion:*
The second sentence is an expansion, for example, a more detailed description of the first. (Clue words include conjunctions such as *sorede* 'then' and *dakara* 'therefore.')

2. *Opposition:*
The second sentence expresses an opposing view toward the first. (Clue words include conjunctions *ga* 'but,' *shikashi* 'but,' and *tokoroga* 'however.')

3. *Addition:*
A related statement is added to the first sentence. (This is achieved by the [V*te*] form, and other conjunctions, such as *de* 'and,' *soshite* 'and,' and *sonoue* 'in addition.')

4. *Apposition:*
   The first and the second sentence both describe the identical item. (This is marked by conjunctions, such as *tsumari* 'in other words' and *tatoeba* 'for example.')

5. *Supplement:*
   The second sentence is a supplement to the first. (Recall how the predicate with explanatory mode adds relevant cause and reason associated with the statement made earlier.)

6. *Contrast:*
   The second sentence represents a view or meaning contrasting with the first. (The contrastive use of *wa* and particles expressing alternation, such as *ka* and *mata wa*, are useful for this purpose.)

7. *Diversion:*
   The second sentence diverts from the first. (For this purpose sentential adverbs and conjunctions, including *tsugini* 'next' and *tokorode* 'by the way,' are used.)

In the discussion above we focused on the semantic connections between consecutive sentences only, and ignored the overall global structure in discourse. It is important to look for the global organization when reading a group of connected sentences, but that is beyond the scope of this book.

128. The Extended Use of the Verb *Suru* and *Da*

■ Grammatical Explanation

The verbs *suru* 'to do' and *da* 'to be' have many extended uses that occur quite frequently. These conventional uses should be learned with care.

Idiomatic use of the verb *suru*.

1. [adverbial form of Adj-*i* + *suru*] 'to make':
   Change [Adj-*i*] to adverb form by replacing the final -*i* with -*ku*, for example, *ookii* → *ookiku*; *ookiku suru* (to enlarge).

   (1a) テレビの音をもう少し**大きくして**ください。
   Terebi no oto o moo sukoshi ***ookiku shite****-kudasai.*
   (Please turn up the volume of the television a little.)

2. [adverbial form of Adj-*na* + *suru*] 'to make':
   Change [Adj-*na*] to adverb form by replacing the final -*na* with -*ni*, for example, *kireina* → *kireini*; *kireini suru* 'to clean up.'

   (2a) 公園を**きれいにしましょう**。
   *Kooen o **kireini shimashoo**.*
   (Let's clean up the park.)

3. [N + *ni suru*] 'to decide':
   This pattern should be used when you are choosing from several available alternatives.

   (3a) **ビールにします**。[ordering at a restaurant]
   Biiru ni shimasu.
   ([lit., I decided on beer] I'll take beer.)

   (3b) 試験は**来週にしましょう**。
   *Shiken wa **raishuu ni shimashoo**.*
   (Let's decide that the exam will be next week.)

   Recall the structure [Vinformal non-past + *koto ni suru*] which is similar to this pattern, also meaning 'to decide to do.'

4. [loan word + *suru*] (changes the word into a verb):

   (4a) **ノックして**ください。
   ***Nokku-shite**-kudasai.*
   (Please knock.)

5. [Adv + *suru*] (changes the adverb into verbs associated with them):

   yukkuri 'slow, leisurely' + *suru* = stay leisurely, stay long

   (5a) **ゆっくりして**いってください。
   ***Yukkuri shite**-itte-kudasai.*
   (Please stay for a long time.)

   burabura 'rambling' + *suru* = to walk aimlessly, to walk around

   (5b) 町を**ぶらぶらして**いたんです。
   *Machi o **burabura shite**-ita n desu.*
   (I was just walking around the town.)

6. Idiomatically, when accompanied by phrases indicating prices, it means 'to cost':

   (6a) このコートは**十万円もした**。
   *Kono kooto wa **juu-man-en mo shita**.*
   (This coat cost a hundred thousand yen.)

7. Idiomatically, when accompanied by phrases associated with appearance, it means 'to appear':

(7a) その男は**青い顔をしていた**。

Sono	otoko	wa	**aoi**	**kao**	**o**	**shite-ita.**
that	man	T	pale	face	O	appeared

(The man's face was pale.)

Extended use of the *be*-verb, *da*. The *be*-verb is frequently used as an auxiliary verb to replace verbs and adjectives. This is in some sense similar to the English auxiliary verb *do* when used as an answer "Yes, I do," to the question, "Do you watch television?" In order to use *da* for this purpose, there must be a context suitable for it, where what is not mentioned is understood between the communicators. Examine how the *be*-verb is used in the second pair-part of the following pairs of interaction.

(a) A: 私は朝はトーストを食べますが、山崎さんは？
Watashi wa asa wa toosuto o tabemasu ga, Yamazaki-san wa?
(I have toast for breakfast; how about you, Yamazaki-san?)

B: やはり和食でごはんとみそしる**です**。
Yahari washoku de gohan to misoshiru ***desu.***
(I have a Japanese-style breakfast [after all], rice and miso soup.)

(b) A: 今夜はどこで食事しますか。
Kon'ya wa doko de shokuji-shimasu ka.
(Where will you eat tonight?)

B: 駅の近くのレストラン**です**。
Eki no chikaku no resutoran ***desu.***
(At the restaurant near the station.)

(c) A: 和食では何が一番好き？
Washoku de wa nani ga ichiban suki?
(Among Japanese dishes, what do you like most?)

B: 天ぷら**です**。
Tenpura ***desu.***
(I like *tempura* most of all.)

(d) A: 若い頃は何をよく飲みましたか。
Wakai koro wa nani o yoku nomimashita ka.
(When you were young, what did you usually drink?)

B: 日本酒**です**。
Nihonshu ***desu.***
(I used to drink [Japanese] *sake.*)

(e) **A:** 着きましたよ。
Tsukimashita yo.
(It arrived.)

B: 何が**です**か。
*Nani ga **desu** ka.*
(What [arrived]?)

A: 手紙が。
Tegami ga.
(The letter!)

(f) **A:** いつまで東京にいらっしゃいますか。
Itsu made Tookyoo ni irasshaimasu ka.
(Until when will you be in Tokyo?)

B: あさってまで**です**。
*Asatte made **desu**.*
(Until the day after tomorrow.)

In all of B's utterances, the *be*-verbs do not logically equate the subject/topic with its complement. Obviously in B's utterance in (a), the sentence does not make sense if we translate literally—'I am Japanese-style breakfast, and I am rice and miso soup.' Yet by interpreting the *be*-verb in its extended meaning, it makes sense.

More specifically, the *be*-verb can replace verbs and adjectives (as in (c)) when what precedes *da* is in focus. Note that in all of these pairs, the answers are in focus; they constitute information specifically sought by the question. *Da* also replaces tense as shown in (d), where *Nihonshu desu* corresponds to the past tense of the question and is interpreted as 'I used to drink *sake*.' Note that in B's utterance in (f), *da* is preceded immediately by a particle. The particles *made* and *kara* are primary examples of particles used in this structure.

Even when there is no obvious context in which the *da* expression replaces a verb, when such an expression is used, it is assumed that a predictable relationship exists between the *da* predicate and the noun. For example, if someone says *Tanaka-sensei wa Tookyoo desu*, a literal translation 'Professor Tanaka is Tokyo' does not make sense; appropriate interpretation is 'Professor Tanaka is in Tokyo' or 'Professor Tanaka is from Tokyo' or whatever semantically appropriate interpretation applies within the general context.

■ Warning

Recall that *da* cannot replace an adjectival predicate when used with *soo*.

(a) **A:** 大きいですか。
Ookii-desu ka.
(Is it large?)

B: はい（、大きいです）。
Hai (, ookii desu).
(Yes, it is large.)

*はい、そうです。
Hai, soo desu.

(b) **A:** 便利ですか。
Benri desu ka.
(Is it useful?)

B: いいえ（、便利ではありません）。
Iie (, benri dewa-arimasen).
(No, it isn't useful.)

*いいえ、そうではありません。
Iie, soo dewa-arimasen.

129. Various Uses of the Word *Tokoro*

■ Target Expression

I was just about to leave.

今ちょうど出かけようとしていたところです。
Ima choodo dekakeyoo to shite-ita tokoro desu.

■ Grammatical Explanation

Using *tokoro.* The noun *tokoro* 'place' is often used in various idiomatic expressions. Fundamentally, *tokoro* means 'place.' In more abstract terms, however, *tokoro* refers to 'the central issue of focus,' or 'the most important point or aspect' as exemplified below:

(a) 言いたい**ところ**はそういうことだったのね。

Ii-tai	***tokoro***	*wa*	*sooyuu*	*koto*	*datta*	*no*	*ne.*
want to say	point	T	such	fact	was	IP	IP

(What [the important point] you want to say was that, right?)

(b) 今日はそんな**ところ**で……
Kyoo wa sonna ***tokoro*** *de . . .*
(Well today let's leave it at that point . . .)

In casual rapid speech, *toko* may replace *tokoro*.

Idiomatic use of *tokoro*. *Tokoro* appears in many idiomatic constructs.

1. [Adj + *tokoro*] 'although ...' (with only limited number of adjectives):

   (1a) **お忙しいところ**をすみませんねえ。
   Oisogashii tokoro *o sumimasen nee.*
   (Although you are busy, thanks for coming.)

2. [Vbasic + *tokoro* + *da*] 'be about to ...':

   (2a) これから**出かけるところです**。
   Kore kara ***dekakeru tokoro desu.***
   (I am about to leave now.)

3. [Vvolitional + *to shite-ita tokoro* + *da*] 'was about to do ...':

   (3a) 今電話を**しようとしていたところです**。
   Ima denwa o ***shiyoo to shite-ita tokoro desu.***
   (I was about to give you a call.)

4. [Vinformal past + *tokoro da*] 'just did ...':

   (4a) 今**起きたとこ**なんだ。
   Ima ***okita toko*** *nan da.*
   (I just got up now.)

5. [V*te* + *-iru* + *tokoro da*] 'is in the middle of doing ...':

   (5a) 今手紙を**書いているとこ**。
   Ima tegami o ***kaite-iru toko.***
   (I am in the middle of writing a letter.)

In patterns 2 through 5, verbs must be active (non-stative).

■ Additional Information

The difference between [Vinformal past + *tokoro da*] 'just did' and [Vinformal past + *bakari da*] 'just did ...' (in Entry 119) is that while *tokoro* implies ensuing action already in progress, *bakari* implies the action has just completed and any following action has not yet begun.

130. Order of Sentence-final Elements

■ Grammatical Explanation

How to end sentences. As our final entry, we review how the sentence-final elements themselves are organized. These include verbs, various types of verb endings, auxiliary verbs, verb compounds, and final particles. The general principle is that the more personal and emotional the element expresses, the more likely it is to appear toward the very end. Thus starting with the verb, which carries the referential meaning, other elements such as causative, passive, and negative follow and so on until the final particle.

Here is a chart that shows the order of sentence-final elements. Under each member the expressions, if used, must be chosen in the order listed. *Soo da* (1) is the predicate of the conjecture [*soona*], while *soo da* (2) represents 'hearsay.' *Yoo* (1) is the volitional form of the verb, and *yoo da* (2) is the predicate of [*yoona*] for expressing resemblance and likelihood. (Note: Obviously not all elements are required. The chart specifies the order of elements if they appear.)

Order of Sentence-final Elements

1		2		3		4		5		6		7		8
Verb	→	*seru* *saseru*	→	*reru* *rareru*	→	[Adj] *nai*	→	*soo da* (1) *nai* *rashii*	→	Past-*ta*	→	*yoo* (1) *-daroo* *soo da* (2) *yoo da* (2)	→	IP

Now study the following combination of verb-final elements, paying special attention to the order of sentence-final elements. Knowing the general order of these items will be helpful when you are uncertain of how to combine sentence-final elements. The best way to remember the order is to memorize a few examples as the ones listed here.

(a) 食べさせられそうだ
tabesaseraresoo da

taberu	*saseru*	*rareru*	*soo*	*da*
eat	causative	passive	*soona*	be

(to seem to be forced to eat)

(b) 行きたくないらしいです
ikitakunai rashii-desu

iku	*tai*	*nai*	*rashii*	*-desu*
go	want	negative	*rashii*	formal-marker

(to seem not to want to go)

(c) なぐられたようだね
nagurareta yoo da ne

naguru	*reru*	*ta*	*yoo*	*da*	*ne*
beat	passive	past	*yoona*	be	IP

(to seem to have been beaten)

(d) むずかしくはなかったそうですよ
muzukashiku wa nakatta soo desu yo
(to hear that it wasn't difficult)

And as a final note to the final entry, how about:

(e) 日本語、本当はそれほどむずかしくはないようですね。
Nihongo, hontoo wa sorehodo muzukashiku wa nai yoo desu ne.
(In truth Japanese looks like it is not so difficult.)

The end, at last! You have come a long way covering 130 entries. Although there is always more to learn, these entries offer a basic knowledge of Japanese grammar and communication strategies. Let me close this entry with that ubiquitous Japanese phrase: *Ganbatte-kudasai*. I hope you will continue to make every effort. Best wishes!

Appendixes:

Pennsylvania Autumn Hills

Appendix 1. Parts of Speech and Definitions of Grammatical Terms

The parts of speech adopted in this book mostly correspond with those in English. The categories nonexistent in English—including two different types of adjectives and the particles—are explained in detail in relevant entries. Although obviously there are some differences between Japanese and English parts of speech, for practical purposes we use most of the grammatical terms across these two languages. Here is a list of parts of speech and grammatical terms (alphabetically ordered) with definitions and examples. Definitions of these and other terms are also given throughout the book.

Active durative verb. A verb describing an action whose process is expressed by its progressive form, e.g., 食べている *tabete-iru* 'to be eating.'

Active verb. A verb describes (dynamic) action, e.g., 食べる *taberu* 'to eat.'

Adjective. Any member of a class of words that independently, without combination with other words, functions as modifier of a noun, e.g., 新しい *atarashii* 'new.'

Adverb. Any member of a class of words that functions as modifiers of verbs, of adjectives, or adverbs or adverbial phrases, e.g., ゆっくり *yukkuri* 'slowly.'

Apposition. A clause or a phrase which modifies a noun and explains what the modified noun is, e.g., 友だちの佐野さん *tomodachi no Sano-san* 'Ms. Sano, my friend.'

Auxiliary adjective. An adjective used after the stem of a verb/adjective or the [V/Adj pre-Aux] forms of predicates, e.g., 使いやすい *tsukai-yasui* 'easy to use,' おいしそうだ *oishi-soo da* 'seems delicious,' 使うらしい *tsukau rashii* 'seems to use,' and おいしいみたいな *oishii mitaina* 'seems delicious.'

Auxiliary verb. A verb used after the [V*te*], the stem of a verb/adjective, or the [V/Adj pre-Aux] forms of predicates, e.g., 落としてしまう *otoshite-shimau* 'to drop,' むずかしすぎる *muzukashi-sugiru* 'too difficult,' 話すだろう *hanasu daroo* 'perhaps will talk,' and むずかしいでしょう *muzukashii deshoo* 'perhaps difficult.'

***Be*-verb.** Similar to English *be,* a copula. Refers to *da* and its conjugated forms.

Casual style. Style used for casual speech among familiar members.

Causative. A relation in which the actor of the causative action causes or forces someone else to act.

Conditional. A relation where an event or state is presented as a condition for another event or state to occur.

Conjunction. A phrase that connects clauses and sentences, e.g., それで *sorede* 'then.'

Controllable verb. A verb describing an action that its performer can control as to whether the action or state takes place or not, e.g., 泳ぐ *oyogu* 'to swim.'

Demonstrative. A word indicating or singling out the thing referred to, e.g., この *kono* 'this.'

Feminine speech. Style of speech used frequently by female speakers, often considered soft and other-accommodating.

Formal style. Style used in formal, often official situations; style used toward those to whom you should show respect in less formal situations; used for formal letter writing.

Informal style. Style used in casual non-official settings. A superior may use this style toward subordinates in formal situations; often used for writing novels and essays.

Interjection. A word expressing emotion, distinguished by its usage in grammatical isolation, e.g., まさか！ *Masaka!* 'No kidding!.'

Interrogative. Of questioning. Interrogative words are those equivalent to English words, such as *why, what, how, when,* and so forth.

Intransitive verb. A verb that describes an action in the framework of "agent-conducts-itself," e.g., 行く *iku* 'to go.'

***I*-type adjective.** Adjectives ending in *-i*, e.g., 新しい *atarashii* 'new.'

Masculine speech. Style of speech used frequently by male speakers, often considered blunt.

***Na*-type adjective.** Adjectives that end with *-na*, e.g., 便利な *benrina* 'convenient.'

Noun. A class of words referring to persons, places, and things which grammatically become subjects and objects by themselves, e.g., うち *uchi* 'house,' パソコン *pasokon* 'personal computer.'

Numeral. A word or words expressing number and quantity, e.g., 五 *go* 'five,' 6万 *roku-man* 'sixty thousand.'

Particle. A group of words typically consisting of a small number of syllables that mark grammatical case relations (grammatical particle) or interpersonal expressions (interactional particle), e.g., the grammatical particle が *ga* (subject marker) and the interactional particle よ *yo* (marker for new information with some emphasis).

Passive. A sentence which describes an action from the point of view of someone who is influenced or affected by the action.

Predicate. A group of words that function as one of the main constituents of a simple sentence, the other being subject. It normally contains a verbal element, and the predicate as a whole typically expresses the action performed by, or the state attributed to, the subject, e.g., 友だちが<u>あした来ます</u> *tomodachi ga <u>ashita kimasu</u>* 'my friend will come tomorrow.'

Progressive. A verb form that describes the continuation of action or continuation of state resultant of the action.

Proper noun. A noun that refers to only specific person(s) or thing(s) that bear the specific name(s), e.g., 山田 *Yamada* 'Yamada,' ニューヨーク *Nyuuyooku* 'New York.'

Proposition. A statement in which something is affirmed or denied, and which one can judge whether the statement is true or false.

Potential form. A verb form that describes the performer's potential and ability to do the act, e.g., かける *kakeru* 'to be able to write.'

Spontaneous verb. A verb which describes the event that spontaneously and naturally occurs without the actor's initiation, e.g., 見える *mieru* 'can be seen.'

Stative durative verb. A verb describing a state that can be expressed by its progressive form, e.g., 似る *niru* 'to resemble.'

Stative verb. A verb that describes the state of things, e.g., ある *aru*, いる *iru* 'to be, to exist.'

Subject. An element within a sentence or an utterance of "primary predicate focus," normally marked by *ga*, unless topicalized, e.g., ケンが来る *Ken ga kuru* 'Ken is coming' and 音楽が聞こえる *ongaku ga kikoeru* 'the music is heard.'

Topic. Something which language users are talking about and commenting on.

Transitive verb. A verb that describes an action in the framework of "agent-operates-on-another-entity," e.g., 本を<u>読む</u> *hon o <u>yomu</u>* 'to read a book.'

Verb. A word that typically expresses action or state. This category includes existential verbs *iru* and *aru*, as well as the *be*-verb *da*, e.g., 歌う *utau* 'to sing,' 食べる *taberu* 'to eat,' だ *da* 'to be.'

Volitional form. A verb form that expresses the will of its actor, e.g., 勉強しよう *benkyoo-shiyoo* 'will study.'

Written style. Style used primarily and sometimes exclusively for writing.

Appendix 2. Basic Verb and Adjective Conjugation

(1) Basic Verb Conjugation

* Verb stem [Vstem] is obtained by deleting final *-masu* from formal non-past form of the verb.

		U-verb		*RU*-verb	
Informal	non-past (Basic)	書く	*kaku*	食べる	*taberu*
	past	書いた	*kaita*	食べた	*tabeta*
	non-past negative	書かない	*kakanai*	食べない	*tabenai*
	past negative	書かなかった	*kakanakatta*	食べなかった	*tabenakatta*
Formal	non-past	書きます	*kakimasu*	食べます	*tabemasu*
	past	書きました	*kakimashita*	食べました	*tabemashita*
	non-past negative	書きません	*kakimasen*	食べません	*tabemasen*
	past negative	書きませんでした	*kakimasen-deshita*	食べませんでした	*tabemasen-deshita*
[V*te*]		書いて	*kaite*	食べて	*tabete*
Conditional		書けば	*kakeba*	食べれば	*tabereba*
Volitional		書こう	*kakoo*	食べよう	*tabeyoo*
Passive		書かれる	*kakareru*	食べられる	*taberareru*
Causative		書かせる	*kakaseru*	食べさせる	*tabesaseru*

Irregular verbs

Informal	non-past (Basic)	来る	*kuru*	する	*suru*
	past	来た	*kita*	した	*shita*
	non-past negative	来ない	*konai*	しない	*shinai*
	past negative	来なかった	*konakatta*	しなかった	*shinakatta*
Formal	non-past	来ます	*kimasu*	します	*shimasu*
	past	来ました	*kimashita*	しました	*shimashita*
	non-past negative	来ません	*kimasen*	しません	*shimasen*
	past negative	来ませんでした	*kimasen-deshita*	しませんでした	*shimasen-deshita*
[V*te*]		来て	*kite*	して	*shite*
Conditional		来れば	*kureba*	すれば	*sureba*
Volitional		来よう	*koyoo*	しよう	*shiyoo*
Passive		来られる	*korareru*	される	*sareru*
Causative		来させる	*kosaseru*	させる	*saseru*

Existential verbs

Informal	non-past (Basic)	いる	*iru*	ある	*aru*
	past	いた	*ita*	あった	*atta*
	non-past negative	いない	*inai*	ない	*nai*
	past negative	いなかった	*inakatta*	なかった	*nakatta*
Formal	non-past	います	*imasu*	あります	*arimasu*
	past	いました	*imashita*	ありました	*arimashita*
	non-past negative	いません	*imasen*	ありません	*arimasen*
	past negative	いませんでした	*imasen-deshita*	ありませんでした	*arimasen-deshita*
[V*te*]		いて	*ite*	あって	*atte*
Conditional		いれば	*ireba*	あれば	*areba*
Volitional		いよう	*iyoo*		—
Passive		いられる	*irareru*		—
Causative		いさせる	*isaseru*		—

(2) Basic Adjective Conjugation

		[Adj-*i*]		[Adj-*na*]	
Basic		新しい	*atarashii*	便利な	*benrina*
Informal	non-past (Basic)	新しい	*atarashii*	便利だ	*benri da*
	past	新しかった	*atarashikatta*	便利だった	*benri datta*
	non-past negative	新しくない	*atarashikunai*	便利でない 便利じゃない	*benri denai* *benri ja-nai*
	past negative	新しくなかった	*atarashiku-nakatta*	便利ではなかった 便利じゃなかった	*benri dewanakatta* *benri ja-nakatta*
Formal	non-past	新しいです	*atarashii-desu*	便利です	*benri desu*
	past	新しかったです	*atarashikatta-desu*	便利でした	*benri deshita*
	non-past negative	新しくないです 新しくありません	*atarashikunai-desu* *atarashiku-arimasen*	便利ではないです 便利じゃないです 便利ではありません 便利じゃありません	*benri dewanai-desu* *benri ja-nai-desu* *benri dewa-arimasen* *benri ja-arimasen*
Formal	past negative	新しくなかったです 新しくありませんでした	*atarashiku-nakatta-desu* *atarashiku-arimasen-deshita*	便利ではなかったです 便利じゃなかったです 便利ではありませんでした 便利じゃありませんでした	*benri dewanakatta-desu* *benri ja-nakatta-desu* *benri dewa-arimasen-deshita* *benri ja-arimasen-deshita*
[Adj *te*]		新しくて	*atarashikute*	便利で	*benri de*
Conditional		新しければ	*atarashikereba*	便利なら(ば)	*benri nara(ba)*

*Adjective stem [Adj stem] is obtained by deleting the final *-i* from [Adj-*i*] and the final *-na* from [Adj-*na*].

*The Adjective *yoi* (or *ii*) is an exception to be noted.

Basic		よい/いい	*yoi / ii*
Informal	non-past	よい/いい	*yoi / ii*
	past	よかった	*yokatta*
	non-past negative	よくない	*yokunai*
	past negative	よくなかった	*yokunakatta*
Formal	non-past	よいです/いいです	*yoi-desu/ii-desu*
	past	よかったです	*yokatta-desu*
	non-past negative	よくないです よくありません	*yokunai-desu* *yokuarimasen*
	past negative	よくなかったです よくありませんでした	*yokunakatta-desu* *yokuarimasen-deshita*
[Adj *te*]		よくて	*yokute*
Conditional		よければ	*yokereba*

Appendix 3. Verb and Adjective Connecting Forms: Pre-nominal and Pre-Aux Forms

Verbs

	[V/Adj pre-nominal] forms		[V/Adj pre-Aux] forms	
Non-past	泳ぐ	*oyogu*	泳ぐ	*oyogu*
Past	泳いだ	*oyoida*	泳いだ	*oyoida*
Non-past negative	泳がない	*oyoganai*	泳がない	*oyoganai*
Past negative	泳がなかった	*oyoganakatta*	泳がなかった	*oyoganakatta*

***Be*-verb**

Non-past	の	*no*	(deletion)	
Past	だった	*datta*	だった	*datta*
Non-past negative	ではない	*dewanai*	ではない	*dewanai*
Past negative	ではなかった	*dewanakatta*	ではなかった	*dewanakatta*

[Adj-*i*]

Non-past	赤い	*akai*	赤い	*akai*
Past	赤かった	*akakatta*	赤かった	*akakatta*
Non-past negative	赤くない	*akakunai*	赤くない	*akakunai*
Past negative	赤くなかった	*akakunakatta*	赤くなかった	*akakunakatta*

[Adj-*na*]

Non-past	便利な	*benrina*	便利	*benri*
Past	便利だった	*benri datta*	便利だった	*benri datta*
Non-past negative	便利ではない	*benri dewanai*	便利ではない	*benri dewanai*
Past negative	便利ではなかった	*benri dewanakatta*	便利ではなかった	*benri dewanakatta*

*Both pre-nominal and pre-Aux forms have only informal forms. The difference between [V/Adj pre-nominal] and [V/Adj pre-Aux] forms are:
(1) *Be*-verb: pre-nominal takes *no* while for pre-Aux, *da* is totally deleted;
(2) [Adj-*na*]: pre-nominal takes basic form with *na*, while pre-Aux takes [Adj stem] without *na*.

*Forms that follow pre-nominal forms are:

[Vpre-nominal] + { nouns (clausal modification) (Entry 83)
nouns (clausal explanation) (Entry 114) }

[V/Adj pre-nominal] +	*no da/wake da*	(Entry 74)
	tame ni (cause)	(Entry 77)
	toki, koro	(Entry 84)
	aida ni	(Entry 84)
	yoona	(Entry 89)
	tsumori	(Entry 103)
	—excluding [Vnon-past]	
	hazu	(Entry 104)
	koto, no	(Entry 105)
	hoo ga ii	(Entry 118)
	koto ga aru (occurs occasionally)	(Entry 120)
	—with [V/Adj pre-nominal non-past] only	
	mono da (surprise)	(Entry 120)

*Specially noted cases where [N + *da*] changes to [N + *na*]:

[N + *na*] +	*node, noni*	(Entry 56)
	n(o) da	(Entry 74)
	no	(Entry 105)
	—Also note that when preceding *koto*, [N + *da*] changes to [N + *da to yuu*].	

*Forms that follow pre-Aux forms:

[V/Adj pre-Aux] +	*-daroo/-deshoo*	(Entry 41)
	mitaina	(Entry 89)
	rashii	(Entry 91)
	nara(ba)	(Entry 92)
	kamoshirenai	(Entry 99)
	kashira	(Entry 99)
	ka na	(Entry 99)
	ni chigainai	(Entry 108)

Appendix 4. Some Verb and Adjective Connecting Forms: [Vstem], [V*te*], and others

Those that follow [Vbasic]:

[Vbasic] +	*tame ni* (goal)	(Entry 62)
	koto ga dekiru	(Entry 75)
	mae ni	(Entry 84)
	to	(Entry 88)
	beki	(Entry 106)
	bakari da (be ready to)	(Entry 119)
	mono da (mild command)	(Entry 120)
	koto wa nai	(Entry 120)
	tokoro da (about to happen)	(Entry 129)

Those that follow [Vinformal non-past]

[Vinformal non-past] +	*tsumori* (intention)	(Entry 103)
	yotei, keikaku	(Entry 103)
	koto ni suru	(Entry 120)
	koto ni naru	(Entry 120)

Those that follow [Vinformal past]:

[Vinformal past affirmative] +	*ato de*	(Entry 84)
	bakari da (just did)	(Entry 119)
	tokoro da (just happened)	(Entry 129)

Those that follow [V/Adj informal]:

[V/Adj informal] +	*to yuu, to omou* (indirect quotation)	(Entry 112)
	soo da	(Entry 115)

Those that follow [V/Adj informal past]:

[V/Adj informal past] +	*-ri*	(Entry 81)
	-ra	(Entry 93)
	mono da (reflection)	(Entry 120)
	koto ga aru (past experience)	(Entry 120)

Those that follow [V/Adj informal non-past]:

[V/Adj informal non-past] +	*hoo*	(Entry 64)
	yori	(Entry 64)

Those that follow [Vstem]:

[Vstem] +	*-mashoo*	(Entry 44)
	ni iku, ni kuru	(Entry 62)
	-tai, -tagaru	(Entry 65)
	-nasai	(Entry 79)
	-nagara	(Entry 84)
	-kakeru	(Entry 121)
	-hajimeru, -dasu	(Entry 121)
	-naosu/-kaesu	(Entry 121)
	-yasui, -nikui	(Entry 123)

Special cases of [Vstem]:

o + [Vstem] +	*ninaru*	(Entry 86)
	suru	(Entry 86)

Those that follow [V/Adj stem]:

[V/Adj stem] +	*-soona*	(Entry 87)
	-sugiru	(Entry 121)

Those that follow [V*te*]:

[Vte] +	*-kudasai*	(Entry 40)
	-iru	(Entry 51)
	-shimau	(Entry 54)
	-iku, -kuru	(Entry 55)
	hoshii	(Entry 65)
	-ageru, -kureru, -morau	(Entry 73)
	kara	(Entry 84)
	-aru, -oku	(Entry 95)
	-miru	(Entry 121)

Those that follow [V/Adj *te*]:

[V/Adj *te*] +	*mo*	(Entry 97)
	mo ii	(Entry 110)
	wa ikenai	(Entry 111)

*Specially noted are Entries 119, 120, 121, 128, and 129 in which these and additional idiomatic adjective and verb connecting forms are introduced.

Appendix 5. Predicates for "Reactive" Description

1. Natural Phenomena

降る *huru*	雨が降る。 *Ame ga huru.*	(Rain falls.)
吹く *huku*	風が吹く。 *Kaze ga huku.*	(Wind blows.)

2. Sense/Perception/Physical Condition

する *suru*	においがする。 *Nioi ga suru.*	(It smells.)
すく *suku*	おなかがすく。 *Onaka ga suku.*	(I'm hungry.)
かわく *kawaku*	のどがかわく。 *Nodo ga kawaku.*	(I'm thirsty.)
出る *deru*	せきが出る。 *Seki ga deru.*	(I cough.)
痛い *itai*	頭が痛い。 *Atama ga itai.*	(I have a headache.)

3. Existence/Possession

ある *aru*	大きい建物がある。 *Ookii tatemono ga aru.*	(There is a large building.)
	田中さんにはお金がある。 *Tanaka-san ni wa okane ga aru.*	(Ms. Tanada has money.)
いる *iru*	子供がいる。 *Kodomo ga iru.*	(There is a child.)

4. Emotional Response

好きな/きらいな *sukina/kiraina*	あの人のことが好きだ。 *Ano hito no koto ga suki da.*	(I like that person.)
ほしい *hoshii*	お金がほしい。 *Okane ga hoshii.*	(I want money.)
～たい *-tai*	おいしいものが食べたい。 *Oishii mono ga tabetai.*	(I want to eat something delicious.)

5. Spontaneous Occurrence

見える *mieru*	海が見える。 *Umi ga mieru.*	(The ocean can be seen.)
聞こえる *kikoeru*	音楽が聞こえる。 *Ongaku ga kikoeru.*	(The music is heard.)

6. Potential

できる *dekiru*	テニスができる。 *Tenisu ga dekiru.*	(I can play tennis.)
作れる *tsukureru*	かわいい人形が作れる。 *Kawaii ningyoo ga tsukureru.*	(I can make a cute doll.)
上手な *joozuna*	日本語が上手だ。 *Nihongo ga joozu da.*	(I'm good at Japanese.)
下手な *hetana*	テニスが下手だ。 *Tenisu ga heta da.*	(I'm not good at tennis.)

7. Other

わかる *wakaru*	日本語がわかる。 *Nihongo ga wakaru.*	(I can understand Japanese.)
かかる *kakaru*	時間がかかる。 *Jikan ga kakaru.*	(It takes time.)
いる *iru*	お金がいる。 *Okane ga iru.*	(Money is needed.)

In all these types of predicates, except the first natural phenomena, the experiencer may be added followed by *ga*. For spontaneous and potential predicates the experiencer may be marked by *ni*. Remember that particle *ga* in these patterns may be replaced by *wa* (or other topic markers) if it is topicalized.

Appendix 6. Interrogative Words in Combination with *Ka, Mo,* and *De mo*

Interrogative words in question	With *ka* in affirmation	With *mo* in affirmation	With *mo* in negation	With *de mo*
いくら *ikura* (how much)	いくらか *ikura-ka* (some amount)	いくらも *ikura-mo* (plenty, as much as)	いくらも *ikura-mo* (not much)	いくらでも *ikura de mo* (any amount)
いつ *itsu* (when)	いつか *itsu-ka* (sometime, some day)	いつも *itsu-mo* (always)	いつも *itsu-mo* (never)	いつでも *itsu de mo* (any time)
誰 *dare* (who)	誰か *dare-ka* (somebody)	誰も *dare-mo* (everybody)	誰も *dare-mo* (nobody)	誰でも *dare de mo* (anybody)
どこ *doko* (where)	どこか *doko-ka* (somewhere)	どこも *doko-mo* (everywhere)	どこも *doko-mo* (nowhere)	どこでも *doko de mo* (anywhere)
どちら *dochira* (which [one of the two])	どちらか *dochira-ka* (either one)	どちらも *dochira-mo* (both)	どちらも *dochira-mo* (neither)	どちらでも *dochira de mo* (either)
どれ *dore* (which [among more than two])	どれか *dore-ka* (some [one])	どれも *dore-mo* (every one)	どれも *dore-mo* (none)	どれでも *dore de mo* (any one)
何 *nani* (what)	何か *nani-ka* (something)	—	何も *nani-mo* (nothing)	何でも *nan de mo* (anything)

List of Author's Works

Senko K. Maynard
(泉子・K・メイナード)

Books (written in English)

1989. *Japanese Conversation: Self-contextualization through Structure and Interactional Management*. Norwood, NJ: Ablex.

1990. *An Introduction to Japanese Grammar and Communication Strategies*. Tokyo: The Japan Times.
(1998. Thai translation of *An Introduction to Japanese Grammar and Communication Strategies* (Tokyo: The Japan Times). Part I and Part II. Translated by Preeya Ingkaphirom Horie and Kanok Singkarin. Bangkok, Thailand: Samakkhiisaan Co. Ltd.)

1993. *Discourse Modality: Subjectivity, Emotion and Voice in the Japanese Language*. Amsterdam: John Benjamins.

1993. *101 Japanese Idioms: Understanding Japanese Language and Culture through Popular Phrases*. With Michael L. Maynard. Hightstown, NJ: Mcgraw-Hill.

1997. *Japanese Communication: Language and Thought in Context*. Honolulu: University of Hawai'i Press.

1998. *Principles of Japanese Discourse: A Handbook*. Cambridge, England: Cambridge University Press.

2002. *Linguistic Emotivity: Centrality of Place, the Topic-Comment Dynamic, and an Ideology of Pathos in Japanese Discourse*. Amsterdam: John Benjamins.

2005. *Expressive Japanese: A Reference Guide to Sharing Emotion and Empathy*. Honolulu: University of Hawai'i Press.

2007. *Linguistic Creativity in Japanese Discourse: Exploring the Multiplicity of Self, Perspective, and Voice*. Amsterdam: John Benjamins.

Books (written in Japanese)

1993. 『会話分析』くろしお出版

1997. 『談話分析の可能性：理論・方法・日本語の表現性』くろしお出版

2000. 『情意の言語学：「場交渉論」と日本語表現のパトス』くろしお出版

2001. 『恋するふたりの「感情ことば」：ドラマ表現の分析と日本語論』くろしお出版

2004. 『談話言語学：日本語のディスコースを創造する構成・レトリック・ストラテジーの研究』くろしお出版

2005. 『日本語教育の現場で使える　談話表現ハンドブック』くろしお出版

2008. 『マルチジャンル談話論：間ジャンル性と意味の創造』くろしお出版

Dissertation

1980. Discourse Functions of the Japanese Theme Marker *Wa*. Northwestern University.

Articles, etc. (written in English)

1981. The Given/New Distinction and the Analysis of the Japanese Particle *Wa* and *Ga*. *Papers in Linguistics,* 14, 1, 109-130.
1981. Teaching *Wa* from a Discourse Perspective. *Proceedings of the Sixth Hawaii Conference on Japanese Linguistics and Language Teaching,* 89-98.
1982. Hiroshima Folktales: Text-typology from the Perspective of Structure and Discourse Modality. *TEXT: An Interdisciplinary Journal for the Study of Discourse,* 2, 375-393.
1982. Theme in Japanese and Topic in English: A Functional Comparison. *Forum Linguisticum,* 5, 235-261.
1982. Analysis of Cohesion: A Study of the Japanese Narrative. *Journal of Literary Semantics,* 11, 19-34.
1983. Flow of Discourse and Linguistic Manipulation: Functions and Constraints of the Japanese and English Relative Clause in Discourse. *Proceedings of the 13th International Congress of Linguists.* Ed. by Shiro Hattori and Kazuko Inoue, 1028-1031. Tokyo: Tokyo Press Co.
1984. Functions of *To* and *Koto-o* in Speech and Thought Representation in Japanese. *Lingua,* 64, 1-24.
1985. Choice of Predicate and Narrative Manipulation: Functions of *Dearu* and *Da* in Modern Japanese Fiction. *Poetics,* 14, 369-385.
1985. Contrast Between Japanese and English Participant Identification: Its Implications for Language Teaching. *International Review of Applied Linguistics,* 23, 217-229.
1985. Review of *Ellipsis in Japanese* by John Hinds. *Journal of Pragmatics,* 9, 847-851.
1986. The Particle *-O* and Content-oriented Indirect Speech in Japanese Written Discourse. In *Direct and Indirect Speech, Trends in Linguistics, Studies and Monographs.* Vol. 31. Ed. by Florian Coulmas, 179-200. Berlin: Mouton de Gruyter.
1986. Interactional Aspects of Thematic Progression in English Casual Conversation. *TEXT: An Interdisciplinary Journal for the Study of Discourse,* 6, 73-105.
1986. On Back-channel Behavior in Japanese and English Casual Conversation. *Linguistics,* 24, 1079-1108.
1986. Review of *Japanese Women's Language* by Janet Shibamoto. *The Journal of Asian Studies,* 45, 860-862.

1987. Thematization as a Staging Device in Japanese Narrative. In *Perspectives on Topicalization: The Case of Japanese Wa*. Ed. by John Hinds, Senko K. Maynard and Shoichi Iwasaki, 57-82. Amsterdam: John Benjamins.
1987. Interactional Functions of a Nonverbal Sign: Head Movement in Japanese Dyadic Casual Conversation. *Journal of Pragmatics*, 11, 589-606.
1987. Review of *Japanese* by John Hinds. *Linguistics*, 25, 1192-1196.
1987. (ERIC Microfiche.) Variability in Conversation Management: Fragmentation of Discourse and Back-channel Expressions in Japanese and English. Microfiche, ED 283 407. Educational Resources Information Center (ERIC), U.S. Department of Education, Office of Educational Research and Improvement.
1987. Pragmatics of Interactional Signs: A Case of *Uh-huh*'s and the Like in Japanese Conversation. *The Fourteenth LACUS (Linguistic Association of Canada and the United States) Forum*, 67-76.
1989. Functions of the Discourse Marker *Dakara* in Japanese Conversation. *TEXT: An Interdisciplinary Journal for the Study of Discourse*, 9, 389-414.
1990. Understanding Interactive Competence in L1/L2 Contrastive Context: A Case of Back-channel Behavior in Japanese and English. In *Language Proficiency, Defining, Teaching, and Testing*. Ed. by Louis A. Arena, 41-52. New York and London: Plenum Press.
1990. Conversation Management in Contrast: Listener Response in Japanese and American English. *Journal of Pragmatics*, 14, 397-412.
1990. TEXT: An Open Forum for International Scholarship. *TEXT Special 10th Anniversary Issue, Looking ahead: Discourse Analysis in the 1990s*. 10, 61-62.
1990. Expression of Appeal in the Utterance Design of Japanese Conversational Language. *Journal of Japanese Linguistics*, 12, 87-114.
1991. Pragmatics of Discourse Modality: A Case of the Japanese Emotional Adverb *Doose*. *Pragmatics*, 1, 371-392.
1991. Pragmatics of Discourse Modality: A Case of *Da* and *Desu/Masu* Forms in Japanese. *Journal of Pragmatics*, 15, 551-582.
1991. Discourse and Interactional Functions of the Japanese Modal Adverb *Yahari/Yappari*. *Language Sciences*, 13, 39-57.
1992. Speech Act Declaration in Conversation: Functions of the Japanese Connective *Datte*. *Studies in Language*, 16, 63-89.
1992. Cognitive and Pragmatic Messages of a Syntactic Choice: A Case of the Japanese Commentary Predicate *N(o) Da*. *TEXT: An Interdisciplinary Journal for the Study of Discourse*, 12, 563-613.
1992. Review of *Aspects of Japanese Women's Language*. Ed. by Sachiko Ide and Naomi Hanaoka McGloin. *Discourse & Society*, 3, 519-522.
1992. Where Textual Voices Proliferate: A Case of *To Yuu* Clause-Noun Combination in Japanese. *Poetics*, 21, 169-189.

1992. Toward the Pedagogy of Style: Choosing between Abrupt and Formal Verb Forms in Japanese. In *Japanese-Language Education Around the Globe*. Vol. 2. Ed. by The Japan Foundation Japanese Language Institute, 27-43. Urawa, Japan: The Japan Foundation Japanese Language Institute.

1993. Interactional Functions of Formulaicity: A Case of Utterance-final Forms in Japanese. *Proceedings of the 15th International Congress of Linguists*, Vol. 3, 225-228. Quebec City, Canada: Laval University Press.

1993. Declaring Speech Act in Conversation: A Study of Japanese Connective *Datte*. *Proceedings of the 15th International Congress of Linguists*, Vol. 1, 355-357. Quebec City: Laval University Press.

1993. The Meaning of Teaching Japanese in the United States. *The Breeze* (The Japan Foundation Language Center Newsletter), September, 3-4.

1994. (Abstract) Images of Involvement and Integrity: Rhetorical Style of a Japanese Politician. *The Association for Asian Studies, Abstracts of the 1994 Annual Meeting*. Ann Arbor: The Association for Asian Studies, 127.

1994. Images of Involvement and Integrity: Rhetorical Style of a Japanese Politician. *Discourse & Society*, 5, 233-261.

1994. Thematic Suspension and Speech Act Qualification: Rhetorical Effects of Stray Interrogative Clauses in Japanese Text. *Poetics*, 22, 473-496.

1994. The Centrality of Thematic Relations in Japanese Text. *Functions of Language*, 1, 229-260.

1995. "Assumed Quotation" in Japanese. *Gengo Hen'yoo ni okeru Taikeiteki Kenkyuu, oyobi sono Nihongo Kyooiku e no Ooyoo*. Ed. by Misato Tokunaga, 163-175. Tokyo: Kanda Gaikokugo Daigaku.

1995. Commentary Questions in Japanese: Cognitive Sources and Pragmatic Resources. *Studies in Language*, 19, 447-487.

1995. Interrogatives that Seek No Answers: Exploring the Expressiveness of Rhetorical Interrogatives in Japanese. *Linguistics*, 33, 501-530.

1995. Review of *Situated Meaning: Inside and Outside in Japanese Self, Society, and Language*, ed. by Jane M. Bachnik and Charles J. Quinn, Jr. *Language in Society*, 24, 611-614.

1995. Japanese Discourse, a new journal. *Japanese Discourse: An International Journal for the Study of Japanese Text and Talk*, 1, 1-5.

1995. Conversation Analysis and the Essence of Language. *Japanese Discourse: An International Journal for the Study of Japanese Text and Talk*, 1, 47-52.

1996. Contrastive Rhetoric: A Case of Nominalization in Japanese and English Discourse. In *Contrastive Semantics and Pragmatics*. Ed. by Katarzyna Jaszczolt and Ken Turner, 933-946. Oxford: Elsevier Science, Ltd.

1996. Multivoicedness in Speech and Thought Representation: The Case of Self-quotation in Japanese. *Journal of Pragmatics*, 25, 207-226.

1996. Presentation of One's View in Japanese Newspaper Columns: Commentary Strategies and Sequencing. *TEXT: An Interdisciplinary Journal for the Study of Discourse*, 16, 391-421.
1996. Contrastive Rhetoric: A Case of Nominalization in Japanese and English Discourse. *Language Sciences*, 18, 933-946.
1997. Manipulating Speech Styles in Japanese: Context, Genre, and Ideology. *Proceedings of the Fifth Princeton Japanese Pedagogy Workshop*, 1-24. Ed. by Seiichi Makino.
1997. Analyzing Interactional Management in Native/Non-native English Conversation: A Case of Listener Response. *International Review of Applied Linguistics and Language Teaching*, 35, 37-60.
1997. Synergistic Structures in Grammar: A Case of Nominalization and Commentary Predicate in Japanese. *Word: Journal of the International Linguistic Association*, 48, 15-40.
1997. Meta-quotation: Thematic and Interactional Significance of *Tte* in Japanese Girls' Comics. *Functions of Language*, 4, 23-46.
1997. Textual Ventriloquism: Quotation and the Assumed Community Voice in Japanese Newspaper Columns. *Poetics*, 24, 379-392.
1997. Shifting Contexts: The Sociolinguistic Significance of Nominalization in Japanese Television News. *Language in Society*, 26, 381-399.
1997. Rhetorical Sequencing and the Force of the Topic-Comment Relationship in Japanese Discourse: A Case of *Mini-Jihyoo* Newspaper Articles. *Japanese Discourse: An International Journal for the Study of Japanese Text and Talk*, 2, 43-64.
1998. Understanding and Teaching Japanese Discourse Principles: A Case of Newspaper Columns. In *Japanese-Language Education Around the Globe*. Vol. 8. Ed. by The Japan Foundation Japanese Language Institute, 67-86. Urawa, Japan: The Japan Foundation Japanese Language Institute.
1998. Ventrioloquism in Text and Talk: Functions of Self- and Other-Quotation in Japanese Discourse. (Keynote Speech) *Japanese/Korean Linguistics*, Vol. 7, 17-37. Ed. by Noriko Akatsuka et al. Stanford, CA: Center for the Study of Language and Information.
1998. Review of *Love, Hate and Everything in Between*, by Mamiko Murakami. *Journal of the Association of Teachers of Japanese*, 32, 2, 69-71.
1999. Discourse Analysis and Pragmatics. In *The Handbook of Japanese Linguistics*. Ed. by Natsuko Tsujimura, 425-443. London: Blackwell.
1999. On Rhetorical Ricochet: Expressivity of Nominalization and *Da* in Japanese Discourse. *Discourse Studies*, 1, 57-81.
1999. A Poetics of Grammar: Playing with Narrative Perspectives and Voices in Japanese and Translation Texts. *Poetics* 26, 115-141.
1999. Grammar, With Attitude: On the Expressivity of Certain *Da*-sentences in Japanese. *Linguistics*, 37, 215-250.

2000. Speaking for the Unspeakable: Expressive Functions of *Nan(i)* in Japanese Discourse. *Journal of Pragmatics*, 32, 1209-1239.

2001. Sources of Emotion in Japanese Comics: *Da, Nan(i)*, and the Rhetoric of *Futaku*. In *Exploring Japaneseness: On Japanese Enactments of Culture and Consciousness*. Ed. by Ray T. Donahue, 225-240. Westport, CT: Ablex.

2001. Expressivity in Discourse: Cases of Vocatives and Themes in Japanese. *Language Sciences*, 23, 679-705.

2001. Mitigation in Disguise: *Te-yuu-ka* as Preface to Self-revelation in Japanese Dramatic Discourse. *Poetics*, 29, 317-329.

2001. Falling in Love with Style: Expressive Functions of Stylistic Shifts in a Japanese Television Drama Series. *Functions of Language*, 8, 1-39.

2002. In the Name of a Vessel: Emotive Perspectives in the Reporting of the Ehime Maru-Greeneville Collision in a Japanese Newspaper. *Journal of Linguistics*, 40, 1047-1086.

2004. Poetics of Style Mixture: Emotivity, Identity, and Creativity in Japanese Writings. *Poetics*, 32, 387-409.

2005. Thematization as a Staging Device in the Japanese Narrative. Reprinted in *Japanese Linguistics*: *Pragmatics, Sociolinguistics and Language*. Ed. by Natsuko Tsujimura, 143-164. London: Routledge.

2005. Another Conversation: Expressivity of *Mitaina* and Inserted Speech in Japanese Discourse. *Journal of Pragmatics*, 37, 837-869.

2008. Playing with Multiple Voices: Emotivity and Creativity in Japanese Style Mixture. In *Style Shifting in Japanese*. Ed. by Kimberly Jones and Tsuyoshi Ono, 91-129. Amsterdam: John Benjamins.

Articles, etc. (written in Japanese)

1987. 「日英会話におけるあいづちの表現」『言語』11月号 88-92.

1991. 「文体の意味：ダ体とデス・マス体の混用について」『言語』2月号 75-80.

1993. 「アメリカ英語」『日本語学』5月臨時増刊号（特集「世界の女性語 日本の女性語」）13-19.

1994. 「『という』表現の機能：話者の発想・発話態度の標識として」『言語』11月号 80-85.

1997. 「アメリカ英語」『女性語の世界』井出祥子編　明治書院 130-140.

1998. 「パトスとしての言語」『言語』6月号 34-41.

2001. 「心の変化と話し言葉のスタイルシフト」『言語』6月号 38-45.

2001. 「日本語文法と感情の接点：テレビドラマに会話分析を応用して」『日本語文法』1, 90-110.

2003. 「談話分析の対照研究」『朝倉日本語講座7：文章・談話』北原保雄監修、佐久間まゆみ編　朝倉書店 227-249.

2005. 「会話導入文：話す『声』が聞こえる類似引用の表現性」『言語教育の新展開：牧野成一教授古稀記念論集　鎌田修他編　ひつじ書房 61-76.

2005.『新版日本語教育事典』担当事項　「会話のしくみ」337-338,「レトリック」361-362,「命題」584-585,「モダリティの研究」585-586,「トピック・コメント」581-582.　日本語教育学会編　大修館書店

2006.「指示表現の情意：語り手の視点ストラテジーとして」『日本語科学』19, 55-74.

2006.（ブログ）「言語についての誤解と正解！」言語学出版社フォーラム http://www.gengosf.com/dir_x/modules/wordpress/index.php?p=16

2007.「言語学と日本語教育学：知の受容から知の創造へ」『日本語教育』132, 23-32.

Subject Index

(For the definition of grammatical terms, see also Appendix 1.)

O

P

Q

R

W

Y

Japanese-English Word List

The following list contains Japanese words and phrases appearing in this book in alphabetical order with their English semantic equivalents, or in some cases with a description of their grammatical functions. The number following each item refers to the page where it first appears. Use main or key words to locate phrases consisting of multiple words. The verb types (*U*, *RU*, or Irregular) and adjective types (*-i* or *-na*) are indicated in brackets.

a(a) oh 262
aa that way 29
aaa whew 262
aayuu such as that 29
achira that way over there 29
ageru [*RU*] to give 36, 183
  te-ageru (giving a favorable action to someone) 188
Ahurika Africa 103
aida between 72
aida ni while 221
aisukuriimu ice cream 23
aite companion 198
aitsu that guy 118
akarui [*-i*] light 293
akemashite omedetoo gozaimasu Happy New Year 248
akeru [*RU*] to open [transitive] 36, 128
aki fall 59
akireru [*RU*] to be surprised, to be astounded 87
akiru [*RU*] to get bored, to get tired of 87
akogareru [*RU*] to long for, to pine for 87
aku [*U*] to open [intransitive] 35, 128, 140
amaeru [*RU*] to be dependent upon 87
amai [*-i*] sweet 79
a(n)mari (not) so much 78, 80
ame rain 68
Amerika America (United States of) 22
Amerika taishikan American embassy 299
Amerika-jin American 47
anata[1] husband [address term] 160
anata[2] you 40
ane elder sister 160
ani elder brother 160
ano that 28
ano hito he, she 146
ano ne (for getting attention) 159
anoo uh, well 98, 158, 210
anta you 40
apaato apartment 327
arau [*U*] to wash 35, 139
are that one over there 28
aree oh my! 262
ari short form of *aru* 39
arienai impossible 39
arigataku choodai itashimasu I accept your gift with gratitude 187
arigatoo (gozaimasu) thank you 162, 250
arigatoo gozaimashita thank you for … 162
arihureru [*RU*] to be common 143
aru[1] one 284
aru[2] [*U*] there exists 32, 38, 139
arubaito part-time job 24
aruku [*U*] to walk 54, 127
asa morning 58
asaban mornings and evenings 151
Asagaya (a place name in Tokyo) 29
Asagaya Apaato (a name of an apartment building) 29
asaneboo o suru to oversleep 153
asatte the day after tomorrow 59
asebamu [*U*] to sweat 307
ashita tomorrow 50, 59
asobu [*U*] to play 35, 139
asoko over there 28
asu tomorrow 59
ataeru [*RU*] to give 185
atama head 175
  atama ga itai to have a headache 175
  atama ni kuru to bet mad 237
atarashii [*-i*] new 14
atashi I [feminine speech] 40
atatakai [*-i*] warm 14
atatakana [*-na*] warm 104
atatakasa warmth 316
ato de[1] after doing 221
ato de[2] later 134
atsui[1] [*-i*] hot 14

atsui[2] [*-i*] thick, heavy 14
atsumaru [*U*] to gather 54
atsusa heat 88
au [*U*] to meet, to see 35
awarena [*-na*] pitiful 104

-ba if 241, 246, 303
  -ba yokatta I wish I had done so … 244
baa bar 24
bai bai bye-bye 224
(aru)baito part-time job 24
baka fool 209
bakari[1] about 97, 306
bakari[2] only 306
  bakari da[1] just did 306, 334
  bakari da[2] ready to 306
  bakari de naku … mo not only but also 306
ban turn 302
-ban (counter for order) 95
banshuu late fall 257
basu bus 24
basudai bus fare 316
basuke(ttobooru) basketball 24
beki ought to 273, 276
benkyoo(-suru) (to) study 37, 111, 140
benrina [*-na*] convenient, useful 105
benrisa convenience 316
biiru beer 23
bijuarukei visually pleasing 317
bijutsukan art museum 118
-biki (phonological change of *-hiki*) 96
bin bottle 297
Biru Bill 23
biru building 21
boku I [masculine speech] 40
-bon (phonological change of *-hon*) 96
boonasu bonus 263
booshi hat 213
Bosuton Boston 23
bubun part, section 135
buchoo manager 228
bunka culture 62
burabura rambling 330
  burabura-suru [Irr] to walk aimlessly 330
Buraun Brown 23
butchake to be totally frank [casual speech] 209
-byoo seconds 85, 96
byooin hospital 65
byooki illness 106, 175
  byooki ni naru to become sick 175

cha (contraction of *te wa*) 289
chau (colloquial version of *te-shimau*) 149
chichi my father 70, 160
chigainai lit., there is no mistake 280
  ni chigainai (guessing with confidence) 280
chigau [*U*] to differ 139
chiisai [*-i*] small 15
chikai [*-i*] near 15
chikaku near 72
chikoku being late 237
chikushoo damn (cursing word) 237
chin-suru [Irr] to cook in the microwave 145
chittomo (not) at all 80
Choo Cho 23
choo extremely 81
chooshuu audience 288
choppiri very little, a wee bit 80
chosha author 60
chotto[1] (for getting attention) 159
chotto[2] a little 80
chotto[3] uhh… 126
  chotto muzukashii naa, sore wa … it's a bit too difficult, I'm afraid … 205
  sore ga, chootto nee … well, it's a bit of a problem 205
Chuugokugo Chinese language 174
Chuugokumuke bound for China, catered to China 317
chuui warning 288
chuumon-suru [Irr] to order 269
chuurippu tulip 325
chuushi cancellation 212

da be (am, is, are) 26, 329
dai fare 316
-dai (counter for vehicles, etc.) 95
daigaku university 89
daigaku kyooju university professor 26
daigakusei university student 86
daijoobu all right 137, 250
  daijoobu desu I'll be fine 137
daikiraina [*-na*] abhorring 177

daisukina [*-na*] favorite 177
dakara[1] and so 153, 328
dakara[2] (emphatic) I'm telling you 157
dake only, just 80
  dake de naku ... mo not only but also 306
damasu [*U*] to deceive 283
dame 87
  nakereba dame must 279
  te wa dame must not 286
dandan gradually 150
dano and 87
dansu dance 24
dare who 64
dare de mo any parson 102
dare-ka someone 102, 268
dare-mo anyone 77, 102
-daro(o) (tagged auxiliary verb) 116, 119
-daroo ([AuxV] for uncertainty) 71, 259
-dasu something begins to occur 312
de[1] in, at, by, through 53, 89
de[2] so 153, 209, 328
  de kyoo wa ... so, today ... 209
de[3] then 157
de (mo) ii it is fine 287
  de-gozaimasu to be 227
dearinagara despite 223
dearu be [written style] 39, 217
dejikame digital camera 24
dekakeru [*RU*] to go out 214, 334
dekiru [*RU*] can do 36, 195
demo[1] but 153
demo[2] or something 98
densha train 57
denshi jisho electronic dictionary 173
denwa-suru [Irr] to make a phone call 70
depaato department store 24
deru[1] [*RU*] to appear, to be served 291
deru[2] [*RU*] to go out 36
-desho(o) (tagged auxiliary verb) 116, 119, 179
-deshoo ([AuxV] for uncertainty) 71, 259
desu (formal of *da*) 26
-desu (formal ending of [Adj-*i*]) 16
desu ne (insertion phrase) 101
desukara and so 153
dewa then 154
dewa-nakute no ... rather 216
dii-bui-dii DVD 222
-do times 95
doa door 127
dochira which one, where 29, 64, 170
dochira-mo both 102
Doitsu Germany 22
doko where 28, 64
doko e mo anywhere 77
doko-ka somewhere 102
doko-mo anywhere 102
dokushin bachelor 197
dono which 28
doo how 29, 64
doo desu ka how about ...ing? 46
doo itashimashite you are welcome 163
doo? saikin wa how are you doing these days? 251
doogu tool 204
doomo (doomo) thanks 162
doomo arigatoo gozaimashita thank you very much 250
doomo arigatoo gozaimasu thank you very much 162
doomo sumimasen thank you 137, 162
doomo sumimasen-deshita thank you for doing ... 162
dooryoo colleague 327
doose anyway, after all 182
dooshite why 64
dooyuu such as what, of what kind 29
doozo please 285
doozo okamainaku please don't go to any trouble 294
doozo yoroshiku (onegai-shimasu) how do you do? 30
doraibu(-suru) (to) drive 22
dore which one 28, 64
dore-mo any one 102
-doru dollar 94
doyoobi Saturday 59

e to, toward 53
e(e)? what? 180, 214, 262
ee yes 20, 93, 180
ee ... uhh ... 210
  ee, maa ... well, uhh, so ... 216
eeto ... well, let's see ... 210
eiga movie 235
eigo English 20
eki station 72
ekimae in front of a station 88
-en yen 81

enjinia engineer 26
-eru (potential verb ending) 195
ett what? 261

famiresu family restaurant (diner) 103
fookasu(-suru) (to) focus 37
fooku fork 73

ga[1] (exhaustive listing) 47
ga[2] (subject marker) 35, 41
ga[3] but 92, 153, 156, 328
gabugabu nomu to drink thirstily 144
gaikoku foreign countries 143
gakkoo school 53
gakkooyoo for consumption at school 316
gakusei student 26
gakusha scholar 26
ganbaru [*U*] to do one's best 151
gankona [*-na*] stubborn 104
garasu glass 297
-gatsu (indicating month) 85
genki? how have you been? 251
(o)genkina [*-na*] healthy, well 201
geragera warau to laugh boisterously 144
getsuyoobi Monday 59
ginkoo bank 72
ginkooin banker, bank employee 26
go five 82
go- (respectful prefix) 110
go-gatsu May 85
gobusata-shite-orimasu I haven't seen you for a long time 249
gochisoosama deshita thank you for the delicious food/drink 295
gogo afternoon 58
gohan cooked rice 331
gokazoku family 160
gokuroosama (desu/deshita) thank you for your effort 164
gokuroosan thank you for your effort 164
gokyoodai sibling 160
gomen sorry, excuse me 132
gomenkudasai hello, excuse me 159, 294
gomennasai I'm sorry 132
gookaku-suru [Irr] to pass an exam 238
gookei total, sum 274
goranninaru [*U*] to look 227
goruhu golf 24
goshujin(-sama) husband 160
gozenchuu morning, before noon 58
guai wa doo desu ka how are you feeling? 250
gurai about 97
-guramu gram 95
gutaiteki ni yuu to more concretely 209
guuzen unexpectedly, coincidentally 134

ha tooth 175
  ha ga itai to have a toothache 175
haa? uh? 214
hachi eight 82
hachi-gatsu August 85
hachi-ji eight o'clock 34
hadena [*-na*] showy 105
hageshii [*-i*] pouring (rain) 109
haha mother 160
hai yes 93, 180, 205
-hai (counter for liquid) 95
haikensuru [Irr] to look 227
hairu [*U*] to enter 33, 54
haishakusuru [Irr] to borrow 227
hajimaru [*U*] to begin 34
hajimemashite how do you do? 30
-hajimeru something begins to occur 312
hakaru [*U*] to measure 317
Hakata Hakata 56
hakken-suru [Irr] to discover 275
hakkiri (to) clearly 135, 235
hako box 72
hakobu [*U*] to carry 54
hamueggu ham-and-eggs 53
han thirty minutes 85
hana[1] flower 185
hana[2] trunk 50
hanashi talk 111
  hanashi chigau kedo to change the subject 209
hanasu [*U*] to talk 195
hanbaagaa hamburger 23
hanbaagu hamburger 23
hanbai(-suru) (to) sell 37
hankachi handkerchief 21
hannin criminal 293
happyoo-suru [Irr] to make a presentation 254
Hara (last name) 25
hara ga heru to be hungry [masculine speech] 168
hara ga tatsu to be angry 237
hareru [*RU*] to clear up 68

haru spring 59
hashiru [*U*] to run 139, 150
hatarakimono hard worker 39
hataraku [*U*] to work 36
hate na? I wonder 262
hatsuka 20th [date] 84
hayai [*-i*] early, quick 15
hayaku[1] early 59
hayaku[2] right away 207
haya-tt quick 16
hazu be supposed to 272
hee is that right, really! 262
heibonna [*-na*] commonplace 105
henna [*-na*] strange 281
herahera warau to laugh condescendingly 144
heru [*U*] to decrease 33
heya room 39
hibi days 315
-hiki (counter for animals) 95
hikidashi drawer 73
hikooki airplane 150
hikui [*-i*] low 15
himitsu secret 239
hinpanni frequently 134
hinshu variety 61
hiraku [*U*] to open, to be opened 128
hirogaru [*U*] to expand 327
hiroi [*-i*] wide, spacious 15
hirosa size 316
hiruma daytime 58
hiruyasumi lunch break 223
hisho secretary 26
hito person 22
hitobito people 315
hitori one person 96
hitotsu one 82
hitsuyoona [*-na*] necessary 301
hodo[1] about 97
hodo[2] degree, extent 170, 307
  hodo dewa nai not so 307
Hokkaidoo Hokkaido 292
hon book 29
-hon (counter for long objects) 95
hon'ya(-san) bookstore 73
hondai book expense 316
honno just 187
  honno sukoshi just a little 187
Honoruru Honolulu 23
honto? really? 180
hontoni really (colloquial) 235
hontoo truth 207
hontoo? Really? 73
hontooni really, indeed 20
hoo direction 169, 172
  hoo ga ii it would be better 170, 305
  no hoo (indirect marker) 172
  no hoo ga (comparative expression) 169
hora see (requesting attention) 117
horeru [*RU*] to fall in love, to be infatuated 88
hoshigatte-iru a third person wants 172
hoshii [*-i*] to want 172
  te hoshii (expressing a desire) 174, 204
hoteru hotel 24
hubenna [*-na*] inconvenient 105
hukami depth 316
hukasa depth 316
hukin vicinity 328
huku [*U*] to blow 151
hukusoo o suru to wear clothes 234
hukutsuu stomachache 175
  hukutsuu ga suru to have a stomach pain 175
-hun minutes 85, 96
Huransu France 22
Huransupan French bread 22
huroshiki furoshiki 263
huru[1] [*U*] to fall 68
huru[2] [*U*] to wave 275
hurui [*-i*] old 15
hurusato hometown 69
husagaru [*U*] to be clogged up 128
husagu [*U*] to clog up 128
hushigina [*-na*] strange 235
hutari two persons 96
hutatsu two 82
hutsuka 2nd [date] 84
hutsukayoi hangover 310
huukei scenery, scene 235
huun I see 180
huyu winter 59
hyaku one hundred 84
hyaku-man one million 84
hyaku-oku ten billion 84

ichi one 82
ichi-gatsu January 85

ichi-man ten thousand 84
ichi-oku one hundred million 84
ichiban most 89, 170
  (no naka) de ichiban (superlative expression) 170
Ichikawa (last name) 25
ichinichijuu all day long 69
idaina [*-na*] great 104
Igirisu England 22
Igirisu-jin English person 173
ii [*-i*] good 15
  ii n desu yo, sonnani ki o tsukatte-itadakanakute it isn't necessary to be so kind and considerate 186
  ii-desu nee that will be nice 125
iie no 93
  iie, kekkoo desu no, thank you 136
iikaereba in other words 209
iikaeruto in other words 209
ijiwaruna [*-na*] mean 104
ijoo nobeta yoo ni as stated above 157
ika under 279
ikaga how 64
  ikaga desu ka how about ...? 98
  okaze wa ikaga desu ka how is your cold? 250
ikenai
  nakereba ikenai must 278
  nakute wa ikenai must 278
  te wa ikenai must not 286, 288
ikiru [*RU*] to live 270
iku [*U*] to go 33
  ni iku go for the purpose of 165
ikura how much 64
ikutsu how many 64
ima now 58
ima de mo even now 178
imi meaning 146
imooto(san) younger sister 121, 160
inko parakeet 170
inshuunten drunken driving 289
intaanetto Internet 24
ip-pai lit., one cup 98
  ip-pai doo how about drinking? 98
ippai da to be filled 257
irasshaimase welcome (to our place) 250
irassharu [*U*] there exists 227
ireru [*RU*] to pour in, to put in 36
iroirona [*-na*] various 59
iru[1] [*RU*] there exists 33, 36, 38, 139
iru[2] [*U*] to need 33
is-sen-man ten million 84
is-sen-oku one hundred billion 84
isha medical doctor 26
isogashii [*-i*] busy 14
isoge (command form of *isogu*) 235
isogu [*U*] to hurry 113
isoide hurriedly 109
isshitsu one room 327
isshoni together 98
isshookenmei hard, diligently 34
itadakimasu I'll help myself, thank you 295
itadaku[1] [*U*] to eat 227
itadaku[2] [*U*] to receive from someone 184
  te-itadakemasen(-deshoo) ka (expressing request) 204
  te-itadaku (receiving a favorable action) 191
itai [*-i*] painful 175
  atama ga itai to have a headache 175
  ha ga itai to have a toothache 175
  koshi ga itai to have a lower back pain 175
  nodo ga itai to have a sore throat 175
  onaka ga itai to have a stomachache 175
Itaria Italy 22
Itaria-jin Italian 78
Itarian Italian 147
itasu [*U*] to do 227
Itoo (last name) 25
itsu when 63
itsu-mo any time 102
itsuka[1] 5th [date] 84
itsuka[2] someday 189
itsumo always 58, 134
itsutsu five 82
ittai how, what, why on earth, in the world 134, 182
itte-kimasu I will go and return 224
itte-mairimasu I will go and return 224
ittoo first prize 189
i(i)ya no 93
iyaa, chotto ... well ... I'm afraid not 286
iyana [*-na*] distasteful 104
iyoiyo all the more, increasingly 257

ja (contraction of *de wa*) 289
ja(a), ashita see you tomorrow 224
ja(a), ato de well then, see you later 224
ja(a), mata see you again 224
-jan (interactional particle) 118
janiizukei young nice-looking males 317
jau (colloquial version of *de-shimau*) 149
jazu jazz 178
jeiaaru Japan Railways 22
ji handwriting 279
-ji hours 85
jibun self 207
-jikan duration of hours 85, 96
jinjika personnel division 215
jinsei life, lifetime 105
jirojiro mirareru to be stared at 284
jishin earthquake 39
jisho dictionary 152
jissai ni actually 275
jitsu wa ... seriously though 209
jiyuu freedom, liberty 166
jogingu jogging 24
Jon John 23
joobuna [*-na*] strong, durable 274
jookyuu upper class 274
joozuna [*-na*] be good at, skillful 48, 105
josei woman 219
jugyoo class, lecture 152
jugyoochuu during the class 292
juu ten 82
juu ichi-gatsu November 85
juu ni-gatsu December 85
juu yokka 14th [date] 84
juu-gatsu October 85
juu-ji ten o'clock 34
juu-man one hundred thousand 84
juu-oku one billion 84
juusho address 126
juusu juice, fruit drinks 23
juutai traffic jam 203

ka[1] (question marker) 63, 268
 ka doo ka whether or not 269
ka[2] or 53, 86, 329
ka na I wonder 261
kaasan mother 160
kaban bag 279
kaeri returning 327
kaeru [*U*] to return 33, 35
-kaesu repeating something 312
kafe café 124
kagi key, lock 131
kagu furniture 200
kai[1] (informal question marker) 65
kai[2] meeting 302
-kai[1] (counter for the stories) 95
-kai[2] times 95
kaigairyokoo overseas travel 130
kaigi meeting 34
kaimono shopping 79, 316
kaisha company 34
kaishain company employee 26
kaji fire 177
kakaru [*U*] to cost
 (jikan ga) kakaru to take (time) 257
kakeru (megane o) to wear glasses 219
-kakeru start doing something 312
kakomareru [*RU*] to be surrounded by 284
kaku [*U*] to write 54, 76
kamaimasen all right 285
kamera camera 24
kamo (a shortened version of *kamoshirenai*) 260
kamoshirenai might be, may be 259
-kan (indicating duration) 84
Kanada Canada 22
kanai wife 160
kanari considerably 80
kanashii [*-i*] sad 236
kanashimu [*U*] to grieve 238
kanata beyond 150
(o)kane money 38
kangae idea 151
kangaeru [*RU*] to think 293
 kangaete-okimasu I will think about it 267
kankei relationship 142
kankookyaku tourist 222
kantanna [*-na*] easy, simple 104
kao face 288
kara[1] after doing 220
kara[2] because 46, 70, 202
kara[3] from 53, 88
karaoke karaoke bar 141
karee curry with rice 211
Kariforunia California 287
kashira I wonder 261
kashu singer 26

kasu [*U*] to lend 191
kasukana [-*na*] faint 104
kasutera sponge cake 23
-*kata* the way of doing 316
Katoo (last name) 26
kau [*U*] to buy 35
kawa river 56
kawaii [-*i*] endearing, cute 170
kawaisooni poor thing 180
kawakasu [*U*] to dry 128
kawaku [*U*] to be dried up 128
kayoobi Tuesday 59
kayou [*U*] to commute 141
kaze[1] cold 89
kaze o hiku to catch a cold 175
kaze[2] wind 151
kazoku family 160
kedo although 153, 303
keeki cake 23
keetai cell phone 143
keetai shoosetsu cell-phone novel 221
kehai sign, indication 257
-*kei* (adjective marker) 317
keikaku plan 272
Keioo Daigaku Keio University 143
kekkon marriage 111
kekkon-suru [Irr] to get married 140
kekkoo more than expected 136
kekkoo desu[1] it is all right 285
kekkoo desu[2] no, thank you 136
kekkyoku in the end, after all 155
kenchikuka architect 26
kenka-suru [Irr] to fight 289
kenkoona [-*na*] healthy 106
kenkooteki healthy 317
kenkyuu(-suru) (to) research 37
kenkyuushitsu (professor's) office 296
keredo(mo) but 153
kesa this morning 58
kesshin-suru [Irr] to decide 292
kesu [*U*] to extinguish, to turn off 128
ki tree 218
kibishii [-*i*] strict, demanding 15
kichinto appropriately 240
kieru [*RU*] to be extinguished, to be turned off 128
kigi trees 284
kikai machine 299
kikenna [-*na*] dangerous 104
kikoeru [*RU*] to be heard 176
kiku [*U*] to hear, to inquire 35, 140
kimeru [*RU*] to decide 269
kimi you 40
kimochi feelings 118
kin'yoobi Friday 59
Kinkakuji the Golden Pavilion 284
kinodokuni I'm sorry to hear that 180
kinoo yesterday 30, 59
kiotsukeru [*RU*] to be careful 208
kippu ticket 161
kiraina [-*na*] disliked 104, 178
kirakira kagayaku to shine and glitter 144
kireina [-*na*] pretty, clean 104
kireini cleanly 253
kireru [*RU*] to be cut 176
-*kiro* kilometers, kilograms 95
kiru[1] [*U*] to cut, to slice 33, 128
kiru[2] [*RU*] to wear 36, 140
kitte postage stamp 97
kitto surely 189, 281
kizuku [*U*] to notice 87
ko child, kid 142
-*ko* (counter for small objects) 95
Kobayashi (last name) 26
kochira this way 29
kochira koso same to you, same here 30, 249
kodawaru [*U*] to be bothered, to be concerned about 87
kodomo(san) child 33, 160
kodomo-tachi children 56
kodomoyoo for use by children 316
koe voice 198
koinu puppy 231
koko here 28
kokoa cocoa 247
kokonoka 9th [date] 84
kokonotsu nine 82
kokuhaku-suru [Irr] to confess 293
komaru [*U*] to be troubled 87
komarimashita nee it's a problem, isn't it? 180
nakereba komaru must 279
kome rice 284
kon'ya tonight 58
kon'ya wa chotto . . . tonight isn't the best time 126
konbanwa good evening 12
kondo this time, next time 134

kongetsu this month 59
konkuuru *concours* (contest) 189
konnichiwa good afternoon 12
kono this 28
kono aida recently 163
konshuu this week 59
koo this way 29
koocha (black) tea 53
koodoo-suru [Irr] to behave 240
kooen[1] lecture 212
kooen[2] park 78
koohii coffee 23
koohii kappu coffee cup 120
koojichuu under construction 193
koojoo factory 156
kookana [*-na*] expensive 104
koomuin public servant, government employee 26
kooru [*U*] to freeze 34
koosoo high-rise 327
kooto coat 330
kootsuujiko traffic accident 203
kooyuu such as this 29
koppu glass 133
kore this one 28
koriru [*RU*] to learn by experience 87
koro approximate time 220
Koronbusu Columbus 275
korosu [*U*] to kill 42, 128
koshi lower back 175
  koshi ga itai to have a lower back pain 175
koshoo-suru [Irr] to break down 263
kotae answer 246
kotaeru [*RU*] to answer 36
koto thing(s), fact(s) 59, 274, 308
  koto ga aru I have experienced it, there are some occasions 310
  koto ga dekiru can do 195
  koto ni naru it has been decided to 310, 324
  koto ni suru to decide to do 310
  koto wa nai there is no need to 310
  to yuu koto o (to write) that 293
kotoba word 215
kotoshi this year 59
kowareru [*RU*] something breaks 282
kowasu [*U*] to break something 282
kozutsumi package 273
ku nine 82
ku-gatsu September 85
kudamono fruit 47
kudasai please give 90
  te-kudasai (expressing request) 112, 206
kudasaru [*U*] someone gives to self 184
  te-kudasaru (receiving a favorable action) 190
kuma bear 291
kuni country 151
kurai[1] [*-i*] dark 15
kurai[2] about 97
kurashikku ongaku classical music 177
kureru [*RU*] someone gives to self 184
  te-kureru (giving a favorable action to self) 188
kurisumasu Christmas 55
kuroo toil 164
kuru [Irr] to come 33
  ni kuru come for the purpose of 165
kuruma car 55
kuso shit (cursing word) 237
kusukusu warau to giggle 144
kutsu shoes 73
kuu [*U*] to eat [masculine speech] 110
kuukoo airport 90
-kyoku (counter for songs) 302
kyonen last year 59
kyoo today 19, 59
kyoodai sibling 160
kyooju university professor 26
kyoojuu within the day 206
kyookai church 52
kyookasho textbook 165
kyooshitsu classroom 152
kyuu nine 82
kyuujitsu holiday, off-duty day 327
kyuuni suddenly 203
Kyuushuu Kyushu 92
kyuuyoo emergency 302

maa[1] oh my! 262
maa[2] more or less 255
  ee, maa yeah, I guess 255
  maa maa (desu) it's OK, more or less 255
  maa maa da ne so-so 251
maa . . . well, say . . . 210
  maa, ano well . . . 209

maa, soo desu ne … Oh, I guess … 210
maa, sorede … so, then … 210
machigai mistake 131
mada not yet 141
mada ii ja-nai-desu ka it's still early 225
mada mada desu I still have a lot to learn 254
made till, up to 54
made ni by 54
mado window 112
mae[1] before [time] 85
mae[2] front 72
mae ni before doing 221
magaru [*U*] to turn 55
-mai[1] (counter for thin objects) 95
-mai[2] (negative intention) 79
maiasa every morning 34
maiku microphone 21
mainen every year 59
mainichi every day 59
mairu [*U*] to come, to go [humble] 33, 227
maishuu every week 50, 59
maitsuki every month 59
maji? seriously? 180
maji de seriously 181
makeru [*RU*] to lose 291
mama mother 160
mamonaku soon, in no time 136
mamoru [*U*] to keep 274
man ten thousand 84
manga comic 122
mangabon comic book 161
maniau [*U*] to be in time 183
manshon upscale apartment 24
masaka! it can't be! 180, 262
-mashoo (formal volitional verb ending) 123
-mashoo ka shall I …? 137
masukomi mass communication 46
mata additionally 157
mata doozo please come again 250
mata wa or 329
mata yoosu o mite to yuu koto de we will see what happens 267
matsu [*U*] to wait 36, 140
Matsumoto (last name) 26
matsuri festival 222
mawari surrounding 234
mayonaka midnight 58
mayou [*U*] to be puzzled 88
mazu first 277
mazui [*-i*] with bad taste 15
mazushii [*-i*] poor 150
me eye 143
me ga mawaru to feel giddy 175
-meetoru meter 95
megane glasses 219
meishi business card 31
memai ga suru to feel dizzy 175
memo memo 166
meshiagaru [*U*] to eat 227
metcha very much, extremely 81
mezamashidokei alarm clock 203
mi (nominalizing suffix) 316
midori green 284
mieru[1] [*RU*] to be seen 176
mieru[2] [*RU*] to visit, to come 259
mijikai [*-i*] short 15
mikakeru [*RU*] to see in passing 193
mikan tangerine 55
mikka 3rd [date] 84
minami south 151
minasama everyone 201
minasan you all 256
minna everyone 120
miru [*RU*] to see 36
miruku milk 23
mise store 55
misoshiru miso soup 331
mitaina[1] it seems 235
mitaina[2] (quotation marker) 235
mitsukaru [*U*] to be found 128
mitsukeru [*RU*] to find 128
mittsu three 82
(o)miyage small gift 186
mizu water 34
mo also, in addition (topic marker) 51, 86, 214, 256
mochiron of course 187
moderu (fashion) model 26
modoru [*U*] to return, to come back 218
mokuyoobi Thursday 59
mondai question 104
mono[1] thing(s) 87, 308, 316
mono da[1] (expressing surprise) 308
mono da[2] (to convey mild, indirect command) 309
mono da[3] used to do 308

nanto ... daroo! how/what ...! 263
nantoka I've been fine 251
naoru [*U*] to be corrected 128
naosu [*U*] to correct 128
-naosu repeating something 312
nara (topic marker) 52
nara(ba) if 241
naru[1] [*U*] to become 151, 322
  koto ni naru to have been decided 325
  yooni naru reach the point where 325
naru[2] [*U*] to ring 203
naruhodo I see 180, 262
-nasai (expressing a command) 207
nasaru [*U*] to do 227
natsu summer 59
natsukashii [*-i*] nostalgic 130
natsuku [*U*] to become attached to 88
natsuyasumi summer vacation 53
naze why 64
ne(e) don't you? (interactional particle) 16, 99, 179, 303
neage price hike 237
nee (for getting attention) 158
neesan elder sister 160
neko cat 38
nemuru [*U*] to sleep 197
-nen kan for ... years 60, 96
-nen kan ni in/within ... years 60
nendai 282
  san-juu nendai 30's 282
neru [*RU*] to sleep, to go to bed 36
netsu fever 175
  netsu ga aru to have a fever 175
(intaa)netto Internet 24
ni[1] (indirect object marker) 42
ni[2] (marking a causee) 300
ni[3] additionally (enumerative particle) 86
ni[4] in, at, from 53
ni[5] two 82
ni chigainai (guessing with confidence) 280
ni iku go for the purpose of 165
ni kuru come for the purpose of 165
ni suru to decide 330
ni tsuite about 267
ni-gatsu February 85
ni-juu yokka 24th [date] 84
-nichi (indicating date/days) 84
-nichi-kan for ... days 84
nichiyoobi Sunday 59
nigiyakana [*-na*] bustling 105
Nihon-jin Japanese 27
Nihonshu Japanese *sake* 331
Nihonteki Japan-like 317
niisan elder brother 160
nikoniko suru to smile 144
niku meat 296
-nikui difficult to do 315
nimotsu luggage 137
-nin (counter for people) 96
ningen human beings, person 277
ninki ga aru to be popular 200
ninki no aru to be popular 194
nioi smell 296
niru [*RU*] to resemble 139
nishuukan two weeks 55
niyaniya suru to grin 144
niyotte by 282
no[1] (indefinite pronoun) 74
no[2] (interactional particle) 100
no[3] (linker) 60
no[4] (nominalizing clauses) 274
no da (predicate with explanation) 191
no kai (informal question marker) 65
noberu [*RU*] to state 293
noboru [*U*] to climb 55
node since, and so 154, 202
nodo throat 175
  nodo ga itai to have a sore throat 175
  nodo ga kawaku to be thirsty 167
nomimono drink 98
nomu [*U*] to drink 33, 36
  gabugabu nomu to drink thirstily 144
  sake o nomu to drink (*sake*) 153
noni in spite of 154, 303
nooto notebook 73
nozoku [*U*] to exclude 327
-nu (negative suffix [written]) 79
nugu [*U*] to take off (clothes) 36
nukeru [*RU*] to came off, to pass through 176
nyuugakushiken entrance exam 46, 62, 253
Nyuujaajii New Jersey 55
nyuujooryoo admission fee 316

nyuusha-suru [Irr] to be newly employed by the company 238
nyuushi entrance examination 46
nyuusu news 142
nyuuyoku(-suru) (to) take a bath 37
Nyuuyooku New York 23

o[1] (marking location) 56, 88
o[2] (marking a causee) 300
o[3] (object marker) 35, 41
o- (respectful prefix) 110
o…da (respectful form) 228
o…ninaru (respectful form) 225
o…suru (humble form) 225
oba(san) aunt 160
obaasan old woman, grandmother 160
oboete-iru to remember 276
ocha green tea 136
ochiru [*RU*] to drop [intransitive] 36
ochuugen the summer gift-giving 187
odaiji ni take care of yourself 250
odoroku [*U*] to be surprised 35
odoru [*U*] to dance 35
Ogawa (last name) 25
ogenki de take care of yourself 224
ohayoo (gozaimasu) good morning 12, 251
ohiru lunch 126
ohisashiburi desu long time no see 249
oideninaru [*U*] there exists, to come, to go 227
oikakeru [*RU*] to chase 281
oishii [*-i*] delicious 15
ojama-shimashita excuse me 295
ojama-shimasu excuse me 294
oji(san) uncle 160
ojiisan old man, grandfather 160
ojoosan (someone's) daughter 160
okaasama (someone else's) mother 259
okaasan mother 160
(no) okage with the help from 256
okane money 38
okashi sweets 283
okiru [*RU*] to get up 36, 128
okkee OK 205
okoru [*U*] to be angry 35
okosu [*U*] to wake 128
oku[1] one hundred million 84
oku[2] [*U*] to put 73
okureru [*RU*] to be last for 149
okurimono personal gift 186
okuru [*U*] to send 35
okusan wife 160
omae[1] wife [address term] 160
omae[2] you [masculine speech] 40
omedetoo (gozaimasu) congratulations 238
  akemashite omedetoo gozaimasu Happy New Year 248
  (gokekkon) omedetoo gozaimasu congratulations on your wedding 249
  tanjoobi omedetoo happy birthday 249
omenikakaru [*U*] to meet 227
omocha toy 190
omoidasu [*U*] to recall 293
omoide memories 298
omoshiroi [*-i*] interesting, funny 15
omou [*U*] to think 79, 313, 314
  to omou to think that 206, 313
onaka stomach 175
  onaka ga itai to have a stomachache 175
  onaka ga suku to be hungry 167
oneesan elder sister 160
onegai request 100
  moo ichido onegai-shimasu could you repeat it one more time? 215
  moo sukoshi yukkuri onegai-shimasu could you speak a little more slowly? 215
  onegai da kara I'm pleading with you 206
  onegai-shimasu I make a request 90
ongaku music 142
oniisan elder brother 160
onna no hito woman 194
onna no ko girl 240
-(y)oo (informal volitional verb ending) 123
  -(y)oo ka shall I…? 137
  -(y)oo to omotte-iru thinking to do 125
oogoe o agete to shout 288
ooi [*-i*] many, much 15
ookii [*-i*] large 15
ookisa size 279
Oosaka Osaka 50
oozei many (people) 80

Oranda Holland 22
ore I [masculine speech] 40
oru [*U*] there exists 227
osakini (shitsurei[-shimasu]) excuse me for leaving early 224
osara dish 253
oseibo the winter gift-giving 187
osewa ni narimashita thanks for taking care of me 163
oshaberi chatter 292
oshieru [*RU*] to teach 36
osoi [*-i*] late, slow 15
ossharu [*U*] to say 227
osushi polite form of *sushi* 110
otaku(-sama) you 40
oto sound 297
otoko man 109
otoosan father 160
otooto(san) younger brother 160
otosu [*U*] to drop 35
ototoi the day before yesterday 59
ototoshi the year before last 59
otsukare sama (deshita) thank you for your effort 225
otsuri change 297
otto husband 219
owaru [*U*] to end 35
oya oh my! 262
oyogikata style of swimming 316
oyogu [*U*] to swim 56

paatii party 39
pan bread 23
papa father 160
Pari Paris 23
pasokon personal computer 24
pasuta pasta 23
Pekin Beijing 174
perapera fluent (in language) 155
petto pet 170
pianisuto pianist 26
-piki (phonological change of *-hiki*) 96
pikunikku picnic 303
pinpon-suru [Irr] to ring the door bell 145
-pon (phonological change of *-hon*) 96
-pun (phonological change of *-hun*) 85
purezento present, gift 55
purintaa printer 274
puro yakyuu professional baseball 275

raamen *raamen* noodles 211
raigetsu next month 59
raimugipan rye bread 22
rainen next year 59
raishuu next week 59
rajio radio 24
ranchi lunch 119
-rareru[1] (passive verb ending) 281
-rareru[2] (potential verb ending) 195
-rareru[3] (respectful verb ending) 225
rashii it seems 238
  sensei rashii teacher-like 240
rei zero 84
reido zero degree 34
reiseina [*-na*] cool (in disposition) 105
renraku-suru [Irr] to contact 253
renshuu practice 254
renshuuyoo used for practice purposes 316
repooto report 154
-reru[1] (passive verb ending) 281
-reru[2] (respectful verb ending) 225
resutoran restaurant 24
ringo apples 20
-rittoru litter 95
riyuu reason 302
rokku bando rock band 260
roku six 82
roku-gatsu June 85
Rondon London 23
roopu rope 274
roorupan rolls 22
Rosanzerusu Los Angeles 23
ryokoo(-suru) (to) travel 37, 165
ryokoo trip 156
ryoo(kin) fare 316
(o)ryoori cooking 255
ryooshin parents 292

sa (interactional particle) 99
-sa (nominalizing suffix) 316
saa well, let's see ... 101, 180
saabisu service 50
sabishii [*-i*] lonely 15
saigo end 223
saihu wallet 206
saikin recently 193
Saitoo (last name) 26
sakana fish 109
sake *sake* (rice wine) 81
  sake o nomu to drink (*sake*) 153

saki ahead 72
sakkaa soccer 24
sakki a while ago 58, 134
saku [*U*] to bloom 231
sakuban last night 58
sakura cherry blossoms 231
samasu [*U*] to cool 128
sameru [*RU*] to become cool 128
samui [-*i*] cold (atmosphere) 15
san three 82
-san Mr., Ms., Miss, Mrs. 25
san-gatsu March 85
sandoitchi sandwich 23
Sanhuranshisuko San Francisco 23
sankyu(u) thank you 162
sanpo-suru [Irr] to go for a walk 221
sansei agreement 267
saraigetsu the month after next 59
sarainen the year after next 59
saraishuu the week after next 59
sarani furthermore 157
sarariiman businessman 234
sarasara nagareru to flow smoothly 144
saru monkey 257
-saseru (causative verb ending) 299
sashiageru [*RU*] to give to someone 184
sasou [*U*] to invite 314
Satoo (last name) 26
-satsu (counter for books) 95
sayo(o)nara goodbye 224
sazukeru [*RU*] to award, to confer 185
seijika politician 26
seiyoo Western world 62
seiyoobunka Western culture 62
seki cough 175
  seki ga deru to have a cough 175
sekkaku with much trouble and effort 182
  sekkaku desu kara I will thankfully receive this 186
semai [-*i*] narrow, small (in space) 15
sen one thousand 84
-senchi centimeter 95
sengetsu last month 59
sensei teacher, professor 26
sensengetsu the month before last 59
sensenshuu the week before last 59
senshuu last week 59
-seru (causative verb ending) 299
sesshi centigrade 34
setsu opinion 290
shaberu [*U*] to chat 33, 36
shachoo company president 225
shanpuu(-suru) (to) shampoo 37
shi four 82
-shi[1] (expressing enumerations) 211
-shi[2] incomplete sentence marker 214
shi-gatsu April 85
shiageru [*RU*] to finish, to complete 206
shiai match (of sports) 291
shiawase! I am happy! 236
Shibuya Shibuya 30
shichi seven 82
shichi-gatsu July 85
shigen resources 88
shigoto work, job 20
shika no more than 80
Shikago Chicago 23
shikashi but, however 153, 328
shiken examination 46
shimaru [*U*] to close [intransitive] 36
shimeru[1] [*RU*] to close [transitive] 36
shimeru[2] [*U*] to dampen 33
shimin citizen 309
shinbun newpaper 152
shinjiru [*RU*] to believe 36, 252
Shinkansen Bullet Train 56
shinsenna [-*na*] fresh 109
shinu [*U*] to die 127, 140
shippai-suru [Irr] to fail 223
shiraberu [*RU*] to examine 269
shiraseru [*RU*] to notify 190
shirimasen I don't know 145
shita under 72
shitagatte therefore 157
shiten branch office 146
shitoshito huru to rain quietly and steadily 144
shitsumon question, inquiry 87
shitsurei sorry, excuse me 132
  shitsurei desu ga … sorry to be rude 158
  shitsurei-shimasu[1] excuse me 294
  shitsurei-shimasu[2] to leave 295
shizukana [-*na*] quiet 104
shokuba job, employment 278
shokuji meal 98
shokupan loaf of bread 22
shoochi-shimashita certainly 205
(o)shoogatsu New Year's days 256

supiichi speech 288
supootsu sports 166
suru [Irr] to do 33, 323, 329
kawaii kao o suru to have a cute face 143
ni suru to decide 330
nikoniko suru to smile 144
niyaniya suru to grin 144
-suru (making verbs) 37
sushi *sushi* 110
suteeki steak 23
suteru [*RU*] to throw away 36
sutoraiki strike 21
sutoraiku strike 21
sutoresu kaishoo relieving stress 166
suu (*tabako o*) to smoke 112
suupaa supermarket 24
suwaru [*U*] to sit down 36
Suzuki (last name) 26
suzushii [*-i*] cool 15
suzushisa coolness 316

Taanaa Turner 23
tabako cigarette 112
tabako o suu to smoke 112
tabekata manner of eating 316
tabemono food 178, 316
taberu [*RU*] to eat 33, 128, 139
tabun perhaps 180, 259
-tachi (plural suffix for persons) 41
tada no just 297
tadashii [*-i*] correct 243
-tagatte-iru a third person wants to 173
-tai to want to 172
-takute tamaranai I am dying to 263
taihen much 80
taihenna [*-na*] serious 249
taihen desu nee it's tough 249
taisetsuna [*-na*] precious 279
taisetsuni suru to treasure 298
taishikan embassy 299
Takahashi (last name) 25
takai[1] [*-i*] expensive 15
takai[2] [*-i*] tall 15
takasa height 316
takusan many, much 80
takushii taxi 24
takushiiryookin taxi fare 316
tamanegi onion 34
tamani occasionally 134
(-takute) tamaranai I am dying to 263
tamaru [*U*] to accumulate, to be saved 247
tame ni[1] because 203
tame ni[2] for, in order to 166
Tanaka (last name) 25
tanjoobi birthday 190
tanomu [*U*] to ask 204
tanomu kara please, I beg you 206
tanoshimi fun, pleasure 316
-tara when, if 245, 303
-tara doo (desu ka) how about ...? 247
tari ... tari ... suru (expressing enumerations) 211
tasu [*U*] to add 231
tatakau [*U*] to fight 166
tatemono building 21
tateru [*RU*] to build 282
tatoeba for example 182, 209, 329
te[1] (colloquial quotation marker) 289
te[2] hand 275
(t)te (colloquial topic marker) 20, 67
te hoshii (expressing a desire) 174, 204
te ka short form of *te yuu ka* 211
te kara after doing 221
te mo even though, whether ... or not 258
te mo ii it is all right 285
te yuu ka (hesitation marker) 211
te-ageru (giving a favorable action to someone) 188
te-aru (resulting state) 251
te-iku (expressing actions involving a direction) 148
te-iru (progressive form) 140, 252
te-itadakemasen(-deshoo) ka (expressing request) 204
te-itadaku (receiving a favorable action) 191
te-kudasai (expressing request) 112, 204, 207
te-kudasaru (giving a favorable action to self) 190
te-kureru (giving a favorable action to self) 188
te-kuru (expressing actions involving a direction) 148
te-miru try and see by doing something 311
te-moraitai (expressing request) 204

te-morau (receiving a favorable action) 188
te-oku (state for future purpose) 251
te-shimau (indicating completion and finality) 148
te-yaru (giving a favorable action to someone) 189
teeburu table 38
tegami letter 54
teineina [*-na*] polite 105
teki enemy 38
-teki (adjective marker) 317
Tekisasu Texas 92
ten'in store attendant 26
tenisu tennis 24
tenki weather 78
tenpura fried vegetables and fish 331
terebi television 24
tetsudau [*U*] to help 136
to[1] (quotative particle) 292
to[2] door 231
to[3] when, whenever 231
to[4] with, and 53, 86, 214
to ieba speaking of 52
to omou to think that 206, 313
to yuu to say that ... 289
  to ieba speaking of 292
  to iimasu to speaking of 292
  to yuu to speaking of 292
tobidasu [*U*] to jump out 231
toboshii [*-i*] poor 88
tobu [*U*] to fly 56
todokeru [*RU*] to deliver 226
todoku [*U*] to arrive, to be delivered 273
tojiru [*RU*] to close, to be closed 128
toka[1] and 87
toka[2] or something 90
tokai large city 103
toki time 117, 220
tokidoki sometimes 134
toko short form of *tokoro* 333, 334
tokoro place 333
  [Adj] + *tokoro* although 333
  te-iru tokoro da be in the middle of doing 334
  to shite-ita tokoro da was about to do 333
  tokoro da[1] be about to 334
  tokoro da[2] just did 334
tokorode by the way 156, 209, 329
tokoroga however 154
-toku (colloquial version of *te-oku*) 253
tomaru[1] [*U*] to say overnight 219
tomaru[2] [*U*] to stop 140
tomodachi friend 30
tonari next door, neighbor 72
tonikaku at any rate 182
too ten 82
-too[1] (counter for animals) 95
-too[2] (counter for order) 95
Toodai The University of Tokyo 46
tooi [*-i*] distant 15
tooka 10th [date] 84
Tookyoo Tokyo 20
Tookyoo Daigaku The University of Tokyo 62
Tookyoo-eki Tokyo Station 54
tooreru [*RU*] to be able to pass through 193
toori street 88
tooru [*U*] to pass though 55
toosan father 160
toosuto toast 53
Toronto Toronto 23
toshokan library 57
totemo very, extremely 78
tozasu [*U*] to shut 128
tsubureru [*RU*] to go bankrupt 155
tsugini next 182, 329
tsuini finally, at last 134
tsuitachi 1st [date] 84
tsukareru [*RU*] to be tired 175
tsukau [*U*] to use 219
tsukeru [*RU*] to attach, to install 54
tsuku [*U*] to arrive 54
tsukue desk 72
tsukuru [*U*] to make, to build 135
tsuma wife 160
tsumaranai mono desu ga ... here's something for you 186, 295
tsumari in other words 182, 329
  tsumari, anoo ... in other words, uh ... 216
tsumetai [*-i*] cold (to touch) 15
tsumori intention 271
tsutomeru [*RU*] to work at, to be employed 292
-tsuu (counter for letters) 95
tsuu ka colloquial form of *te yuu ka* 210
tsuzuku [*U*] to continue 203

tte (colloquial quotation marker) 289

uchi[1] house 54, 124
uchi[2] inside 18
ue on 72
Ueda (last name) 25
uisukii whiskey 23
ukabu [*U*] to appear (an idea) 151
ukagau [*U*] to come, to go 227
umi ocean 327
un yeah, uh-huh 93, 180
untenshu(-san) driver 25
ureshii naa! great! 236
urikire sell-out 193
urusai [*-i*] noisy, bothersome 189
ushiro behind 72
uso! I don't believe it! 180, 262
ussoo! I can't believe it! 261, 262
usuku thinly 34
uta song 141
utau [*U*] to sing 35
utsukushii [*-i*] beautiful 15
utsukushisa beauty 316
uun nope 93
uwasa rumor 297

wa[1] (contrastive) 51, 327
wa[2] (interactional particle) 99
wa[3] (topic marker) 19, 50
-wa (counter for birds) 95
wain wine 23
waishatsu solid colored dress shirt 24
wakai [*-i*] young 15
wakamonomuke catered to young people 317
wakarimasen I don't understand 145
wakarimashita I'll take care of it 205
wakaru [*U*] to understand, to be solved 130, 139, 246
wake da (predicate with explanation) 191
warau [*U*] to laugh 36, 140
  geragera warau to laugh boisterously 144
  herahera warau to laugh condescendingly 144
  kusukusu warau to giggle 144
wareru [*RU*] to be broken 176
waru [*U*] to break 297
warui [*-i*] bad 15
washoku Japanese-style meal 331
wasureru [*RU*] to forget 113, 140
watakushi I 40
Watanabe (last name) 26
wataridori migratory bird 151
watashi I 40
watasu [*U*] to hand (over) 246

ya and 86, 214
yabai [*-i*] risky 15
yahari after all, as expected 331
yakeru [*RU*] to be burned, to be grilled 176
yaku[1] about 97
yaku[2] [*U*] to grill 296
yakusoku promise 216
yakyuu baseball 275
yama mountain 143
Yamada (last name) 26
Yamanaka (last name) 26
Yamanashi Yamanashi 69
yamaoku deep in the mountains 291
Yamashita (last name) 26
yameru [*RU*] to stop 275
yappari that's what I thought 180
yara and 86
yare yare oh, boy! 262
yarite achiever 157
yaru [*U*] to give to someone 184
  te-yaru (giving a favorable action to someone) 189
yasashii [*-i*] kind, easy 15
yasui [*-i*] inexpensive 15
-yasui easy to do 315
yasumi day(s) off 303
yasumu [*U*] to be absent 50
yattaa success (exclamation) 238
yatto at last, with difficulty 182
yattsu eight 82
yo (interactional particle) 65, 99
yoi [*-i*] good 15
yoi otoshi o (omukae kudasai) I wish you'll have a good new year 248
yokka 4th [date] 84
yoko beside 72
yokogiru [*U*] to cross 56
yoku frequently, well, a lot 68, 135
yokunai (negative of *ii*) 93
yomimono things to read 316
yomu [*U*] to read 36

yon four 82
yoo for the use by 317
yoo! hi! 249
-yoo (informal volitional verb ending) 123
  -yoo ka shall I …? 137
  -yoo to omotte-iru thinking to do 125
yooji ga dekiru a chore comes up 203
yooka 8th [date] 84
yookini cheerfully 231
yoona it resembles, it looks like 232, 240
  yooni naru reach the point where 325
yooni as, so that 166, 233
Yooroppa Europe 293
yooyaku with toil 135
yori than 170
yorokobu [*U*] to be pleased, to rejoice 190
yorokonde with pleasure 126
(ni) yoroshiku please give my regards (to) 224
yoroshiku yuu to give regards 247
yoru[1] night 58
yoru[2] [*U*] to stop by, to visit 247
yotei plan 272
yottsu four 82
yowaru [*U*] to be troubled
  yowatta naa what troubled 180
yukaina [*-na*] pleasant, funny 105
yuki snow 212
yukkuri slowly, leisurely 135
yukkuri-suru [Irr] to relax 213
yume dream 235
yuniikuna [*-na*] unique 22
yurusu [*U*] to approve, to forgive 189
yushutsu(-suru) (to) export 37
yuu [*U*] to say 36, 289
yuu mada mo naku needless to mention 157
yuube last night 58
yuubinkyoku post office 313
yuugata evening 58
yuumeina [*-na*] famous 52
yuushoku dinner 119

zannenna [*-na*] sorry, regrettable 291
  zannen (desu) nee I'm sorry to hear that 180, 236
ze (interactional particle) 99
zehi by all means 126
zeitakuna [*-na*] extravagant 105
zenbu everything, every part 149
zenzen (not) at all 307
zero zero 84
zettai certainly 281
zonjiru [*RU*] to think 227
zoo elephant 50
-zu (negative suffix [written]) 79
zubunure being soaked, drenched 284
zuibun very much 80
zutto for a long time 197